T0311818

Partnerships for Regional Innovation and Development

This monograph presents the experience in the implementation of smart specialization strategies (S3) from multilevel policy governance, as well as from the bottom-up perspectives of firms, clusters, and networks in selected European countries. The presented research focuses on the relevance and feasibility of the S3 adoption, emphasizing the importance of linking policy considerations with partnerships at lower governance levels.

The major contribution of the presented research rests in theoretical implications and practical recommendations relevant for the implementation of regional S3 in the European context, with the possibility of place-based adoption in other environments. The book is also valuable for synthesizing the most recent advancements in smart specialization as a policy concept and the concept of transformation and growth for territorial units and economic entities. This book aims to further diffuse and expand the academic community's learning of the new S3 approach in Europe and beyond.

The book will be of interest and useful to the academic community of researchers and doctoral students focused on regional innovation development and related policy, as well as on entrepreneurship, networks, and clusters. Public sector professionals dealing with regional development, regional innovation policies, and industrial transformation will also benefit from its content.

Marta Gancarczyk is Associate Professor at the Institute of Economics, Finance, and Management, Jagiellonian University in Krakow, Poland.

Anna Ujwary-Gil is Associate Professor at the Institute of Economics, Polish Academy of Sciences in Warsaw, Poland.

Manuel González-López is a researcher and Associate Professor at the Department of Applied Economics of the University of Santiago de Compostela and a member of the ICEDE Research Group.

Routledge Studies in Business Organizations and Networks

For more information about this series, please visit: www.routledge.com

Partnerships for Regional Innovation and Development
Implementing Smart Specialization in Europe

Edited by Marta Gancarczyk,
Anna Ujwary-Gil, and Manuel
González-López

Routledge
Taylor & Francis Group

NEW YORK AND LONDON

First published 2021
by Routledge
605 Third Avenue, New York, NY 10158

and by Routledge
2 Park Square, Milton Park, Abingdon, Oxon, OX14 4RN

*Routledge is an imprint of the Taylor & Francis Group, an
informa business*

Library of Congress Cataloging-in-Publication Data
Names: Gancarczyk, Marta, editor. | Ujwary-Gil, Anna, editor. |
    González López, Manuel, editor.
Title: Partnerships for regional innovation and development:
    implementing smart specialization in Europe/edited by Marta
    Gancarczyk, Anna Ujwary-Gil, and Manuel González-López.
Description: New York, NY: Routledge, 2022. | Series: Routledge
    studies in business organizations and networks | Includes
    bibliographical references and index.
Identifiers: LCCN 2021007130 (print) | LCCN 2021007131 (ebook) |
    ISBN 9780367352646 (hardback) | ISBN 9781032053752
    (paperback) | ISBN 9780429330261 (ebook)
Subjects: LCSH: Entrepreneurship—Europe. | Regional
    planning—Europe. | Research and development partnership—
    Europe. | Europe—Economic policy.
Classification: LCC HB615 P3738 2022 (print) |
    LCC HB615 (ebook) | DDC 338/.04094—dc23
    LC record available at https://lccn.loc.gov/2021007130
    LC ebook record available at https://lccn.loc.gov/2021007131

ISBN: 978-0-367-35264-6 (hbk)
ISBN: 978-1-032-05375-2 (pbk)
ISBN: 978-0-429-33026-1 (ebk)

Typeset in Sabon
by Apex CoVantage, LLC

Contents

Part 2

Figures

Tables

Acknowledgments

The editors would like to extend deep thanks to *the authors* who contributed with chapters to this monograph. That volume is entirely based on their high research standards, creativity, and involvement.

We address our grateful thanks to the reviewers, who greatly supported us with their expertise and insightful evaluations. These special thanks go to Björn Asheim, University of Stavanger; Jadwiga Berbeka, Cracow University of Economics; Ondřej Dvouletý, University of Economics, Prague; Robert Hassink, University of Kiel; Silje Haus-Reve, University of Stavanger; Michał Jasieński, Nowy Sącz Business School-National-Louis University; Miren Larrea, University of Deusto; Marta Najda-Janoszka, Jagiellonian University; Roger Normann, University of Agder; Artur Rosa Pires, University of Aveiro; Ida Rašovská, University of Brno; Marina Solesvik, Western Norway University of Applied Sciences; Richard Tuffs, European Regions Research & Innovation Network; Jon Mikel Zabala-Iturriagagoitia, University of Deusto.

Contributors

Marta Gancarczyk, Ph.D., Hab., Associate Professor at the Institute of Economics, Finance, and Management, Jagiellonian University in Krakow, Poland. Her research, publication, and consulting activities focus on entrepreneurship, firm growth, technology management and commercialization, industrial clusters, as well as innovation systems and policies. She is an Associate Editor of the international scientific journal entitled Journal of Entrepreneurship, Management and Innovation (JEMI), and a Member of the Editorial Advisory Board of the Journal of Organizational Change Management.

Anna Ujwary-Gil, Ph.D., Hab., Associate Professor at the Institute of Economics, Polish Academy of Sciences (Laboratory of Process and Network Analysis) in Warsaw, Poland, where she is also a director of two MBA programs. She earned her Ph.D. in economics and management from the Warsaw School of Economics, Poland. She is the Editor-in-Chief of the international and scientific journal named Journal of Entrepreneurship, Management, and Innovation (JEMI). She is also the founder and president of the Cognitione Foundation for the Dissemination of Knowledge and Science. Her research interests include organizational network analysis, knowledge management, intellectual capital, resource-based views, and dynamic approaches to organization and management.

Manuel González-López, Ph.D., is a researcher and Associate Professor at the Department of Applied Economics of the University of Santiago de Compostela and a member of the ICEDE Research Group. He has published many papers in the field of regional development and innovation with a focus on the EU regions. He has also participated in several national and EU projects about innovation policies, regional innovation systems, and other similar topics.

Krzysztof Klincewicz is a Professor at the Faculty of Management, University of Warsaw. He specializes in the management of technology and innovation, with a particular interest in strategies of technology firms and R&D management. Prior to joining the University, he had worked in high-tech industry in Poland, Finland, the UK, and at the Tokyo Institute of Technology. Expert in analyzing innovation policies of EU member states in the Research and Innovation Observatory of the European Commission. Former member of the UN Technology Executive Committee and management board of EIT Food.

Magdalena Marczewska, Ph.D., is Assistant Professor at the Faculty of Management, University of Warsaw. She specializes in innovation and technology management, as well as project management, with a focus on environmental technologies. Participant in research projects commissioned by the Polish Ministry of Environment, European Commission, the World Intellectual Property Organization, the Polish Patent Office, and the National Science Centre. Participant in numerous international research and education programs, such as the University of Kentucky, London School of Economics and Political Science, University of Padova, Vienna University of Economics and Business, Harvard Business School, University of Ferrara, and Lund University.

Christopher L. Tucci is Professor of Digital Strategy & Innovation at Imperial College Business School and former Chair in Corporate Strategy & Innovation, Ecole Polytechnique Fédérale de Lausanne (EPFL). His primary area of interest is in how firms make transitions to new business models, technologies, and organizational forms. He also studies crowdsourcing, Internetworking, and digital innovations. He has published articles in, among others, *Academy of Management Review, Strategic Management Journal, Management Science, Research Policy, Communications of the ACM*, and the *Strategic Entrepreneurship Journal.*

María del Carmen Sánchez-Carreira is a researcher and Associate Professor at the Department of Applied Economics, University of Santiago de Compostela, and member of ICEDE Research Group. Her main research topics are state-owned enterprises, privatization, innovation policies, regional policies, and public procurement. Apart from academic publications, she has participated in several international and national projects.

Pedro Varela-Vázquez is a researcher and lecturer at the Department of Applied Economics of the University of Santiago de Compostela and member of GESPIC Research Group. His research focuses on wind sectoral policies, socioeconomic impact of renewable energies, and their market diffusion. In this regard, he has led a research project to quantify the potential economic effects of offshore wind on the Spanish economy. Moreover, his research topics are also related to public procurement for innovation, as well as innovation policies in peripheral areas.

Elżbieta Wojnicka-Sycz, Ph.D., Hab. in Economics, Associate Professor at the University of Gdansk and Associate Professor at the Gdansk University of Technology. Her specialization is in the analysis of innovation and technology transfer, spatial management from the point of view of innovation, the impact of structural funds on economic development, and the development of cities and regions. She is a coordinator and/or expert in numerous projects for central and local government administration as well as international organizations.

Korneliusz Pylak, Ph.D. in economics in the field of management. He works at the University of Marie Curie-Sklodowska in Lublin as a lecturer. He runs an expert activity in the field of Regional Innovation Strategies, innovation policies assessment, business support organizations activity, and so on, prepared for the Ministry of Regional Development and Offices of the Marshal. He runs also expert activity in the field of programs' evaluations. He has huge practical experience as a project author, project manager, and project coordinator.

Piotr Sliż, Ph.D. Eng., Assistant Professor at the Faculty of Management at the University of Gdańsk. He specializes in assessing the process maturity of an organization and the implementation of modern information technologies in process-oriented organizations, as well as measuring processes using statistical methods and the implementation of artificial intelligence technology, robotics process management, and data mining in process organizations. Experienced consultant in the field of business process improvement, after-sales process analysis, and audits of warranty processes in the automotive sector in Europe.

Piotr Sycz, Master in Management, Engineer in Computer Science, Assistant, and Ph.D. candidate at the University of Gdansk. He is a researcher on various projects for public administration, and his main fields of interest are lean project management and innovation management.

Elisabeth Baier is a Professor for Business Administration and head of the study location Baden-Baden of the VICTORIA | International University of Applied Sciences. She studied economics at the University of Stirling, UK, and the University of Mannheim, Germany. In 2011, she obtained her doctoral degree (Dr. rer. nat.) jointly from the University of Strasbourg, France and the Karlsruhe Institute of Technology, Germany. Her research interests include international management, innovation economics, economic geography, and regional innovation policy. She focuses on the application of mixed-methods approaches in her empirical work.

Xiang Ying Mei, Ph.D., is an Associate Professor in marketing at Inland Norway University of Applied Sciences. She received her doctorate in tourism management from the University of Queensland, Australia. In addition to years of practical experiences in the service industries, her research interests range from government policies, innovation, regional development, tourism management and development, experience economy, consumer behavior, and marketing, to digital learning tools and student engagement in higher education.

Victoria Konovalenko-Slettli, Ph.D., is an Associate Professor in Organization and Management at the School of Business and Social Sciences, Inland Norway University of Applied Sciences. She holds a doctoral degree in Business Economics from the University of Nord, Bodø, Norway, and a master's degree in Business Administration from the Baltic State Technical University "VOENMEH," St-Petersburg, Russia. Victoria is teaching and doing research in the areas of communication, organizational change, development and innovation, and knowledge management. In the research, she is especially interested in topics such as organizational and individual learning, knowledge sharing, and intellectual capital.

Jacek Gancarczyk is a researcher and Associate Professor at the Department of E-entrepreneurship and Innovation, Institute of Entrepreneurship, Jagiellonian University in Krakow. His research, publications, and consulting focus on entrepreneurship, small and medium enterprises (SMEs), regional development, networks, and clusters. He has some experience in national and international (EU, the United States, Japan) research projects (Erasmus+ Jean Monnet/EURIPER, Euro-Found, USAID/USIA, Sasakawa), both as a partner and as a coordinator. He has published several articles in peer-reviewed journals and books on the topics such as entrepreneurship, small and medium-sized enterprises, SME strategies in clusters, networks, and innovation systems. He is a member of the European Council of Small Business and Entrepreneurship ECSB).

Vanda Maráková is a Full Professor and Head of the Department of Tourism at the Faculty of Economics, Matej Bel University in Banska Bystrica. She has 20 years of experience in the research areas and education of tourism studies. Her main research topics include tourism management, corporate social responsibility in the tourism sector, sustainability and competitiveness in destination management, innovations in tourism, and marketing communication. She was the head of the project team that leaded the unit to the UNWTO TedQual scheme award for the period 2019–2022. She is a representative in an international knowledge alliance IREST Triangle knowledge network focused on sustainable tourism development and Slovak office of standards, metrology, and testing.

Ewa Wszendybył-Skulska is a researcher and Associate Professor at the Department of Tourism and Sport Management of the Jagiellonian University. She has published many articles on human resources management, quality management, innovation, and modern management in tourism enterprises. She also participated in several research projects. Actively participated in numerous national and international scientific conferences. She is a member of IFITT (International Federation for IT and Travel&Tourism) and the Hotel Rating Team at the Marshal of Małopolskie Voivodship and an expert on the estimation of the applications as part of the Małopolskie Regional Operational Program between 2007–2013 and 2014–2020.

Ivano Dileo, Ph.D., MSc, Assistant Professor in Applied Economics. He was a visiting researcher at the Department of Town and Regional Planning (Sheffield, UK), Department of Applied Economics (Santiago de Compostela, SP), and UniBocconi (IT). His research interests are entrepreneurship, regional development and policy, and innovation. He teaches in Italy and abroad, coordinated international programs such as Interreg, and participated in research projects on several programs such as 7FP, Jean Monnet, Interreg IPA CBC, Ministry of Economy, POR, ESF, ERDF, and Erasmus+ Programme. Member of ICEDE research group collaborates actively with the Universities of Krakow, Warsaw, Olsztyn and Lodz (Poland), Bucharest (Romania), Santiago de Compostela (Spain), Agder (Norway), Lund (Sweden).

Marco Pini, Economist at the "Centro Studi delle Camere di Commercio Guglielmo Tagliacarne" (Rome, Italy). He is a Ph.D. student in Political Studies at Sapienza University (Rome, Italy). He was a visiting researcher at the Department of Management of Warsaw University (Poland) and the Department of Human Geography and Planning of Utrecht University (Netherlands). He teaches at LUISS Guido Carli (Rome, Italy). A regular speaker at institutional conferences, workshops, and policy seminars. He has published in international peer-reviewed journals in the fields of family businesses, internationalization, innovation, industry 4.0, green economy, and corporate social responsibility. He is coauthor of a book on innovation and regional disparities.

Anna Maria Lis, Ph.D., is Associate Professor and Head of the Department of Industrial Management of the Faculty of Management and Economics, at Gdańsk University of Technology. Her scientific and research interests have been focused on problems related to institutional forms of support provided for the development of interorganizational cooperation (including cluster organizations and business environment institutions). She has participated in numerous research projects implemented at academic centers, as well as in projects requested by the public authorities.

Arkadiusz Michał Kowalski, Ph.D., is Associate Professor and Head of the Department of East Asian Economic Studies in the SGH Warsaw School of Economics. He holds a habilitation degree in Economics (2013) from the Collegium of World Economy and a Ph.D. in Economics (2006) from the Collegium of Economic Analysis. His research and academic teaching focus on innovation policy, clusters, and international competitiveness, internationalization of firms, and economies in East and Southeast Asia. He has been involved as a manager or researcher in different European or domestic research projects, which resulted in more than 80 publications.

Marta Mackiewicz, Ph.D., is Assistant Professor in the SGH Warsaw School of Economics, World Economy Research Institute. Her research focuses on innovation policy, clusters, and international competitiveness. She was the head of the Policy and Research Department at Ecorys Polska (2006–2019). She led several evaluation studies related to the implementation of programs financed with ERDF funds and studies related to the implementation of entrepreneurship and innovation policies.

Aleksander Jakimowicz is Institute Professor of economics at the Department for World Economy, Institute of Economics, Polish Academy of Sciences, Warsaw, Poland. His research interests include mathematical economics, complexity economics, econophysics, nonlinear dynamics, econometrics, economic methodology, and wikinomics. He has proven that markets and economies function properly only close to the edge of chaos, which they seek in the long term as a result of the simultaneous operation of the law of increasing complexity and the principle of emergence. He has published more than 80 scientific papers in leading journals and authored four scientific books. For his research, in 2004 he received the Bank Handlowy Award, referred to as the Polish Economic Nobel Prize, and a medal for the Most Famous Pole of the Year.

Daniel Rzeczkowski is Adjunct Professor at the Department of Market and Consumption at the University of Warmia and Mazury in Olsztyn, Poland. He received his Ph.D. degree at this University in 2013. His research interests include mathematical economics, wikinomics, econometrics, statistics, information technology, and public administration. He is the author of one book and several other scientific publications. At the Faculty of Economic Sciences, he is involved in research and teaching and also acts as an IT Administrator.

Foreword

Dominique Foray

The idea of smart specialization strategy was born within the framework of the *Knowledge for Growth* expert group of the European Commission around 2009 (Foray et al., 2009). The issue addressed at that time was— *how regional economies in the European Union can change and develop into areas with high growth potentials ?*—and the initial paper already proposed four ideas which then became mainstream in the S3 literature:

The idea of priorities that involve the need for any region to make explicit what transformation is desirable for what kind of sectors;

The idea of concentration and strategic focuses on a small number of transformational goals—in order to generate density, agglomeration, and critical mass—all essential determinants of innovation and creativity;

The idea of a bottom-up entrepreneurial discovery process as an essential mechanism to identify transformational roadmaps and activities;

The idea of related diversification and regional differentiation: not all regions need a biotech cluster but all regions can recognize and realize region-specific capacities and opportunities.

Based on this seminal paper, a massive policy experiment was undertaken between 2014 and 2020—involving almost all regions and countries in designing and implementing the S3 approach.

We have made a lot of progress since 2009 both in theory and in practice. The book edited by Marta Gancarzyk, Anna Ujwary-Gil, and Manuel González-López is particularly welcomed to illustrate and concretize such evolution both in theory and in practice. Its collection of chapters also makes a great contribution to the argument that there is today a certain disparity between, on the one hand, the most recent academic work that concerns the S3 concept, its rationality, its basic principle, and policy design and, on the other, the actual S3 policy implementation which was characterized by several difficulties that were in fact very predictable.

The book shows very clearly that recent academic work has enabled considerable progress to be made, regarding both the concept and its implementation, thanks to the unique opportunity academic scholars have had to observe real experiences, participate in them and then, based on this, take another look at our initial work. The book's Introduction, in particular, does an excellent job of illuminating the various ways in which academics have improved the understanding, analysis, and more practical implication of the S3 approach.

On the other hand, however, the actual practical implementations have not evolved very much and remain strongly marked by the historical conditions and circumstances in which the S3 policy experiment was launched and several chapters of the book illustrate very well some of the effects of a lack of preparation and understanding in the early stage of the S3 period.

The initial formulation of the concept was actually fairly general; there was no time to test the approach (no pilot study) and at that time there was no market for S3 expertise—or, to put it more bluntly—there was simply no expertise. Regions and countries did their best to design and implement the S3 approach but because of these unfavorable conditions, the outcomes were imperfect let's say.

In many cases, regional strategies led to too broad priorities at the sectoral level (tourism, agriculture, digital economy) or to priorities that were confused with the so-called Grand Challenges (healthy society, circular economy). However, such broad priorities are another way of providing "coffee for all"—so that one of the key objectives of an S3 approach (generating density, agglomeration, and complementarities between actors and projects) was never achieved.

In many cases too, regions experienced great difficulty in materializing and concretizing the selected priorities into actions, programs, and projects. So in a sense, the plan was just not executed.

Finally, the entrepreneurial discovery process, which is a key mechanism to address the information and uncertainty problems that arise from any kind of policy that includes a planning component (which is clearly the case in S3), was viewed more as an administrative or bureaucratic condition to fulfill than an effective policy practice.

Several chapters in the book thus describe these difficulties in policy design and implementation that have characterized early S3 history. Chapters on the general case of Central and Eastern Europe as well as on Galicia or Kosice are particularly interesting in this regard.

But the positive side of the first S3 period is that, thanks to the commitment demonstrated by the regions, a massive and unique policy experiment took place—involving more than 100 cases—and this has been an extraordinary opportunity to learn and significantly improve the policy design and implementation process. And this is the other aspect of the book, which is to identify some pockets of S3 excellence—that can now be used to build a better policy concept for the next period. The cases of Baden Württemberg, Krakow, or Inland County in Norway illustrate well regional S3s that have already delivered valuable results in the regional economies concerned.

At the end of this first learning period, the S3 concept today seems clearer, simple, and easy to understand for regional policymakers—which does not mean, however, that it is easy to do. Various recent contributions (Foray et al., 2020; Gancarczyk et al., 2021, which incidentally is the introductory chapter of this book) illustrate this academic dynamism leading to better understanding, analysis, and application of the S3 concept. In particular, the S3 toolbox now provides an efficient design and implementation process to effectively manage the tension between top-down prioritization (the planning logic of S3) and bottom-up decentralized actions (the entrepreneurial discovery logic of S3). It also highlights the right level of granularity at which the S3 process needs to materialize—which is neither a whole sector nor an individual project—but a collection of related projects—all oriented toward the same transformational goal—the so-called transformative activity.

Such academic progress—as reflected in the book of Gancarczyk, Ujwary-Gil, and González-López—represents a great source of optimism. One can predict that the next period of regional innovation policy within the EU will benefit from better S3 design and implementation processes, and this will help European regions to succeed in their structural transformations and transitions. This book will clearly play a key role in the diffusion and learning of the new S3 approach in Europe and beyond.

Dominique Foray

Full Professor of Economics and Management of Innovation at the École Polytechnique Fédérale de Lausanne (EPFL), Switzerland

References

Foray, D., David, P. A., & Hall, B. (2009). *Smart specialisation: The concept, knowledge for growth: Prospects for science, technology and innovation.* European Commission, EUR 24047 EN.

Foray, D., Eichler, M., & Keller, M. (2020). Insights gained from a unique European policy experiment on innovation and industrial policy design. *Review of Evolutionary Political Economy*. doi:10.1007/s43253-020-00026-z

Gancarczyk, M., Ujwary-Gil, A., & González-López, M. (2021). The expansion of the smart specialization concept and practice. In M. Gancarczyk, A. Ujwary-Gil, & M. González-López (Eds.), *Partnerships for regional innovation and development: Implementing smart specialization in Europe*. New York: Routledge.

The Expansion of the Smart Specialization Concept and Practice

Marta Gancarczyk, Anna Ujwary-Gil, and Manuel González-López

Introduction

Within slightly more than 10 years of its dissemination, the smart specialization concept managed to revitalize, reconfigure and energize a set of interrelated policies, notably industrial, innovation, R&D, regional, and entrepreneurship policies (Morgan & Marques, 2019; Barzotto et al., 2019). In that period of dynamic expansion, SS refined its core concepts and agenda for implementation (Foray, 2019, 2020). This conceptual advancement was accomplished in parallel with putting SS into practice as a rationale for the distribution of the EU Structural Funds. The practical experience drove the conceptual progress of SS, both in terms of its major constructs, assumptions, and implementation guidelines. Still, the implementation guidelines have not been fully integrated into the practice of smart specialization strategy as policy based on the SS concept (Foray, 2020). The evidence on this implementation is growing at the level of countries and regions. However, the research on the application of S3 at the bottom-up level of local governments, industries, clusters, and enterprises remains scarce. Therefore, more studies are needed to fill in the research gap in the understanding of 3S processes to inform policy practice.

The conceptual advancement of SS raises one more direction for the expansion of this idea. Namely, it broadens its reach from the policy-focused perspective toward a general transformation and growth concept for multi-scalar entities, such as the EU, countries, regions, local governments, as well as enterprises, clusters, networks, and industries (Biagi et al., 2020; Cai et al., 2018; Caragliu & Del Bo, 2018; D'Adda, Guzzini, Iacobucci, & Palloni, 2019). This might be another fruitful direction of SS impacts, namely, to be become a framework to understand and drive innovation and development at different spatial levels, and to guide the choices of not only public but also private entities. Consequently, SS as economic concept might inspire and affect strategies of enterprises, clusters, and networks (Foray, 2013, 2014, 2017; Varga et al., 2018; Galbraith, McAdam, Woods, & McGowan, 2017). This can be expected both as a consequence of purposeful SS-based policies, and regardless of them, as spontaneous, private choices of economic agents (Nguyen et al., 2020). The research in this nascent area is scarce and explorative (Caragliu & Bo, 2018; Crescenzi, de Blasio, & Giua, 2020).

The current chapter aims to synthesize the essence and expansion of SS as policy approach and as transformation and growth concept. Moreover, it will present the contribution of this monograph to the research gap and policy challenges in implementing SS. In the following sections, we discuss the advancements in the SS and highlight the major research areas and research gaps. Furthermore, we emphasize the major argument and methodological approach of this book, and we establish a framework that will organize the presentation of research evidence and findings in the volume. Then, the contributions from the individual chapters and outlook for further academic and policy-related research have been discussed.

Smart Specialization as Policy and Growth Concept

The Expansion of SS as Policy Concept

Smart specialization was launched as industrial policy concept targeted at restoring the proactive role of government in prioritizing the objectives, selecting proper measures, and implementation guidelines (Morgan & Marques, 2019; Barzotto et al., 2019). This proactive role and vertical intervention in industrial growth processes proved to be particularly relevant after the economic crisis of 2007–2009 (European Commission, 2020). The earlier largely horizontal and indirect approach was considered as insufficient, although the development of the framework conditions for innovation, such as R&D infrastructures and legal environment, continues to be relevant in the policy agenda (Foray, 2016; Bailey et al., 2019a; Bailey et al., 2019b; Aiginger & Rodrik, 2020). The recognized strengths of SS include comprehensiveness of its theoretical framework, as well as integration and reconfiguration of the earlier concepts of innovation and regional development (Foray, 2019, 2020). This enabled the absorption and continuation of the earlier development concepts, however, within a new framework. The new framework structured the development directions based on key concepts and assumptions. Industry growth through specialized diversification, entrepreneurial discovery process (EDP), and critical mass in identifying targets and policy measures were recognized as frames for a nexus of related policies, in particular, regional innovation policies.

The adoption of regional innovation policies contextualized the SS-based industrial policy in diverse spatial, economic, and institutional environments. First of all, however, it launched the challenges of implementation. Smart specialization rapidly transformed from the concept to the EU innovation policies and measures based on the Structural Funds (Estensoro & Larrea, 2016). Therefore, its conceptual development and adoption were interrelated and mutually reinforcing processes. Due to a comprehensive and consistent view, SS expanded as regional transformation and growth concept. Thus regional and innovation policies have been observed as converging into one policy framework that aims to accomplish cohesion through the development of innovation (Asheim, 2019; González-López et al., 2019).

The implementation experience matched with the academic, policy-related research enabled clarification and refinement of the major constructs. Specialized diversification was specified as related diversification, a sustainable growth strategy based on region-specific capacities and region-specific entrepreneurial opportunities (Foray, 2019; Hassink & Gong, 2019). This concept promotes the regional new path creation through developing higher value adding and more technology advanced activities (Grillitsch & Asheim, 2018; Balland et al., 2019). The enabling tools in this regard are technological fields and specialized R&D rather than particular industries (D'Adda et al., 2019; Iacobucci & Guzzini, 2016). The regional industrial path development can be accomplished through upgrading, diversifying the extant industrial profile, and the emergence of radically new industries (Asheim, 2019; Isaksen et al., 2019).

One of the major accomplishments of extant experimentation with S3 is its implementation guidelines. They assume neither purely top-down nor purely bottom-up method, but rather a processual adoption (Foray, 2020). The latter starts from the top design with the participation of stakeholders and is followed by bottom-up entrepreneurial discovery process, engaging all relevant actors of the quadruple helix innovation system. EDP resonates with the currently developing framework of entrepreneurial ecosystems as an auxiliary idea for regional transformation and growth (Stam, 2015; Mason & Brown, 2014; Brown et al., 2017; Brown & Mawson, 2019).

When progressing from the industrial policy approach to a comprehensive framework that guides regional and innovation policies, SS expanded its scope. It requires a holistic approach that acknowledges regional as well as international and global contexts for industrial transformation (Hassink et al., 2019; Foray, 2019, 2020). New regional path creation through S3 should engage social and political processes, such as bottom-up initiatives of communities and organizations and multi-level governance of local, regional, as well as national and cross-border agents. Consequently, regions and clusters are facing the challenge of specializing smartly within global production networks and global value chains (Gancarczyk & Gancarczyk, 2018; OECD, 2020).

The advancements in the theory and practice of SS are mainly based on the experience in formulating the regional smart specialization strategy

(S3), implementing S3 at the level of regions and countries, and evaluations of the EU funding in the area of S3 and related policies, that is, R&D, industrial, and innovation policies (Reimeris, 2016; Iacobucci & Guzzini, 2016; Radosevic, Curaj, Gheorghiu, Andreescu, & Wade, 2017; Crescenzi et al., 2020; Cai et al. 2018; Varga, 2018; D'Adda et al., 2019). Nevertheless, smart specialization acknowledges a bottom-up approach in formulating and implementing the policies (Foray, 2016; McCann & Ortega-Argilés, 2015). Relatedness, embeddedness, and connectivity of actors at the local level, as well as their links with external actors, form the basis for entrepreneurial discovery processes (McCann, 2015; Ujwary-Gil & Potoczek, 2020). Bottom-up and micro-level approaches in EDP need to be supported by a place-based perspective that recognizes the idiosyncrasy of territories (Hassink, 2020). However, the extant research and policy analyses focus on country and regional levels, while micro-foundations of S3 are underexplored (Grillitsch, 2019; Aranguren, Magro, Navarro, & Wilson, 2019; Grillitsch & Asheim, 2018; Borrás & Jordana, 2016). Consequently, there is a research gap in investigating how S3 is implemented at the level of local governments, firms, networks, clusters, and individual industries (Grillitsch & Asheim, 2018; Grillitsch, 2019; Ujwary-Gil, 2019; Ujwary-Gil, 2017).

Another important outcome from the extant implementation experience is recognition that S3 does not apply to all types of regions. It is relevant for those moderately rather than highly or less developed regions (Foray, 2019, 2020; González-López & Asheim, 2020). Moderately developed regions need prioritization of resources to accomplish growth and differentiation (Lin & Wang, 2020). The pathway of SS goes from the general concept of industrial policy to its place-based focus on regional innovation policies and regional development policies, to tightening its focus to regions with particular development needs. Based on the experience in implementation matched with ongoing research, and after advancing in terms of theory and implementation guidelines, SS has been recently reabsorbed as a conceptual basis for New Industrial Policy (NIP) (European Commission, 2020; Aiginger & Rodrik, 2020). NIP follows the SS approach regarding the proactive role of government, that is, a mission-oriented animator in industrial transformation and growth. Consistent with SS are vertical intervention measures not to pick up winning enterprises or industries, but to support fields and domains and thus derive synergetic effects in industries. Moreover, critical mass in targets and related sets of measures are promoted to accomplish structural change and transformation in view of the systemic failure. This method of intervention departs from ad hoc, incidental instruments to address market failure only (Gancarczyk & Ujwary-Gil, 2020). NIP follows the logic of S3 guidelines in the design rather from the top, and in the implementation closer to the bottom-up governance (Fagerberg & Hutschenreiter, 2019). Consequently, we have observed the dynamic growth and evolution of SS throughout a set of related policies that were affected by this concept. Through this experience, in turn, SS gained in comprehensiveness and universality.

SS as Transformation and Growth Concept

Smart specialization integrates, reconfigures, and expands a number of concepts related to economic transformation and growth (Foray, 2013, 2017, 2019, 2020). The integrative approach brings benefits, such as the opportunity to draw upon earlier achievements and accumulated experience, and to advance these accomplishments. In the area of regional innovation, transformation and growth, it integrates such perspectives as innovation systems, cluster policies, regional specializations, place-based and evolutionary approaches, and the theories of polarized growth. Moreover, its framework reveals complementarity with the ideas of regional, innovation, and entrepreneurial ecosystems (Porto Gomez, Otegi Olaso, & Zabala-Iturriagagoitia, 2016). The integrative approach mutually benefits SS and these related concepts. Specialized diversification as vertical approach to intervention, directed at industrial structural change and branching out, expands and complements the horizontal intervention of system approaches (Morgan & Marques, 2019). Innovation systems and ecosystems are examples of horizontal measures directed at particular system components, such as financing (Brown & Mawson, 2019). SS explains how growth might be accomplished in ecosystems through vertical relationship, such as branching out (Capello & Kroll, 2016; Nguyen et al., 2020). Evolutionary approaches to industrial change, such as cluster evolution models, acknowledge the dynamics of vertical industrial relationships, and thus contribute to SS (Gancarczyk, 2015; Gong & Hassink, 2019). Regional industrial clusters represent spatial concentration of specialized domains and knowledge, thus might form a sound platform for the identification of target domains with critical mass, and for branching out advocated in S3 (Ciffolilli & Muscio, 2018; Götz, 2020). Smart specialization, in turn, helps to go beyond extant spatial concentrations toward prospective activities that might be non-clustered, and toward clusters based on intellectual, technological, and institutional match rather than on spatial proximity (Barzotto et al., 2019; Ujwary-Gil, 2017, 2019).

As a comprehensive growth and transformation concept, SS also represents a fruitful framework for private choices, reflected in strategies of enterprises, networks, clusters, and industries. It builds upon and expands economic approaches relevant to these private choices (Foray, 2013, 2017). The idea of related diversification refers to the microeconomics literature in growth based on investment in indivisibilities to accomplish economies of scope, economies of scale, and economies of expansion (Foray, 2020; Penrose, 1959; Panzar & Willig, 1977; Gancarczyk, 2019).

On the one hand, it resonates with the strategic management literature in related diversification through exploration of extant core capabilities to ensure synergies. On the other hand, it also invokes unrelated diversification through exploration, to avoid risky complementarities. The aforementioned literature informs micro-foundations for branching out in SS. At the same time, this literature might gain by perceiving diversification in a systemic way rather from the approach of an individual enterprise. SS promotes branching out based on the systemic approach that acknowledges the specificity of spatial environment, and place-based opportunities (Hassink, 2020). In this vein, firm growth through diversification can be understood as entrepreneurial discovery process assisted by other actors in innovation system. Moreover, from the angle of SS, branching out toward new domains should be perceived as an interindustrial and mutually reinforcing process (EOCIC, 2019). In this process, new product or service innovation (e.g., a software application) as a response to demands in one of the regional domains (such as tourism) opens a new market segment in the ICT (Biagi et al., 2020). At the same time, by launching new products or services in the customer industry, it stimulates new segments in this industry (new tourism segments). These mechanisms of partnerships and enterprise interactions in a particular environment also specify and enrich such perspectives as population ecology and evolutionary approaches to firm and industrial growth.

Ultimately, entrepreneurial discovery process refers to the entrepreneurship literature (Brown & Mawson, 2019). It enhances this literature by contextualization of entrepreneurial processes, that is, placing them within the framework of public and private partnerships in innovation systems (Brown, Mawson, & Mason, 2017). The contextualization of entrepreneurship process benefits also strategic entrepreneurship perspective that recommends concurrent pursuit of exploitation of extant capabilities and exploration toward new domains to avoid rigidities and lock-in (MCann & Ortega-Argilés, 2015).

The Rationale, Purpose, and Methodological Design of the Monograph

On the basis of the earlier sections, we can state that policy practice still faces the challenge of comprehensive adoption of the latest conceptual developments in assumptions and implementation guidelines of SS. Therefore, there is a recognized research gap in the implementation of S3. In particular, more evidence and conclusions are needed regarding S3 adoption processes after the design phase, toward particular activities (actions, projects, and processes), and toward the evaluation of these activities (Foray, 2019, 2020; Wojnicka-Sycz, 2020).

The implementation of S3 is still a vital issue, because it has been started ahead of the operationalization of the concept (Rodrik, 2014;

McCann & Ortega-Argilés, 2015; Foray et al., 2018; Estensoro & Larrea, 2016). Therefore, theory and practice are mutually reinforcing and require the ongoing synthesis (Capello & Kroll, 2016). The book intends to address the research and policy gaps of how to implement regional smart specialization strategies. Its general argument states that successful implementation of S3 depends on linking regional innovation policies with local activities of enterprises, regional networks, as well as with initiatives of private and public actors. The geographic scope of the presented research focuses on European countries, although SS and related policies reach out the European context. This focus is justified by more coherent approach to the implementation practice of S3 that enables comparative analyses. Despite recognized diversity, the European context features relative institutional similarities. In particular, the EU countries adopted common guidelines and measures of S3.

Consequently, *the purpose of this monograph is to present the experience of the S3 implementation from multilevel policy governance, as well as from the bottom-up perspectives of firms, clusters, and networks in selected European countries.*

The presented research will also reflect on SS as transformation and growth concept that can be investigated in the development paths of territorial units, enterprises, and industries. Therefore, the focus of the current monograph is on feasibility in adoption and relevance of SS implemented through smart specialization strategies.

In the first part, this volume broadens the understanding of S3 design, implementation, and monitoring in European regions. The second part presents the insights on the S3 adoption in the subregional, and local contexts. The third part focuses on the implementation of SS at the level of enterprises, clusters, and networks. Correspondingly to the focus of each part, three sets of research questions (RQs) will be addressed:

> *RQ Set 1: What are the current theoretical developments and practical experiences in the design implementation, and monitoring of S3 at the European regions' level? What theoretical contributions and policy recommendations can be derived from these developments and experiences?*
>
> *RQ Set 2: How is S3 implemented in the context of subregions and local governments and what are theoretical and policy implications in this regard? How does SS explain the transformation and growth of these territorial units? How can the S3 approach be enhanced through the experience from the transformation and growth at the local level?*
>
> *RQ Set 3: How is the smart specialization concept reflected in the activities of firms, clusters, and public–private networks? What theoretical implications and policy recommendations can be derived in this regard? How can the S3 approach be enhanced through the*

> experience from the transformation and growth of firms, clusters, and networks?

The *methodologies applied in this monograph* range from quantitative (e.g., surveys, analyses of statistics) to qualitative (e.g., case studies, content analysis of secondary information) approaches. The value of this mix-method approach rests on the possibility to address multi-scalar perspectives (macro, mezzo, and micro views). The book offers unique insights from matching the general overviews from secondary data sets, surveys, and document analyses with in-depth investigations through interviews and case studies. Multidimensional insights can also be derived from confronting cross-sectional large data sets with evolutionary approach in explorative single cases or multiple cases.

When considering the methodological approach to the research on implementing S3, we need to acknowledge that ex post evaluations are rare, as yet. However, the theoretical lens of smart specialization can be used to investigate programs and policies, as well as industrial strategies that are not purposefully designed and declared as driven by 3S. We can extrapolate from this experience toward new SS-based policies and strategies and thus evaluate the adaptability and feasibility of S3 (Crescenzi et al., 2020; Gancarczyk et al., 2020). Therefore, this volume enhances the understanding of the S3 implementation based on two approaches. One approach is direct experience and learning from the adoption of S3 at different governance levels, that is, from the policies formally declaring the SS direction. The other approach is based on pattern-matching and uses SS as concept and theoretical lens, through which the experience of development policies and strategies are analyzed, even though they do not formally follow S3. This perspective is useful in particular at the local level, where SS is not explicitly present in strategies, but rather invoked by reference to regional policies. We match this bottom-up evidence with SS assumptions, reflecting on their adaptability and usefulness, as well as on how this experience can inform the practice of S3.

Contributions

In response to the sets of research questions specified in section 3, Part 1 approaches the experiences in designing, implementing, and monitoring smart specialization strategies in European regions. This part starts with the chapter by Klincewicz, Marczewska, and Tucci (2021), which explores whether the choices of specialization of regional S3 in five Central and Eastern European countries were linked to the innovation potential of those regions, using patent application as a proxy. The findings indicate mismatches between the actual inventive activities and priorities selected by many of the regions, with specializations topics being generic and insufficiently differentiated. The analysis offers important insights into the adequacy of political decisions and their relevance for regional stakeholders, as well as methodological contributions that highlight possible ways of mapping the scope of the priorities of RIS 3.

The chapter by Sánchez-Carreira, González-López, and Varela-Vázquez (2021) explores the experience of Galicia, a region in northwest Spain. The authors identify the main drivers and barriers in the prioritization of Galician S3 and derive the implications of the smart specialization approach for the policy-making process and institutional learning. The research highlights some relevant aspects for a proper definition and implementation of S3, which are regional singularities, the level of granularity on prioritization, and the inclusiveness of the entrepreneurial discovery process, among others.

This part ends with the contribution by Wojnicka-Sycz, Pylak, Sliz, and Sycz (2021), who approach the process of S3 monitoring, a poorly discussed area in S3 studies, based on the analysis of S3 in the regions of several European countries. The authors highlight the importance of counting with adequate indicators, which, in addition to context indicators, require an appropriate structure grouped in resources, symptoms, and effect blocks. The challenge is also to ensure the participation of different governmental bodies as well as beneficiaries of the policy in the cooperation on the collection of indicators and on how to better finance and provide human resources for the monitoring system, even in more developed regions. By focusing on the level of region with international, comparative perspective, Part 1 explains some of the framework conditions for the adoption of S3 at lower levels of governance in the following parts.

Part 2 focuses on how S3 is implemented in the context of subregions and local governments. This part starts from the contribution by Baier (2021), who focuses on a particular initiative to enhance entrepreneurial discovery processes at the sub-territorial level of Baden-Wuerttemberg, Germany. The author emphasizes the value of the place-based and bottom-up approach in the initiative of the RegioWIN competition, which cut across governance levels, engaging regions, cities, and municipalities. Besides positive impacts, such as industrial upgrading and institutionalization and professionalization of partnerships for S3, the author points to the shortages in the S3 implementation, that is, excessive costs and difficulties to adopt in localizations with lower institutional and industrial capacity. The identified variety in the EDPs also poses a challenge to convert the unique technological potentials and micro-systems of innovation into a coherent, growth-oriented development. The Baden-Wuerttemberg provides valuable insights into formal S3 implementation and a systemic approach to bottom-up micro-systems of innovation.

The chapter by Mei and Konovalenko-Slettli (2021) presents emergent rather than systemic logics of policy practice in the Hamar Municipality, Norway. The smart city (SC) policy is launched in the local government and spreads toward a wider regional environment with a potential to fulfill at least some of S3 assumptions. In theoretical terms, the authors seek to identify the relationships between SC and S3, and they find these concepts partially overlapping and complementary. This observation points to an important theoretical impact from S3, which not only integrates the earlier regional and innovation development theories but also is generative for novel policy concepts (Caragliu & Del Bo, 2018). Besides the theoretical synthesis, the authors derive practical recommendations. These refer to the role of SC in developing more place-based than administrative partnerships, to linking and coordination among levels of government, as well as to innovation-oriented measures when identifying and evaluating local specialization.

The third chapter by Gancarczyk, Marakova, and Wszendybył-Skulska (2021) also refers to SS as a development concept rather than a formally adopted policy. The authors evaluate the coherence between SS assumptions and tourism growth in two Central European cities of Kraków, Poland, and Košice, Slovakia. The successful growth of tourism in Krakow fits with well with S3, providing a positive test of SS as a concept for an individual industry development. The Košice tourism recorded only modest growth in the referred period, and the pattern of this growth follows SS assumptions only marginally. Nevertheless, mutual lessons for the cities can be derived. Kraków put stress on the vertical industrial policy while neglecting the horizontal policy toward the quality of life and sustainable development. Košice, although weaker in industrial policy, emphasized horizontal measures toward ecological targets and sustainability. The chapter identifies a policy challenge to jointly pursue horizontal and vertical policies for industrial and territorial development.

Due to thematic adjacency, the chapters in Part 2 can also be treated as mutually explaining and reinforcing their theoretical and practical contribution. In terms of advancing the guidelines of S3, Baier (2021) provides an argument toward systemic and place-based linking of multi-scalar governance and agency in the adoption of S3. Moreover, this chapter suggests the activity (a project) as a unit of implementation rather than only framing bottom-up strategies by regional programmatic documents. This approach is directly called for in the chapter by Mei and Konovalenko-Slettli (2022) and invoked in the chapter by Gancarczyk et al. (2021). Moreover, the latter cases add to SS as a development concept. Kraków supports its adaptability and feasibility for an individual industry in an urban location. Mei and Konovalenko-Slettli (2021) emphasize how it inspires theoretical perspectives on urban development by SC, and how SC can enhance S3 in terms of theory and policy practice. At the same time, the cases of Hamar and Košice, as examples of horizontal development policy, can be informative for Kraków to jointly pursue smart industrial and territorial policies toward sustainability and quality of life.

In relation to Parts 1 and 2, Part 3 highlights S3 regardless of administrative units, but referring to partnerships formed by enterprises, clusters, and public–private networks. Dileo and Pini (2021) focus on public support and partnerships by Italian enterprises to generate eco-innovations. The authors refer to the Quadruple Helix (QH) model as instrumental to the implementation of S3, from conceptual and practical angles. The chapter reveals more effective partnership build-up and project outcomes among the enterprises in economically and institutionally advanced regions. Besides the conceptual input to the understanding of the importance of QH efficiency in the implementation of SS, the study offers a number of policy-related implications. These include the recommendation to identify the institutional potential for collaboration and capacities of relevant actors before particular partnership projects are launched. Because some of the less institutionally developed regions can be disadvantaged at the start, the policy measures might deepen economic polarization by strengthening those already competitive.

The chapter by Lis, Kowalski, and Mackiewicz (2021) focuses on the usefulness of the cluster-based approach in the design and implementation of S3 in Germany and Poland. They find the important role of leading clusters in S3 of both countries. They also see differences, such as German approach better exploiting both the accomplished advancements in clusters and continuity in related innovation policies. The chapter conceptually specifies the role of clusters and cluster policies within the framework of S3. It proposes policy directions with long-term view and continuity in those accomplishments that are vital to structural change guided by SS. Moreover, some conditions for the adoption of clusters in S3 were highlighted, such capacity to transcend the sectoral composition and boundaries of extant industrial agglomerations to enable regional transformation.

Jakimowicz and Rzeczkowski (2021) emphasize the importance of digital technologies in forming local public–private partnerships for S3. They conceptualize digital municipality platforms as local growth poles and reflect on their potential to become hubs for S3-oriented collaboration in the Warmia-Mazury, Poland. Based on the spatial graph method, the authors find that the most advanced municipality digital platforms overlap with the territorial development axes rather than with administrative units. Digital platforms for partnerships are then contemporary growth poles complementing, but also partially substituting for spatial development axes that rely on tangible infrastructures. The findings enabled an interesting proposition that the concepts of wikinomics are useful in developing public–private partnerships for EDP and S3 adoption. The policy implications comprise the recommendation for extensive use of digital public administration to enhance collaboration for S3. On the other hand, potential threats have been identified, such as the current digital growth poles petrifying the polarization of local development (McCann, & Ortega-Argilés, 2015).

Alike in Part 3, the chapters represent a set of mutually reinforcing ideas. The three studies emphasize local partnerships for S3 as path dependent. Dileo and Pini (2021) find the enterprise collaboration with academia and society as dependent on historical economic polarization of Italy. Lis et al. (2021) point to clusters being both embedded structures and outcomes of earlier innovation policies. Jakimowicz and Reczkowski (2021) reveal the overlap between the most advanced ICT platforms of local governments and historically the most developed communities. Policy makers need to acknowledge these historical conditions when designing partnerships and assigning them with S3-related objectives. Moreover, the authors point to longevity and historically established structures that condition local development and partnerships. Consequently, it is advisable that new policy directions, such as S3, build upon the earlier accomplishments and enable their continuity so that these investments could be comprehensively exploited.

Implications for Further Research

The volume also offers some avenues for further research in terms of both thematic areas and proposed methodologies to explore these areas. Chapters from part 1 highlight the importance of counting with more comparative studies of regional S3 based on similar methodologies as the one used by Klincewicz et al. (2021), which adopts patent data to address the linkages between S3 and the innovative potential of regions. Another field for further research could be the analysis of structural impacts of S3, as the time scope will soon allow such analysis (Sánchez-Carreira et al., 2021). Finally, regarding the monitoring process, a stronger effort is needed to define standards for monitoring indicators and methodologies (Wojnicka-Sycz et al., 2021).

As it stems from Part 2, future research on local and bottom-up implementation of S3 might be oriented toward individual projects and actions that enable to clearly assign inputs and outcomes of policy (Baier, 2021). Another important thematic focus might be the relationships between SS and other adjacent concepts. This refers to both earlier perspectives on innovation and regional development, and those inspired by S3, such as the smart city concept (Mei & Konovalenko-Slettli, 2021). Ultimately, more research can be postulated in the area of adaptability and validity of S3 as development concept for individual industries. In particular, innovation-driven branching out and synergies with extant and novel industry segments need to be explained in depth (Gancarczyk et al., 2021).

Part 3 sets out such promising research themes, as cross-country and cross-sectoral comparisons of enterprise partnerships in innovation processes, regarding their formation conditions and effectiveness (Dileo & Pini, 2021). It would also be relevant to obtain more evidence as to real processes of involving extant clusters in the design and implementation of S3 (Lis et al., 2021). Another avenue of research might be processes of integrating clusters in S3, as entities embodying specialized knowledge and stakeholder networks. Moreover, the research in wikinomics models of public–private partnership might be informative for policy makers (Jakimowicz & Rzeczkowski, 2021).

Implications for future research methodologies stem from the characteristics distinguishing the chapters in this monograph. First, they are predominantly explorative and thus case-based investigations. Second, they focus on the S3 implementation, which is a processual phenomenon and thus longer term and often evolutionary in nature. Exploratory case studies are justified by the novelty of the research area, its complexity requiring a plethora of variables, as well as by contextual idiosyncrasies of spatial development. Nevertheless, singular cases call for multiple case study design, and further for quantitative methods to enable generalizations (Baier, 2021; Mei & Konovalenko-Slettli, 2021; Gancarczyk et al., 2021). Moreover, structural change and transformation induced by S3 suggest a longitudinal and evolutionary research approach (Sánchez-Carreira et al., 2021). This requires panel data for quantitative studies (Dileo & Pini, 2021; Klincewicz et al., 2021), as well as longitudinal, in-depth and direct observation of particular policy processes in qualitative studies (Lis et al., 2021; Mei & Konovalenko-Slettli, 2021; Gancarczyk et al., 2021). Traditional statistical measures of industrial structure and performance cannot fully embrace EDP in identifying high potential economic activities, or a number of soft and intermediary outcomes, such as partnership building (Wojnicka-Sycz et al., 2021; Jakimowicz & Rzeczkowski, 2021; Mei & Konovalenko-Slettli, 2021). Consequently, further research needs to seek other adequate measures that would reflect these S3-related phenomena with more accurate variables.

Conclusion

Following the stated aim, the monograph presented the experience of the S3 implementation from multilevel policy governance, as well as from the bottom-up perspectives of firms, clusters, and networks in selected European countries. The unique value of the volume consists in linking policy considerations with the approaches of public and private actors, forming partnerships at the lower governance levels. In particular, Part 1 assumes a broader view, with regions in the international and comparative perspectives. Parts 2 and 3 reveal S3 implementation processes and SS feasibility in organizations and partnerships at the bottom layers of governance.

The major contribution of the presented research rests in theoretical implications and practical recommendations relevant for the implementation of regional S3 with a focus on the European context. Nevertheless, we can assume the possibility to extend the proposed implications to other geographical contexts, acknowledging their place-based specificities. Another contribution from the volume consists in presenting smart specialization as transformation and growth concept for territorial units and economic actors. This input can be treated as a more general theoretical outcome that highlights the potential for smart specialization to further advance its ideas and implementation practice, both in the public policy space and in private choices of economic entities.

References

Aiginger, K., & Rodrik, D. (2020). Rebirth of industrial policy and an agenda for the twenty-first century. *Journal of Industry, Competition and Trade*, 20(2), 189–207.

Aranguren, M. J., Magro, E., Navarro, M., & Wilson, J. R. (2019). Governance of the territorial entrepreneurial discovery process: looking under the bonnet of RIS3. *Regional Studies*, 53(4), 451–461.

Asheim, B. T. (2019). Smart specialisation, innovation policy and regional innovation systems: What about new path development in less innovative regions?. *Innovation: The European Journal of Social Science Research*, 32(1), 8–25.

Baier, E. (2021). The impacts of policy instruments to stimulate bottom-up approaches for smart specialization: The case of Baden-Wuerttemberg. In M. Gancarczyk, A. Ujwary-Gil & M. González-López (Eds.), *Partnerships for regional innovation and development: Implementing smart specialization in Europe*. New York: Routledge.

Bailey, D., Glasmeier, A., & Tomlinson, P. R. (2019a). Industrial policy back on the agenda: Putting industrial policy in its place?. *Cambridge Journal of Regions, Economy and Society*, 12(3), 319–326.

Bailey, D., Glasmeier, A., Tomlinson, P. R., & Tyler, P. (2019b). Industrial policy: New technologies and transformative innovation policies?. *Cambridge Journal of Regions, Economy and Society*, 12(2), 169–177.

Balland, P. A., Boschma, R., Crespo, J., & Rigby, D. L. (2019). Smart specialization policy in the European Union: Relatedness, knowledge complexity and regional diversification. *Regional Studies*, 53(9), 1252–1268.

Barzotto, M., Corradini, C., Fai, F. M., Labory, S., & Tomlinson, P. R. (2019). Enhancing innovative capabilities in lagging regions: An extra-regional collaborative approach to RIS3. *Cambridge Journal of Regions, Economy and Society*, 12(2), 213–232.

Biagi, B., Brandano, M. G., & Ortega-Argiles, R. (2020). Smart specialisation and tourism: Understanding the priority choices in EU regions. *Socio-Economic Planning Sciences*, https://doi.org/10.1016/j.seps.2020.100883.

Borrás, S., & Jordana, J. (2016). When regional innovation policies meet policy rationales and evidence: A plea for policy analysis. *European Planning Studies*, 24(12), 2133–2153.

Brown, R., & Mawson, S. (2019). Entrepreneurial ecosystems and public policy in action: A critique of the latest industrial policy blockbuster. *Cambridge Journal of Regions, Economy and Society, 12*(3), 347–368.

Brown, R., Mawson, S., & Mason, C. (2017). Myth-busting and entrepreneurship policy: The case of high growth firms. *Entrepreneurship & Regional Development, 29*(5–6), 414–443.

Cai, Y., Normann, R., Pinheiro, R., & Sotarauta, M. (2018). Economic specialization and diversification at the country and regional level: Introducing a conceptual framework to study innovation policy logics. *European Planning Studies, 26*(12), 2407–2426.

Capello, R., & Kroll, H. (2016). From theory to practice in smart specialization strategy: Emerging limits and possible future trajectories. *European Planning Studies, 24*(8), 1393–1406.

Caragliu, A., & Del Bo, C. (2018). Much ado about something? An appraisal of the relationship between smart city and smart specialisation policies. *Tijdschrift voor Economische en Sociale Geografie, 109*(1), 129–143.

Ciffolilli, A., & Muscio, A. (2018). Industry 4.0: National and regional comparative advantages in key enabling technologies. *European Planning Studies, 26*(12), 2323–2343.

Crescenzi, R., de Blasio, G., & Giua, M. (2020). Cohesion policy incentives for collaborative industrial research: Evaluation of a smart specialisation forerunner programme. *Regional Studies, 54*(10), 1341–1353.

D'Adda, D., Guzzini, E., Iacobucci, D., & Palloni, R. (2019). Is Smart Specialisation Strategy coherent with regional innovative capabilities?. *Regional Studies, 53*(7), 1004–1016.

Dileo, I., & Pini, M. (2021). The quadruple helix for sustainable growth in more and less developed macro-regions in Italy under the lens of the smart specialization strategy. In M. Gancarczyk, A. Ujwary-Gil & M. González-López (Eds.), *Partnerships for regional innovation and development: Implementing smart specialization in Europe.* New York: Routledge.

EOCIC (European Observatory for Clusters and Industrial Change). (2019). *European cluster and industrial transformation trends report.* Luxemburg: Publications Office of the European Commission.

Estensoro, M., & Larrea, M. (2016). Overcoming policy making problems in smart specialization strategies: Engaging subregional governments. *European Planning Studies, 24*(7), 1319–1335.

European Commission. (2020). *A New Industrial Strategy for Europe.* Retrieved from https://eur-lex.europa.eu/legal-content/EN/TXT/?qid=1593086905382&uri=CELEX:52020DC0102

Fagerberg, J., & Hutschenreiter, G. (2019). Coping with societal challenges: Lessons for innovation policy governance. *Journal of Industry, Competition and Trade, 20*(2), 279–305.

Foray, D. (2013). The economic fundamentals of smart specialisation. *Ekonomiaz, 83*(2), 83–102.

Foray, D. (2014). *Smart specialisation: Opportunities and challenges for regional innovation policy.* New York: Routledge.

Foray, D. (2016). On the policy space of smart specialization strategies. *European Planning Studies, 24*(8), 1428–1437.

Foray, D. (2017). The economic fundamentals of smart specialization strategies. In S. Radosevic, A. Curaj, R. Gheorghiu, L. Andreescu & I. Wade (Eds.), *Advances in the theory and practice of smart specialization* (pp. 38–50). Cambridge, MA: Academic Press.

Foray, D. (2019). In response to 'Six critical questions about smart specialisation'. *European Planning Studies*, 27(10), 2066–2078.

Foray, D. (2020). Six additional replies—one more chorus of the S3 ballad. *European Planning Studies*, 28(8), 1685–1690.

Foray, D., Morgan, K., & Radosevic, S. (2018). *The role of smart specialization in the EU research and innovation policy landscape.* Brussels: European Commission. Retrieved from http://ec.europa.eu/regional_policy/sources/docgener/brochure/smart/role_smartspecialisation_ri.pdf

Galbraith, B., McAdam, R., Woods, J., & McGowan, T. (2017). Putting policy into practice: an exploratory study of SME innovation support in a peripheral UK region. *Entrepreneurship & Regional Development*, 29(7–8), 668–691.

Gancarczyk, M. (2015). Enterprise-and industry-level drivers of cluster evolution and their outcomes for clusters from developed and less-developed countries. *European Planning Studies*, 23(10), 1932–1952.

Gancarczyk, M. (2019). The performance of high-growers and regional entrepreneurial ecosystems: A research framework. *Entrepreneurial Business and Economics Review*, 7(3), 99–123.

Gancarczyk, M., & Gancarczyk, J. (2018). Proactive international strategies of cluster SMEs. *European Management Journal*, 36(1), 59–70.

Gancarczyk, J., Marakova, V., & Wszendybył-Skulska, E. (2021). City smart specializations in tourism: The cases of Kraków, Poland, and Košice, Slovakia. In M. Gancarczyk, A. Ujwary-Gil & M. González-López (Eds.), *Partnerships for regional innovation and development: Implementing smart specialization in Europe.* New York: Routledge.

Gancarczyk, M., Najda-Janoszka, M., & Gancarczyk, J. (2020). Regional innovation system and policy in Malopolska, Poland: An institutionalised learning. In M. González-López & B. Asheim (Eds.), *Regions and innovation policies in Europe* (pp. 225–251). Cheltenham, UK: Edward Elgar Publishing.

Gancarczyk, M., & Ujwary-Gil, A. (2020). Revitalizing industrial policy in the EU through smart, micro-level and bottom-up approaches. In A. Ujwary-Gil & M. Gancarczyk (Eds.), *New challenges in economic policy, business and management* (pp. 11–29). Warsaw: Institute of Economics, Polish Academy of Sciences.

Gong, H., & Hassink, R. (2019). Co-evolution in contemporary economic geography: Towards a theoretical framework. *Regional Studies*, 53(9), 1344–1355.

González-López, M. & Asheim, B. (Eds.). (2020). *Regions and innovation policies in Europe.* Cheltenham: Edward Elgar Publishing.

González-López, M., Asheim, B. T., & Sánchez-Carreira, M. C. (2019). New insights on regional innovation policies. *Innovation: The European Journal of Social Science Research*, 32(1), 1–7.

Götz, M. (2020). Cluster role in industry 4.0—a pilot study from Germany. *Competitiveness Review: An International Business Journal.* https://doi.org/10.1108/CR-10-2019-0091

Grillitsch, M. (2019). Following or breaking regional development paths: On the role and capability of the innovative entrepreneur. *Regional Studies*, 53(5), 681–691.

Grillitsch, M., & Asheim, B. (2018). Place-based innovation policy for industrial diversification in regions. *European Planning Studies*, 26(8), 1638–1662.

Hassink, R. (2020). Advancing place-based regional innovation policies. In M. González-López & B. T. Asheim (Eds.), *Regions and innovation policies in Europe. Learning from the margins* (pp. 30–45). Cheltenham, UK: Edward Elgar Publishing.

Hassink, R., & Gong, H. (2019). Six critical questions about smart specialization. *European Planning Studies*, 27(10), 2049–2065.

Hassink, R., Isaksen, A., & Trippl, M. (2019). Towards a comprehensive understanding of new regional industrial path development. *Regional Studies*, 1–10.

Iacobucci, D., & Guzzini, E. (2016). Relatedness and connectivity in technological domains: Missing links in S3 design and implementation. *European Planning Studies*, 24(8), 1511–1526.

Isaksen, A. O., Jakobsen, S. E., Njøs, R., & Normann, R. (2019). Regional industrial restructuring resulting from individual and system agency. *Innovation: The European Journal of Social Science Research*, 32(1), 48–65.

Jakimowicz, A., & Rzeczkowski, D. (2021). Municipality digital platforms and local development in the Warmia and Mazury region: Implications for smart specialization. In M. Gancarczyk, A. Ujwary-Gil, & M. González-López (Eds.), *Partnerships for regional innovation and development: Implementing smart specialization in Europe* (pp. 00–00). New York: Routledge.

Klincewicz, K., Marczewska, M., & Tucci, Ch. L. (2021). Regional smart specializations in Central and Eastern Europe: Between political decisions and revealed technological potential. In M. Gancarczyk, A. Ujwary-Gil & M. González-López (Eds.), *Partnerships for regional innovation and development: Implementing smart specialization in Europe*. New York: Routledge.

Lin, J. Y., & Wang, Y. (2020). Structural change, industrial upgrading, and middle-income trap. *Journal of Industry, Competition and Trade*, 20(2), 359–394.

Lis, A. M., Kowalski, A. M., & Mackiewicz, M. (2021). Smart specialization through cluster policy: Evidence from Poland and Germany. In M. Gancarczyk, A. Ujwary-Gil & M. González-López (Eds.), *Partnerships for regional innovation and development: Implementing smart specialization in Europe*. New York: Routledge.

Mason, C., & Brown, R. (2014). Entrepreneurial ecosystems and growth oriented entrepreneurship. *Final Report to OECD, Paris*, 30(1), 77–102.

McCann, P. (2015). *The regional and urban policy of the European Union: Cohesion, results-orientation and smart specialisation*. Cheltenham, Northampton: Edward Elgar Publishing.

McCann, P., & Ortega-Argilés, R. (2015). Smart specialization, regional growth and applications to European Union cohesion policy. *Regional Studies*, 49(8), 1291–1302.

Mei, X. Y., & Konovalenko-Slettli, V. (2021). Exploring the relationship between smart specialization strategy (S3) and Smart City (SC) initiatives in the context of Inland Norway. In M. Gancarczyk, A. Ujwary-Gil & M. González-López (Eds.), *Partnerships for regional innovation and development: Implementing smart specialization in Europe*. New York: Routledge.

Morgan, K., & Marques, P. (2019). The public animateur: Mission-led innovation and the "smart state" in Europe. *Cambridge Journal of Regions, Economy and Society*, 12(2), 179–193.

Nguyen, N., Mariussen, Å., & Hansen, J. Ø. (2020). The role of smart specialization in providing regional strategic support for establishing sustainable start-up incubation ecosystems. In *Research handbook on start-up incubation ecosystems*. Cheltenham: Edward Elgar Publishing.

OECD. (2020). *Broadbased innovation policy for all regions and cities*. Paris: OECD Publishing.

Panzar, J. C., & Willig, R. D. (1977). Economies of scale in multi-output production. *The Quarterly Journal of Economics*, *91*(3), 481–493.

Penrose, E. (1959). *The theory of the growth of the firm*. Oxford: Oxford University Press.

Porto Gomez, I., Otegi Olaso, J. R., & Zabala-Iturriagagoitia, J. M. (2016). ROSA, ROSAE, ROSIS: Modelling a regional open sectoral innovation system. *Entrepreneurship & regional development*, *28*(1–2), 26–50.

Radosevic, S., Curaj, A., Gheorghiu, R., Andreescu, L., & Wade, I. (Eds.). (2017). *Advances in the theory and practice of smart specialization*. Cambridge, MA: Elsevier, Academic Press.

Reimeris, R. (2016). New rules, same game: The case of Lithuanian smart specialization. *European Planning Studies*, *24*(8), 1561–1583.

Rodrik, D. (2014). Green industrial policy. *Oxford Review of Economic Policy*, *30*(3), 469–491.

Sánchez-Carreira, M. C., González-López, M., & Varela-Vázquez, P. (2021). The implementation of the smart specialization approach in the peripheral region of Galicia. In M. Gancarczyk, A. Ujwary-Gil & M. González-López (Eds.), *Partnerships for regional innovation and development: Implementing smart specialization in Europe*. New York: Routledge.

Stam, E. (2015). Entrepreneurial ecosystems and regional policy: A sympathetic critique. *European Planning Studies*, *23*(9), 1759–1769.

Ujwary-Gil, A. (2017). Intra-organizational two-mode networks analysis of a public organization. *Economics & Sociology*, *10*(3), 192–205.

Ujwary-Gil, A. (2019). Organizational network analysis: A study of a university library from a network efficiency perspective. *Library & Information Science Research*, *41*(1), 48–57.

Ujwary-Gil, A., & Potoczek, N. (2020). A dynamic, network and resource-based approach to the sustainable business model. *Electronic Markets*, *30*, 717–733.

Varga, A., Sebestyén, T., Szabó, N., & Szerb, L. (2018). Estimating the economic impacts of knowledge network and entrepreneurship development in smart specialization policy. *Regional Studies*, 1–12.

Wojnicka-Sycz, E. (2020). Theory-based evaluation criteria for regional smart specializations and their application in the Podkarpackie voivodeship in Poland. *Regional Studies*, *54*(11), 1612–1625.

Wojnicka-Sycz, E., Pylak, K., Sliż, P., & Sycz, P. (2021). Challenges for monitoring smart specialisation in the European Union. In M. Gancarczyk, A. Ujwary-Gil & M. González-López (Eds.), *Partnerships for regional innovation and development: Implementing smart specialization in Europe*. New York: Routledge.

Part 1

Regional Smart Specialization Policies

An Experience in Planning, Implementation, and Monitoring

1 Regional Smart Specializations in Central and Eastern Europe

Between Political Decisions and Revealed Technological Potential

Krzysztof Klincewicz, Magdalena Marczewska, and Christopher L. Tucci

Introduction

Regional authorities endorse smart specializations based on heterogeneous processes of analysis, planning, and stakeholder dialogue. The choice of specializations often appears linked to observed concentrations of innovative activities or declared interests of R&D actors in a nascent thematic field. In this chapter, we use the examples of Estonian, Latvian, Lithuanian, Polish, and Romanian regions (28 regions in total) and their declared specializations related to the agri-food and health sectors. We aim to discuss how political decisions regarding supported priorities correspond to the actual technological potential of different regions. This will be explored using patent data—with a particular focus on the patenting activities of companies—with a view to better understand how regional smart specialization strategies relate to the innovative development of firms operating in the analyzed sectors.

The linkage between science/technology policy and economic development is a critical one to explore (Nelson, 1993). As *Smart Specialization* has become an increasingly important component of different countries' development strategies, evaluating its effectiveness and the conditions under which it is performing well has lagged behind its diffusion and adoption. In a highly effective smart specialization region, one might expect the companies within that region to be highly attuned to the specialization, differentiated from other regions, and as a result, performing well due to their agglomeration and their interactions with the entire ecosystem that would have developed around the specialization. One way of examining the nature of corporate and ecosystem innovation is to explore the inventive activities of these actors in and around smart specialization regions. Without such a feedback loop, the policy, while appealing, remains in a vacuum, untested, and is difficult to improve.

As a first step in this process of clusters and policy evaluation, we can study a geographic region that exhibits variance in policy approaches, smart specialization foci, and potential innovation outcomes: Central and Eastern Europe. We can document the level of activity, the coherence of smart specialization, and the ecosystem's role, both vertical (different actors along the innovation chain) and horizontal (joint work with other similar organizations). Thus, our analysis addresses the following research questions (RQs):

> *RQ1: Do the agri-food and health-related smart specialization strategies of the 28 analyzed regions of Central and Eastern Europe match their technological potential revealed by inventive activity?*
>
> *RQ2: How intensive were the inventive activities related to the agri-food and health sectors in the analyzed regions in 2006–2015?*
>
> *RQ3: What was the role of different R&D actors representing specific sectors of business enterprises, individuals, universities, and research institutes in the agri-food and health outputs of the analyzed regions?*
>
> *RQ4: How important was cross-sectoral cooperation leading to joint inventive outcomes in the analyzed sectors and regions?*

The chapter makes several contributions. It presents an up-to-date list of regional smart specializations of 28 regions in five countries of Central and Eastern Europe. It also identifies discrepancies between the declared specializations and regional patenting, offering important insights for policy makers, who need to consider the technological potential of stakeholders to stimulate regional innovative capacities. The chapter is structured as follows. First, the literature review concerning the regional development and implementation of smart specialization strategies is presented. Subsequently, the research methods and data are introduced, followed by the research results. The chapter ends with conclusions and research limitations, supplemented by implications for theory and policy.

Literature Background

The concept of Research & Innovation Smart Specialization Strategy (RIS3) was introduced by the European Commission as a means to *"help regions to concentrate resources on few key priorities rather than spreading investment thinly across areas and business sectors"* (EC, 2010, p. 6). The subsequently developed theoretical framework of RIS3 emphasized the importance of experimentation, involvement of multiple stakeholders, and bottom-up processes of "entrepreneurial discovery." These activities were planned with the view to lead to the selection of specific regional priorities, which would be continuously monitored and refined. The processes were supposed to involve local stakeholders, in particular, innovative companies, counterbalancing the power of public authorities, unable to aspire to the role of an *"omniscient planner"* (Foray, 2016, p. 1432). Specializations could address emerging opportunities or existing critical mass in technology development in each region.

RIS3 as place-based innovation strategies were supposed to leverage specific competitive advantages and unique assets of regions (Capello & Kroll, 2021, p. 1402). The methodological guidance recommended to specialize in sufficiently granular fields that for a subset of a single industrial sector or have inter-sectoral nature and correspond to an emerging or existing innovation potential (Foray & Goenaga, 2013, p. 3). Prioritizations based on broadly defined industrial sectors (e.g., food, medicine, energy) were discouraged, with recommendations to focus on finer levels of aggregation (Foray, 2016).

Starting from 2014, the adoption of RIS3 became a necessary precondition for gaining access to the European Structural and Investment Funds of 2014–2020, and the RIS3 approaches became more common and formalized. RIS3 turned out to be particularly important for Central and Eastern European countries, heavily reliant on access to EU funds. The European Commission expected that RIS3 would limit the duplication of project themes and eliminate investments insufficiently related to local innovation ecosystems (Berkowitz, 2017, p. XVII). In the wake of RIS3 development, the regions of Central and Eastern Europe were hoped to benefit from the financial stimulus coupled with improvements in policy-making capacities (Muscio et al., 2015). RIS3 was defined on national or regional levels. For example, Poland and Romania identified specializations at the regional level, alongside sets of nationwide priorities. At the same time, Estonia, Latvia, and Lithuania, as smaller countries, had only single lists of specializations per country.

In accordance with the RIS3 approach, specializations should be "smart," aiming to exploit unique regional strengths to further develop its innovation system, and thus specialization was to be coupled with differentiation (Foray et al., 2018), ensuring a regional competitive advantage. The lack of selectivity was considered an essential threat to RIS3 success (Foray et al., 2011). Still, the definition and implementation of thematically focused innovation support proved difficult owing to the limited experiences of regional authorities (Foray et al., 2018).

In many cases, RIS3 priorities turned out to be insufficiently specific or differentiated. RIS3 development and implementation were faced with challenges related to the lack of relevant skills of the coordinating authorities (Radosevic, 2017, p. 23). Regions operated under time pressure to adopt RIS3 as pre-requirements for accessing EU funding but did not have opportunities to acquire the necessary knowledge about this novel approach or carry out extensive stakeholder consultations (Kroll, 2015, pp. 2080–2082). As a consequence, many regions used simplistic, generic priorities, disregarding methodological guidance and selecting broad sectors or technologies (e.g., medicine or biotechnology) instead of the recommended, fine-grained specializations. Such tendencies were observed both in Southern Europe (Tsipouri, 2017, p. 150) and in the Central and Eastern European countries, which often relied merely on economic data to select priorities, with only limited private sector consultations. This resulted in the selection of broad, imprecise, and ambiguous specializations (Karo et al., 2017, p. 271), without observed changes in innovation policies (Reimeris, 2016) and with an overly generic character (Klincewicz, 2018). For example, a patent-based analysis of northern Portugal proved a mismatch between selected RIS3 priority areas and regional potential (Duque Estrada Santos, 2018). Although the logic behind selecting RIS3 priorities seems to be well understood by policy makers, the results of its adoption do not always meet initially set objectives and goals (Kleibrink et al., 2016). Another example of the limited differentiation was the recurring selection of three thematic fields across most EU regions: health, energy, and agri-food (Sörvik & Kleibrink, 2015, p. 10). In general, regions with sufficient technological and entrepreneurial capabilities and strong networks are more likely to benefit from opportunities associated with RIS3 selection and adoption (McCann & Ortega-Argilés, 2015). In contrast, due to insufficient innovation and entrepreneurial capabilities of lagging regions, these are not capable of running smoothly the entrepreneurial discovery process and selecting fitting priorities (Barzotto et al., 2019). Bulgaria is an example of such a region (Krammer, 2017).

Methodological Approach

The research is based on a content analysis of RIS3 documents and quantitative patent analyses. A comparable approach was adopted by D'Adda et al. (2019) to verify the consistency between smart specialization priorities and patents in Italy. Patent data were extracted from databases maintained by the European Patent Office (PATSTAT: for Estonia, Latvia, Lithuania, and Romania) and the Polish Patent Office (for Poland). The data sets were disaggregated into patents filed by companies and other actors and compared with regional smart specializations selected in the process of implementing the European Structural and Investment Funds, 2014–2020.

In what follows, we describe the use of patent data as a stand-in for inventive activity and indeed innovative activity. In the past, researchers often used R&D spending or other R&D metrics as a gauge of innovation, but as Schmookler (1966) pointed out, R&D spending is actually an input into the innovation and not really an output. In this chapter, we are concerned with economic development as a potential outcome of regional smart specialization policies, so we would prefer to study innovation outcomes that have economic potential. Hasan and Tucci (2010), discussing the pros and cons of using patent data as a proxy for innovation, start with the pros: patent data are widely used in innovation studies because (1) patents represent inventive output that is usually intended to be commercialized; (2) extensive data have been carefully collected for years; and (3) there appear to be some financial benefit to having a patent, given how costly they are to obtain and defend. On the other hand, Hasan and Tucci (2010) also develop some of the cons: (1) patents do not cover all innovations; (2) many companies prefer secrecy to disclosure and therefore do not patent some important inventions; (3) some patents are used "defensively" to block competitors rather than for commercialization; and (4) certain sectors are more completely covered than others. However, on the whole, the reason that patent data are so widely used is that, while "noisy," they are the best and the most replicable large-scale measures of innovation activity that exist (see Freeman & Soete, 1997, pp. 112–120; Tidd & Bessant, 2009, pp. 555–560).

Priority patent applications filed in a given national patent office were identified in accordance with methods for matching patents with industrial sectors, developed for Eurostat (Van Looy et al., 2014).[1] We selected food, beverages, pharmaceuticals, and medical technologies, because not only are they empirically important for smart specialization but they are also considered to have strong intellectual property protection in the form of patents (Scherer, 2000; Lesser, 1998). All patents filed between the years 2006 and 2015 in a given country were selected and subsequently decomposed into subsets for specific regions (based on a manual process of matching addresses of applicants, as stated on the patent applications, or identifying the addresses of organizations in external sources when not explicitly listed in the patent documents). The analyzed period was considered relevant for the 2014–2020 financial perspective of the EU, as these 10 years, 2006–2015, directly preceded the new programming period and the time when RIS3 documents were drafted, thus corresponding to the accumulated technological capabilities in the beginning of the RIS3 implementation. The queries were carried out in the autumn 2017 edition of PATSTAT (available in early 2018) and in the spring 2018 version of the Polish Patent Office database. The research followed a methodological approach applied previously to the Polish regions by Klincewicz (2018). Details of smart specializations of analyzed regions were obtained through analysis of official documents published by authorities, mainly in local languages (Table 1.1).

Since the beginning of the EU perspective 2014–2020, these documents have been modified in some regions, with names and scopes of some specializations revised. The S3Platform maintained by the European Commission contains data on smart specializations of EU regions (JRC, 2020), but an up-to-date list of regional smart specializations is not available. The content analysis was used to interpret the scope of prioritized support areas, using a list of identified RIS3 documents from the analyzed countries, based on the following documentary sources: ADR București-Ilfov (2019), ADR Centru (2017), ADR Nord-Est (2017), ADR Nord-Vest (2018), ADR Sud Muntenia (2015), ADR Sud-Est (2017),

Table 1.1 Smart specializations and patent applications related to agri-food and health in Estonia, Latvia, Lithuania, Poland, and Romania

Region	Smart specializations		Total	Patent applications (2006–2015)			
	Agri-food	Health		Food	Beverages	Pharmaceuticals	Medical technologies
EE	Resource efficiency (including food)	Health technology and services	3	12	0	58	29
LV	–	Biomedicine, medical technologies, biopharmaceuticals, and biotechnologies (Knowledge-intensive bioeconomy)	5	5	0	32	20
LT	Agro-innovation and food technologies	Health technologies and biotechnologies [Chemistry] [Life sciences]	6	5	3	20	36
PL21: Małopolskie	–		7	70	17	173	136
PL22: Śląskie	–	Medicine Emerging industries (including personalized medicine)	5	51	11	124	304
PL41: Wielkopolskie	Bio-based raw materials and food	Modern medical technologies	6	109	19	289	102
PL42: Zachodniopomorskie	Modern agri-food processing [Health and quality of life]	[Products of chemical and materials engineering]	8	46	13	147	61
PL43: Lubuskie	Health and quality of life	Health and quality of life	4	10	2	3	20
PL51: Dolnośląskie	High-quality food	Chemical and pharmaceutical industry	6	90	8	773	195

Region	Specialization	Health specialization					
PL52: Cpolskie	Agri-food technologies	Processes and products for health and environmental protection	6	6	2	28	21
PL61: Kujawsko-Pomorskie	Healthy and safe food	Health and health tourism	8	40	2	61	80
PL62: Warmińsko-Mazurskie	High-quality food	–	3	40	4	17	25
PL63: Pomorskie	–	Medical technologies related to lifestyle diseases and aging	4	57	5	144	79
PL71: Łódzkie	Innovative agriculture and agri-food processing	Medicine, pharmacy, cosmetics	6	89	14	214	213
PL72: Świętokrzyskie	Modern agriculture and food processing	Health tourism	7	5	4	17	35
PL81: Lubelskie	[Bioeconomy]	Medicine and health [Quality of life]	4	37	18	183	67
PL82: Podkarpackie	[Quality of life]		4	24	9	24	46
PL84: Podlaskie	Agri-food and related sectors	Medical, life sciences and related sectors [Quality of life]	4	19	1	27	62
PL91–92: Mazowieckie	Food safety [Quality of life]	[Quality of life]	4	245	40	659	405
RO11: Nord-Vest	Agri-food Cosmetics and food supplements	Health	6	8	0	41	29
RO12: Centru	Agri-food sector	Medical and pharmaceutical sectors; Balneary tourism	9	6	0	9	22
RO21: Nord-Est	Agri-food sector	Biotechnologies Health and tourism	6	0	1	22	20

(*Continued*)

Table 1.1 (Continued)

Region	Smart specializations		Patent applications (2006–2015)				
	Agri-food	Health	Total	Food	Beverages	Pharmaceuticals	Medical technologies
RO22: Sud-Est	Agro-food industry and fishery	Biotechnologies	7	10	6	5	1
RO31: Sud-Muntenia	Agriculture and food industry [Bioeconomy]	–	6	3	0	6	3
RO32: București-Ilfov	Food industry and food safety	–	5	34	0	132	83
RO41: Sud-Vest Oltenia	Agriculture and food industry	Innovative medicine	5	2	0	3	6
RO42: Vest	Agri-food sector	–	5	3	0	16	9

Source: Own elaboration based on ADR București-Ilfov (2019), ADR Centru (2017), ADR Nord-Est (2017), ADR Nord-Vest (2018), ADR Sud Muntenia (2015), ADR Sud-Est (2017), ADR Vest (2016), C ACZ Consulting SRL (2015), Lapienis and Reimeris (2016), MEC (2014), Ministry of Education and Research (2014), MOES (2018), SWM (2015), UMWD (2015), UMWKP (2016), UMWL (2014), UMWŁ (2015), UMWO (2016), UMWPod (2015), UMWPom (2015), UMWŚ (2014), UMWW (2015), UMWWM (2014), UMWZ (2016), ZWM (2015), ZWP (2016), ZWŚ (2018). Patent data from PATSTAT and the Polish Patent Office databases.

ADR Vest (2016), C ACZ Consulting SRL (2015), Lapienis and Reimeris (2016), MEC (2014), Ministry of Education and Research (2014), MOES (2018), SWM (2015), UMWD (2015), UMWKP (2016), UMWL (2014), UMWL (2015), UMWŁ (2015), UMWO (2016), UMWPod (2015), UMWPom (2015), UMWŚ (2014), UMWW (2015), UMWWM (2014), UMWZ (2016), ZWM (2015), ZWP (2016), ZWŚ (2018). The use of patent analysis/bibliometric techniques revealed the technological strengths of regions and allowed the assessment of the accuracy of political decisions related to smart specializations.

Results

Smart Specializations and Patenting Activities in Estonia, Latvia, Lithuania, Poland, and Romania

Countries and regions of the European Union include agri-food and health specializations amongst the most popular priorities in RIS3 documents (Sörvik & Kleibrink, 2015, p. 10). Table 1.1 presents smart specializations related to the agri-food and health sectors in Estonia, Latvia, Lithuania, Poland, and Romania. The lists reveal the original names of the specializations, as presented in the original policy documents establishing RIS3 in a given region or country. Names in *italics* indicate priorities that are only partially related to the analyzed fields of agri-food or health, but the linkages were established on the basis of detailed descriptions of the RIS3 documents. Among the 28 analyzed regions, only three do not include agri-food-related smart specializations (Latvia and the two Polish regions of Pomorskie and Śląskie). Accordingly, the health sector is indicated as a priority by most regions, with the exception of one region in Poland (Warmińsko-Mazurskie) and three in Romania (Sud-Muntenia, Bucureşti-Ilfov, and Vest). Most of the priorities are very broad, referring to the general name of the sector (an exception is the Polish region of Pomorskie, specializing in medical technologies related to lifestyle diseases and aging). The names and scopes of specializations do not correspond to the previously discussed methodological recommendations, which emphasized the need to adopt a fine-grained approach, identifying priorities that help differentiate a region, and correspond to emerging technologies or demonstrated innovation potential. Most of the analyzed regions simply used the broad definitions of agri-food and health sectors, encompassing various technologies and innovative activities, without explicitly identified strengths or differentiators.

Table 1.1 helps answer RQ1, addressing the relations between selected priorities and revealed the technological potential of regions. It presents the counts of patent applications filed in 2006–2015 in areas corresponding to agri-food (columns: "Food" and "Beverages") and health (columns "Pharmaceuticals" and "Medical technologies"). No systematic linkages could be identified between the selected specializations and the scope of patenting activities for the 28 analyzed regions. Regions seem to significantly differ in patenting propensity, with the Baltic states of Estonia, Latvia, and Lithuania demonstrating in general rather limited interests in patenting, alongside some of the less developed regions of Poland and Romania. In general, regions tend to be more active in filing patents for health-related inventions rather than in the agri-food field. It must also be remembered that apart from patented technologies, in agri-food and health sectors, innovations might also result from other creative processes, particularly for market-level innovations (e.g., food products novel in a given region but known elsewhere and thus no longer patentable, dietary supplements and OTC (over-the-counter) drugs based on widely known active substances but marketed in novel ways) or for innovation in services (e.g., related to therapeutic, agricultural or food preparation techniques). RQs focus on patent applications, but regional smart specializations might also manifest themselves in other ways than patented inventions.

RQ2 referred to the intensity of inventive activities in the analyzed regions. Polish regions display the most intensive patenting activities in both sectors (in total, 1063 agri-food patent applications and 4222 health applications). Romania is also relatively active (90 agri-food applications, 624 health applications). In contrast, counts of patent applications in Estonia, Latvia, and Lithuania remain limited (in total, 25 agri-food patent applications from these three Baltic states and, respectively, 195 health-related patent applications).

For Poland, every fourth agri-food patent application in 2006–2015 was filed by applicants from Mazowieckie (285 patent applications, 26.8% of all Polish agri-food applications). Other regions of Poland active in agri-food patenting include Wielkopolskie (128 patent applications; 12%), Łódzkie (103 patent applications, 9.7%), Dolnośląskie (98 patent applications, 9.2%), Małopolskie (87 patent applications, 8.2%). In the health sector, strong patenting activities are observed in Mazowieckie (1,064 applications from 2006 to 2015, 23.4% of all Polish health-related patent applications) and Dolnośląskie (968 applications, 21.3%). Other active regions include Łódzkie (427 applications, 9.4%), Śląskie (408 applications, 8.9%), and Wielkopolskie (391 applications, 8.6%).

In Romania, the largest share of patent applications related to the agri-food sector from 2006 to 2015 was filed by applicants from București-Ilfov region (34 patent applications, 37.8%). Other regions active in agri-food patenting include Sud-Est (16 applications, 17.8%), Nord-Vest (8 applications, 8.9%), and Centru (6 applications, 6.7%). 34.5% of Romanian patent applications in the health sector were filed by applicants from București-Ilfov (215 applications), 11.2% from Nord-Vest

(70 applications), 6.7% from Nord-Est (42 applications), and 5% from Centru (31 applications).

Figure 1.1 summarizes the findings by presenting a scatterplot with counts of patent applications respectively in agri-food and health fields. It uses names of NUTS2 regions and graphical symbols that indicate whether a given region has agri-food or health priorities in its official RIS3 document.

In all of the analyzed regions, agri-food and health patent applications were primarily filed by local entities (organizations operating in the region), and applications filed by international entities were of marginal importance (the analysis did not include validations of foreign patents but only priority applications submitted to the national patent office of each region). Only a few patent applications related to agri-food or health sectors were filed with international co-owners, and the patenting had an overwhelmingly local character.

The analysis indicates a mismatch between the RIS3 priorities and the actual technological potential, revealed by an analysis of patents from the 10 years preceding the adoption of RIS3 in 28 analyzed regions. There were only a few regions performing strongly in agri-food and health

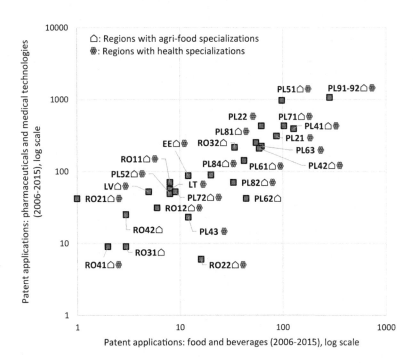

Figure 1.1 Patent applications related to agri-food and health in the regions of Estonia, Latvia, Lithuania, Poland, and Romania, 2006–2015

patenting, but most regions identified food and health as their innovation priorities, regardless of the revealed scale of regional inventive activities or technological potential.

R&D Actors in Regional Patenting Activities

RQ3 refers to the role of R&D actors representing specific sectors of the innovation system in agri-food and health patenting. It was addressed through an extensive analytical process involving decomposition of the patent data set into four types of applicants: business enterprises (BES), higher education institutes including universities (HEI), individual inventors–applicants (IND), and public research institutes including public hospitals (PRO). The process required a manual allocation of 3,426 affiliations, identified in the agri-food and health patent data sets (240 affiliations in Estonia, 70 in Latvia, 77 in Lithuania, 2,302 in Poland, and 737 in Romania). Results of this process are presented in Figure 1.2, which outlines sectoral shares of patent applications related to food, beverages, pharmaceuticals, and medical technologies in the regions of Estonia, Latvia, Lithuania, Poland, and Romania, filed by applicants representing

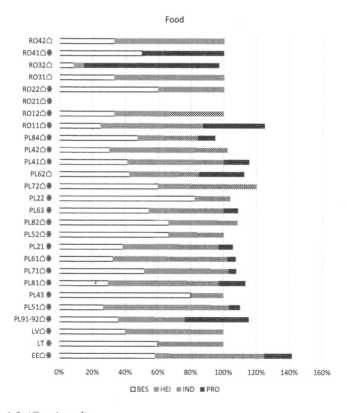

Figure 1.2 (Continued)

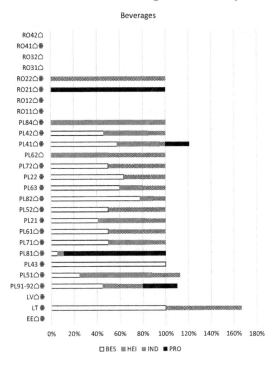

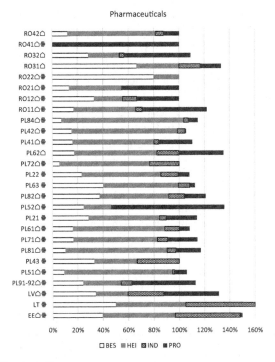

Figure 1.2 (Continued)

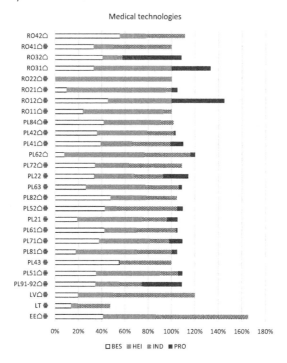

Figure 1.2 Sectoral shares of patent applications in food, beverages, pharmaceuticals, and medical technologies for each of the 28 analyzed regions

sectors of business enterprises (BES), higher education (HEI), individual inventors (IND) and public research organizations (PRO), 2006–2015. Shares do not add to 100% (due to some applications being filed jointly by representatives of more than one sector).

At the national level, companies play a leading role in agri-food patenting activities (combining food and beverages) in Lithuania (75% of patent applications had at least one company applicant), Estonia (58.3%, the share is equal to the share of applications filed by individuals), Poland (43.6%), and Latvia (40%, equal to the individual applicants). In Romania, the lead role was played in turn by public research organizations (35.6%) and individual applicants (31.1%).

In the health sector (combining pharmaceuticals and medical technologies), the significance of specific sectors or R&D performers is more regionally diversified. Individual inventors-applicants turned out to be the most prolific health patent applicants in Estonia (60.9% of applications had at least one individual applicant), Latvia (44.2%), Romania (38.1%), and Lithuania (37.5%), but their overall outputs were relatively limited. In Poland, universities took the lead role (51.5% of all health-related patent applications). However, these tendencies differ when health-related patent applications are decomposed into pharmaceuticals and medical technologies. The field of pharmaceutical inventions is dominated by universities in Poland (61.6% of patent applications), Estonia (56.9%), and Lithuania (55%, the same share as individual applicants), and strong relevance of public research organizations can be observed in Latvia (43.8% of patent applications) and Romania (32% of patent applications, with the share of patent applications filed by individuals at 32.3%). Medical technologies tend to originate primarily in filings by individual inventors–applicants in Estonia (79.3% of patent applications), Latvia (70.0%), Romania (44.9%), and Lithuania (27.8%), albeit counts of their patent applications are low. In contrast, Polish patent applications in the field of medical technologies were primarily submitted by higher education institutes (36.2%) and companies (35.0%).

Regional data presented in Figure 1.2 confirm that for 12 out of 16 Polish regions, business enterprises were the dominant source of agri-food patent applications in 2006–2015. Exceptions were: Dolnośląskie and Zachodniopomorskie (dominated by university patenting), Lubelskie (with the strongest role of research institutes), and Kujawsko-Pomorskie (with the largest share of applications filed by individuals). In health-related applications, universities turned out to play the lead role in 12 out of 16 regions of Poland. Other sectors dominated in Lubuskie, Podkarpackie, and Mazowieckie (business enterprises) and Opolskie (public research organizations).

In Romanian regions, agri-food patent applications were dispersed among R&D sectors, without clearly observable tendencies, owing to the small counts of patent documents. Bucureşti-Ilfov was the only Romanian region with a notable count of applications (corresponding to 37.7% of all Romanian agri-food patent documents from 2006 to 2015), and the majority of applications from this region were filed by public research organizations (82.4% of applications from Bucureşti-Ilfov). For health-related patent applications, counts were higher and tendencies more distinct. In pharmaceuticals, public research organizations play important roles in Nord-Vest, Centru, Nord-Est, Bucureşti-Ilfov, and Sud-Vest Oltenia, accompanied by universities in Vest and companies in Centru and Sud-Muntenia. The field of medical technologies is dominated by universities (in Nord-Vest, Centru, Nord-Est, Sud-Est, Sud-Muntenia), joined by research institutes (Bucureşti-Ilfov). Companies account for the largest shares of applications only in two regions (Sud-Vest Oltenia and Vest), but the counts of applications are very limited.

The findings could be interpreted in the context of regional innovation policies, which stimulate the development and introduction of new products, services, and business processes, enacted primarily by local companies. A regional technological strength would be revealed by dominant shares of patent applications filed by business enterprises or individuals who might pursue entrepreneurial opportunities. Patenting activities of scientific organizations (higher education institutes and public research institutes) do not necessarily indicate genuine technological strengths. Science systems in Central and Eastern Europe rely on academic patents as signals of research excellence, in ways similar to scientific publications.

Public science organizations from these regions are incentivized to file patents disregarding their commercial applicability, in order to improve their standing in national scientific evaluations, and the occurrence of successful commercialization of R&D results is still limited. Hence, the observed scientific rather than commercial character of patenting in many of the 28 analyzed regions, particularly with respect to health-related inventions, does not seem to offer compelling evidence of a critical mass in innovations, accumulated in a region that could be easily leveraged as the basis for a priority in a regional RIS3.

In response to RQ4, patent data were analyzed to trace the importance of cross-sectoral cooperation that led to joint patenting (patent co-applications and co-ownership). In particular, the technology transfer between science and industry and joint R&D efforts of companies with universities or research institutes would be of interest as indicators of emerging innovative strengths in a specific region. The findings are presented in Figure 1.3, revealing relatively low counts of cross-sectoral applications representing the following sectors of the innovation system: business enterprises (BES), higher education institutes (HEI), individual inventors–applicants (IND), and public research organizations (PRO).

In agri-food patenting, the occurrence of inter-sectoral patenting is very limited, with the exception of Poland (22 applications filed jointly by companies and universities, 13 by companies and research institutes, 26 by universities and research institutes). The health sector turned out to attract more cases of cross-sectoral patenting, observed in all of the analyzed countries. Counts of the applications filed by companies and universities were as followed: 4 in Estonia, 4 in Latvia, 3 in Lithuania, 59 in Poland, and 2 in Romania, and cross-sectoral applications by companies and research institutes included: 1 in Latvia, 61 in Poland and 2

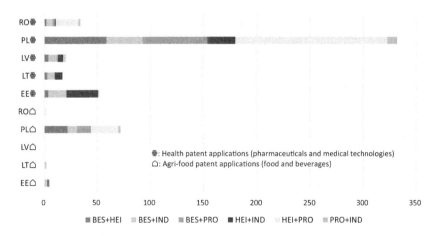

Figure 1.3 Counts of cross-sectoral applications of agri-food and health patents from Estonia, Latvia, Lithuania, Poland and Romania, 2006–2015

in Romania. Cases of cooperation between scientific organizations (HEI or PRO) and individual inventors–applicants were also observed: 31 in Estonia, 6 in Latvia, 7 in Lithuania, 35 in Poland, and 3 in Romania. Research collaboration between higher education institutes and public research organizations was also prevalent in Poland (143 joint cross-sectoral patent applications) and Romania (21 applications).

When interpreting the data, it must be remembered that joint patent applications present only one of the possible forms of R&D and patenting cooperation between science and industry, as technology transfer could also involve licensing of technologies owned by scientific organizations or changing the ownership of patented inventions, and these scenarios would not be identifiable as cross-sectoral patent ownership.

Discussion of Research Findings

This research was based on a unique data set combining patent data analyzed at the regional level and contents of RIS3 documents from 28 regions of five Central and Eastern European countries. Its originality is also linked to the critical assessment of prioritization decisions made at the regional level, contrasted with the revealed technological potential of companies and other stakeholders active in fields related to the selected regional smart specializations. Patent analyses were conducted in response to four specific RQs that allowed a better understanding of the inventive activities and R&D interests of various actors in the regional innovation systems. The obtained results were contrasted with the contents of smart specialization strategies of the analyzed regions.

The analysis focused on smart specializations related to agri-food and health, which belong to the most popular themes prioritized in RIS3 documents in various EU member states. Both themes were also almost uniformly popular in the researched regions, with topics of the selected smart specializations being very broad and undifferentiated, referring to the generic names of sectors or technologies, such as: *"agri-food,"* *"high-quality food,"* and *"food safety"* (in the case of agri-food-related specializations), and *"health,"* *"health technologies,"* *"medical technologies,"* *"medicine,"* *"biotechnologies,"* *"pharmaceutical sector,"* *"life sciences,"* and *"quality of life"* (for health-related specializations). A notable exception was the Polish region of Pomorskie, which prioritized *"medical technologies related to lifestyle diseases and aging."* Still, it was the only region that decided to narrow down the focus of its innovation support activities. The priorities adopted at the regional level do not seem to adequately implement the notion of smart specializations, as they do not correspond to specific thematic specializations nor differentiate regions from each other. They are mostly abstract, generic, and defined on a high level, not allowing to easily track relevant economic outcomes or innovation performance at a regional level. Furthermore, the research confirmed that for most regions, the selected priorities remain disjoint from their actual innovative potential, revealed by patenting activities (RQ1).

The observed approach to RIS3 prioritization suggests that from the financial perspective of 2014–2020, most of the analyzed regions implemented horizontal, undifferentiated support for their entire agri-food and health sectors, which remained contrary to the official guidance for RIS3 development. The selected priorities remained overwhelmingly undifferentiated, so regions could not easily achieve a critical mass in innovation development, benchmark their performance against directly comparable regions, or identify sources of competitive advantage. The analysis also revealed limited levels of ambition, with only a few regions interested in emerging technologies or specific societal challenges.

RQ2 offered an overview of patenting activities related to the agri-food and health sectors in the analyzed regions from 2006 to 2015. For most of the 28 regions, patenting outputs were scarce. In particular, patenting played a marginal role for all three of the Baltic states as well as some of the less economically developed Polish and Romanian regions. For Poland and Romania, inventive activities were strongly cumulated in some regions, including the central regions with the capital cities— the regions of Mazowieckie in Poland and Bucureşti-Ilfov in Romania— which dwarfed other regions' patenting efforts.

The analysis of the roles of R&D actors representing specific sectors of business enterprises, individuals, universities, and research institutes (RQ3) offered further insights into the development of regional innovation systems related to the agri-food and health fields. For agri-food, patenting was overwhelmingly driven by private sector organizations, but the field of health was dominated by public science, including universities and research institutes. In some of the most prolific regions, patenting outputs were dominated by public sector entities (e.g., in the Romanian region of Bucureşti-Ilfov). Patent applications filed by universities and research institutes do not necessarily correspond to commercially viable inventions, for which implementation efforts are actively pursued. The rules of institutional evaluation of scientific organizations in various Central and Eastern European countries incentivize patent filings, and cases of successful commercialization of scientific inventions remain scarce (either through the formation of spinoff companies or through a formal technology transfer to private-sector organizations).

This can further be linked to the answer to RQ4, which referred to the extent of cross-sectoral cooperation that led to joint patenting in the analyzed sectors and regions. As demonstrated in the preceding section, the patenting involving both scientific organizations and companies was in general limited, with some exceptions. At the same time, more cases of R&D collaboration were confirmed for scientific organizations among themselves (including universities and research institutes) as well as scientific organizations co-patenting with individual inventor–applicants. Altogether, the sectoral analysis of patenting tendencies in 28 regions of Central and Eastern Europe suggests that aggregate patent statistics could not be directly considered a sufficient basis for identifying potential regional specializations, because some technological fields might be overrun with patent applications by public science, not business. The sectoral decomposition of patent data sets, presented in this chapter, offers a more reliable approach to identifying the interests of companies that could spur entrepreneurial discovery processes.

Conclusion

Implications for Theory

Empirical and theoretical papers related to RIS3 tend to take for granted their methodological soundness and their compliance with recommendations put forward by theorists and the European Commission. This study casts doubts on such an approach. It has overviewed RIS3 priorities of 28 regions from Central and Eastern Europe and demonstrated that these priorities were overly general, referring to broad agri-food and health sectors rather than to specific, identified specializations. Furthermore, most of these priorities do not meet the requirements for "smart" specializations because they do not guide regional stakeholders in their pursuit of differentiation or leveraging unique resources for innovation.

The analyzed lists of priorities related to agri-food and health lacked an identification of genuine regional strengths or potential competitive advantages (such mismatch has also been observed by other scholars researching other regions, for example, Duque Estrada Santos, 2018). Based on the sample of 28 regions, RIS3 appears to promote traditionally conceived, horizontal support for entire industrial sectors (Sörvik & Kleibrink, 2015) rather than examples of successful implementation of the smart specialization model. These findings pose a significant challenge for scholars researching smart specializations because they might be researching a phenomenon that actually failed to materialize in at least some regions and countries (e.g., Tsipouri, 2017; Karo et al., 2017), and the analytical frameworks of smart specializations might not adequately capture the actual developments in innovation policies. A particularly worrisome tendency is the widespread occurrence of specializations defined on the basis of a sector (agri-food or health), because the very premise of the RIS3 approach was the replacement of sectoral support by more focused, "smart" priorities, resulting from entrepreneurial discovery processes and corresponding to differentiated, ambitious innovation fields, embedded in the regional context.

Despite the enthusiasm of the European Commission and some policy makers for the smart specialization approach, it seems to be wishful thinking for innovation scholars to assume that the RIS3 implementation in EU member states generates major enhancements of economic competitiveness or yields breakthroughs for regional innovation policies.

This study calls into question the applicability of the smart specialization model to the innovation policies of numerous regions in Central and Eastern Europe.

Implications for Policy

The chapter highlighted the disparities between technological potential revealed by patent analyses and the contents of smart specialization strategies of the analyzed regions from Central and Eastern Europe. It must be noted that RIS3 documents developed in the beginning of the 2014–2020 EU programming period were the first attempts at regional innovation policies in most of the analyzed regions, so their contents were bound to be imperfect and learning processes are likely to yield superior results for the financial perspective of 2021–2027. Nevertheless, it appears that most of the analyzed regions have actually disregarded the methodological guidance put forward by the European Commission while developing their Research & Innovation Smart Specialization Strategies, pursuing broad support for the entire sectors of agri-food and health. In many regions, the RIS3 priorities seem to have been selected without a solid grounding in empirical evidence, including the accumulated stocks of thematic patent applications. Hence, it is difficult to argue that RIS3 of all of the 28 sampled regions from Central and Eastern Europe were developed as outcomes of solid analytical processes. Paraphrasing the famous Solow productivity paradox, you can see agri-food and health almost everywhere but in the innovation statistics.

Interestingly, the RIS3 documents of the analyzed regions were also not strongly supported by in-depth entrepreneurial discovery processes that would involve significant numbers of private sector stakeholders. It indicates that the declared RIS3 priorities might have been selected in an overwhelmingly arbitrary, top-down manner by regional or national authorities, without sufficient linkages to any revealed technological strengths (confirmed by patent statistics) or declared aspirations of business enterprises. This, in turn, sheds light on the existing capacities of regional policy makers, the adopted governance models, and approaches to innovation policy programming. All these imperfections offer important lessons learned for the new financial perspective 2021–2027 and opportunities for further improvement as part of the RIS3 monitoring and update cycles.

When discussing the shortcomings of the RIS3 implementation in the samples' Central and Eastern European regions, one should also remember that in the beginning of the 2014–2020 EU programming period, the regions had very limited time to develop their RIS3 documents, and it is likely that they had not received detailed, individual guidance or feedback concerning the strategy design. The requirement to define RIS3 priorities was imposed on regions by the European Commission as a "door opener," an *ex ante* condition that enabled subsequent access to the European Structural and Investment Funds, and obviously, regions made efforts to remove any factors inhibiting the launch of their operational programs. Consequently, smart specialization strategies were developed in a hasty manner, without extensive stakeholder consultations or genuine entrepreneurial discovery processes, merely to satisfy the formal requirements and ensure that they would not hamper access to EU funding. This presents an important implication for the European Commission, regarding the effectiveness of coercion in policy processes through the explicit use of *ex ante* conditions. The requirements for prompt compliance with formal requirements for the definition of RIS3 priorities did not translate into extensive, evidence-based analytical processes, nor genuinely inclusive stakeholder consultations. Such processes could only have started after the initial RIS3 documents were adopted in the beginning of the 2014–2020 financial perspective of the European Union, and will hopefully yield promising results for the 2021–2027 regional programs.

Limitations

Some limitations of the research presented in this chapter should be taken into consideration. First of all, the analyzed period of filing patent applications (2006–2015) coincides with as many as three subsequent financial perspectives of the European Union. Each of them was associated with different focus of regional public interventions, addressing the specific identified challenges in the national and regional innovation systems. Furthermore, Romania only joined the European Union in 2007.

Second, EU regulations regarding smart specialization strategies were introduced in 2013, and most of the analyzed regions embarked on the strategy development in 2014–2015, when they realized that RIS3 priorities would become a formal requirement to access EU funds, so the analyses and entrepreneurial discovery processes took place toward the end of the period that is covered by our patent analysis. For this reason, the current assessment of the accuracy of prioritization decisions in the countries and regions is based on data that have not yet been available to policymakers at the time of drafting their RIS3 documents. As of 2014–2015, authorities of the analyzed countries and regions could also not have seen the most recent patent data due to the legally required time lags between the filing and publication dates (patent applications only become publicly available 18 months after their submission).

As another pertinent limitation, the analyzed regional sample is not an extensive coverage of EU member states from Central and Eastern Europe. The sample covers 28 regions and 30 NUTS2 entities (with the state of Lithuania and the Polish region of Mazowieckie decomposed into 2 NUTS areas, despite having one RIS3 document and one dedicated operational program per region), representing 41.8% of NUTS2 entities in Central and Eastern Europe. The sample did not include regions of Bulgaria (6 NUTS2 entities), Croatia (2), Cyprus (1), the Czech Republic (14), Hungary (8), Slovakia (4), and Slovenia (2), altogether 37 NUTS2 entities. It must, however, be stated that for these remaining regions, no dedicated regional operational programs were defined for 2014–2020 (with the only exceptions of Prague in the Czech Republic and the region of Central Hungary, which were both classified as more developed regions, exceeding the level of 90% of GDP average for the EU and thus requiring another set of measures and differentiated support intensity than the remaining regions of Central and Eastern Europe, belonging to the categories of poorly developed or transition regions). Furthermore, the above-mentioned countries have not defined separate smart specialization strategy documents at the regional level. The linkages between patent data and regional smart specializations would be difficult to explore. The present study focused on a sample consisting of two countries with a sizeable number of subnational RIS3 documents and three member states where the entire country belongs to one region with its dedicated RIS3 and an operational program.

Another limitation of the study is linked to its focus on patent applications, which also includes filings that were unlikely to successfully progress toward effective intellectual property protection. The analysis of patent applications (as opposed to granted patents) allows researchers to explore the R&D interests of actors in the regional innovation system, but does not provide an objective picture of the actual innovative potential because many of the filed patent applications might be of inferior quality, lacking the required inventive steps or not being genuinely novel. An even broader interpretative restriction is the study's reliance on patentable inventions, whereas some innovations might not meet the patenting criteria (including novel sensory aspects of food products, marketing innovations in the pharmaceutical sector, or service innovations in healthcare and medical tourism). In general, the reliance on patent data for the analysis of innovation potential can be challenged due to various limitations of this method (Griliches, 1990), for example, patents usually represent a specific knowledge base and may not correspond to all innovative activities (Barzotto et al., 2019). However, this method is widely used, thus it has been accepted by multiple authors as relevant and reliable (Acs et al., 2002; Faber & Hesen, 2004; Ronde & Hussler, 2005; Kogler et al., 2017; Krammer, 2017).

Finally, patent protection in some of the analyzed countries does not appear to be particularly popular among R&D performers (with higher patenting propensity observed in Poland and drastically low in the Baltic states). Hence, many innovative companies from Central and Eastern Europe might not think about legal protection of their intellectual property, and many important innovations might not be subject to patent protection.

Future Research Directions

Researchers might consider possible applications of the analytical method used in this chapter to other countries, with a view to verify the empirical basis for the selected smart specializations. Comparisons could also be made with more recent patent data as time goes by, particularly during the 2021–2027 financial perspective. A potentially inspiring research direction would also be a benchmarking of the "new" EU member states from Central and Eastern Europe (which joined the EU between the years of 2004 and 2013) with "older" member states—countries far more experienced in programming the EU funding on national and regional levels, having longer track records in setting innovation policies aligned with the formal requirements of the European Commission. The proposed research method could also be extended to other smart specialization topics such as energy or specific priorities identified in individual, regional RIS3 documents (albeit only agri-food and health were widely selected across all EU regions and at the same time, are relatively easy to delineate through queries in patent databases). Last but not least, more attention of researchers could be placed on the detailed contents of RIS3 documents, including the actual scope of selected priorities, the compliance with official guidance concerning RIS3 prioritization, and the substance behind the developments surrounding smart specialization strategies to ensure that the phenomenon dubbed "smart specialization strategies" are not merely artifacts. These artifacts might not correspond to significantly new directions in regional innovation support or sufficiently specific and differentiating topics that could be pursued by actors in the regional innovation system.

Note

1. Based on the following classes of the International Patent Classification (IPC):
   Food: A01H, A01J, A21D, A23B, A23C, A23D, A23F, A23G, A23J, A23K, A23L 1/*, A23L 3/*, A23P, C12J, C13B, C13F, C13J, C13K;
   Beverages: A23L 2/*, C12C, C12F, C12G, C12H; Pharmaceuticals: A61K (except A61K 8/*), A61P, C07D, C07H, C07J, C07K, C12N, C12P, C12Q; Medical technologies: A61B, A61C, A61D, A61F, A61G, A61H, A61J, A61L, A61M, A62B, B01L, B04B, C12M (except A61K, including only A61K 8/*), G01T, G21G.

References

Acs, Z., Anselin, L., & Varga, A. (2002). Patents and innovation counts as measures of regional production of new knowledge. *Research Policy*, *31*, 1069–1085. https://doi.org/10.1016/S0048-7333(01)00184-6

ADR Bucureşti-Ilfov. (2019). *Strategia de specializare inteligenta—analiza potenţialului regiunea de dezvoltare Bucureşti-Ilfov*. Retrieved from www.adrbi.ro/media/1817/ris3-bi_varianta_11122019-copyprotected.pdf

ADR Centru. (2017). *Strategia de Specializare Inteligentă a Regiunii Centru 2014–2020 (RIS3)*. Retrieved from www.adrcentru.ro/wp-content/uploads/2018/07/ajxyl_1.-RIS3.pdf

ADR Nord-Est. (2017). *Strategia pentru Cercetareşi Inovare Regiona lăprin Specializare Inteligentă RIS3 Nord-Est*. Retrieved from https://adrnordest.ro/user/file/news/17/RIS3_Nord-Est_05_12_2017.pdf

ADR Nord-Vest. (2018). *Strategia de specializare inteligentă regiunea de dezvoltare Nord-Vest (RIS3 NV)*. Retrieved from www.nord-vest.ro/wp-content/uploads/2018/07/RIS3-NV-190301.pdf

ADR Sud-Est. (2017). *The Smart Specialization Strategy of the South-East Development Region*. Retrieved from www.adrse.ro/Documente/Planificare/RIS3/Smart_Specialization_Strategy_SE.pdf

ADR Sud Muntenia. (2015). *Smart Specialization Strategy of South Muntenia Region. Innovative instrument devoted to regional economic development*. Retrieved from https://adrmuntenia.ro/index.php/download_file/article/76/regioengprint.pdf

ADR Vest. (2016). *Regiunea Vest Romania—strategia regionala de specializarea inteligenta*. Retrieved from https://adrvest.ro/wp-content/uploads/2016/09/RIS3-septembrie-2016.pdf

Barzotto, M., Corradini, C., Fai, F. M., Labory, S., & Tomlinson, P. R. (2019). Enhancing innovative capabilities in lagging regions: An extra-regional collaborative approach to RIS3. *Cambridge Journal of Regions, Economy and Society*, *12*(2), 213–232. https://doi.org/10.1093/cjres/rsz003

Berkowitz, P. (2017). Preface. In S. Radosevic, A. Curaj, R. Gheorghiu, L. Andreescu & I. Wade (Eds.), *Advances in the theory and practice of smart specialization* (pp. XVII-XXIV). London, UK: Academic Press—Elsevier.

C ACZ Consulting SRL. (2015). *Studiu strategia regionala de inovare pentru specializare inteligenta*. Retrieved from www.adroltenia.ro/wp-content/uploads/2020/01/Studiu-Strategia-Regionala-de-Specializare-Inteligenta.pdf

Capello, R., & Kroll, H. (2016). From theory to practice in smart specialization strategy: Emerging limits and possible future trajectories. *European Planning Studies*, *24*(8), 1393–1406. https://doi.org/10.1080/09654313.2016.1156058

D'Adda, D., Guzzini, E., Iacobucci, D., & Palloni, R. (2019). Is Smart Specialisation Strategy coherent with regional innovative capabilities? *Regional Studies*, *53*(7), 1004–1016. https://doi.org/10.1080/00343404.2018.1523542

Duque Estrada Santos, R. A. (2018) *Patent output as an evaluating factor for RIS3 strategies: A case study of North of Portugal*. Retrieved from https://repositorio-aberto.up.pt/bitstream/10216/114212/2/278146.pdf

EC. (2010). Communication from the Commission to the European Parliament, the Council, the European Economic and Social Committee and the Committee of the Regions. *Regional policy contributing to smart growth in Europe 2020*. Retrieved from https://ec.europa.eu/regional_policy/sources/docoffic/official/communic/smart_growth/comm2010_553_en.pdf

Faber, J., & Hesen, A. B. (2004). Innovation capabilities of European nations. Cross-national analyses of patents and sales of product innovations. *Research Policy*, *33*, 193–207. https://doi.org/10.1016/S0048-7333(03)00122-7

Foray, D. (2016). On the policy space of smart specialization strategies. *European Planning Studies*, *24*(8), 1428–1437. https://doi.org/10.1080/09654313.2016.1176126

Foray, D., David, P. A., & Hall, B. H. (2011). *Smart specialisation from academic idea to political instrument, the surprising career of a concept and the difficulties involved in its implementation* (EPFL Working Paper No. 170252). École Polytechnique Fédérale de Lausanne. Retrieved from https://infoscience.epfl.ch/record/170252/files/MTEI-WP-2011-001-Foray_David_Hall.pdf

Foray, D., & Goenaga, X. (2013). *The goals of smart specialisation* (JRC S3 Policy Brief Series, No. 1/2013). European Commission, Joint Research Centre, Institute for Prospective Technological Studies. Retrieved from http://publications.jrc.ec.europa.eu/repository/bitstream/JRC82213/jrc82213.pdf

Foray, D., Morgan, K., & Radosevic, S. (2018). *The role of smart specialisation in the EU Research & Innovation Policy Landscape*. European Commission. Regional and Urban Policy. Retrieved from http://ec.europa.eu/regional_policy/en/information/publications/brochures/2018/the-role-of-smart-specialisation-in-the-eu-research-innovation-policy-landscape

Freeman, C., & Soete, L. (1997). *The economics of industrial innovation*. Cambridge, MA: MIT Press.

Griliches, Z. (1990). Patent statistics as economic indicators: A survey. *Journal of Economic Literature, 28*, 1661–1707.

Hasan, I., & Tucci, C. L. (2010). The innovation—economic growth nexus: Global evidence. *Research Policy, 39*, 1264–1276.

JRC. (2020). *Registered countries and regions in the S3 Platform*. European Commission, Joint Research Centre. Retrieved from https://s3platform.jrc.ec.europa.eu/s3-platform-registered-regions

Karo, E., Kattel, R., & Cepilovs, A. (2017). Can smart specialization and entrepreneurial discovery be organized by the government? Lessons from Central and Eastern Europe. In S. Radosevic, A. Curaj, R. Gheorghiu, L. Andreescu & I. Wade (Eds.), *Advances in the theory and practice of smart specialization* (pp. 269–292). London, UK: Academic Press—Elsevier.

Kleibrink, A., Gianelle, C., & Doussineau, M. (2016). Monitoring innovation and territorial development in Europe: Emergent strategic management. *European Planning Studies, 24*(8), 1438–1458. https://doi.org/10.1080/09654313.2016.1181717

Klincewicz, K. (2018). Aktywność patentowa w sektorze rolno-spożywczym a inteligentne specjalizacje województw Polski. *Problemy Zarządzania—Management Issues, 16*(6), 37–82. https://doi.org/10.7172/1644-9584.79.2

Kogler, D. F., Essletzbichler, J., & Rigby, D. L. (2017). The evolution of specialization in the EU15 knowledge space. *Journal of Economic Geography, 17*(2), 345–373. https://doi.org/10.1093/jeg/lbw024

Krammer, S. M. S. (2017). Science, technology, and innovation for economic competitiveness: The role of Smart Specialisation in less-developed countries. *Technological Forecasting and Social Change, 123*, 95–107. https://doi.org/10.1016/j.techfore.2017.06.028

Kroll, H. (2015). Efforts to implement smart specialization in practice—Leading unlike horses to the water. *European Planning Studies, 23*(10), 2079–2098. https://doi.org/10.1080/09654313.2014.1003036

Lapienis. J., & Reimeris. R. (2016). *Lithuanian RIS3: How it was designed*. Retrieved from https://strata.gov.lt/images/Lithuanian_RIS3_Framing_Process.pdf

Lesser, W. (1998). Intellectual property rights and concentration in agricultural biotechnology. *AgBioForum*, *1*(2), 56–61. www.agbioforum.org/v1n2/v1n2a03-lesser.htm

McCann, P., & Ortega-Argilés, R. (2015). Smart specialization, regional growth and applications to European Union cohesion policy. *Regional Studies*, *49*(8), 1291–1302. https://doi.org/10.1080/00343404.2013.799769

MEC. (2014). *Strategia națională de cercetare. Dezvoltareşi inovare 2014–2020*. Romanian Ministry of Education and Research. Retrieved from www.edu.ro/sites/default/files/_fi%C8%99iere/Minister/2016/strategii/strategia-cdi-2020_-proiect-hg.pdf

Ministry of Education and Research. (2014). *Estonian Research and Development and Innovation Strategy 2014–2020*. Knowledge-based Estonia. Republic of Estonia Ministry of Education and Research. Retrieved from www.hm.ee/sites/default/files/estonian_rdi_strategy_2014-2020.pdf

MOES. (2018). *Informative Report. Monitoring of Smart Specialization Strategy*. Latvian Ministry of Education and Science. Retrieved from https://izm.gov.lv/images/statistika/petijumi/RIS3_progress-report_LV_2018.pdf

Muscio, A., Reid, A., & Rivera L. (2015). An empirical test of the regional innovation paradox: Can smart specialisation overcome the paradox in Central and Eastern Europe? *Journal of Economic Policy Reform*, *18*(2), 153–171. https://doi.org/10.1080/17487870.2015.1013545

Nelson, R. R. (Ed.). (1993). *National systems of innovation*. Oxford, U.K.: Oxford University Press.

Radosevic, S. (2017). Assessing EU Smart Specialisation policy in a comparative perspective. In S. Radosevic, A. Curaj, R. Gheorghiu, L. Andreescu & I. Wade (Eds.), *Advances in the theory and practice of smart specialization* (pp. 1–36). London, UK: Academic Press—Elsevier.

Reimeris, R. (2016). New rules, same game: The case of Lithuanian smart specialization. *European Planning Studies*, *24*(8), 1561–1583. https://doi.org/10.1080/09654313.2016.1179722

Ronde, P., & Hussler, C. (2005). Innovation in regions: What does really matter? *Research Policy*, *34*, 1150–1172. https://doi.org/10.1016/j.respol.2005.03.011

Scherer, F. M. (2000). The pharmaceutical industry. In A. J. Culyer & J. P. Newhouse (Eds.), *Handbook of health economics* (pp. 1297–1338). Amsterdam, the Netherlands: Elsevier Science.

Schmookler, J. (1966). *Invention and economic growth*. Cambridge, MA: Harvard University Press.

Sörvik, J., & Kleibrink, A. (2015). *Mapping innovation priorities and specialisation patterns in Europe* (JRC Technical Reports, No. 08/2015). European Commission, Joint Research Centre. Retrieved from www.kooperation-international.de/uploads/media/Mapping_Smart_Specialisation_Priorities.pdf

SWM. (2015). *Regionalna strategia innowacji dla Mazowsza do 2020 roku. System wspierania innowacyjności oraz inteligentna specjalizacja regionu*. Sejmik Województwa Mazowieckiego. Retrieved from www.funduszedlamazowsza.eu/wp-content/uploads/2017/12/zalacznik-nr-10-inteligentna-specjalizacja-wojewodztwa-mazowieckiego-do-regionalnej-strategii-innowacji-dla-mazowsza-do-2020-roku.pdf

Tidd, J., & Bessant, J. (2009). *Managing innovation: Integrating technological, market and organizational change*. Hoboken, NJ: Wiley.

Tsipouri, L. J. (2017). Innovation policy in Southern Europe: Smart specialisation versus path dependence. In S. Radosevic, A. Curaj, R. Gheorghiu, L. Andreescu & I. Wade (Eds.), *Advances in the theory and practice of smart specialization* (pp. 125–155). London, UK: Academic Press—Elsevier.

UMWD. (2015). *Ramy strategiczne na rzecz inteligentnych specjalizacji Dolnego Śląska*. Urząd Marszałkowski Województwa Dolnośląskiego. Retrieved from www.umwd.dolnyslask.pl/fileadmin/user_upload/Gospodarka/zdjecia/ RAMY_STRATEGICZNE_NA_RZECZ_INTELGENTNYCH_SPECJALIZACJI_DOLNEGO_SLASKA.pdf

UMWKP. (2016). *Inteligentne specjalizacje województwa kujawsko-pomorskiego. Charakterystyka obszarów inteligentnych specjalizacji dla projektów realizowanych w ramach Regionalnego Programu Operacyjnego Województwa Kujawsko-Pomorskiego na lata 2014–2020.* Urząd Marszałkowski Województwa Kujawsko-Pomorskiego. Retrieved from www.innowacje. kujawsko-pomorskie.pl/wp-content/uploads/2016/06/charakterystykaobszarow-inteligentnych-specjalizacji-dla-projektow-w-ramach-rpo-wk-p.pdf

UMWL. (2014). *Regionalna strategia innowacji województwa lubelskiego do roku 2020.* Urząd Marszałkowski Województwa Lubelskiego. Retrieved from http://rsi.lubelskie.pl/images/794_RSI.pdf

UMWL. (2015). *Inteligentne specjalizacje województwa lubuskiego. Urząd Marszałkowski Województwa Lubuskiego—Lubuskie Regionalne Obserwatorium Terytorialne.* Retrieved from https://obserwuj.lubuskie.pl/uploads/ documentsearch/id240/um%20lubuskie%20inteligentne%20specjalizacje.pdf

UMWŁ. (2015). *Wykaz regionalnych inteligentnych specjalizacji województwa łódzkiego oraz wynikających z nich nisz specjalizacyjnych.* Urząd Marszałkowski Województwa Łódzkiego. Retrieved from https://rpo.lodzkie. pl/images/konkurs_2.3.1_cop_28122015/Wykaz_Regionalnych_Inteligentnych_Specjalizacji.pdf

UMWO. (2016). *Specjalizacje inteligentne województwa opolskiego oraz potencjalne specjalizacje inteligentne województwa opolskiego z wyszczególnieniem.* Urząd Marszałkowski Województwa Opolskiego. Retrieved from http://rpo. ocrg.opolskie.pl/uploads/zamowienia/assets/2_1_3/Opracowanie_%E2%8 0%9ESpecjalizacje_inteligentne_wojew%C3%B3dztwa_opolskiego_oraz_ potencjalne_specjalizacje_inteligentne_wojew%C3%B3dztwa_Opolskiego_z_ wyszczeg%C3%B3lnieniem%E2%80%9D.pdf

UMWPod. (2015). *Regionalna strategia innowacji województwa podkarpackiego na lata 2014–2020 na rzecz inteligentnej specjalizacji* (RIS3). Urząd Marszałkowski Województwa Podkarpackiego. Retrieved from www.rpo.podkarpackie.pl/images/dok/15/RSI_WP_2014–2020_przyj%C4%99ty.pdf

UMWPom. (2015). *Inteligentne specjalizacje Pomorza.* Urząd Marszałkowski Województwa Pomorskiego. Retrieved from https://drg.pomorskie.eu/documents/102005/ 129070/broszura/06625c62-965e-40a3-b829-48cb6b866218

UMWŚ. (2014). *Uszczegółowienie inteligentnych specjalizacji województwa świętokrzyskiego. Załącznik 1 do planu wykonawczego do RIS3.* Urząd Marszałkowski Województwa Świętokrzyskiego. Retrieved from www.2014-2020.rpo-swietokrzyskie.pl/dowiedz-sie-wiecej-o-programie/ zapoznaj-sie-z-prawem-i-dokumentami/dokumenty-regionalne/zapisz/682- uszczegolowienie-inteligentnych-specjalizacji-wojewodztwa-swietokrzyskiegopdf/16/210

UMWW. (2015). *Regionalna strategia innowacji dla Wielkopolski na lata 2015–2020. Aktualizacja.* RIS3. Urząd Marszałkowski Województwa Wielkopolskiego—Wielkopolskie Obserwatorium Innowacji. Retrieved from https://bip.umww.pl/artykuly/2822092/pliki/20160920145457_regionalnastrategiainnowacjidlawielkopolski20152020ris32.pdf

UMWWM. (2014). *Proces identyfikacji inteligentnych specjalizacji województwa warmińsko-mazurskiego.* Urząd Marszałkowski Województwa Warmińsko-Mazurskiego. Retrieved from https://rpo.warmia.mazury.pl/plik/send/?id=261&v=1

UMWZ. (2016). *Wykaz inteligentnych specjalizacji województwa zachodniopomorskiego.* Urząd Marszałkowski Województwa Zachodniopomorskiego. Retrieved from http://smart.wzp.pl/sites/default/files/wykaz_inteligentnych_specjalizacji_pomorza_zachodniego_20160928.pdf

Van Looy, B., Vereyen, C., & Schmoch, U. (2014). *Patent statistics: Concordance IPC V8—NACE Rev.2. Eurostat.* Retrieved from http://ec.europa.eu/eurostat/ramon/documents/IPC_NACE2_Version2_0_20150630.pdf

ZWM. (2015). *Inteligentne specjalizacje województwa małopolskiego. Uszczegółowienie obszarów wskazanych w regionalnej strategii innowacji województwa małopolskiego 2014–2020.* Zarząd Województwa Małopolskiego. Retrieved from www.rpo.malopolska.pl/download/BONY%202015/Zal_nr_09_do__Regulaminu_konkursu_Uszczegolowienie_RIS.pdf

ZWP. (2016). *Plan rozwoju przedsiębiorczości w oparciu o inteligentne specjalizacje województwa podlaskiego na lata 2015–2020+ (RIS3).* Zarząd Województwa Podlaskiego. Retrieved from https://rpo.wrotapodlasia.pl/resource/file/download-file/id.2507

ZWŚ. (2018). *Lista Inteligentnych specjalizacji Województwa Śląskiego* (Aktualizacja). Zarząd Województwa Śląskiego. Retrieved from www.scp-slask.pl/czytaj/zaktualizowana_lista_inteligentnych_specjalizacji_wojewodztwa_slaskiego

2 The Implementation of the Smart Specialization Approach in the Peripheral Region of Galicia

María del Carmen Sánchez-Carreira, Manuel González-López, and Pedro Varela-Vázquez

Introduction

Smart specialization (SS) has become a key pillar of the EU regional policy; thus, the regions must develop their own smart specialization strategies (S3) as a condition for accessing European funds. This fact poses opportunities for place-based regional policies founded on local capabilities, but also relevant challenges, which are higher for peripheral regions. In this regard, peripheral regions are characterized by a low innovation performance, lack of critical mass, and institutional thinness (Tödtling & Trippl, 2005; Copus, 2011).

This chapter addresses the implementation of the S3 in Galicia, a northwest Spanish region, which can be considered a peripheral region in geographical, economic, and innovation terms. This region presents a high degree of regional autonomy concerning innovation policies. It is considered an example of implementation of the S3 by the European Commission (EC) (Gianelle, Kyriakou, & Cohen, 2016). In particular, this research addresses two main aims: first, to identify the main drivers and barriers which affect the Galician S3 implementation; second, to understand the implications of the SS approach in the policy-making process, effectiveness, and institutional learning.

This research combines the literature review about SS, the analysis of the Galician innovation system (GIS), and policies with in-depth semi-structured interviews carried out with 12 policymakers and other stakeholders involved in the process of design, definition, and implementation of the Galician Research and Innovation Smart Specialization Strategy (Galician RIS3).

This chapter provides useful inputs to improve the design and implementation of the regional innovation policies and S3. This diagnosis might also foster policy making and institutional learning. Furthermore, it may help understand the particularities of the S3 implementation in peripheral regions. Although some works deal with the Galician innovation system and policies (Vence, 2001; González-López, 2019, 2020), the Galician RIS3 is not analyzed enough. It is worthy of study due to the mixed character of this case: it is a good example in the formal S3 implementation, but it presents poor results concerning innovation performance. Moreover, this case study is an illustration of peripheral region, meaning that the conclusions could also be extended to other structurally similar regions in Europe. However, it should be regarded as a general frame, which needs specific adaptation to each regional singularity. This chapter focuses mainly on the policy and learning processes, as well as the results of Galician RIS3 implementation. The information collected in the interviews also provides useful insights for improving the design, implementation, and effectiveness of the innovation policies.

The chapter is organized as follows. After this introduction, the second section deals with the SS from a theoretical perspective and focusing on the relevance of these strategies for peripheral regions. The methodological section describes the process of design and implementation of the Galician RIS3, after approaching the main characteristics of the regional innovation system and policies. The next sections analyze and discuss the Galician RIS3 case study, focusing on the main drivers and barriers. Finally, the last section presents conclusions and implications.

Literature Background

The Smart Specialization as a New Approach in the Framework of the European Union Regional and Innovation Policies

The EC policy-making experience was important for adopting the SS concept. Thus, different Innovation Actions funded by the Structural Funds, such as Regional Technological Plans (RTPs), Regional Innovation Strategies (RIS), or Regional Innovation and Technology Transfer Infrastructures and Strategies (RITTS), had already been implemented during the 90s and 2000s, aiming at establishing and strengthening regional innovation capacities in less favored regions and involving all regional innovation actors in the definition of local priorities (Landabaso & Reid, 1999; Fernández et al., 2007; Morgan & Nauwelaers, 2003; Zabala-Iturriagagoitia et al., 2008; Sánchez-Carreira, 2020). In this sense, they could be considered the basis of the current S3 (Sánchez-Carreira, 2020). The process is similar because it is based on a strategic and bottom-up approach, interaction with regional stakeholders, and assessment by the EC and experts; as well as the phases of building consensus, identifying and selecting prioritized projects in the framework of the strategy and evaluation (Landabaso & Reid, 1999; Morgan & Nauwelaers, 2003; Zabala-Iturriagagoitia et al., 2008; Sánchez-Carreira, 2020).

The SS approach is rooted in a report commissioned by the EC Directorate General of Research and Innovation (DG RTD) to the Knowledge for Growth Expert Group in 2005, within the framework of the Innovative Europe initiative. The purpose was to explain and confront the EU productivity and technological gap with the US and Japan. At that time, different studies and reports highlighted the good EU R&D and technological basis; but it showed evident problems with translating technologies into products due to intrinsic deficiencies within many sectors (Kroll, 2017).

The SS concept, first launched by Foray and Van Ark (2007), refers to "the capacity of an economic system (a region for example) to generate new specialties through the discovery of new domains of opportunity and the local concentration and agglomeration of resources and competences in these domains" (Foray, 2014, p. 1). SS should not be confused with S3. SS refers to structural changes that happen in economic systems, which take different forms, such as transition, diversification, modernization, or radical change (Foray, 2014). Nevertheless, S3 refers to those actions and measures (policies) that promote this kind of process (Foray, 2014; McCann, 2015). The policy should involve productive and institutional stakeholders that, from a bottom-up perspective, identify and develop potential domains for SS that governments could support. S3 is committed to concentrate and prioritize resources on a few initiatives.

Two crucial concepts concern SS: entrepreneurial discovery and critical mass. The goal of SS policies could be understood as a successful replication of market-driven structural transformation. Therefore, it is important to replicate the actions of entrepreneurs, understood in a broad sense, in launching such processes. It means that the policy should involve productive actors (firms) and other institutional actors (universities, public agencies, etc.). They can identify and develop potential domains for SS from a bottom-up perspective, which governments will eventually support. Secondly, the policy should aim at generating critical mass; otherwise, the structural change will not be achieved. This idea explains why S3 is committed to concentrating resources on (relatively) few initiatives (Foray, 2014).

It should be underlined that SS was not originally a spatial concept but also a science, technology, and innovation-related concept. However, its rationale was quickly translated into regional policy when the EC Directorate-General for Regional and Urban Policy embraced the concept (McCann, 2015). Its rationale was used as an enabling principle for investing Structural Funds more efficiently (Foray, 2014). When translating the SS logic into spatial and economic geography terms, McCann (2015) indicates the relevance of concepts as relatedness, embeddedness, and connectivity, which mainly come from the evolutionary economic geography. Relatedness describes the technological proximity among different activities. The more related are activities the easier is to switch between them and provoking structural change, through adjusting production systems, organizational changes, and so on. Embeddedness refers to "the extent to which particular activities display depth linkages with a broad range of other local activities, local skills or local institutions" (McCann, 2015, p. 174). The key point is that structural changes do not happen "in the air," but in specific places where there are multiple linkages with existing activities and institutions. Finally, connectivity concerns the ability of actors to absorb knowledge from a wide range of connections, both with internal and external actors. Based on these three spatial concepts, McCann (2015) notes that "the smart specialization logic argues that in order to foster innovation and growth regions should aim to prioritize those activities fostering and enhancing entrepreneurial search initiatives in activities which are aimed at technologically diversifying those activities which are both highly embedded within a region and also highly connected to other regions" (McCann, 2015, p. 175).

S3 rationale fitted well with the EU cohesion policy due to two reasons (McCann, 2015). First, it provides a policy prioritization framework aligned with the Europe 2020 Strategy. Secondly, it follows a place-based logic, like the Cohesion Policy. The place-based approach assumes that policy priorities should vary in different types of regions (Tödtling & Trippl, 2005). It also suggests that regional policies should build on local capabilities and promote innovative strategies based on local and nonlocal actors and knowledge (Rodrik, 2005; Barca et al., 2012; Varela-Vázquez et al., 2019; Hassink, 2020). This is the case of the S3 bottom-up entrepreneurial discovery process.

The SS approach has become the main link, theoretical and practical, between the EU regional development and innovation policies. Thus, SS became a key pillar for the EU cohesion policy in the programming period 2014–2020. It was also implicitly admitted by the EU institutions. For instance, the European Council recognized SS as a key concept in its conclusions of the "Innovation Union" flagship initiative (European Commission, 2012). This understanding also has a practical expression with the establishment of the Synergies Expert Group by the DG RTD, which argues that "the concept is an important instrument for ensuring synergies between Horizon 2020 and the Structural Funds in the interest of building and providing a stairway to excellence" (European Commission, 2012, p. 8). SS is viewed as the existing most complete European industrial and decentralized innovation policy.

The practical implementation of S3 faces different challenges. One of the common misunderstandings was to confuse specialization with sectorial specialization, when the SS approach referred to knowledge domains, which are mainly cross-sectorial, at the interfaces of technologies and economic activities. Thus, relevant domains are activities, tasks, or specific technological functions in firms and production processes rather than sectors or industries. For the same reason, specialization does not refer to an opposite trend to diversification. This process refers to choosing the right domains for policy support that can lead to more specialized or diversified structures, depending on the region. Thus, specialization and diversifications are complementary, arising different combinations, such as related variety, unrelated variety, specialized diversification, or diversified specialization (Foray, 2014; McCann, 2015; McCann & Ortega-Argilés, 2015; Foray et al., 2018; Asheim, 2019; Hassink & Gong, 2019). In this regard, finding the right granularity level in the selection of priorities becomes a crucial aspect related to the S3 implementation (McCann & Ortega-Argilés, 2015; Foray et al., 2018).

Smart Specialization Strategies in Peripheral Regions

Another recurrent debate about S3 concerns the aforementioned apparent incompatibility between innovation and cohesion. The argument is that aiming at creating technological hubs at the European level, SS favors concentration of capabilities on a limited number of regions. This objective seems contradictory with the cohesion policy aims, particularly with the need to improve socioeconomic well-being in less developed regions. There is mutual interaction between innovation and regional development. As it has already indicated, the S3 adoption has come together with a change (at least rhetorically) in the rationale of the cohesion policy toward promoting competitiveness and effectiveness of investments. Nevertheless, this change does not imply the exclusion of the cohesion perspective, as in practice, the main beneficiaries of cohesion funds continue to be lagged regions. As Kroll (2015) indicates, the logic is that the ex ante conditionality obligates these regions to develop and adopt a coherent, prioritizing, and place-based innovation strategy, which otherwise they might not have embraced.

The S3 adoption raises opportunities as well as challenges. The S3 implementation has been quick and often ignoring its experimental nature (Morgan, 2017; Foray et al., 2018; Gianelle et al., 2016) and the lack of experience makes difficult its effectiveness; it is in an ongoing policy process. The complex and innovative approach also requires resources and competences to identify local assets and potential domains for specialization. In addition, the strategy should be flexible enough to adapt to a changing context and the emergence of new combinations of knowledge and capabilities. It involves an effective and diagnostic monitoring (Kuznetsov & Sabel, 2017; Foray et al., 2018).

The challenges inherent to S3 are higher for peripheral regions. The existence of some features help identifies them, such as locational disadvantage, deficiencies in infrastructures, slow economic growth, institutional thinness, low innovation performance, or limited absorption capacity (Landabaso & Reid, 1999; Copus, 2011; Morgan & Nauwelaers, 2003; Tödtling & Trippl, 2005). Concerning innovation, Fernández et al. (2007) identify the following characteristics of peripheral regional innovation systems: low effort on R&D&I, high weight of public sector, low R&D business innovation pattern, small firms, traditional sectors, and low skilled works.

For peripheral regions, S3 provides an opportunity of identifying their specific development path based on local assets and capabilities (McCann & Ortega-Argilés, 2016). A more prioritized approach constitutes a good opportunity for designing and implementing tailored policies for the specificities and challenges of each region. Moreover, the recent financial crisis and the consequent reduction of resources leads to a new approach of policies, seeking to achieve the higher returns of public resources, through a strategic approach, prioritization, cooperation, and generating synergies.

The process of setting up S3 priorities is based on identifying capacities, potential, and opportunities to transform economic structures. Thus, the right information is key to construct own regional competitive advantages (European Commission, 2012; Asheim et al., 2020). In this sense, the specific regional preconditions are different, given that the regional innovation policies differ in several aspects. The causes of these differences are multiple; however, they can be summarized in three dimensions (OECD, 2011): the institutional context, the regional innovation system, and the strategic choices. There are notable differences concerning the institutional context in the degree of autonomy, level of competences, and governance among EU regions. Governance is a crucial issue to design and implement regional innovation policies. Accordingly, the regional capacities differ in several aspects, such as legislative autonomy, budget autonomy, national framework, human resources, competences, tradition, and experience in the design and implementation policies, the existing institutions and their role, relations and interactions with policy makers of other levels; the horizontal and vertical coordination; and the sociocultural aspects (Uyarra et al., 2007; Walendowski et al., 2011; Baier & Zenker, 2020). Concerning regional innovation systems, the different features result from several factors, such as development paths; productive structure; historical and cultural patterns; institutional capacity; knowledge creation, diffusion, exploitation and absorption; connectivity and internal and external linkages; sources of funding; innovation actors and institutions (OECD, 2011). Finally, the strategic choices lead to identify challenges and opportunities for regional development and setting key priorities, which should be tailored to the regional context singularities (OECD, 2011).

The shortcoming on regional capabilities, competences, and resources can limit and hinder the definition and adoption of an appropriate regional S3. Peripheral regions are precisely those that present more weaknesses concerning the institutional context and capacities because they have less competences, resources, capabilities, and experience to deal with this complex policy process. In such cases, the mismatch between the policy ambition and the policy delivery process widens (McCann & Ortega-Argilés, 2015; Foray et al., 2018; Trippl et al., 2019). Since the EU embraced this policy approach, tools, concepts, and support in the S3 policy process were provided, through different ways: experts, S3 Platform[1] or Vanguard Initiative for New Growth through Smart Specialization[2] (Foray et al., 2018). Moreover, because the process of setting up S3 priorities is based on identifying capacities, potential, and opportunities to transform economic structures, the need for right information is key. The experimental nature of S3 and the need of prioritization as a result of a discovery entrepreneur process is more challenging for less developed regions (Foray et al., 2018; Kroll, 2019). Building capacities for design and implementing strategic bottom-up place-based regional innovation policies is needed, which conflicts with the rapid implementation of the process, limiting the operationalization of SS (Balland et al., 2018). However, it provides capabilities and learning useful for the next policy implementation (McCann & Ortega-Argilés, 2016).

Methodological Approach

The Context of the Design and Implementation of the Galician Smart Specialization Strategy

This section describes the process of design and implementation of the Regional Innovation Smart Specialization Strategy (RIS3) in Galicia. Before that, the main characteristics of the Galician innovation system and policies are briefly approached. This contextualization, as well as the description, are based on the revision of the limited literature about the Galician case and the own analysis of the policy documents and evolution of the indicators of the GIS.

An Approach to the Galician Innovation System and Policies

Galicia is a northwest Spanish region, which can be considered peripheral in geographical, economic, and innovation terms. This region has a high level of autonomy, specifically concerning innovation. It involves a multilevel level governance system with the national and EU levels. According to the Regional Innovation Scoreboard, the region is considered a moderate innovator, ranking 190 out of the 238 regions (European Commission, 2019).

The Galician Regional Innovation System (GIS) can be considered weak. Its main characteristics before launching the Galician RIS3 are the following ones: low efforts in inputs (R&D expenses or personnel); predominance of public efforts; limited cooperation, interaction, and articulation; low weight of intensive technology activities; and low absorption capacity. Thus, the GIS presents the typical pattern of peripheral regions (Vence, 2001; Fernández et al., 2007; González-López, 2019, 2020).

Concerning innovation policies, the level of regional competences is high, as well as in education or industrial fields, according to the Spanish Constitution and the Galician Statute of Autonomy. The general framework for innovation policy is completed by the regional Law on the Promotion of Research and Innovation in Galicia, approved in 2013. The regional government plays a key role in the GIS, which follows a top-down approach (González-López, 2020). The research plans are the main instrument of the innovation policy. Since the first plan, which was running in the period 1999–2001 until the current Galicia Innova 2020, there were five plans. The Galician innovation policy evolves, showing certain continuity patterns in a path-dependent process, albeit affected by external shocks and interaction with other governance levels (Spain and EU), highlighting the imitation path of the national innovation policies and governance structure (González-López, 2020).

Design and Implementation of the Galician Smart Specialization Strategy

The SS policy process involves effort and resources, and it was leaded by the Galician Innovation Agency (GAIN), the entity responsible for regional innovation policies in Galicia. The Galician RIS3 implementation follows the methodology established by the EC Guide Research and Innovation Strategies for Smart Specialization (European Commission, 2012). The process is divided into six steps (European Commission, 2012; Xunta de Galicia, 2014).

Analysis of the Regional Context and Potential for Innovation

The first step consists of a diagnosis of the regional context and the potential for specialization in economic, technological, and scientific fields. It covers the three dimensions indicated in the EC Guide (European Commission, 2012): regional assets, entrepreneurial environment dynamics, and the region position within the European and global economy. It focuses on the interaction among different players and the identification of systemic failures. The elaboration of a map of available resources and capacities regarding the productive system, the identification of agents and infrastructures by specialization areas, make it easier to identify the potential and competitive advantage (Xunta de Galicia, 2014; European Commission, 2012).

Governance: Ensuring Participation and Ownership
Collaborative Leadership

The second step refers to the creation of a formal governing structure for the S3, attempting to be participative and representative of the GIS. It was established in 2013 pivoting around GAIN. It is composed of an Executive Board, a Management Team, seven Working Groups, and Forums (Xunta de Galicia, 2014; European Commission, 2012).

The Executive Board manages and supervises the SS process, as well as reviews the strategy and coordination with other national and regional S3. This board, named GAIN Governing Council, is comprised of 12 members, one from each Xunta de Galicia Department, and one from the Galician Universities System. The Management Team conducts the daily strategy development, encourages Working Groups, and organizes the Forums. Several Working Groups were created in different areas for strategic reflection and participation of the GIS agents (enterprises, science, and knowledge sector, as well as users, citizens, and organizations) in the S3 definition. These groups attempt to identify the current and future situation of their activity areas, propose of potential niches and priority lines of action in such areas, from a cross-specialized approach and open policy focused on practice. Finally, several Forums were organized to obtain wider participation of the GIS agents and citizens.

There are other two supporting tools, which are consulting councils: the S3 Advisory Council and the S3 International Advisory Council. The S3 Advisory Council addresses the supervision and evaluation of the Galician RIS3 implementation. It is composed of members from knowledge-generating agents (Galician University System, technological centers, health foundations, or others, accounting for 40% of the representation), renowned business sector representatives (20%), public sector representatives (20%), and citizens' representatives (20%). Thus, there is a predominance of knowledge members. The S3 International Advisory Council contributes to give a global strategic vision of interregional cooperation within the framework of S3. It consists of national and international regional representatives that cooperate in the innovation field and a representative from DG Regio.

Elaboration of an Overall Vision for the Future of the Region

This step focuses on defining a shared vision of the Galician economy. The process followed to define it is relevant, being crucial to the involvement of different agents. Three milestones in that process are the prioritization of niches, the proposal of the challenges, and the building of the shared vision (Xunta de Galicia, 2014; European Commission, 2012).

Based on the diagnosis of the first step, seven working groups were created to think about key ideas and opportunities for a regional development path from a participatory perspective. There are three thematic working groups in the following fields: Health, Welfare and Life; Food, Agriculture, Fishing and Biotechnology; and Energy, Environment and Services. Moreover, two working groups are focused on Facilitators Technologies, one devoted to ICT Facilitating Technologies, and another related to Nanotechnologies, Materials, and Manufacturing Technologies. Moreover, two transversal working groups were created: Citizen Participation and Horizontal Policies. Following the participatory method, each Working Group was formed with different profiles: a coordinator, which leads the group; participants, which are between 4 and 10 representatives of the regional administration, steering the political leadership; interlocutors, which are between 15 and 25 representatives from enterprises, science and knowledge sectors, citizens and transversal organizations; and a motivator, from the management team, which is responsible for supporting the coordinator, encouraging and guiding the meetings. The followed methodology consisted of eight sequential actions, including meetings, round tables, and surveys.

As a result of the working groups and forums, 30 potential niches were identified. They were fined-tuned and reduced to 18 prioritized niches, which serve as a basis for finding the regional transformative path. Moreover, five capacities inventories were prepared by each thematic working group (Xunta de Galicia, 2014).

In the light of the previous steps, the work of the GAIN technical team, a crossing sectorial approach, and the relation with S3 strategies, three challenges were proposed for regional specialization. There was a validation process by the interlocutors and GIS agents involved in the Galician RIS3 participatory process. As a consequence of this step, the vision is defined as follows: "to consolidate the economy of Galicia for 2020 on a socially recognizable route for improving growth and competitiveness based on transformation of the production model from a medium–low technological intensity production model to a model characterized by medium–high technological intensity, via absorption of Key Enabling Technologies (KET) into settled sectors, and by positioning the region as a benchmark in Southern Europe in providing knowledge-intensive services and products related to active aging and a healthy lifestyle" (Xunta de Galicia, 2014, p. 66).

Identification of Priorities

The fourth step consists of defining the Galician RIS3 priorities. The prioritization process was based on the criteria set by the Management Team to structure, coordinate and make convergent the identified priorities. These criteria are three: value chain, beneficiaries, and instruments. (Xunta de Galicia, 2014; European Commission, 2012). Thus, the priorities were appraised based on the capacities and ranked.

There were meetings among motivators from GAIN technical team to validate the results, homogenize the sources of scores, and calibrating the results depending on the specific sector weight. Moreover, there were meetings among GAIN technical team, GAIN political heads, and Working Group coordinators, to involve them in the result of the process. The selected objectives were validated by the political heads from the different Regional Departments. The process culminated in a list of 10 priorities aligned with the defined vision and grouped into three challenges (Xunta de Galicia, 2014). Table 2.1 shows these challenges and priorities.

Definition of Coherent Policy Mix, Roadmaps, and Action Plan

This step refers to the policy-mix definition, specifically the programs, instruments, and action plan. The proposal was drawn by GAIN, based on a consultation process through questionnaires to representative GIS agents, and three dialogue round tables (Xunta de Galicia, 2014; European Commission, 2012).

The Working Group Horizontal Policies works on the identified potential niches to define the support measures. This working group held an initial meeting with 27 aid beneficiaries and 15 fund managers to present the methodology and the questionnaires. The aim is to assess the appropriateness of different support instruments and measures used in previous budget periods and gather proposals for new instruments. Once validated, the instruments considered most appropriate were grouped by the GAIN management team on Strategic Axes, and Programs, depending on their influence in the different stages of the innovation value chain or their final purpose. As a result, the policy mix is composed of four programs and 20 instruments (Xunta de Galicia, 2014). They are grouped into five strategic axes: Knowledge Generation, Knowledge Transfer, Knowledge Absorption, Entrepreneur Discovery, and Commercialization.

Integration of Monitoring and Evaluation Mechanisms

The last step addresses the definition of the Galician RIS3 evaluation and monitoring system. The proposed system follows a dual approach, but also complementary: the process of implementation of the own strategy or follow-up; and the evaluation of the effects of the undertaken actions.

A panel of indicators is proposed to measure the progress to achieve the Galician RIS3 objectives. It is composed of 74 implementation indicators, 50 for results, and 12 for impact. These indicators are divided into three groups, following the EC recommendations (European Commission, 2012): performance indicators, which address the progress in the strategy; result indicators, which measures the outcomes concerning the strategic

Table 2.1 Challenges and priorities of GRIS3

Description	Priorities
Challenge 1: New model for management of natural and cultural resources based on innovation	
Modernization of traditional Galician sectors by introduction of innovations that provide higher yield and efficiency in the use of endogenous resources and their reorientation toward alternative high added value uses in energy, aquaculture, drug, cosmetic, food, and cultural activities	—**Valorization sea**: Valorization of by-products and waste generated by production chains linked to the sea, through the use of their components for cosmetic products; food additives; pharmaceutical applications; in order to achieve a significant decrease in generated waste and attain a position in the market for innovative products with added value —**Aquaculture**: Development of the Galician aquaculture sector to convert the region into an international reference for the generation of new technology-based products and services applied to aquaculture —**Biomass and marine energies**: Diversification in the Galician energy sector in order to gain significant improvement in the efficiency of natural resources use in Galicia, giving priority to biomass and marine energy —**Primary sectors modernization**: Modernization of the Galician primary sectors (agriculture, fishing, livestock, and forestry) aimed at sustainable improvement of the efficiency and profitability indicators for operations and creation of innovative products and services —**ICT–tourism**: Modernization of the tourism sector and Galician cultural industries by means of intensive use of ICTs to achieve a tourist sector that is competitive at a European level based on cultural and nature tourism

Challenge 2: New industrial model based on competitiveness and knowledge

Increase the technological intensity of the Galician industrial sector through hybridization of Key Enabling Technologies

—**Diversification of driving sectors:** Diversification in the Galician driving sectors and its auxiliary sectors via an intensive use of Enabling Technologies (KETs), geared toward the supply of new processes and high value-added products that enable us to explore new markets based on hybridization, knowledge, and technology

—**Competitiveness in the industrial sector:** To promote the competitiveness of the Galician industrial sector under the concepts of the "Factory of the Future" and Eco-innovation to improve efficiency and environmental behavior in the industry

—**Knowledge economy: ICT and KETs:** Boost ICTs as the driving sector of the Galician knowledge-based economy just like in the case of other KETs

Challenge 3: New healthy lifestyle model based on active aging of the population

Position Galicia in 2020 as a lead region in Southern Europe that offers knowledge-intensive products and services linked to a healthy lifestyle model: active aging, therapeutic application of fresh and marine water resources, and functional nutrition

—**Active aging:** Galicia as the leading region in Southern Europe in the implementation of new technologies in the field of active aging and healthy living, and in the promotion of personal autonomy

—**Food and nutrition:** Diversification of the Galician food sector in order to position it as an international reference around innovation in nutrition as the key for healthy living

Source: Own elaboration based on Xunta de Galicia (2014).

priorities; and impact indicators, which aims at innovation progress regarding Galician RIS3 challenges and vision (Xunta de Galicia, 2014). In addition, qualitative methods may complement the evaluation system through questionnaires or focus groups. This proposal will be updated considering the periodic evaluation and monitoring to enhance the effectiveness of the policies, the synergies, and the achievement of the goals. It is planned an interim evaluation and a final evaluation, an annual follow-up to assess the ongoing implementation, and an assessment report about the achieved results and the qualitative information gathered about the application of the Galician RIS3 through surveys and discussion groups (Xunta de Galicia, 2014). The monitoring concerns the Management Team of the Galician RIS3. It is planned an external team to evaluate at different times: at the beginning, middle, and end (Xunta de Galicia, 2014).

The estimated budget for the overall 2014–2020 period accounts for 1,624 million euros, considering the own regional funds, the EU Structural and Investment Funds (the main resources), the national funds, and other resources expected from European and national programs (Xunta de Galicia, 2014).

Results and Discussion of Research Findings

Once described the process of Galician RIS3 implementation, this subsection analyses and discusses some relevant issues, identifying its main drivers and barriers. This analysis is based on the former section, and the case study of the Galician RIS3, based on the revision of the policy documents, as well as the qualitative information provided by the in-depth semi-structured interviews. This input is useful to identify the main drivers and barriers, the successful and failed policy tools, as well as sources for improving the design and implementation of RIS3. The implementation of the Galician RIS3 was considered a good practice by the EC in 2014. However, it is needed to differentiate the process of implementation of the strategy and its impact.

Concerning the first issue, the Galician RIS3 process follows well the formal approach, procedures, and recommendations established by EC Guide (European Commission, 2012). The first driver is the EU cohesion policy, which puts S3 as an ex ante condition. The high regional autonomy concerning innovation policy and the tradition of implementing innovation policies can help the Galician RIS3 definition and implementation. It can also contribute to make easier the political commitment to the Galician RIS3. Nevertheless, a deep analysis raises critical issues to the implementation. As a result of the desk and field research, the main concerns involve the entrepreneurial discovery process, the prioritization, the coordination with existing innovation plans, and the evaluation.

A key element in the SS approach is the entrepreneurial discovery process to identify the strengths and appropriate domains for the regional specialization path (Foray, 2014; Gianelle, Guzzo, & Mieszkowski,

2019; Trippl et al., 2019). Around 240 GIS agents were involved in the working groups and the forums, together with public participation. However, some doubts arise about its representativeness and inclusiveness. Table 2.2 presents the composition of working groups, showing the predominance of scientific and technological fields. Beyond clusters, the business sector appears underrepresented in a landscape where there are

Table 2.2 Involvement and participation in the working groups

Working Group	Participants*	Interlocutors
Participation of Citizens	Regional Dept. of Finance & Industry Vice president's Office Deputy Directorate-General for Emigration	Universities (3) Technological Centres (6) Clusters (13) Local Entities/ FEGAMP (1)
Horizontal Policies Commission	Regional Dept. of Finance &Industry Galician Institute for Economic Promotion Regional Dept. of Labour and Welfare Regional Dept. of Taxation Regional Dept. of Education and Culture Vice president's Office Agency for Technological Modernization of Galicia	Business (1) Xunta de Galicia-Funds Managers (15) Others (2) Citizens (180)
Health, Welfare, and Life	Regional Dept. of Health Regional Dept. of Labor and Welfare Regional Dept. of Education and Culture Agency for Technological Modernization of Galicia Deputy Directorate-General for Sports Regional Dept. of Rural and Marine Affairs	Universities (3) Clusters (2) Hospital Foundations and health-related ones (3) Technological Centers (1) Health experts (3)
Food, Agriculture, Fishing and Biotechnology	Regional Dept. of Rural and Marine Affairs Regional Dept. of Education and Culture Regional Dept. of Health Agency for Technological Modernization of Galicia	Universities (3) Technological Centers (9) Clusters (4) Enterprises (4) Galician Agency for Rural Development (1)

(Continued)

Table 2.2 (Continued)

Working Group	Participants*	Interlocutors
Energy, Environment, and Services	Regional Dept. of Finance & Industry Regional Dept. of Environment, Infrastructures, and Territory Deputy Directorate-General for Tourism Agency for Technological Modernization of Galicia Vice president's Office Regional Dept. of Rural and Marine Affairs, and Galician Energy Institute	Universities (3) Clusters (3) Associations (9) Technological Centers (4) Foundations (2) Enterprises (11) Experts on Tourism and ICC (2)
ICT	Agency for Technological Modernization of Galicia Galician Innovation Agency Galician Institute for Economic Promotion Regional Dept. of Education and Culture	Universities (3) Clusters (1) Associations (5) Technological Centers (3) Other Centers (4)
Nanotechnologies. Materials and Manufacturing Technologies	Regional Dept. of Finance & Industry Regional Dept. of Environment, Infrastructures, and Territory Regional Dept. of Education and Culture Galician Institute for Economic Promotion	Universities (3) Clusters (5) Associations (2) Technological Centers (5) Spin-offs (2) Independent Expert (1)

* The participant who appears first on each list is the coordinator of the working group.
Source: Own elaboration based on Xunta de Galicia (2014, p. 26).

around 200,000 firms, being 99.9% of them SMEs (mainly microenterprises, 96%).

Moreover, the selection of participants in each working group followed a coherent way, depending on their relationship with regional activities for generation and exploitation of knowledge, interrelation, and connectivity (Xunta de Galicia, 2014). In addition, questionnaires were sent to 42 GIS agents. However, the process does not allow an active role within the workings group or build consensus. This is due to the coordinating role concerning the results of the working groups and the selection of priorities by the Management Team, which later are validated together with the coordinators of working groups. Although a strong institutional leadership is needed in this process, it seems that GAIN assumes a dominant and interventionist role. Thus, the bottom-up approach is contested by this technical leadership.

Concerning the citizen participation, 140 people attended the Forum to present the Galician RIS3 process and starting the citizen consult, representing 119 GIS agents. Regarding the Forum focused on presenting the Galician RIS3 policies proposal, 36 people attended, representing 27 GIS agents. They are not open events because the attendants to the forums were selected. Therefore, the participatory process seems more formal and technical than inclusive. It should be noted that there is no tradition of participatory processes for citizens or specifically for designing policies. The involvement of the stakeholders should be widened and engaged to avoid vested interests (Gianelle et al., 2016; Foray et al., 2018; Trippl et al., 2019), as well as the inclusiveness of the governance system (Trippl et al., 2019).

The limited time available to define the strategy can be considered a barrier for a more participatory, interactive, dynamic, and deliberate process, as well as to narrow the priorities. Thus, the participative process was undertaken in approximately 3 months and the prioritization in approximately 1 month. Moreover, this entrepreneurial discovery process is limited to the time of designing the strategy. The entrepreneurs and participants in the initial discovery process have not been involved in its development. The discovery and experimental process do not sustain during the implementation to improve the process or evaluation, as sources for updating and fine-tuning the priorities and instruments, as Trippl et al. (2019) highlight.

Another foundation of the SS approach is prioritization. In this sense, the Galician RIS3 identifies ten priorities aligned with the three challenges (see former Table 2.1). This selection shows a high number of priorities; and overall, they are generic. Apart from the broad nature of the Key Enabling Technologies, most of the priorities are wide, defined for at the sector level, or even more aggregated. Only a few priorities show a right granularity level, such as Valorization–Sea (1.1), Aquaculture (1.2), ICT–Tourism (1.5), Food and Nutrition (3.2). Two main issues arise concerning the SS rationale: the granularity is not appropriate, and the concentration of resources on the prioritized niches is discussed. Thus, the resources invested from 2014 until mid-2019 are mainly aimed at challenge 2 (New industrial model based on competitiveness and knowledge), which accounts for 72% of the total Galician RIS3 investment. Challenge 1 (New model for management of natural and cultural resources) represents 16.1% of the investment, and challenge 3 (New healthy lifestyle model based on active aging of the population) the remaining 11.9%. This distribution is uneven, concentrating most of the resources on one challenge, which comprises three generic priorities. This fact together with the low resources allocated to two challenges (and seven priorities) contests the rationale of concentration and the potential benefits of reaching critical mass. This threatens the SS rationale: specialization in local domains as a potential path for regional development and concentration to search for complementarities, and synergies. Moreover, those trends hinder the identification of regional assets and potential (Iacobucci, 2014; McCann & Ortega-Argilés, 2016).

It should highlight that the Galician RIS3 priorities are mainly linked with the traditional specialization of the Galician economy. Only very few priorities target new domains with future potential, in line with the trend outlined by Trippl et al. (2019). The Galician RIS3 priorities are aligned with the existing specialization campuses in the Galician University System, which can contribute to generate synergies.

The coordination of the strategy with other policies, and specifically with innovation plans, is limited. It should underline that the Galician RIS3 design and implementation of the strategy concentrates most of the GAIN resources and efforts. Thus, when the Galician RIS3 started, the innovation plan then in force was the Galician Plan for Research, Innovation, and Growth 2011–2015, known as I2C. The new plan Galicia Innova 2020 was presented in 2018. According to the 2013 law, the R&D Plans are the "fundamental instrument" for planning and coordinating innovation policies in Galicia. The long delay in approving the current plan seems to be to the concentration of resources and efforts on the Galician RIS3, as most of the interviewees suggest. Because the Galician RIS3 has completely absorbed the innovation efforts of the regional government, the plan was left in a secondary place, which is contrary to the 2013 law. Indeed, the plan and Galician RIS3 were not understood as complementary and synergic, but also as substitutes. Therefore, Galician RIS3 undermines the principle of prioritization because it attempts to cover all the sectors, confusing with the purpose of the plan. Although a plan must consider all sectors, and S3 must select and prioritize. Thus, a relevant barrier was the absence of regional innovation plan during most of the strategy's duration because the plan should be instrumental for achieving the Galician RIS3 goals. Beyond the links of the new plan with the Galician RIS3, there are not found changes in the definition of this plan, taking advantage of the S3 methodology, the entrepreneurial discovery process, and the institutional learning. The regional innovation policy has traditionally followed a rationale opposite to the S3. Thus, it lacked well-defined and strategic aims, spreading, and dispersing the limited resources among a multitude of beneficiaries without targeted goals, instead of the SS logic of concentration resources on priorities. In this sense, the Galician RIS3 involves the main shift in the Galician innovation policy.

Concerning policy instruments, the Galician RIS3 proposal comprises 20 instruments, most of them new ones. However, there is a mismatch between those planned instruments and the implemented ones. The majority of the utilized instruments previously existed, and they were reformulated, being most of them horizontal. The key issues are the effectiveness of the instruments, which are not assessed, and their alignment with the Galician RIS3 priorities and with regional, national, and EU policies. Most of the annual calls mention RIS3 priorities, however, it seems more a formal issue than a requirement to get funds. This can be at least partially explained by some unusual circumstances, such as not having a new plan until 2018; and that the strategy has not differentiated its instruments from the innovation plans. However, this merger does not necessarily imply coordination, but rather an uneven competition in the calls between initiatives aligned with Galician RIS3 and others that are not. It can also affect the results on Galician RIS3 prioritization, undermining this logic due to part of its resources are allocated without considering the Galician RIS3 priorities. Thus, it shows limited embeddedness in regional policies (not only innovation policies), such as Hassink and Gong (2019) underline.

Some policy instruments can be underlined in the Galician RIS3 implementation, despite most of them are not in the proposal of linked instruments. Innova SME and Innovator Accelerators are interesting initiatives focused on strengthening business innovation. Public procurement of innovation is an emerging instrument with potential to develop new activities and useful within the S3 framework (Uyarra et al., 2017; Sánchez-Carreira et al., 2019). In this sense, Galicia has a pioneer experience in health mainly developed by the Galician Health System (SERGAS) since 2012 through three plans. The regional government used public procurement to tackle active aging as one of the Galician RIS3 challenges. This challenge represented an opportunity for regional enterprises to develop innovations for the Galician Healthcare System (GHS) through the public demand pull (Sánchez-Carreira et al., 2019). Based on this former experience, GAIN leads the development of the Civil UAVs (Unmanned Aircraft Vehicle Initiative) to develop an aerospace industrial pole. Galicia has no specific industrial capabilities in this field but in other branches of transport equipment manufacturing, such as automobiles or shipbuilding. For promoting this industrial pole, public procurement of innovation is one of the policy tools utilized, together with other industrial and innovation tools. Thus, the investment of around 164 million euros in the field develops about 400 high-skilled employments, 35 R&D&I projects with more than 50 stakeholders involved in the initiative. Thus, it can be aligned with the Galician RIS3 becoming a new domain and transformative activity of the Galician economy with a growing global market. Concerning collaboration among the agents of the innovation system, two initiatives highlight: the Mixed Research Units, aimed at promoting cooperation between research entities and the business sector to develop joint and coordinated research, innovation, and development activities; and Connecta SME, which addresses to promote cooperation among SMEs and other agents in the regional innovation system, through support for market-oriented research, development and innovation projects. Finally, but not least, the current plan includes the tool Innovation Digital Hubs, a new instrument enhanced by the EC. It aims at grouping and organizing all the agents of the R&D&I ecosystem in strategic areas through generating open and intelligent public–private collaboration dynamics. There are two Innovation Digital Hubs since 2019 in the fields of biotechnology and automotive, in which there are strengths and alignment with the Galician RIS3 priorities.

Another relevant issue to analyze is the Galician RIS3 evaluation. Nowadays, evaluation of any policy is needed in different moments to know the impact, to propose changes and improvements, and to learn to design and implement more effective policies. The Galician RIS3 proposes an evaluation and monitoring system. However, advances in this area have been limited. There were no meetings of the working groups to follow the progress or assess the needed adjustments or entrepreneurial process during the implementation. There are no published reports about the annual follow-up of the implementation or the evolution of the indicators or some assessment of the impact. It should be assessed the changes in the innovation performance and its relationship with the Galician RIS3 implementation, as well as the results of the policy actions (e.g., additionality), focusing on the prioritized areas and the main beneficiaries. Thus, the monitoring system is more formal than focused on results and impact. Only three forums were celebrated in mid-2019, as part of a wider process of monitoring and interim evaluation of GRIS3. The aims of this evaluation process, which follows a formal participatory process, are to identify deviations in the execution of RIS3 that allow introducing corrective measures or refining the priorities. It will also serve to lay the foundations for starting the process of defining the next RIS3 for the period 2021–2027.

Therefore, the Galician RIS3 implementation does not follow a dynamic and interactive process. Thus, the strategy has not been updated and adapted to a changing context in economic or innovation terms. It avoids improvements and adaptations derived from the reflection and analysis of the progress, difficulties, and hindrances, as well as strengthening the commitment of the stakeholders involved in the initial entrepreneurial discovery process.

Concerning the evaluation, the Galician RIS3 experience has been recognized as good practice by the European Commission, due to its participation as leader of the European Interreg project MonitorRIS3, aimed at improving the S3 policy delivery through the exchange of experiences and policy learning on monitoring strategies on policy instruments among regional relevant actors on S3. This project is relevant for building the monitoring indicators system, only approached in the definition of the Galician RIS3.

Although the efforts and the resources devoted to Galician RIS3, the changes in the economic structure and innovation performance are not sufficiently noted. The recent economic recession started in 2008 has affected the Galician RIS3 implementation and the expected effects on innovation. Thus, the own innovation performance in Galicia has not improved in the last years and its situation worsened in the EU context, as the Regional Innovation Scoreboard shows. Galicia scores 58.3 in innovation index in 2019, belonging to the group of moderate innovators, showing a negative trend in the last years (European Commission, 2019).

Finally, three additional considerations should be raised. First, the definition of the Galician RIS3 is supported by external assessment, both from a DG REGIO external expert and consultancy. This helps the implementation but can also lead to select broad and common priorities, in the face of local priorities. Second, the Galician RIS3 was designed and implemented in the context of a financial crisis, which reduced public and private resources for innovation and hits the GIS severely. However, the SS rationale gives an opportunity to allocate resources more efficiently. Third, to assess the Galician RIS3 impact is required more quantitative and qualitative information. Beyond the impact in the innovation system, the building of capabilities and institutional learning can improve the performance of innovation, the effectiveness of policies, and upgrade the regional development. The new EU programming period, becoming SS an enabling condition, is a good opportunity to use these capabilities and learning.

Discussion of Research Findings

SS is a strategic bottom-up approach that has been adopted for the EU Cohesion Policy. S3 seems a good tool to combine innovation and regional development. It involves a shift on the regional policy rationale, following a place-based perspective. This result-oriented approach provides an opportunity to optimize resources, concentrating them on local strengths to achieve critical mass in a context of limited resources due to the recent financial crisis. However, this complex policy process, which is innovative, faces several challenges (McCann & Ortega-Argilés, 2015; Kroll, 2017; Foray et al., 2018; Gianelle et al., 2019; Trippl et al., 2019; Hassink & Gong, 2019).

This chapter analyzes these challenges in the light of the Galician experience, which is interesting because it is a good example in S3 implementation from the formal perspective, but it presents poor results concerning innovation performance. Moreover, other relevant features of the region are its nature as a peripheral region, and it has own competences concerning innovation.

The main drivers of the Galician RIS3 have been the cohesion policy rationale and the existence of regional innovation policies with the intrinsic resources and competences, which makes easier the Galician RIS3 definition. Thus, the region has followed in right terms the different steps set by the EC. However, the results in the innovation performance are not promising. This suggests the existence of a mismatch between the definition and the implementation, raising deficiencies in the implementation. Besides the economic crisis, the main barriers that hinder the SS rationales arise. One of the most relevant is limited prioritization. There are a high number of priorities and most of them are generic and broad, with an inappropriate granularity level, based on sectors and traditional specializations. The high degree of generalization poses the risk of losing the local specificities, as well as the specialization rationale (Foray, 2014; Gianelle et al., 2019; Trippl et al., 2019). The entrepreneurial discovery process is formally followed in the definition of the strategy, but it is not an inclusive process. The engagement of the stakeholders is not high, mainly due to the novelty of the approach and the lack of experience in participatory processes (Gianelle et al., 2016; Foray et al., 2018; Trippl et al., 2019). Likewise, it seems that the university system is overrepresented in the policy-making process. The regional government assumes a leading role that challenges the bottom-up approach. In this sense, the process seems more technocratic and open to consults than truly participatory.

Another shortcoming refers to the limited coordination with other policies because there are no specific instruments to achieve the goals and priorities (Hassink & Gong, 2019). Moreover, the evaluation process is focused on formal issues and implementation, more than on results. An ongoing monitoring that helps to refine priorities or instruments has not developed, as it happens in other cases (Trippl et al., 2019).

Although Galicia made significant efforts in the Galician RIS3, the results are not promising. Thus, the innovation system performance and the policy design and implementation have hardly improved in the light of the Galician RIS3, which undermines the result-oriented approach. It is true that it coincides with a context of economic crisis. Apart from its own shortcomings, the approach presents several challenges for any region, which can be higher in the peripheral regions, as happens in this case. In this sense, one of the critical aspects is that the practical implementation of the RIS3 does not undermine the rationale of regional specialization and concentration of resources to achieve critical mass and scale economies. It is advisable to carry out a dynamic process of reviewing, adapting, and updating the strategy, as an element of flexibility. It can help to leverage the RIS3 efforts, as well as to target new opportunities that may arise during the 7-year period of implementation of the strategy. Thus, the risk of not identifying potential interesting specialization fields can be overcome with this dynamic approach.

Some relevant insights from the Galician case study are the following ones: the prioritization structure is based on challenges, which is a strength of the Galicia RIS3, that can facilitate the process of intersectoral and interdisciplinary entrepreneurial discovery; and the existence of a specific entity, such as GAIN, responsible for innovation policies and RIS3 is considered positive because it has the experience and necessary capacities to design and implement policies and strategies.

Conclusion

Implications for Theory

Given common characteristics in peripheral regions, this chapter contributes to understanding the challenges of S3 for regions and, in particular, for peripheral regions both from the theoretical and implementation perspectives. It identifies the main drivers and barriers of this new approach, and it focuses on the policy and learning processes. Despite these singularities, suggested policy recommendations should be regarded as general frame because there could be more missing or additional elements and interactions. A minimum adaptation is usually required due to endogenous dynamics.

Implications for Policy

The Galician experience is useful to improve the design and implementation of the regional innovation policies and S3 in peripheral regions. The need to adapt the S3, as well as to continue with the entrepreneurial process during all the implementation arises. In addition, the process of discovery process and prioritization need more time to think strategically and to find synergies. The search for synergies among S3, as well as with other regional, national, and EU policies is also suggested.

Limitations and Future Research

Concerning the main limitations of this research, more time is needed to find the long-term results and to improve the implementation. Moreover, there is a lack of sufficient data to evaluate the impact of the Galician RIS3, and the available information concerning the different policy tools is not homogeneous to compare its effectiveness. In addition, the intermediate evaluation has started in mid-2020 and it has not yet been published. In this sense, new research is needed to assess the long-term impact of Galician RIS3, as well as the learning of this process for the design and implementation of the new Galician RIS3 for the period 2021–2027. The next programming period provides an opportunity to put in practice the learning and the capacities built in this process and assess if the S3 can provoke structural change, a process that requires time and it is path dependent.

Acknowledgments

The authors would like to thank the valuable cooperation of the people and institutions that have collaborated in the field research. This work is supported by Xunta de Galicia (Consellería de Cultura, Educación e Ordenación Universitaria: Consolidation and structuring of competitive research units. Mode A: competitive reference groups GRC GI-1178, ED431C 2018/23; Aids for the improvement, creation, recognition, and structuring of strategic groups of the Galician University System Cross-Research in Environmental Technologies CRETUS, 2018-PG100); and by the Eramus+ Programme of the European Union Project EURIPER, under grant number 587410-EPP-1–2017–1-ES-EPPJMO-PROJECT].

Notes

1. www.s3platform.eu/
2. www.s3vanguardinitiative.eu/

References

Asheim, B. T. (2019). Smart specialisation, innovation policy and regional innovation systems: What about new path development in less innovative regions?. *Innovation: The European Journal of Social Science Research*, 32(1), 8–25.

Asheim, B. T., Isaksen, A., & Trippl, M. (2020). The role of the regional innovation system approach in contemporary regional policy: Is it still relevant in a globalized world? In M. González-López & B. T. Asheim (Eds.), *Regions and innovation policies in Europe. Learning from the margins* (pp. 12–29). Cheltenham: Edward Elgar.

Baier, E., & Zenker, A. (2020). Regional autonomy and innovation policy. In M. González-López & B. T. Asheim (Eds.), *Regions and innovation policies in Europe. Learning from the margins* (pp. 66–91). Cheltenham: Edward Elgar.

Balland, P.-A., Boschma, R., Crespo, J., & Rigby, D. L. (2018). Smart specialization policy in the European Union: Relatedness, knowledge complexity and regional diversification, *Regional Studies*, 53(9), 1252–1268.

Barca, F., McCann, P., & Rodríguez-Pose, A. (2012). The case for regional development intervention: Place-based versus place-neutral approaches. *Journal of Regional Science*, 52(1), 134–152.

Copus, A. K. (2011). From core-periphery to polycentric development: Concepts of spatial and aspatial peripherality. *European Planning Studies*, 9, 539–552.

European Commission. (2012). *Guide to research and innovation strategies for smart specialisation*. Luxembourg: Publications Office of the European Union.

European Commission. (2019). *Regional innovation scoreboard*. Luxembourg: Publications Office of the European Union.

Fernández, I., Castro, E., & Zabala, M. (2007). Estrategias regionales de innovación: El caso de regiones europeas periféricas. In X. Vence (Ed.), *Crecimiento y políticas de innovación. Nuevas tendencias y experiencias comparadas* (pp. 157–189). Madrid: Pirámide.

Foray, D. (2014). *Smart specialisation: Opportunities and challenges for regional innovation policy.* New York: Routledge.

Foray, D., Morgan, K., & Radosevic, S. (2018). *The role of smart specialization in the EU research and innovation policy landscape.* DG Regio Working Paper, European Union. Retrieved from https://ec.europa.eu/regional_policy/sources/docgener/brochure/smart/role_smartspecialisation_ri.pdf

Foray, D., & Van Ark, B. (2007). *Smart specialisation in a truly integrated research area is the key to attracting more R&D to Europe.* Knowledge Economists Policy Brief, No. 1. Retrieved from http://ec.europa.eu/invest-in-research/pdf/download_en/policy_brief1.pdf.

Gianelle, C., Guzzo, F., & Mieszkowski, K. (2019). Smart specialisation: What gets lost in translation from concept to practice?. *Regional Studies.* https://doi.org/10.1080/00343404.2019.1607970

Gianelle, C., Kyriakou, D., & Cohen, C. (2016). *Implementing smart specialisation strategies. A Handbook.* Luxembourg: Publication Office of the European Union.

González-López, M. (2019). Understanding policy learning in regional innovation policies: Lessons from the Galician case. Change of the Galician innovation system and policies. *Innovation: The European Journal of Social Science Research, 32*(1), 104–118.

González-López, M. (2020). Evolution and change of the Galician innovation system and policies. In M. González-López & B. T. Asheim (Eds.), *Regions and innovation policies in Europe. Learning from the margins* (pp. 188–206). Cheltenham: Edward Elgar.

Hassink, R. (2020). Advancing place-based regional innovation policies. In M. González-López & B. T. Asheim (Eds.), *Regions and innovation policies in Europe. Learning from the margins* (pp. 30–45). Cheltenham: Edward Elgar.

Hassink, R., & Gong, H. (2019). Six critical questions about smart specialization. *European Planning Studies, 27*(10), 2049–2065.

Iacobucci, D. (2014). Designing and implementing a smart specialization strategy at regional level: Some open questions. *Scienze Regionali. Italian Journal of Regional Science, 13*(1), 107–126.

Kroll, H. (2015). *Weaknesses and opportunities of RIS3-type policies: Seven theses.* Kahlsruhe: Fraunhofer ISI.

Kroll, H. (2017). The policy challenge in smart specialisation. A common approach meets European diversity. In J. Bachtler, P. Berkowitz, H. Sally & T. Muravska (Eds.), *EU cohesion policy: Reassessing performance and direction* (pp. 115–126). London: Routledge.

Kroll, H. (2019). Smart specialisation in economically and institutionally less favoured regions. In I. Kristensen, A. Dubois & J. Teräs (Eds.), *Strategic approaches to regional development. Smart experimentation in less-favoured regions* (pp. 36–51). London: Routledge.

Kuznetsov, Y., & Sabel, C. (2017). Managing self-discovery: Diagnostic monitoring of a portfolio of projects and programs. In S. Radosevic, A. Curaj, R. Gheorghiu, L. Andreescu & I. Wade (Eds.), *Advances in the theory and practice of smart specialization* (pp. 51–72). Cambridge, MA: Academic Press.

Landabaso, M., & Reid, A. (1999). Developing regional innovation strategies: The European Commission as animateur. In K. Morgan & C. Nauwelaers

(Eds.), *Regional innovation strategies: The challenge for less favoured regions* (pp. 18–38). London: The Stationery Office.

McCann, P. (2015). *The regional and urban policy of the European Union: Cohesion, results-orientation and smart specialisation.* Cheltenham, UK, and Northampton, MA: Edward Elgar Publishing.

McCann, P., & Ortega-Argilés, R. (2015). Smart specialization, regional growth and applications to EU cohesion policy. *Regional Studies, 49*(8), 1291–1302.

McCann, P., & Ortega-Argilés, R. (2016). The early experience of smart specialization implementation in EU Cohesion Policy. *European Planning Studies, 24*(8), 1407–1427.

Morgan, K. (2017). Nurturing novelty: Regional innovation policy in the age of smart specialisation. *Environment and Planning C: Government and Policy, 35*(4), 569–583.

Morgan, K., & Nauwelaers, C. (Eds.). (2003). *Regional innovation strategies: The challenge for less-favoured regions.* London: Routledge.

OECD. (2011). *Regions and innovation policy. OECD reviews of regional innovation.* Paris: OECD.

Rodrik, D. (2005). Growth strategies. In P. Aghion & S. Durlauf (Eds.), *Handbook of economic growth* (pp. 967–1014). Amsterdam: Elsevier.

Sánchez-Carreira, M. C. (2020). An overview of the European Union innovation policy from the regional perspective. In M. González-López & B. T. Asheim (Eds.), *Regions and innovation policies in Europe. Learning from the margins* (pp. 113–138). Cheltenham: Edward Elgar.

Sánchez-Carreira, M. C., Peñate-Valentín, M. C., & Varela-Vázquez, P. (2019): Public procurement of innovation and regional development in peripheral areas. *Innovation: The European Journal of Social Science Research, 32*(1), 119–147.

Tödtling, F, & Trippl, M. (2005). One size fits all? Towards differentiated regional innovation policy approach. *Research Policy, 34*, 1203–1219.

Trippl, M., Zukauskaite, E., & Healy, A. (2019). Shaping smart specialization: The role of place-specific factors in advanced, intermediate and less-developed European regions. *Regional Studies.* https://doi.org/10.1080/00343404.2019.1582763

Uyarra, E., Flanagan, K., Magro, E., & Zabala-Iturriagagoitia, J. M. (2017). Anchoring the innovation impacts of public procurement to place: The role of conversations. *Environment and Planning C: Politics and Space, 35*(5), 828–848.

Uyarra, E., Koschatzky, K., & Héraud, J. A. (2007). *Understanding the multi-level, multi-actor governance of regions for developing new policy designs.* Position paper the ERASpaces/ERISP projects prepared for the PRIME Annual Conference, Pisa, 29.01.-01.02.2007. Manchester: PREST, University of Manchester.

Varela-Vázquez, P., González-López, M., & Sánchez-Carreira, M. C. (2019). The uneven regional distribution of projects funded by the EU Framework Programmes. *Journal of Entrepreneurship, Management and Innovation, 15*(3), 45–72. https://doi.org/10.7341/20191532

Vence, X. (2001). El sistema de innovación de Galicia: Debilidades y especificidades de un sistema periférico. In M. Gómez & M. Olazarán (Eds.), *Sistemas regionales de innovación* (pp. 327–374). Bilbao: Universidad del País Vasco.

Walendowski, J., Kroll, H., Stahlecker, T., Baier, E., Wintjes, R., & Hollanders, H. (2011). *Regional innovation monitor. Innovation patterns and innovation policy in European regions—Trends, challenges and perspectives.* 2010 Annual Report. Brussels: Technopolis, Fraunhofer ISI, UNU Merit.

Xunta de Galicia. (2014). *Smart specialisation strategy in Galicia.* Santiago de Compostela: Xunta de Galicia.

Zabala-Iturriagagoitia, J. M., Jiménez-Sáez, F., & Castro-Martínez, E. (2008). Evaluating European Regional Innovation Strategies. *European Planning Studies, 16*(8), 1145–1160.

3 Challenges for Monitoring Smart Specialization in the European Union

Elżbieta Wojnicka-Sycz, Korneliusz Pylak, Piotr Sliż, and Piotr Sycz

Introduction

Monitoring is a process of comparing characteristics over different periods to measure improvement after the implementation of policies. Monitoring provides information for ongoing outputs and results without further analysis of the reasons for their possible unintended level. A less frequent evaluation is the process of assessing policy characteristics according to a specific objective or perspective. Evaluation is a periodic assessment of the adequacy and results of the policy. Evaluation is usually carried out by entities external to the authorities responsible for the policy (Ostašius & Laukaitis, 2015; Annecke, 2008).

Research and Innovation Strategy for Smart Specialization Strategies (RIS3) is an active, bottom-up, entrepreneurial discovery of new, innovative subsectors of the economy, assessing their potential and supporting their development (Foray, 2012). The choice of smart specializations should be considered as a multifaceted continuous study; hence the appropriateness of the applied approach and the way it is implemented by a given region will have an impact on the effectiveness of using EU funds to support smart specializations. Smart specializations indicated in the regions will often escape traditional statistical classifications; therefore, it is a challenge to develop appropriate systems for their monitoring and evaluation.

Good management of domestic and regional smart specializations will be the prerequisite for receiving by countries and regions of the EU support for R&D&I via cohesion policy in the years 2021–2027. One of the assessed criteriums will be having tools for monitoring and evaluation of SS. The monitoring should be based on comprehensive performance data, open to the public.[1]

According to European Commission, RIS3 monitoring system should strike a balance between complexity and usefulness as it should diagnose whether the strategy is implemented as planned; support decisions on possible changes or maintenance of priority areas and the ways the strategy is implemented; disseminate information on strategic achievements.

To cover the whole period of RIS3 implementation, the European Commission recommended three types of indicators for use in the monitoring system: (1) input indicators—measuring the budget allocated to support a given area; (2) output indicators—describing the "physical" product produced from resources as a result of the policy intervention; and (3) result indicators—measuring a positive change in a specific characteristic that reflects an improvement in well-being (European Commission, 2014).

RIS3 and their monitoring systems are elaborated in multidimensional processes and can be adjusted by learning processes during their implementation. The monitoring system should, however, serve such learning (Kleibrink, Gianelle, & Doussineau, 2016; McCann & Ortega-Argilés, 2016). On the one hand, the *Fifth report on economic, social, and territorial cohesion* recommends the minimalist, conservative, and realistic selection of the monitoring indicators (European Commission, 2010). On the other hand, RIS3 monitoring indicators should measure several areas, such as: conducting Research and Development and Innovation (R&D&I) activity, cooperation between businesses, science, innovative intermediaries, administration, society and environment (sixtuple helix), international competitiveness, the development of a critical mass of R&D activity in the region, entrepreneurial discovery, interdisciplinarity potential and the degree of novelty/niche specialization that allows for related diversification (Wojnicka-Sycz, 2020). Reconciling the objectives of the monitoring system with the available indicators is therefore another challenge.

This chapter seeks to discuss the challenges for the RIS3 monitoring system from an international perspective and to present a case study of modification of RIS3 monitoring in the less developed region of Pomerania (Poland). It responds to the lack of research on RIS3 monitoring, especially from an international perspective. The aim of the research for this chapter was to assess how RIS3 monitoring was planned in the strategic documents and to what extent and how it is carried out and what are the challenges of its implementation. Therefore, based on the expert research of 102 RIS3 documents and the literature review we analyzed different perspectives of the design of monitoring systems and applied indicators. To assess the implementation of the monitoring we conducted a Computer-Aided Web Interview (CAWI) with 37 regional authorities in 13 European countries. The outline of this chapter comprises a literature review, research methods, results, and discussion section: construction of monitoring systems, the results of the survey, and the case study of the Pomeranian region. This chapter closes with the conclusions.

Literature Background

Monitoring usually requires a continuous examination of activities carried out during the implementation of the strategy to ensure that it remains on track to achieve its objectives. The strategy should be flexible to take into account emerging events or shocks and adapt to new conditions following the results of the basic analysis of monitoring data. This is especially important for evolving strategies, such as RIS3, although the possibility of changes in such a strategy will be less likely than for private sector strategies, where we usually experience a combination of intended and emerging strategies while allowing part of the intended strategies not to be implemented. Iannacci et al. (2009) define monitoring as the continuous process of examining the delivery of program outputs to the intended beneficiaries and is carried out during the execution of a program to immediately correct any deviation from operational objectives. Because it is impossible to manage something that cannot be measured, monitoring by establishing and gathering information on performance indicators reflecting the objectives and logic of public intervention (results, outputs, activities, and inputs) is the basis for responsible public management.

Monitoring activities enables quick learning of what is not working. It reveals the extent to which policy objectives have been achieved and thus provides the evidence necessary to ensure strong government responsibility to external actors. Continuous monitoring of performance indicators allows comparisons to be made over time. The disadvantage of monitoring information is that it provides little insight into the causes of good or bad performance. Such understanding can be ensured through evaluation.

The development of effective monitoring systems requires a well-defined formulation of performance indicators. Indicators should be selected according to criteria of relevance, periodicity, timeliness, reliability, quality control of indicators; methods of data collection, reporting, and dissemination (Lopez-Acevedo, Krause, & Mackay, 2012). Lopez-Acevedo et al. (2012) differentiate between high (macro) and low (micro) performance indicators. The high level refers to external influences and includes impacts, results, and outcomes. The low level includes outputs, activities, and inputs that are internal to the program. Outputs connect the high and low levels in the policy implementation chain. Performance indicators reflect changes in intervention-related variables. A common weakness of monitoring systems is the excessive number of performance indicators. It is better to have a small number of reliable and widely used performance indicators than large collections of dubious quality and not fully utilized.

Evidence-based policymaking, as a policy of smart specialization, is defined as making informed policy decisions. It requires the systematic use of data, evidence, statistics, and machine learning methods. To establish a monitoring system, it is important to integrate different data sources, which have increased in diversity and quantity in recent years. The monitoring systems can use such sources as digital records of companies and citizens, use of service applications, social media, company websites, digital sensors, and the Internet of Things, as well as big data volumes (Gruzauskas et al., 2020; Wojnicka-Sycz, 2020).

To collect monitoring information, existing databases within or outside the managing agency should be identified and used. Surveys of citizens and procedures for evaluating by trained observers may also be used. For each performance indicator, data sources, data collection procedures, and frequency of collection and reporting should be planned. Lopez-Acevedo et al. (2012) recommend a periodic review of data monitoring and data collection procedures to introduce improved measurements. Current events and decisions are "path-dependent"; that is, they are conditioned by past events and decisions. Authorities learn with experience and adapt systems over time. Typically, monitoring committees are established in each region to oversee the monitoring activities and implementation of the program and to verify that the objectives are being met; they also approve the implementation reports (Iannacci et al., 2009).

The monitoring system is designed to provide analytical feedback on the results and impact of implemented policies. Based on Foray et al. (2012) three types of monitoring indicators have been identified: (1) Context indicators reflecting the objectives of the strategy, which assess the region concerned against the background of the EU or other similar regions; (2) Performance indicators for each component of the strategy, which make it possible to check that the actions are effective—specific indicators; (3) Output indicators measuring the progress of the measures taken (Angelidou et al., 2017). The European Commission and the S3 Platform recommend that the indicators should be specific and achievable and should be developed taking into account the initial and target values. The indicators should also be policy-relevant, normative, and robust. The existing national monitoring system should be considered to ensure comparison with other regions. Annual monitoring and data collection are recommended. The data sources for each indicator must be identified from the beginning. The results should be published and regularly communicated to all stakeholders and the public at large (4th Smart-watch Minibook, 2019).

RIS3 monitoring involves several key challenges. It faces organizational barriers, such as inefficiency of existing structures, staffing constraints, and overload of tasks, the unsustainability of structures built within projects; lack of dedicated funding for the monitoring system; barriers to awareness and knowledge of local government decision makers about the importance of continuous monitoring of RIS3 implementation, information needs of different stakeholder groups and the shape of the monitoring system (Pylak, 2013).

Indeed, we have noticed that the literature on RIS3 monitoring is scarce and therefore does not contribute to a better understanding of how the system should be composed, implemented, and managed. This observation is confirmed by bibliometric analysis and systematic

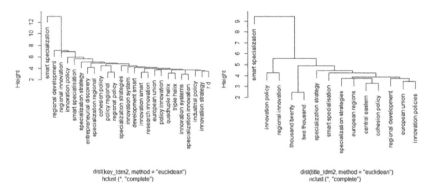

Figure 3.1 Dendrogram of keywords and title words most related to smart specialization within the collection of publications on smart specialization

Source: Own study based on WoS using R.

literature review based on the Web of Science Core Collection (WoS) database. We searched for publications and quotations from the term "smart specialization" (SS) and found 345 publications and 1,769 quotations (h-index 15). Interestingly, most of the publications and quotations were made between 2015 and 2017, when all the systems were developed and should already be operational. In 2020, this is again a key moment for discussion on monitoring systems for the period 2021–2027.

Figure 3.1 shows a dendrogram of keywords and titles containing the most common phrases related to the term "smart specialization" (SS) in 335 examined documents. Unfortunately, the quantitative bibliometric analysis did not reveal any areas related to monitoring and methodology for measuring the performance of RIS3 implementation.

This small number of publications on the concept of measurement methodologies and monitoring of the potential of smart specializations indicate a still unfilled research gap. At the same time, the present moment of investigation is ideal for preparing monitoring systems for subsequent RIS3 updates.

Methodological Approach

The analysis of monitoring systems in the EU regions (which correspond to the NUTS2 level) and countries included desk research of 102 RIS3 strategy documents available on the Regional Innovation Monitor and S3 Platform websites.[2] Most of these documents were only available in the national languages, so they were translated into English. Then we searched the keywords "monitoring" and "indicators" to find the appropriate parts of the documents. We also searched about 50 websites of regional authorities of EU regions to find monitoring reports (also in original languages), but usually, we were not able to find them. Moreover, it was often difficult to find any department/unit responsible for smart specialization. We analyzed whether the documents contain a description of the monitoring system and the system of indicators together with estimated baseline and target values. We conducted more precise research for 16 regions of Poland. The collected RIS3 documents as well as implementation records and resources from regional authorities' websites allowed to analyze the level of decision making regarding the involvement of the regional board, steering committee, innovation council, economic and entrepreneurship council, and various working groups and observatories. We also examined the level of implementation of RIS3 concerning its management and monitoring, whether it is integrated into the government structure or whether it is a project, and whether regional research centers, innovation support centers, and an innovation fund have been established. We conducted these studies both during the planning stage of RIS3 and its implementation. As a result of the survey, the systems' compliance with the evaluation criteria for the sustainability of structures and partnerships was assessed.

We then surveyed European regional authorities in all European Union countries to examine RIS3 monitoring in practice. We sent a CAWI questionnaire to all authorities with documents on the S3 Platform together with emails to officials, as well as regional offices, to about 150 regions in total. We received replies from 37 regions in 13 countries, which are mainly less developed (16), but also medium (11) and highly developed (10). In particular, these regions belong to Belgium (1 region), Finland (1), Hungary (1), Netherlands (1), Czech Republic (2), France (2), Greece (2), Austria (3), Italy (4), Portugal (4), Romania (4), Spain (4), Poland (7). The survey was conducted in April and May 2020 using CAWI and included 8 closed and 2 open questions on the approach to identify and monitor SS, the monitoring activities carried out, the costs of these activities, the indicators planned and used, as well as obstacles, advantages, and weaknesses of RIS3 monitoring systems.

Finally, we conducted a case study for the Pomeranian SS presenting how the monitoring of specific indicators for areas of smart specialization was improved there. It reflects the changing nature of S3 monitoring and the necessity of modification of the initial set of performance indicators. This modification was based on the analysis of various statistical indicators proposed initially for the monitoring system based on their strengths and weaknesses and the proposal of new indicators based not only on statistical sources. The analysis also aimed at proposing a narrow set of indicators for each area of smart specialization, which in most cases differed from one SS area to another. In the description of the monitoring system of Pomerania, we also used source documents of the authorities of the Pomeranian region concerning the construction of the monitoring system and the monitoring activities carried out as well as information from interviews with three officials involved in the management and implementation of the RIS3 in the Pomeranian region daily.

Results and Discussion

Different Perspectives on the Design of Smart Specialization Indicator System

Our analysis of 102 S3 documents shows that 78 of them specified a monitoring system with indicators, mostly with baseline and target values. Seventeen regions did not describe their monitoring systems in their strategies and 7 defined them very generally. This means that most of the EU regions have designed monitoring systems for their strategies from the very beginning. However, it was usually not possible to find the monitoring reports on the regions' websites or the S3 platform.

Angelidou et al (2017) propose that output and result indicators should be defined using the system of common indicators established in the Structural Funds regulations. The nine Central European regions participating in the Interreg SmartWatch project have developed a set of indicators using context, output, and result indicators, which for most of them have at least indicated baseline and target values. Their RIS3 result indicators focus on innovation, research, or economics. Monitoring with these indicators is in most cases planned as an ongoing procedure. The output indicators measure project-specific values and give a certain amount as a target value to be achieved over a given period. Examples are the number of patents, EU-funded projects, people employed in a given sector, companies with new business products, clusters, R&D grants, supported networks, and so on.

The main monitoring challenges include a lack of data, inadequacy, and delays in existing statistics and difficulties in collecting other information (Plenikowska-Ślusarz & Jurkiewicz, 2017). The monitoring system is mostly strategy specific. National and regional authorities across Europe have made use of some very advanced data sources in the strategy development phase. Current versions of monitoring mechanisms often do not have a comprehensive database. Moreover, they show little innovative approaches, such as using big data analysis (Gianelle & Kleibrink, 2015).

We selected several interesting examples of designing monitoring indicators from RIS3 documents research. We also noticed that often monitoring systems in different regions of individual countries are quite similar, especially in the approach to indicator logic and data sources. The data are gathered from varied sources and by various institutions involved in the process of implementation of the policy as different governmental bodies, banks, regional observatories, specialized institutions, statistical offices, and so on.

Italy

The Emilia-Romagna region (Italy) is an example of a developed and completed system for RIS3 monitoring. This system also includes transformation indicators, that is, indicators specific to each priority area, but these indicators are linked to the priorities and thematic focus of the strategy. Also, it is evident, especially at the level of transformation indicators, that different data sources are used, mainly collected by specialized regional institutions or business associations, as well as those based on current direct surveys. It should be noted that in Italy there is an obligation to belong to associated institutions, such as an association of a given industry, and therefore it is easier for these institutions to collect data. The system for monitoring areas of specialization in Emilia-Romagna (E-R) is therefore based on a network of institutions, often financed from regional funds. This also reflects the long tradition of monitoring the variables and topics identified in the RIS3, as the values of the indicators in many cases dating back to 2010. The E-R RIS3 defines five main areas of production on which regional innovation policy should focus, three of which are established activities: (1) agriculture and food; (2) mechatronics and (3) automotive engineering and construction, and two others: (4) health and well-being; (5) culture and creativity—are areas with great potential for development and change also for other components of the production system. Monitoring in E-R refers to indicators relating to a specific area of specialization and a specific thematic orientation indicated when defining the strategy. The system of indicators for the E-R RIS3 monitoring includes output, specialization, transformation, and result indicators: (1) output indicators measuring the level of implementation of regional policies and related activities; (2) specialization indicators assessing the level of five regional production systems regarding the 19 thematic fields defined by RIS3, in terms of patent applications, research grants, start-ups, and innovative SMEs; (3) transformation indicators measuring the direction and intensity of expected changes in the five production systems (areas of specialization) to the strategy's technological objectives (Table 3.1); (4) result indicators measuring the effectiveness of the strategy with the objectives set, that is, the achievement of results consistent with the desired objectives of the changes. Their values come from the Italian Statistical Office (e.g., share of R&D in GDP). The value of each monitoring indicator and its dynamics are presented publicly on the website of the regional authorities.

In Lazio and Lombardy (Italy), the main monitoring indicators envisaged are contextual indicators; impact indicators: strategy indicators; result indicators: progress/implementation indicators (measuring the

Table 3.1 Examples of transformation indicators in RIS3 of Emilia-Romagna

Specialization area and source of data	Innovation engine	Transformation indicator
Construction Data: Regional Development Agency of E-R, Smart City Index Report, GreenEr Observatory, Lepida—institution for ICT network development	Sustainable development	Construction of new buildings. Construction of buildings with low energy consumption. Environmental certificates of the construction process. Environmental product declarations.
	Information society	Share of ultrafast Internet connections. Smart city index.
Health and well-being Data: Regional Health Service, Ministry of Health, Assobiomedica—Health Service Association, AIFA—Italian Pharmaceutical Agency, Italian Statistical Office	Companies operating in the medical equipment industry. Start-ups. Electronic distribution of health data (ESF). Laboratories certified by BPL. Innovative medicines undergoing clinical trials. Local units operating in the supply chain. Employees in local supply chain units.	

Source: Retrieved June 22, 2020, from www.regione.emilia-romagna.it/s3-monitoraggio

percentage progress of the process related to the action, the financial progress, and the products intended as "physical" results obtained through the use of the resources used for regional interventions); "observational" indicators relating to the use or development of enabling technologies and the hybridization of value chains. Also, the following indicators are envisaged: indicators relating to the regional innovation system; indicators relating to spin-off activities; indicators relating to projects that develop innovation in new emerging niche markets; indicators relating to RIS3's ambitions; and indicators relating to the pollution of specific policy choices by RIS3.

Portugal and Spain

The proposed RIS3 monitoring system in the Norte Region (Portugal) considered the monitoring of individual measures, for example, projects, for the achievement of a specific input, output, and result indicators. This was followed by an examination of whether the strategic and cross-cutting objectives are being achieved utilizing result indicators and indicators for individual priority areas. The third level of monitoring is contextual (impact) indicators, which allow monitoring of the overall level of RIS3 implementation. Contextual indicators reflect key variables related to regional innovation performance and allow for a comparative analysis of performance with other national and European regions (Monteiro, Santos, Guimarães& Silva, 2018).

The RIS3CAT monitoring process in Catalonia (Spain) involves three levels: projects and instruments, a smart specialization process, and an impact. For projects and instruments, the data are linked to the IT systems used by the different bodies managing the RIS3CAT instruments to monitor and follow up projects and instrument operations. Monitoring of SS includes an analysis of EDP, focusing on leading sectors and emerging activities. It uses technology and market surveillance and continuous feedback to stakeholders through specific questionnaires for clusters or business organizations. The monitoring of the overall impact of RIS3CAT is essentially linked to the Regional Operational Program of the European Fund for Restructuring and Development (ERDF). A dedicated team is involved in the monitoring process, which is responsible for preparing the information and results. A revision of the RIS3CAT action plan shall be carried out at least once a year (HIGHER, 2017).

In Navarra (Spain), the following tools have been deployed to monitor RIS3: (1) monitoring the development of the region broken down into (a) general objectives: six indicators for the main goals of RIS3: prosperity, quality of life, and sustainability and (b) intermediate objectives: 20 competitiveness indicators: education and employability, R&D&I, business development, infrastructure and public administration (also analyzed in a territorial perspective); (2) specialization control: key economic variables analyzed for each RIS3 priority (e.g., productivity, employment, exports, etc.), compared with Navarra as a whole and with other regions or countries; (3) challenge monitoring tool, in which the activities under the RIS3 strategy are monitored using output and result indicators; (4) other monitoring tools to control the development of each plan (input and output indicators) and its impact (results).

In Madrid (Spain), indicators are established for each priority, which are (a) financial indicators related to the allocated expenditure; (b) output indicators obtained from the operations supported; (c) performance indicators related to the priorities. Output indicators for the priority areas include private investments induced in parallel to public support for innovation or research and development projects, the number of Madrid companies applying to European and international programs, the number of innovative goods and services purchased by the public sector, the number of SMEs participating in European and international programs. In the health sector, the indicators are the number of professionals and biomedical groups or clinical trials, number of publications, total impact rate on publication, cumulative patents, and so on.

Performance indicators are, for example, supported start-ups based on new technologies, increase in the level of R&D&I in enterprises that received funding, increase in the number of enterprises cooperating with science, publications in an international database, total employment in the R&D sector, number of scientists per million inhabitants, submitted European patents. Interesting detailed indicators for priority areas in the Balearic Islands in Spain related to the energy balance, the energy produced using renewable energy, greenhouse gas emissions, the sustainable development management system implemented in enterprises, the number of supported enterprises in the field of sustainable development technologies, the number of implemented projects for the internationalization of products, services, and technologies.

The following types of indicators are assumed in RIS3 Galicia (Spain): (1) performance indicators, which directly measure everything that has been done with public funds; (2) result (outcome) indicators, which measure the degree of implementation of the proposed Strategic Priorities, in terms of scientific specialization (publications, joint international R&D&I projects), technological specialization (patents, number of established technology companies, etc.), (3) contextual or impact indicators relating to the overall objectives of the Strategy and analyzed employing inputs (resources invested and people involved in R&D activities), results generated by scientific, technological and economic specialization but at a global level for Galicia and the overall economic impact of the RIS3 Strategy on the welfare and improvement of Galicia's society.

Austria and Germany

In Austria, in 2010, the government mandated the Research, Technological Development and Innovation Council to monitor the implementation of the strategy. It prepares an annual report on Austria's science and technology potential. Progress in implementing the strategy is monitored using a comprehensive set of indicators assigned to each objective. All *Länder* report regularly on the economy, location, and innovation. A very advanced set of monitoring and evaluation instruments is the Lower Austrian balanced scorecard model. These processes are usually supported by monitoring bodies with an advisory function, the "Research and Innovation Councils," which include experts from the fields of science, education, and business. Styria, Carinthia, Upper Austria, Salzburg, Vorarlberg have their advisory boards (Gruber, Handler, & Kleinberger-Pierer, 2016).

In Hamburg RIS3 (Germany), contextual indicators relate to the entire federal state. Furthermore, so-called program indicators are used to determine the success of individual support measures. Projects aimed at promoting innovation are measured by a uniform panel of input, output, and result indicators. The Hamburg Investment and Promotion Bank

(IFB) is the implementing authority. IFB has developed a uniform system for collecting data on project financing. This allows the results of the activities to be measured on a case-by-case as well as a program basis through financial input, material output, and result indicators as direct benefits of the activities for the relevant target groups. The financial input indicators include, for example, the approved project costs, the amount of funding provided, or the funding rate. Output indicators provide a further material description of the projects financed. They include, for example, the gender-differentiated number of jobs at the beginning and end of the project, additional sales, or the number of patents as a result of the project. Program indicators are usually presented in an aggregated way in all projects at the level of supporting activities.

In Rhineland-Palatinate (Germany), the RIS3 monitoring concept rests on a system of indicators comprising central result indicators, central observation instruments for the functioning of the regional innovation system, supplemented in particular by a qualitative assessment approach (workshops, expert reviews, etc.). In the state of Mecklenburg-Vorpommern, result indicators at the state level relating to R&D&I results and program indicators are used. Program indicators include financial indicators and physical output indicators, which are collected at the project level. Output indicators are used for the further material description of financed projects. Also, complementary monitoring in these Länder, as well as in Schleswig-Holstein, takes place based on the monitoring of the ERDF Operational Programs 2014–2020. For the ongoing monitoring of the RIS3 strategy, Lower Saxony uses a system of indicators with central result indicators. The selected result indicators are quantitative or qualitative variables to provide information on the success of the strategic direction and areas of RIS3. The strategy control is complemented by output indicators of the multi-fund program of Lower Saxony. In Thuringia, a distinction is made between the levels "Vision with overarching objectives," "Vision and objectives of areas of specialization," and indicators at the level of action plans. The first two levels focus on impact indicators, while the result and output indicators are at the heart of the monitoring of funded activities.

Poland

RIS3 monitoring of Lower Silesia (Poland) is based on (1) general context indicators to assess the overall level of innovativeness and competitiveness of the region and the region itself on a national scale and other regions of the country and the EU; (2) selected context indicators to monitor sectors and fields of science and technology for given areas of SS (cross-sectional data on NACE classification and product groups relating to exports, employment, and concentration of enterprises, location quotient for granted patents; (3) result and output indicators, resulting from public intervention in SS areas based on information system for structural funds (enterprises that increased exports, demonstrated R&D activity, received support for R&D, internationalized, commercialized technologies; patent applications; the number of supported cluster initiatives and cooperative links, the number of applications to national programs related to R&D&I, etc.). A Working Group was also established in the region to study methods of analysis and monitoring the development of SS. Besides, Working Groups for SS periodically update areas and subareas of Lower Silesia's SS based on monitoring and evaluation of adopted indicators, observation of changes, and identification of new and emerging trends and in the regional economy (Lower Silezia 2015).

Different Perspectives on the Design of Smart Specialization Monitoring System

Gianelle and Kleibrink (2015) suggest that regions and countries with experience in monitoring innovation strategies should build on existing monitoring structures and those with limited experience should develop their monitoring system, starting with simple systems. Indeed, our study has shown that developed regions, such as the Austrian or Flanders regions in Belgium, base their RIS3 monitoring activities on preexisting structures.

Kleibrink, Gianelle, and Doussineau (2016) showed that the most frequently used data sources for monitoring RIS3 implementation include official statistics, operational program indicators, participation in Horizon 2020, and European statistics, while only about half of the respondents conduct surveys and focus groups. Other sources used are Regional Innovation Scoreboard, Regional Competitiveness Indicator, data from regional labor offices. The indicators in the strategies we analyzed often referred to patents or patent applications provided by patent offices, but these indicators mainly referred to general regional statistics in this field (per capita patents). An interesting example of the use of keyword data from scientific publications, EU projects, and patents is the analysis of emerging SS areas in Moldova using machine learning carried out by SIRIS Academic (2018). Wojnicka-Sycz, Sliż, and Sycz (2018) used keyword information from patents and publications to monitor SS areas in the Pomeranian Province of Poland, as well as in the case of Internet queries by Wojnicka-Sycz (2020) to analyze SS companies in the Podkarpackie region.

In the monitoring of National Smart Specialization Strategies for Poland and Polish regions apart from existing data, bottom-up, interactive mechanisms are used. They involve entrepreneurs, experts, and scientists in the form of interviews, working groups, and Smart Labs. Monitoring tools are also the Steering Committee, IT platform (smart.gov.pl), Consultative Group, and economic observatory (Otręba-Szklarczyk et al., 2017).

Table 3.2 Analysis of RIS3 management and monitoring systems in 16 Polish regions

		Plan	Implementation
Decision-making level			
Regional Board		16	16
RIS3 Steering Committee		14	11
Innovation Council		7	10
Economic or Entrepreneurship Council		0	2
Unit/working group on innovation development/observatory		6	5
Executive level			
RSI *management*	within the structures of the authority	13	12
	as a project	3	4
RSI *monitoring*	within the structures of the authority/ Monitoring Committee	11	10
	as a project	1	4
Regional Studies Centre		2	2
Innovation Centre/Innovation support office		5	4
Innovators' fund		1	0
Evaluation criteria			
Durability of the structure		NA	12
Partnership		NA	10

Source: Own study based on analysis of RIS3 documents. The numbers in the cells indicate the number of regions (NUTS2) that hold/meet a given element. NA—not applicable.

Table 3.2 presents the results of our study based on official documents and reports from the structure planning stage (described in strategic or executive documents) and the system implementation stage (actual implementation of documents). The study also considers the sustainability of such systems and verifies the application of the partnership principle.

The analysis reveals that RIS3 implementation systems, in particular monitoring systems, are similarly built-in all voivodeships. They all involved the Regional Board as the main decision-making body and several regional actors, thus ensuring partnership in the system. It is worth adding that other structures not provided for in the strategic documents have also been created. At the executive level, RIS3 monitoring units have been created in most regions, although it should be stressed that several voivodships have not created any monitoring structures. As there must be permanent structures in each region that collect and process monitoring data, it is planned to finance them mainly with the assistance of the region's resources (although partly also from project funds). Only a few voivodeships have based these key units of the RIS3 system exclusively on project sources, which may endanger their durability.

Similarly, all nine Central European regions of the SmartWatch project designate a body responsible for implementing and monitoring RIS3. In most cases, working groups, observatories, NGOs, or other types of institutions support these designated bodies. This means that EDP is often used for monitoring purposes. Such qualitative monitoring is complemented by quantitative monitoring, which is often difficult due to problems with the statistical description of SS areas based on NACE, especially in the case of those defined as technology/activity bundles (Plenikowska-Ślusarz & Jurkiewicz, 2017).

Monitoring tools based on EDP are successfully applied in Scandinavian regions (Roman & Mutanen, 2018). The "Innovation picture" is a tool launched in 2013 and has since been implemented annually by the Tampere Regional Council. It integrates quantitative data on key indicators with qualitative analyses and comments from regional stakeholders. The process starts with the collection of data on R&D&I funding, the capacity of the value chain, growth enterprises, higher education institutions, internationalization, digitization, and innovation platforms. This is followed by a series of workshops with representatives of businesses, universities, research institutes, and the public sector to observe, interpret, and develop additional material based on preliminary data. In 2017, a total of 120 people from different organizations were involved to develop a situational picture of innovation. The Partnership Barometer was launched in 2014 in southwest Finland. It is based on a survey sent to 700 key regional stakeholders in the industry, universities, and the public sector. Respondents assess statements on overall regional development and the stage of implementation of key strategic actions. All questions reflect the current stage as well as expectations for future development. The Communication Tool was launched in 2013 in Ostrobothnia. The process includes a survey for regional businesses, science and administration, and interviews to identify their expectations and experiences with other stakeholder groups. Gap analyses are then carried out to compare the differences between expectations and experiences of different stakeholder groups. The Communication Tools provide information on the bottlenecks between different aspects of cooperation. A focus seminar is organized as a joint closing event for different stakeholder groups to collectively plan activities to improve the current basis of cooperation concerning bottleneck areas.

Similarly, an Innovation Advisory Board has been set up in Wales, comprising large and small businesses, public sector innovation bodies, university funding boards, local authorities, and other funding bodies. It examines both individual projects and the entire RIS3 portfolio (Polverari, 2016). As many of the monitoring activities are based on EDP, the challenge is to increase the propensity of SS agents to participate in monitoring activities.

The Challenges of Implementing RIS3 Monitoring in the EU Regions—Survey Results

After we analyzed the perspectives on institutional and indicator systems in the EU, a key question arises regarding the implementation of RIS3 for actual monitoring measures and challenges faced by regions. Most of the regions analyzed identified smart specializations by mixed industries and activity/technologies (23), while only five and four regions defined them separately as domains of technologies and industries, respectively. The mixed nature of smart specializations affects the choice of indicators (see Table 3.3). Most of the regions (11) planned common indicators for all specializations as a result of the identification of SS through the combination of industry and activity/technology and the possible separation of indicators for individual industries. Such identification of specialization

Table 3.3 Linking the classification of smart specializations with the preparation of indicators specific to each specialization in the studied regions

Classification of smart specializations in a region Assignment of indicators to specialization	Domains of technologies (referring to the same knowledge)	Domains of industries (referring to NACE codes)	Domains of activities (referring to the same market/clients)	Mixed domains of industries and activities/technologies	Other approach/not specified	All regions by indicator specification
Indicators planned for each specialization separately	2	1	1	5	2	11
Indicators planned together for all specializations	2	1	0	11	0	14
Indicators planned for each specialization to some extent	1	1	0	6	1	9
Indicators planned not for specializations	0	1	1	1	0	3
All regions by SS classification	5	4	2	23	3	37

Source: Own elaboration based on CAWI [n = 37]. Multiple answers are allowed.

is therefore certain facilitation in the selection of monitoring indicators. Interestingly, such facilitation is more apparent in developed regions than in less developed ones.

The selection of indicators is also made easier by the sources used in monitoring processes (see Figure 3.2). Almost all regions (32) use statistical indicators related to general research, development, and innovation (R&D&I) activities in the region. Most of them also use other sources, such as a patent or scientific databases, which are free of charge. However, only a few regions (28) use project databases that are not permanent and continuous and thus may pose a problem in the proper implementation of monitoring processes. Similarly, 20 regions employ special indicators collected from nonstatistical sources as direct surveys and designated observatories, requiring additional financial resources. The use of paid sources, requiring additional and cyclical effort, is not a domain of more developed regions, there are no differences between regions in this respect. Interestingly, there are also no differences in the number of indicators collected among regions with different levels of development. Most often the regions collect 3–5 indicators for each specific area of smart specialization or all specializations (when specializations are not assessed separately).

Our survey shows that only 27 regions carried out RIS3 monitoring activities, 5 did not at all and 5 only to some extent. Almost all regions have collected data for all their planned indicators. It is also surprising that most regions (21) covered the costs of monitoring activities from the salaries of officials regardless of the level of regional development,

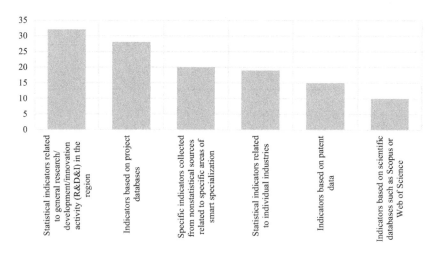

Figure 3.2 Sources of monitoring indicators

Source: Own elaboration based on CAWI (*n* = 37). Multiple answers are allowed

considering the lack of adequate resources to be one of the most important obstacles in the system. The monitoring system lacks automation and digitization, all main tasks are still performed manually. Modernization would make the process more smooth, fast, and reliable. In addition, cooperation with regional actors is not being strengthened to maximize the use of open data sources that would target innovative companies and businesses in the regional economy. Indeed, ten regions pointed to poor cooperation of smart specialization agents in collecting data on their activities.

The regions identified three main obstacles in the monitoring system (see Table 3.4). The first one stems from the fact that the statistical grouping by NACE codes usually does not fit into SS. This raises two of the most serious monitoring issues (identified by 23 regions), namely the lack of appropriate statistical indicators for the selected SS and thus the need to collect additional data through direct surveys or designated observatories. The third main obstacle to the system (also identified by the 23 regions) is quite well known, namely the delays in data collection. The regions have confirmed our concerns about the durability of the monitoring systems, as ten of them have indicated problems in obtaining funding for the operation of these systems. These obstacles do not differentiate regions with different levels of development either.

Table 3.4 The main obstacles to monitoring RIS3 activities in examined regions

	Lack of relevant statistical indicators for the selected smart specialization	Need for additional data collection through direct surveys or designated observatories	Delays in collecting data on statistical indicators for selected areas of smart specialization	Lack of adequate financial resources	Lack of cooperation of smart specialization agents when collecting data on their activities	No need for RIS3 monitoring suggested by policy makers	There are no obstacles in my region
All regions	23	23	23	10	10	3	1
Less developed regions	10	11	10	4	3	2	0
Medium developed regions	6	9	8	6	6	0	0
Highly developed regions	7	3	5	0	1	1	1

Source: Own elaboration based on CAWI [n = 37]. Multiple answers are allowed.

The Challenge of the Modification of a Monitoring System— The Case Study of Monitoring Smart Specializations in Pomerania (Poland)

The following smart specializations have been identified in the Pomeranian region: (1) marine and port and logistics technologies; (2) interactive technologies in an information-intensive environment; (3) eco-efficient technologies in production, transmission, distribution, and consumption of energy and fuels and in construction; (4) medical technologies in the field of civilization diseases and aging. Smart specializations in the Pomeranian region were selected based on competition, in which partnerships of enterprises and scientific entities participated, in a bottom-up manner. The SS areas represent technologies rather than industries.

RIS3 monitoring in the region is carried out by (1) analyzing indicators based on statistical data to assess changes in the social and economic environment of the region, for example, benchmarking Pomerania against other Polish and European regions (context indicators); (2) analyzing the changes arising from the implementation of the coordinated measures (as number of supported entities, number of their patents, volume of investment); (3) specific indicators for each SS area; (4) in-depth interviews (individual or group) with entrepreneurs, coordinators of smart specialization and representatives of local government units; (5) discussion panels with the participation of independent experts to analyze the obtained data, assess the consistency of the monitoring results and explain its causes and recommendations; (6) preparing the peer-2-peer application to exchange experiences in the field of monitoring (Doczekal, Mergner, & Janssen, 2019).

The approach to monitoring proposed in the Pomerania includes the same for each SS area general indicators, based mainly on the Statistics Poland (SP) data and data about supported projects, grouped into indicators reflecting the dynamics of SS, innovativeness and competitiveness indicators, and impact indicators on the Pomeranian economy, as well as specific indicators showing the level of development of particular SS areas. However, the initial set of specific indicators proposed for SS areas was very broad and is comprised of several indicators based on statistical data but also data needed to be gathered in specialized surveys for each of the four SS. Hence we proposed modification of the indicators based on the analysis of weaknesses and strengths of each of the initially proposed indicators. We proposed that the specific indicators used for RIS3 monitoring should be of 4–5 for each of the SS areas and based not only on SP but also on databases of international projects, that is, the Horizon 2020 Framework Program of the European Union and grants from the European Economic Area (EEA). In addition, new data sources are proposed, such as (1) an official register of new entrants in 2014–2018 broken down by NACE classes; analysis of new entrant data over the next few years may help to monitor the entrepreneurial discovery process and identify new potential areas of SS if the number of entrants in a specific NACE class is significantly higher than the average for previous years; (2) project data of the National Science Centre (NSC) in terms of topics and financial resources for basic research projects; (3) the database of the Patent Office of the Republic of Poland in the field of inventions (patents), utility models and industrial designs according to their subject matter; due to the longtime of obtaining many protection rights, in particular patents, it is better to carry out such analysis once every few years; (4) international publication databases, that is, Web of Science and Scopus: number of publications by keywords and scientific category/areas of science related to sub-technologies of smart specializations. This indicator indicates research conducted in the area of SS, mainly basic, but also applied that are not protected and whose applications could be published. Moreover, it shows to what extent this research has been innovative in an international context, which increases the likelihood of developing internationally competitive solutions within SS.

Indicators based on patents, scientific publications, and data concerning NSC projects will allow in particular for monitoring of SS through the prism of individual priority technologies, which is a specificity of the Pomeranian RIS3. On the other hand, the data from SP provide an opportunity to analyze individual economic areas of SS through the prism of NACE sections or classes or other variables specific to individual sub-technologies of individual SS areas. Table 3.5 presents the recommended set of indicators reflecting the logic: resources, symptoms, effects of individual SS areas, together with an indication of whether all SS or individual subtypes of activity/technology within an SS area are concerned and an indication of data sources for these indicators.

Monitoring indicators were proposed based on the following criteria: (1) easy availability of data at low cost; (2) as far as possible, no link with NACE codes, which often do not reflect the actual activity of enterprises; (3) for interactive technologies, it was decided to leave indicators based on data on NACE divisions, but referring to the key human potential for this specialization (jobs and wages); (4) for health technologies, indicators related to research activities in the SS were identified, as well as their effects and showing the level of development of medical services, especially for the elderly.

Mostly indicators specific for a particular SS area were proposed. However, additionally some horizontal indicators but allowing analysis for particular technological subfields shall be used. They are based mainly on not statistical data sources: protection of intellectual property rights, scientific publications, basic research, and international projects. An indicator of newly registered entities was recommended for all SSar-easand their sub-technologies at the level of NACE classes. Participation

Table 3.5 Set of proposed specific monitoring indicators for SS areas in Pomerania

Indicator (data source)	Technologies			
	marine and port logistics	*interactive*	*eco-effective*	*medical*
Resources				
Share of graduates of fields and specializations related to the SS in the total number of graduates (regional statistics, SP)	Sum for the whole individual SS			X
Marine transport fleet by age of vessel (regional statistics)	Port logistics	X	X	X
Basic research projects related to SS (NSC)	Sum for the whole individual SS			
Intramural R&D expenditures by science and technology—total expenditures in the area of medical and health sciences [PLN] (SP)	X	X	X	Total SS
Internal investment in biotechnology activities in enterprises (SP)	X	X	X	Pharmacy and cosmetics
Symptoms				
Share of Pomeranian entities in international projects cofinanced by the EU (Cordis, EEA grants)	Sum for the whole individual SS			
New SS-related entities appearing in particular years (SP register)	Sum for the whole individual SS and for particular subareas of SS			
Working in the ICT industry (SP)	X	Total and NACE divisions	X	X
Production of electricity from renewable energy sources (SP)	X	X	Energetics	X
Biotechnology companies (SP)	X	X	X	Pharmacy and cosmetics
Number of beds in hospices, care, and nursing facilities per 100,000 inhabitants (SP)	X	X	X	Ageing

Indicator (data source)	Technologies			
	marine and port logistics	*interactive*	*eco-effective*	*medical*
Effects				
International trade in seaports in tones (regional statistics)	Port logistics	X	X	X
Production of ships (regional statistics)	Production	X	X	X
Average monthly salary per employee (SP)	X	Total and NACE divisions	X	X
Sales of thermal energy in terms of volume of residential buildings (SP)	X	X	Energy efficiency in construction	X
Total energy consumption per 1 million PLN of GDP (SP)	X	X		X
Share of electricity produced from renewable sources in total electricity production (SP)	X	X		X
Energy balance of the region (SP)	X	X	Total SS	X
Number of patients treated in hospitals and spa sanatoriums in Pomerania (SP)	X	X	X	Ageing
Persons receiving health services aged 65 years and over (SP)	X	X	X	
Average life expectancy at birth for women and men (SP)	X	X	X	Total SS
Death from cancer and cardiovascular disease per 10,000 inhabitants (SP)	X	X	X	Civilization diseases
Protection of intellectual property rights related to SS (Patent Office)	Total SS and SS technology subareas			
Scientific publications in the international database by keywords (Scopus)				

Source: Own study. X—not relevant.

in international R&D and application projects shows the level of internationalization of specializations.

Moreover, for the first three specializations, the share of SS-related graduates in the total number of university graduates in the region was recommended. This indicator has not been chosen for medical technologies, as education policy in this area is overregulated at the national level and, due to study costs, it is not possible to easily adapt it to market requirements.

Conclusion

Implications for Theory

RIS3 monitoring systems are as diverse as the regions in the EU. Therefore, approaches to monitoring the implementation of the strategy are almost incomparable. The first conclusion indicates that the indicators for individual SS should form a system based on intervention logic, that is, they should cover (1) resources: human resources and expenditures on SS activities; (2) symptoms: products of measures within SS; (3) effects: performance of SS activities (Wojnicka-Sycz, Sliż, & Sycz, 2018). Such a monitoring logic will also reflect the recommendations of the European Commission (2014) to monitor input, output, and result indicators in monitoring systems. Input indicators from the resource block reflect human, material, or scientific resources, that is, deliberately conducted work in basic research and university graduates.

The indicators from the symptom block, that is, manifestations of SS activity in the form of research and development projects conducted for practical implementation, that is, in the field of applied research and development works, will be matched to the output/product indicators. Moreover, the symptom of SS activity will also include new entities emerging in the areas of related activities, which will indicate the attractiveness of these areas and new ideas for conducting projects in these areas. Result indicators will first of all be juxtaposed with indicators relating to the effects of SS operations, that is, intellectual property rights obtained, as well as scientific publications in international databases and other specific to particular SS. It is also a good idea to use such tools as the balanced scorecard model for the whole SS and every subarea of SS.

Our research has revealed several challenges for monitoring systems, indicating that they may be common to various regions. Although a number of our interviewees emphasized that their monitoring systems are transparent, structured, and thus comprehensible, as they use a limited number of indicators, they may not, on the other hand, provide precise information. Obtaining information is also problematic because of the lack of automated procedures, software, or delays in data collection. This is certainly due to the lack of constant and sufficient funding of monitoring systems and this is probably due to the lack of involvement of the various regional actors and, above all, the authorities supporting and understanding the monitoring and evaluation processes. For instance, it is necessary to justify and agree on the use of certain permanent networks of institutions that continuously collect the indicators needed for monitoring (see the case of the Emilia-Romagna region), with funding and agreed procedures.

Implications for Policy

The challenge of monitoring RIS3 in several regions is the lack of resources—not only funds but also individuals involved in implementing RIS3. It seems that in many regions of the EU, monitoring and the overall RIS3 strategy are neglected. Evidence of this is the lack of monitoring reports and even the difficulty of finding RIS3 documents or departments/ units dealing with RIS3 or even innovation policy on the websites of EU regional authorities.

Due to lack of resources in less developed regions, the system of indicators for monitoring individual priority areas of the SS should generally be based on publicly available data from statistical offices, databases on international projects and basic research projects, as well as data on scientific publications (in particular the Scopus database), protection of intellectual property rights, available also in relevant online databases. Such a solution has been successfully implemented in the Polish region of Pomerania. Also, it is necessary to use databases on projects cofinanced by the Structural Funds, especially those related to RIS3 support (Kleibrink, Gianelle, & Doussineau 2016). These indicators will reflect both R&D and innovation, as well as international competitiveness or entrepreneurial discovery manifested in the creation of enterprises at completely new intersections of industries and technologies. Regional authorities should strive to cooperate with national institutions (e.g., export data collectors) and convince other regional institutions (e.g., loan funds) to collect data across SS.

Besides, networks of regional authorities should be created to analyze their databases in each SS area. This learning through the development of the SS monitoring system leads to the construction of more permanent regional observatories and monitoring mechanisms, as is the case in more developed regions, which now often use monitoring systems developed for innovation policy purposes before RIS3 (Gruber, Handler, & Kleinberger-Pierer, 2016; Lopes, Farinha, Ferreira, & Silveira, 2018).

Another challenge for monitoring in all types of regions is the stronger use of new technologies, such as the big data and data collected using the various sensors installed within the Internet of Things, as well as text mining methods for Internet queries. This requires both the implementation of ICT innovations and infrastructure development and the availability of individuals able to analyze this type of data (Gruzauskas et al., 2020).

A further challenge is to make more intensive use of data from the beneficiaries of projects supported by authorities related to SS areas, which should be obliged to carry out such monitoring activities or participate in surveys.

The challenge of monitoring new promising areas of SS could be met by analyzing the development of entrepreneurship in various EDP-related initiatives in a bottom-up manner and by analyzing statistical data on newly registered entities (Polverari, 2016; Wojnicka-Sycz, Sliż, & Sycz, 2018). Therefore, EDP initiatives and analyses carried out or commissioned by the authorities should not only be linked to the monitoring of already designated SS areas but also encourage the demonstration of new areas that may become new specializations. The diverse research carried out in the regions could also be used to analyze the data collected from the perspective of existing and emerging innovative areas of the regional economy.

Limitations

The main limitation of the research is only a fragmentary analysis of actions performed by the regions and declarative statements on the results of monitoring. We were not able to verify the actual functioning of the monitoring systems and the quality and relevance of the collected indicators. The lack of monitoring reports on the implementation of RIS3 is considered to be a serious problem, but this may be due to the modest resources that the regions surveyed (with different levels of development) spend on monitoring. Therefore, it seems that the regions rather do not give much importance to monitoring the implemented strategies.

Future Research Directions

Future research should focus on the effectiveness and efficiency of monitoring systems. Firstly, the institutional system should be analyzed to ensure the most effective implementation of monitoring activities and optimal collection of indicators. At this point, it would be interesting to examine whether the monitoring activities require an entrepreneurial discovery process and what are the real benefits of such an approach. As regards monitoring indicators, we propose to develop standards for their review to continuously improve public governance.

Notes

1. See more about the monitoring and comprehensive performance data, open to the public here https://tem.fi/documents/1410877/10387910/Romanska

+MFF+and+cohesion+policy+post+2020.pdf/2b77997e-42a9-41a0-92f5-b32f5140975e/Romanska+MFF+and+cohesion+policy+post+2020.pdf.pdf

2. See more on the Regional Innovation Monitor and S3 Platform websites: https://ec.europa.eu/growth/tools-databases/regional-innovation-monitor/ and https://s3platform.jrc.ec.europa.eu. Accessed May and June 2020.

References

4th Smart-watch Minibook. (2019). *Regional observatories for supporting the development of smart specialization countries, monitoring, future.* Interreg Central Europe. Retrieved from www.interreg-central.eu/Content.Node/4th-SMART-watch-MiniBook.pdf

Angelidou, M., Passas, I., Psaltoglou, A., Tsarchopoulos, P., & Komninos, N. (2017). Monitoring the impact of smart specialisation strategies across EU regions. *International Conference for Entrepreneurship, Innovation and Regional Development*, Thessalonki. Retrieved from www.onlines3.eu/wp-content/onlines3-files/07%20Angelidou%20M,%20Komninos%20N,%20Passas%20I%20A,%20Psaltoglou%20A,%20Tsarchopoulos%20P,%20(2017)%20Monitoring%20the%20Impact%20of%20Smart%20Specialisation%20Strategies%20Across%20EU%20Regions.pdf

Annecke, W. (2008). Monitoring and evaluation of energy for development: The good, the bad and the questionable in M&E practice. *Energy Policy*, *36*(8), 2839–2845.

Doczekal, Ch., Mergner, R., & Janssen, R. (2019). *Best practice report: Smart specialisation strategies and SET plan implementation actions.* TRACER project. Glasgow: European Policies Research Centre.

European Commission. (2010). *Investing in Europe's future: Fifth report on economic, social and territorial cohesion.* Brussels: Publications Office of the European Union.

European Commission. (2014). *Guidance document on monitoring and evaluation.* Retrieved from https://ec.europa.eu/regional_policy/sources/docoffic/2014/working/wd_2014_en.pdf

Foray, D., Goddard, J., Goenaga, B. X., Landabaso, M., McCann, P., Morgan, K., & Ortega-Argiles, R. (2012). *Guide to research and innovation strategies for smart specialisation.* Brussels: European Commission.

Gianelle, C., & Kleibrink, A. (2015). *Monitoring mechanisms for smart specialisation strategies.* Brussels: European Commission.

Gruber, M, Handler, R., & Kleinberger-Pierer, M. (2016). *Policy framework for smart specialisation in Austria.* Retrieved from https://s3platform.jrc.ec.europa.eu/documents/20182/223684/AT_RIS3_201611_Final.pdf

Gruzauskas, V., Krisciunas, A., Calneryte, D., Navickas, V., & Koisova, E. (2020). Development of a market trend evaluation system for policy making. *Journal of Competitiveness*, *12*(2), 22–37.

HIGHER. (2017). *Monitoring and evaluation: The case of Catalonia (Spain). Monitoring process for smart specialization communities.* Interreg Europe. Retrieved from www.interregeurope.eu/fileadmin/user_upload/tx_tevprojects/library/GoodPractice_CataloniaMonitoring.pdf

Iannacci, F., Cornford, T., Cordella, A., & Grillo, F. (2009). Evaluating monitoring systems in the European social fund context: A sociotechnical approach. *Evaluation Review*, *33*(5), 419–445.

Kleibrink, A., Gianelle, C., & Doussineau, M. (2016). Monitoring innovation and territorial development in Europe: Emergent strategic management. *European Planning Studies*, 24(8), 1438–1458.

Krause, P., Lopez-Acevedo, G., & Mackay, K. (Eds.). (2012). *Building better policies: The nuts and bolts of monitoring and evaluation systems.* Washington, DC: The World Bank.

Lopes, J., Farinha, L., Ferreira, J. J., & Silveira, P. (2018). Smart specialization policies: Innovative performance models from European regions. *European Planning Studies*, 26(11), 2114–2124.

Lopez-Acevedo, G., Krause, P., & Mackay, K. (Eds.). (2012). *Building better policies: The nuts and bolts of monitoring and evaluation systems.* Washington, DC: The World Bank.

Lower Silezia. (2015). *Strategic framework for smart specialisations of Lower Silesia.* Attachment to the 2011–2020 RIS for Lower Silesia Province, Wrocław. Retrieved from www.interregeurope.eu/fileadmin/user_upload/tx_tevprojects/library/file_1580811969.pdf

McCann, P., & Ortega-Argilés, R. (2016). Smart specialisation, entrepreneurship and SMEs: Issues and challenges for a results-oriented EU regional policy. *Small Business Economics*, 46(4), 537–552.

Monteiro, R., Santos, P., Guimarães, C., & Silva, A. (2018). *Norte Region smart specialisation strategy* (NORTE RIS3). A monitoring system methodological approach for MONITORIS3 project, S3 Platform. Retrieved from https://s3platform.jrc.ec.europa.eu/documents/20182/201464/Norte+Monitor+RIS3/8f4ae2dc-d76e-4fd5-a49f-f489564b1154

Ostašius, E., & Laukaitis, A. (2015). Reference model for e-government monitoring, evaluation and benchmarking. *Engineering Economics*, 26. https://doi.org/10.5755/j01.ee.26.3.8128

Otręba-Szklarczyk, A., Pierzchała, M., Strzebońska, A., Szklarczyk, D., Ulatowska, R., Winogrodzka, D., & Worek, B. (2017). *Ex-ante evaluation of the non-competitive project "Monitoring of National Smart Specialisation" of the Operational Programme Intelligent Development 2014–2020.* Final report from the evaluation study, PAED, Kraków-Warsaw. Retrieved from www.parp.gov.pl/storage/publications/pdf/2018_POIR_KIS_ewaluacja.pdf

Plenikowska-Ślusarz, T., & Jurkiewicz, T. (2017). *Evaluation of the monitoring model for smart specialisations of Pomerani.* Gdańsk: Centre for Analysis and Expertise of the University of Gdańsk.

Polverari, L. (2016). The implementation of Smart Specialisation Strategies in 2014–20 ESIF programmes: Turning intelligence into performance. *IQ-Net Thematic Paper*, 39(2). European Policies Research Centre December. Retrieved from www.eprc-strath.eu/public/dam/jcr:e14d1ac5-43d4-484f-853f-a6f40b8cd1c2/IQ-Net_Thematic_Paper_39(2).pdf

Pylak, K. (2013). *Management of innovation policy in less developed regions: Impact of the Metropolitan area on innovation of the economy of Lubelskie Region.* Lublin: Lublin University of Technology.

Roman, M., & Mutanen, O. P. (2018). Monitoring the Innovation Ecosystem and the Effectiveness of Smart Specialisation Strategies, *27th International Scientific Conference on Economic and Social Development*, Rome. Retrieved from www.onlines3.eu/wp-content/onlines3-files/16%20Roman%20M,%20Mutanen%20O-P%20(2018)%20Monitoring%20the%20innovation%20 ecosystem%20and%20the%20of%20effectiveness%20smart%20specialisation%20strategies.pdf

SIRIS Academic. (2018). Characterization of preliminary priority areas for smart specialisation in Moldova. *Network analysis for the identification of key stakeholders for preliminary priority areas for smart specialisation in Moldova.* European Commission Joint Research Center (JRC). Retrieved from http://unics.cloud/solutions/priority-areas-for-smart-specialisation-moldova/

Wojnicka-Sycz, E. (2020). Theory-based evaluation criteria for regional smart specializations and their application in the Podkarpackie voivodeship in Poland. *Regional Studies*, *54*(11), 1612–1625.

Wojnicka-Sycz, E., Sliż, P., & Sycz, P. (2018). *Monitoring of smart specialisations in Pomorskie Region (PSI) in 2018—a proposal for modifications in terms of specific indicators.* Report for the Office of the Marshal of Pomorskie Voivodeship in Gdańsk.

Part 2

Smart Specialization in the Subregional and Local Government Context

4 The Impacts of Policy Instruments to Stimulate Bottom-up Approaches for Smart Specialization

The Case of Baden-Wuerttemberg

Elisabeth Baier

Introduction

This chapter presents a regional and practice-oriented case study about the implementation of the smart specialization strategy in the federal state of Baden-Wuerttemberg, Germany. The analyses focus on the effects of the competition "Regional Competitiveness through Innovation and Sustainability—RegioWIN," as an example of a regional innovation policy instrument supported by the European Regional Development Fund (ERDF) that pursues a place-based approach. Within the general context of this book, the chapter focuses on aspects of entrepreneurial search processes and the mobilizing potential of smart specialization strategies (S3) in order to stimulate the formation of regional partnerships. It follows the general argument and working hypothesis that "the successful implementation of smart specialization strategies depends on linking regional and innovation policies with bottom-up activities of enterprises, regional networks, as well as with initiatives of private and public actors" in order to spur regional development and to support cohesion.

To address and finally to overcome undesired social, economic, and territorial disparities the European Union devotes approximately 32.5% of its budget in the programming period 2014–2020 to policy instruments that support cohesion.[1] The idea of policy support for cohesion has a long tradition. It emerged during the founding phase of the European Economic Community with a clear focus on solidarity for less favored and economically weaker parts of Europe. In the early phase of the European regional development policies regional compensation, solidarity, and regional convergence were driving forces. However, the policy rationales for cohesion policy have shifted over time (Ares, 2020). Policy rationales concentrate presently on investment profitability and innovation-driven regional development (Sánchez-Carreira, 2020) in order to achieve the goals set out in the Europe 2020 strategy. Thus, the policy rationales implicitly aim to address static and dynamic efficiency and effectiveness at the same time and leave policy makers with the challenge to find suitable instruments for the development of an economy based on knowledge and innovation, the promotion of a more resource-efficient, greener and more competitive economy and a high-employment economy delivering economic, social, and territorial cohesion (European Commission, 2010). The changing policy rationales have had as a result that nowadays not only lagging regions can benefit from the ERDF but also leading regions such as Baden-Wuerttemberg.

With the beginning of the funding period 2014–2020 smart specialization serves as the major conceptual basis and implementation framework (European Commission, 2009) to accomplish cohesion in Europe and the development of "Research and Innovation Strategies for Smart Specialization" is central in the EU's innovation policy agenda. It should stimulate entrepreneurial discovery processes (EDP) in the regions, in which regional stakeholders from different environments (government, business, academia, administration) jointly identify potential technological and market opportunities and the specialization domains for their territory. In this line, entrepreneurial knowledge and innovation are perceived as important drivers for economic development, growth, and prolonged global competitiveness. Innovation shall induce economic transformation toward higher value activities as well as societal change. With the evolvement of the smart specialization framework the stimulating potential of entrepreneurial identification processes, bottom-up approaches, cooperative activities, and interactive learning for regional innovation gained additional notice (Foray, Morgan, & Radosevic, 2018). In the funding period 2014–2020, it was one of the formulated goals of the European Commission that cohesion policy instruments are managed and delivered in partnerships between the European Commission, the Member States, and stakeholders at the local and regional level.[2] Regions are encouraged to adopt S3, which is a prerequisite (ex ante conditionality) for accessing European Structural and Investment Funds (ESIF) in general and ERDF in particular.

In order to demonstrate how entrepreneurial discovery processes in a place-based policy setting can be stimulated by S3, the chapter is structured as follows. The next section presents a brief literature background on smart specialization, place-based innovation policy making, entrepreneurial discovery processes, and path development, which serve as the theoretical reference frame. This is complemented by a discussion about implementations strategies for S3 and associated challenges. A section explaining the methodological approach follows subsequently. The first part of the successive empirical section provides general insights about the case study region. The results serve for the framing of the analysis in the second part of this section, which contains a discussion of the impacts of the RegioWIN competition with a focus on the bottom-up effects within the S3 framework. The last section reflects the findings and presents recommendations for policy learning.

Literature Background

Smart Specialization, Place-based Innovation Policy Making, and Entrepreneurial Discovery Processes

Based on the origin of the concept of smart specialization by Foray, David, and Hall (2009) and its refinement over the following years smart specialization is now understood as specialized diversification (Foray, 2014; Foray et al., 2018; Foray, 2019; Hassink & Gong, 2019; Valdaliso, Magro, Navarro, Aranguren, & Wilson, 2014). Based on region-specific capacities as well as region-specific entrepreneurial opportunities it should enable regions to concentrate future relevant investments on priorities, which have been identified in localized entrepreneurial search processes and which seem to be promising for future regional development. The concept pursues the underlying goal to empower the regions to trigger processes of economic transformation, leading to structural change and to gain competitive advantage based on their strengths (Foray, 2019). The aspect of self-discovery in finding the right spheres of action is emphasized and the S3 concept intends to evoke bottom-up approaches in regional policy formulation and implementation. Additionally, it should support the formation of capabilities by building micro-systems of innovation (Foray, 2016). Hence, the S3 concept adheres to a place-based policy approach.

According to Barca (2009) places are defined through the policy process from a functional perspective as regions, in which a set of conditions conducive to development apply more than they do in larger or smaller areas. Thus, there is no predefined boundary to a place, according to administrative or government logic. A place is conceptualized by its actors, their recognition, identity, and imagination (Hassink, 2020). It depends on the geographical context, which consists of formal and informal institutions and the influences of cultural, historical, and spatial specificities (Gertler, 2018). From a geographical perspective, place is no container, but it is socially constructed and specified by the relationship between the place, the actors, and drivers for regional development (Hassink, 2020). Place characteristics include the geographic and institutional specificities and particularities, which hold the clues to the most appropriate pathways for development (McCann & Ortega-Argilés, 2013). This implies that policy interventions should rely on local knowledge and capabilities and the regional–local context should be recognized as an important factor in the policy and planning processes.

As stated by McCann & Ortega-Argilés (2013) a place-based approach to designing well-tailored and integrated policy solutions requires first, an identification of the place-specific characteristics of a region. In addition, it is necessary to consider the territorial features of a region, in terms of the interrelationships and interdependencies within or between places. This is important because the combination of the place-specific characteristics and the territorial aspects heavily influences the choice of the appropriate challenges to be addressed. It is important to take into account linkages among places and to differentiate between place-based specialization and regional diversification (Hassink & Gong, 2019). It is necessary to overcome sector-based institutional "silos" and to provide integrated and place-based development policy solutions, to build tailored institutions and intervention strategies based on local knowledge, shared values, and joint practices in order to reach the desired form of path development.

The innovation potential, the demographic and industrial characteristics of a place as well as criteria for system differentiation are important for the identification of path development potentials (Grillitsch & Asheim, 2018; McCann & Ortega-Argilés, 2013). They should form the basis for the formulation of policy priorities, which requires a comprehensive understanding of the regional status quo and an aligned imagination of future development potentials based on entrepreneurial discovery processes, structured knowledge exchange, and region learning. The smart specialization approach and in particular S3 constitute a place-based policy framework, which foregrounds the role of regions and emphasizes research and innovation for building competitive advantage based on the identification of regional strengths and potentials (Fitjar, Benneworth, & Asheim, 2019). It promotes specialized diversification, which in turn can lead to more advanced forms of industrial path development due to smart, deliberate, and selective investments. Entrepreneurial discovery processes provide a basis for a targeted economic structural change and a renewal of the industrial base of a region. The fact that technological and market opportunities are discovered jointly by actors from different environments, enables the diversification into new but related economic fields and higher forms of path development such as path upgrading, path importation, or related path diversification or even new path creation (Asheim, Isaksen, & Trippl, 2019; Grillitsch, Asheim, & Trippl, 2018).

Implementation Strategies for S3 and Associated Challenges

Because the smart specialization framework is the guiding policy principle for the regional innovation and cohesion policy in the European Unions during the programming period 2014–2020 numerous evaluation studies and several academic publications give insights into the experiences of implementing smart specialization in the regions of the different Member States. To complete the discussion about smart specialization it seems important to draw the attention also toward present implementation strategies and associated challenges.

As mentioned in the previous subsection, S3 requires acknowledging territorial diversity by considering regional specificities, in particular economic, sectoral, and institutional settings. In consequence, implementation strategies are highly idiosyncratic. Implementation practices vary greatly concerning the underlying entrepreneurial discovery processes. Papamichail et al. (2019) distinguish between a narrow-to-broad approach with initially very limited participation of local stakeholders or an hourglass model based on a broad-to-narrow approach, followed by widely open and transparent practices. Actor involvement, consultation processes, and decision-making might differ, depending on the regional characteristics.

Thus, regional characteristics such as socioeconomic advancement, governance practice during the implementation process, the degree of professionalization of regional stakeholders or the institutional capacity influence the implementation of S3. The latter presents a main constraint for efficient and effective S3 implementation (Esparza Masana & Fernández, 2019). In particular, sparsely populated areas or catching-up regions face additional challenges. In sparsely populated area strategy development is often designed by representatives from urban centers for the whole territory. As a consequence, entrepreneurial actors in rural areas aren't sufficiently involved in the design and implementation (Teräs, Dubois, Sörvik, & Pertoldi, 2015). In catching up regions, the main barriers to S3 implementation can be related to a limited ability of the local firms to acquire university-generated knowledge and develop a leading role in developing S3 action (Papamichail et al., 2019).

In addition, Pagliacci et al. (2020) stress the importance to take regional heterogeneity into consideration in order to support more effective policy learning. By looking at regional economic advancement Crescenzi and Guia (2016) show that in most disadvantaged regions purely bottom-up policy tools might be inefficient. Capello and Kroll (2016) find that regions without a critical mass in any sectoral or technological domain have difficulties to identify the local specialization pattern and new related activities for a specialized diversification. In some cases, the governance of the S3 processes did not necessarily match the smart specialization policy approach in particular if the implementation processes were assigned to levels of governance that were too high or too low or if member states favored a top-down process instead of promoting a bottom-up approach (Capello & Kroll, 2016). Governance challenges also arise if a region reveals a lack of capability to design and implement strategic regional innovation policies or to engage actively in the process of regional entrepreneurial discovery (Capello & Kroll, 2016) or if the overall institutional framework hampers regional attempts (Kroll, 2015). Although the region of Baden-Wuerttemberg belongs to the group of innovation leaders, it is characterized by intra-regional disparities and an uneven spread of institutional capacities that challenge the implementation of S3.

Based on the theoretical considerations and critical aspects summarized in the previous subsections, the following questions serve as a guiding framework for the empirical investigation. They aim at a better understanding of the mobilizing potential of S3 in a region, which belongs to the group of innovation leaders in Europe. Within this scope of the book the following research questions Q1 and Q2 aim at a better understanding of the implementation processes and intend to generate further insights concerning the implementation practice.

> *Q1: What kind of bottom-up processes and activities are stimulated by the implementation of the S3 approach in Baden-Wuerttemberg?*
> *Q2: Which differences in the stimulation of bottom-up activities can we observe during the different phases of the RegioWIN competition?*

Since the socioeconomic advancement, governance practice or the institutional capacity of a region seems to be relevant for an effective implementation (Esparza Masana & Fernández, 2019) this chapter also intends to contribute to regional and policy learning by addressing the following research questions Q3 and Q4.

> *Q3: Which differences in the stimulation potential and bottom-up activities can we observe according to prior innovation capacities, prior professionalization, and the institutional capacities of the subregions?*
> *Q4: What are the impacts of RegioWIN on regional innovation policymaking?*

Methodological Approach

Methodologically, this chapter pursues a case study approach as proposed by Yin (2013). Such a case study design benefits the generation of knowledge about individual, group, network, organizational, social, and political phenomena. As an empirical identification strategy, it particularly suits a situation when a contemporary phenomenon within its real-life context is to be examined. It relies on multiple sources of evidence and triangulation is used to capture different dimensions of the investigation.

The RegioWIN competition serves as the guiding reference frame for the empirical investigation due to several reasons. First, it is the major regional policy instrument for the distribution of the ERDF funding in Baden-Wuerttemberg. About 30% of the ERDF funding of the of Baden-Wuerttemberg are distributed through the RegioWIN competition

(Ministerium für Ländlichen Raum und Verbraucherschutz Baden-Württemberg, 2013, p. 66). Second, the policy instrument is designed as a two-stage interregional competition. It pursues the goal of spurring the formulation of regional strategic development concepts during the first stage and the development of corresponding lighthouse projects during the second stage. With the design of the competition, the responsible ministries aimed at activating and involving local stakeholders in all parts of Baden-Wuerttemberg to participate in the smart specialization processes (Häberle, 2016). Third, the competition follows a place-based approach. Territorial subunits (regions, cities, and municipalities) were invited to apply for funding and to develop regional strategies for smart and sustainable development. Applications were not limited to administrative units. Instead regional actors were encouraged to define their territorial sphere and the strategic development concepts themselves (Ministerium für Finanzen und Wirtschaft Baden-Württemberg, 2013b). Taken together, the RegioWIN competition provides a profound reference frame for the regional case study both in terms of relevance vis-à-vis the research questions and the general topic of the book but also in terms of its regional importance. The winner regions of the RegioWIN competition serve as the unit of analysis for the subsequent investigation.

The empirical sources that support the case study include the analysis of secondary data from the statistical offices and secondary data from public sources as well as the screening of regional strategy documents, policy documents, the operational program, and financial reports obtained from desk research. In addition, the core data were collected in 17 in-depth, direct, and semi-structured interviews with 19 interviewees, covering all winner regions.[3] The interviewees were selected according to a careful purposive sampling strategy (Patton, 1990; Teddlie & Yu, 2007) and can be considered as key informants. They represent the winner regions with successful proposals in the RegioWIN competition and are directly involved in the first or second stage of the competition. They are project managers, regional key actors, or initiators of the regional development concepts. All interviews lasted between 45 and 90 minutes and the questionnaire (see Appendix A) addressed key aspects of discovery processes and bottom-up approaches. To achieve a higher degree of independence from individual interviewees and possibly biased statements, several key informants per region were interviewed (whenever possible). The combination of multiple perspectives with confirming or contradictory statements in combination with other sources of evidence contributes to a comprehensive analysis of regional self-organizing processes. During the interviews, notes were taken and transcripts were completed afterward. Anonymity was granted.

Because the winner regions vary according to their innovative capabilities, size, population density, sectoral composition, and rural or metropolitan characteristics, regional descriptive statistics provide important background material to grasp intra-regional differences, which serve as contextual factors for the analyses. To answer the research questions and to provide insights into the development of innovation partnerships and bottom-up processes the interview material was structured and analyzed according to the means of a qualitative content analysis (Mayring, 2015). The transcripts were used to identify different practices, which in turn were structured (according to the chronological order of the competition and regional characteristics) in order to identify relevant aspects.

The following section presents a description of the case study region and an introduction to the structural characteristics of the winner regions and its subunits. Subsequent to this, it contains the results of the analysis of the empirical evidence from the interviews. Form the many aspects that were mentioned by the interviewees and which are worthwhile a detailed discussion (e.g., prioritization mechanisms for regional specialization, cofinancing, the organization of the competition by the responsible ministries, administrative restrictions) the following analyses will exclusively focus on the emergence of bottom-up activities as to keep in line with the general topic of this book.

Results and Discussion: S3 in Baden-Wuerttemberg

Baden-Wuerttemberg is one of the 16 federal states of Germany and located in the southwest of Germany. It is Germany's third largest federal state with an area of 35,751 km[2] and 11.07 million inhabitants at the end of 2019. The territory is divided into four territorial units on the NUTS 2[4] level and 44 territorial subunits on the NUTS 3 level. It is by far not homogeneous because it comprises metropolitan areas as well as predominantly rural areas with a low population density. The innovativeness and the transformative capacity of the case study region were subject of debate in the regional science and economic geography literature over the last decades (inter alia Cooke and Morgan (1994), Cooke (2001), Cooke, Heidenreich, and Braczyk (2004), Heidenreich and Krauss (2004), Stahlecker and Muller (2008), Baier, Kroll, Schricke, and Stahlecker (2012), Strambach and Klement (2013)) with different conclusions. In some of the contributions, the innovativeness and transformative powers of the region were questioned (Baier et al., 2012; Stahlecker & Muller, 2008). Despite all doubts, the region belongs to the economic powerhouses of Germany with high innovative potentials as recent numbers from the Regional Innovation Scoreboard reveal (Hollanders & Es-Sadki, 2017; Hollanders, Es-Sadki, & Merkelbach, 2019).

Industrial Specialization

Concerning its industrial structure, Baden-Wuerttemberg is highly industrialized compared to the national average. The manufacturing sector

Table 4.1 Industrial specialization of Baden-Wuerttemberg (percentage share of employment)

	2009	2011	2013	2015	2017
Manufacturing	36.86	36.88	36.30	35.51	34.61
Wholesale and retail trade; repair of motor vehicles and motorcycles	16.31	16.14	16.04	15.64	15.17
Human Health and Social Work Activities	11.21	11.35	10.75	12.15	12.87
Professional, scientific, and technical activities	5.81	5.67	6.29	6.24	6.42
Administrative and support service activities	4.37	5.29	5.20	5.18	5.64
Construction	5.35	5.13	5.18	5.19	5.30
Information and communication	3.57	3.47	3.55	3.55	3.83
Transportation and storage	3.10	3.05	3.14	3.20	3.37
Others < 3%	13.44	13.02	13.54	13.34	12.80

Source: Own presentation based on data from the Statistical Office Baden-Württemberg.

with a location quotient of 1.35 and relatively high total job numbers (1.53 mio of 4.41 mio in the region) forms the region's economic base.[5] Additionally, Baden-Wuerttemberg is traditionally dominated by core technology-oriented sectors such as mechanical and electrical engineering, automobile production, OEMs as well as first- and second-tier suppliers. Table 4.1 presents the sectoral composition of the region over the last years. As regards its industrial structure, Table 4.1 reveals structural transformations. The manufacturing sector has lost weight and other sectors such as human health or professional, scientific, and technical activities gained in terms of higher employment shares.

Additionally, the region's economy is characterized by a strong export orientation. The export volume amounted to almost €203 billion in the year 2018, representing 15.4% of German exports. This reveals that the region's companies are competitive on a global scale. In addition, Baden-Wuerttemberg hosts numerous hidden champions, firms that are world market leaders in international niche markets with high export rates (Audretsch, Lehmann, & Schenkenhofer, 2018; Simon, 2009), even in rural parts of the region (Glückler, Punstein, Wuttke, & Kirchner, 2019).

Innovation, R&D, and the Higher Education Sector

The four NUTS 2 regions of Baden-Wuerttemberg are classified as "innovation leaders," however, with a decreasing innovation performance in some of the sub-indicators in the Regional Innovation Scoreboard 2019 (Hollanders et al., 2019). In detail, the region is characterized by a large share of R&D expenditures as percentage of GDP (5.7% in 2017), with 83.6 % of the R&D expenditures coming from the business sector.[6] According to the Regional Innovation Scoreboard 2019, it is further characterized by a high patent intensity, a strong higher education, and research infrastructure but only a low share of SMEs with innovation co-operation activities. Thus, the innovation system faces certain challenges for sustaining its competitiveness. There is a need for spurring the development of new and more service-oriented business models and the transformation of core technology-oriented sectors at firm level.

With research and development (R&D) expenditures reaching €27.8 billion in 2017, about 28% of the German R&D expenditure can be attributed to Baden-Wuerttemberg.[7] The regional higher education infrastructure is very strong and well differentiated: in 18 universities, 15 colleges of arts and music, 6 colleges of education, 69 universities of applied sciences, and 1 cooperative state university, almost 360,000 students are enrolled.[8] In addition, the region has a large number of public research institutions that are active in the areas of basic and application-oriented research, almost 70 further institutes fulfilling R&D activities, 215,310 R&D personnel and researchers (head count)[9], and an extensive system of transfer institutions.

Innovation Policy and the Implementation of S3

Innovation policy making has a long tradition. In the 1980s, Baden-Wuerttemberg started to establish a comprehensive technology transfer system and the systematic development of a business-related research infrastructure as well as a higher education system with differentiated task profiles. In the 1990s, the innovation policy focused on high-performance research priorities, the promotion of business-related and applied research, structural improvements in technology transfer, and on strengthening the capacity for innovation in SMEs by promoting collaborative research and business start-ups. Since the beginning of the century, the region's research and technology policies focus on the development of systematic networking of innovation actors and the emergence of cluster policy. Fostering the cooperation of people and institutions from the science, business, and political sectors and the establishment of dialogue processes among the various stakeholders are likewise important elements of Baden-Wuerttemberg's innovation policy (Ministerium für Finanzen und Wirtschaft Baden-Württemberg, 2013a).

The region has taken the preparations for the ESIF period 2014–2020 as incentive to summarize the implementation status and the priorities as well as innovation policy challenges in an innovation strategy in the year 2013. In its innovation strategy, the region explicitly addressed the first thematic objective "strengthening research, technological development, and innovation," which constitutes one of the key priorities for the ERDF[10] as well as the ex ante conditionality related to research and innovation. The state gives special attention to the promotion of four sectors of growth: (1) sustainable mobility, (2) environmental technologies, renewable energies and resource efficiency, (3) health care, and information and (4) communication technology, Green IT, and intelligent products. This primary sector-oriented growth strategy is complemented by the support of key enabling technologies such as micro- and nanotechnology, biotechnology or photonics, artificial intelligence, or digitalization. Additionally, activities around the promotion of Industry 4.0 play an important role. The innovation policy mix of Baden-Wuerttemberg comprises traditional regional innovation policy measures as well as measures, which explicitly address the promotion of structural change.

In preparation for the next ESIF period, the innovation strategy of the region was revised and the updated document was published in February 2020 (Ministerium für Wirtschaft, Arbeit und Wohnungsbau Baden-Württemberg, 2020). The S3 concept served as a guiding principle and the amendments to the strategy are developed in dialogue processes. To combine existing strengths with new technological possibilities and to tap into new potentials for higher value creation, the 2020 innovation strategy explicitly addresses digitization, artificial intelligence and Industry 4.0, sustainable mobility, healthcare, resource efficiency and energy transition, and a sustainable bio-economy. The document claims that the region pursues "a place-based and experimentalist policy,"[11] within the S3 framework.

The RegioWIN Competition

In accordance with the operational program "Innovation and Energy Transition" the government of the federal state of Baden-Wuerttemberg has launched the competition "Regional Competitiveness through Innovation and Sustainability—RegioWIN" in 2013 in order to implement S3 in the region. The policy instrument is designed as a two-stage interregional competition and territorial subunits (regions, cities, and municipalities) were invited to develop regional strategies for sustainable development and to derive lighthouse projects for funding. To achieve a broad mobilization, each territorial subunit should participate in only one RegionWIN proposal. Officially, 37[12] out of the 44 NUTS 3 regions of Baden-Wuerttemberg belong to one of the 11 winner regions. The following map in Figure 4.1 presents an overview of the federal state of Baden-Wuerttemberg with the 11 winner regions. The NUTS 3 regions, which belong to a single winner region, are jointed (where applicable) and the areas of the different winner regions appear in different shades of grey. All other NUTS 3 regions (seven) are white.

As we can see from the map, the competition had a broad mobilizing effect, because the vast majority of the NUTS 3 regions are involved. The thematic objectives "strengthening research, technological development

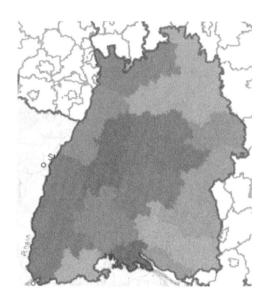

Figure 4.1 Overview of Baden-Wuerttemberg and the RegioWIN winner regions

and innovation" and "supporting the shift toward a low-carbon economy in all sectors" served as a guideline for the development of the regional development concepts in the first stage of the competition. For the second stage of the competition, the regions were invited to develop lighthouse projects, in different funding categories, namely research infrastructure in applied research, cluster funding, technology transfer intermediaries, start-up accelerators, systematic climate protection, or innovation infrastructure.[13]

As mentioned before, the design of the RegioWIN competition serves as the reference frame for the analyses of the emergence of bottom-up activities and the formation of regional partnerships during the competition. In chronological order, the competition can be characterized by four main periods of potential interest for the emergence of bottom-up activities: the initiating phase (0), the preparation phase for the development of the regional proposal (stage 1 of the competition), the development of lighthouse projects (stage 2 of the competition) and the implementation and execution of the projects (3). Figure 4.2 depicts the different periods and the associated tasks and challenges for the territorial units that participated. The phases 0–2 are completed and phase 3 is in some of the winner regions at the time of writing still ongoing.

Baden-Wurttemberg is characterized by intra-regional disparities as regards the innovative potential, density, sectoral composition, and economic performance. These disparities are also reflected in the

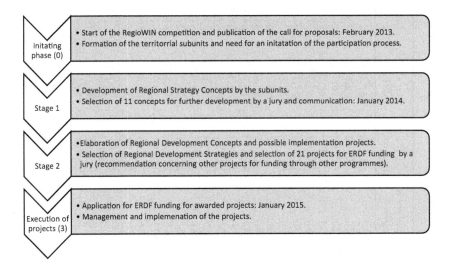

Initating phase (0)
- Start of the RegioWIN competition and publication of the call for proposals: February 2013.
- Formation of the territorrial subunits and need for an initatation of the participation process.

Stage 1
- Development of Regional Strategy Concepts by the subunits.
- Selection of 11 concepts for further development by a jury and communication: January 2014.

Stage 2
- Elaboration of Regional Development Concepts and possible implementation projects.
- Selection of Regional Development Strategies and selection of 21 projects for ERDF funding by a jury (recommendation concerning other projects for funding through other programmes).

Execution of projects (3)
- Application for ERDF funding for awarded projects: January 2015.
- Management and implemenation of the projects.

Figure 4.2 Overview of the organization of the RegioWIN competition

characteristics of the winner regions, which are very heterogeneous in size and innovative and economic capabilities. Table 4.2 provides an overview of the winner regions in order to provide a better understanding of the differences of the winner regions.

As we can see, the number of NUTS 3 regions, which form the winner regions differs between 1 and 6, reflecting the place-based approach in the design of the competition. Based on the composition of the NUTS 3 regions, the winner regions are characterized by intra-regional disparities as regards the population density, GDP/inhabitant, innovation capabilities, but also concerning the institutional capacities for implementation (which are not listed, but this aspect was frequently mentioned during the interviews). The institutional and economic framework conditions were in many cases decisive for the organization of the entrepreneurial discovery processes. The winner regions are highly aware of intra- and interregional disparities and the regional development concepts and project proposals address them explicitly. The interdependencies between metropolitan centers and the rural parts often constitute an essential component of the development strategies, at least in those regions where it applies.

Findings

It was one of the goals of the RegioWIN competition to mobilize regional actors and to trigger regional entrepreneurial search processes for the

Table 4.2 Characteristics of the winner regions

Winner Region	Involved NUTS3 Regions	km² 2014	Inhabitants 2014	Population density	GDP 2014 in mio. €	GDP/inh. 2014	Innol* 2014
Southern Upper-Rhine	Stadtkreis Freiburg	153.1	222,203	1452	10,543	47,448	41.3
	Lörrach	806.8	223,692	277	7,302	32,643	30
	Ortenaukreis	1850.8	415,639	225	15,260	36,715	16.1
	Emmendingen	679.9	159,708	235	4,487	28,095	20.5
	Breisgau-Hochschwarzwald	1378.3	252,749	183	7,039	27,850	17.2
Technology Region Karlsruhe	Stadtkreis Karlsruhe	173.5	300,051	1730	17,737	59,113	37.4
	Landkreis Karlsruhe	1085.0	431,315	398	14,183	32,883	35.9
	Rastatt	738.8	224,687	304	8,702	38,729	36.9
	Baden-Baden	140.2	53,342	380	2,753	51,610	34.7
Stuttgart	Stadtkreis Stuttgart	207.4	612,441	2954	47,149	76,985	64.2
	Böblingen	617.8	374,279	606	21,849	58,376	69.9
	Esslingen	641.5	516,779	806	19,426	37,591	39.3
	Göppingen	642.4	250,117	389	7,959	31,821	25.4
	Ludwigsburg	686.8	526,377	766	21,912	41,628	51.7
	Rems-Murr-Kreis	858.1	414,016	482	13,174	31,820	30.9
Metropolitan Area Rhine-Neckar	Stadtkreis Mannheim	145.0	299,844	2068	17,946	59,851	33.1
	Stadtkreis Heidelberg	108.8	154,715	1421	8,193	52,955	61.8
	Neckar-Odenwald-Kreis	1126.3	141,651	126	4,146	29,269	16.8
	Rhein-Neckar-Kreis	1061.7	534,729	504	16,542	30,935	39.7
Ostalb District	Ostalbkreis	1511.6	308,205	204	12,251	39,750	32.9
Members from Baden-Wuerttemberg of the Swabian League	Alb-Donau	1358.7	189,129	139	5,400	28,552	22.6
	Biberach	1409.8	190,438	135	8,585	45,080	42.3
	Heidenheim	627.1	128,894	206	4,013	31,134	40.9
	Stadtkreis Ulm	118.7	120,714	1017	8,339	69,081	53.9

District	Kreis						
District Lake Constance / Black Forest-Baar-Heuberg	Bodenseekreis	664.8	209,386	315	9,334	44,578	57
	Schwarzwald-Baar-Kreis	1025.3	206,116	201	7,415	35,975	27.1
	Rottweil	769.4	135,912	177	5,384	39,614	25.8
	Tuttlingen	734.4	134,607	183	5,885	43,720	36.4
Constance-Sigmaringen	Konstanz	818.0	275,785	337	8,937	32,406	24.8
	Sigmaringen	1204.3	127,716	106	4,266	33,402	13.4
Northern Black Forest	Enzkreis	573.7	196,066	342	5,288	26,971	27.9
	Pforzheim	98.0	119,291	1217	4,942	41,428	19.1
	Calw	679.9	152,766	225	4,070	26,642	20.4
	Freudenstadt	870.7	115,147	132	4,071	35,355	22.6
Neckar-Alb	Reutlingen	1028.1	278,031	270	10,553	37,956	34
	Tübingen	519.2	218,355	421	6,705	30,707	44.2
	Zollernalbkreis	917.7	186,360	203	5,962	31,992	18.9

Notes: *Innovation Index (Innol) is a composite indicator based on a min–max approach calculated by the statistical office of Baden-Wuerttemberg based on six individual indictors; c.f. www.statistik-bw.de/GesamtwBranchen/ForschEntwicklung/Innovation-I_BW.jsp; accessed 08.07.2020.

Source: Own compilation based on data from the statistical office of Baden-Wuerttemberg.

development of regional strategies, which is regarded as central for a successful implementation of S3. For the development of the regional strategies different actor groups proved to be particularly important: that is, enterprises from various sectors (and of different size), universities and universities of applied sciences, R&D organizations, county administrations, economic development agencies, different chambers, and associations, representatives from municipalities as well as other regional and innovation intermediaries. The engagement of the different actors varied greatly between the different winner regions, due to prior professionalization and the existence of regional networks, thematic orientation, or individual motives. Table 4.3 describes the winner regions in a consolidated manner and gives insights into the areas of specialization identified during the competition. It also sheds light on the initiators of the regional development concepts and informs about the lead partners during the first stage of the competition.

Table 4.3 shows that most of the winner regions have identified local specialization patterns, which are reflected in their regional development concepts for the competition. Only some of the winner regions, in particular, those without a critical mass in specific sectors in the more rural parts of Baden-Wuerttemberg had difficulties to identify a certain specialization pattern. As a consequence, the focus of their development strategies remained in the field of the funding categories in general, for example, systematic climate protection or development of a future-oriented innovation infrastructure. Concerning the technology and sectoral specialization, the industrial structure of Baden-Wuerttemberg with its traditional specialization is reflected quite well in the regional strategies (automotive, aerospace industry, material sciences, medical technologies, networks of supplier firms, biotechnology, life sciences). Although, in many regional development strategies the development of new business models and the development of services to help SMEs to become more innovative are among the goals, the service sector isn't directly mentioned. Otherwise, the regional development concepts are closely related to the operational program "Innovation and Energy Transition" and focus thematically on the topics of energy efficiency, sustainable development, and innovation.

Concerning the initiators, Table 4.3 reveals that the majority[14] come from the system level and belong to the group of regional development intermediaries, which either are independent network organizations (mostly organized as private companies with limited liabilities) or have an official or political function in the governance system. In most of the winner regions, the initiators, that is, the initiating organizations also coordinate the participative processes during phase 0 and become the lead partners during stage 1. In those winner regions where no regional development intermediary existed prior to the competition, new regional organizations were established or actors with an official or political function (i.e., district offices, chambers) became the lead partner. It is

Table 4.3 Regional specialization, initiation, and lead partners at the first stage of the competition

Winner Region	Specialization in the proposal	Initiators during the implementation (phase 0)	Lead partners first stage
Southern Upper Rhine	Sustainable Energy Valley: energy transition and distribution of new enabling technologies in the energy sector.	A manager from Badenova (regional energy supply provider), and a group of actors from research, public administration, and industry.	Strategic partners—climate protection Upper Rhine; membership association of cities, municipalities, municipal firms, innovative SMEs, universities, research organizations.
Technology Region Karlsruhe	Smart Movement: intermodal mobility, autonomous driving, urban logistics.	Karlsruhe Technology Region; for the (lighthouse) projects in Bruchsal: firms and the city of Bruchsal.	Karlsruhe Technology Region—a regional action group made up of businesses, chambers, scientific institutions, and public authorities; tasks: promoting the region as a hub for business, science, and innovation.
Stuttgart	Innovative and sustainable urban-rural cooperation for the environment, energy, transport, industry, and the labor market.	Stuttgart Region Economic Development Corporation	Stuttgart Region Economic Development Corporation: an independent company with limited liability, its strategic tasks include: promoting the region, acquisition of companies, investor services, supporting start-ups, promoting regional technology and innovation networks.
Metropolitan Area Rhine-Neckar	Smart Innovation. Smart distribution. Smart energy. Focus on entrepreneurship support in medical technology, biotech, life sciences.	Verband Region Rhein-Neckar: initiator and coordinator of the participative process and the discussion.	Verband Region Rhein-Neckar; a public corporation based in Mannheim. It is democratically legitimized and thus an institution where political decisions are taken. It is supporting regional planning and development.

(Continued)

Table 4.3 (Continued)

Winner Region	Specialization in the proposal	Initiators during the implementation (phase 0)	Lead partners first stage
Ostalb District	Sustainable Innovation in the Ostalb District.	An initiative group; launched in 2013 by the district office; comprised of universities, chambers, municipalities, the district trade union, business development agencies.	District office Ostalbkreis; the district administrator.
Members from Baden-Wuerttemberg of the Swabian League	Knowledge transfer and network building in certain sectors: pharmaceutical industry, biotechnology, energy systems.	Chamber of Industry and Commerce	Chamber of Industry and Commerce Ulm; a public corporation.
District of Lake Constance	Innovation, quality, and sustainability: small supplier companies, automotive and aerospace industry combined with mobility and tourism.	Bodenseekreis Economic Development Corporation	Bodenseekreis Economic Development Corporation: an independent company with limited liability, its core task is to improve the economic structure, to create and maintain jobs, and to promote the economic power of industry, commerce, trade, and services.
Black Forest–Baar-Heuberg	An industrial region in a rural area focused on microsystem–technology and medical technology.	The regional development agency, the chamber of industry and commerce, the regional assembly, and the chamber of crafts.	Regional assembly Schwarzwald-Baar-Heuberg; a public corporation; regional planning and regional management of the municipalities and districts involved.
Constance-Sigmaringen	Efficiency: sustainable resource management, resource efficiency around water, metal, and energy.	Lake Constance economic development agency	Pan-regional economic development agency Bodensee, independent company with limited liability.
Neckar-Alb	Research, Technology, Environment, Nature: development of new technologies at the intersection of material sciences and life sciences.	The three representatives of the EU units of the three rural districts, which were looking for partners and further actors.	District office and district administrator of Tuebingen.

important to mention that the initiators did not work in isolation but involved numerous regional actors for the development of the regional strategy concepts. These actors often formed the nuclei for regional partnerships during the second stage of the competition.

Most of the winner regions report, that the second stage of the Regio-WIN competition was the most challenging period and that bottom-up activities were very intense. The established networks needed to be enlarged and new participation formats had to be developed to involve further actors in the elaboration of the lighthouse projects. This was a crucial step, because the regions had to mobilize organizational, personal, and financial resources from the region for the application of lighthouse projects. Moreover, after the elaboration of the lighthouse projects, prioritization was necessary, which should come from the regions themselves.[15] This required additional coordination and planning.

Concerning the formation of regional partnerships, most of the winner regions stated, that they organized the participation processes very openly during the second stage of the competition. The involvement of (further) actors happened in different ways. The already existing partnerships from the first stage were utilized to find and activate additional partners. In this context, personal relationships, trust, and working groups were particularly important. Some of the regions tried to enlarge the partnerships by addressing already existing clusters and networks in order to mobilize their participants. In industry-driven networks, large firms operated as multipliers and opened their internal networks for the acquisition of new project partners. Some of the rural regions put additional emphasis on trust building in order to promote the formation of innovation networks with diverse actors in their territory. Thus, the formation and professionalization of regional innovation partnerships through the ERDF means seemed to be of pivotal importance for the rural parts of Baden-Wuerttemberg.

As a result, the number and the diversity of actors in the networks increased during the second state and the interaction of the regional partners gained momentum. Not surprisingly, the enlargement of the regional networks caused an increase in managerial complexity as the number of elements as well as their degree of relatedness increased. The intensification of the knowledge transfer and joint learning within the regional networks resulted in further professionalization of the actors that were involved.

To strengthen the regional innovation partnerships and the bottom-up activities within the regions, the winner regions have developed various measures to spur continuous interaction and knowledge exchange during the second stage of the competition. The establishment of steering groups with regular meetings for the development and monitoring of the projects, the organization of working groups for specific thematic objectives, or the organization of workshops to address and explore differences in the regional subspace are examples of the manifold measures that were developed. Although they resemble each other at first sight, the measures accommodate the specific needs of the winner regions and vary in practice.

Depending on the degree of prior professionalization the winner regions faced certain organizational and management challenges during the second stage of the competition. In those regions where the formation of innovation networks prior to the competition was in its infancy, the mobilization of a critical mass of actors and trust building for a prolonged and intense collaboration was particularly challenging. In regions with established regional innovation and development networks, the overcoming of sectoral silos and the enhancement of collaboration between industry and research was difficult to achieve. Networks with a high industrial engagement were on the brick of becoming closed shops.

During the implementation phase of the lighthouse projects (phase 3) the bottom-up activities have changed compared to the earlier phases of the competition. Project management and the execution of certain implementation steps gained importance over the entrepreneurial search and discovery processed during phase 0 and phase 1 and the formation of regional partnerships in phase 2. Depending on the project category (e.g., research infrastructure in applied research, technology transfer intermediaries, start-up accelerators, systematic climate protection, or innovation infrastructure) the project management had to deal with specific management challenges. In the aftermath of the implementation phase, additional potential for new regional partnerships emerges, that is, in the start-up centers, in B2B partnerships for the implementation of new technologies, or research–industry partnerships in the innovation centers. If moderated and managed in a skillful manner, the projects bear additional potential for further bottom-up activities and the formation of additional partnerships with regional and extra-regional partners. The partnerships that evolved during stage 1 and stage 2 are in most of the regions still existent and form the nuclei for regional entrepreneurial discovery processes for the new ERDF funding period and the competition "RegioWIN 2030," which is already tendered.

Although the intra-regional entrepreneurial search processes were realized independently from each other, in order to identify place-specific development potentials, interregional similarities in the outcomes can be observed. This holds for example for the development and a potential future specialization in the advancement and exploitation of the hydrogen technology. Such aspects of interregional learning were repeatedly mentioned during the interviews. In the course of the RegioWIN competition, the so-called RegioWIN network was established as a platform for interregional learning and in order to support the regional development processes.[16] The network should help to identify synergies in the implementation of the regional development concepts and ensure mutual learning. Lead partners of the regional strategy and development concepts from the RegioWIN competition as well as the project managers of the award-winning lighthouse projects, representative of the regional state associations, as well as representatives from the ministries belong to its members.[17]

Discussion

Turning to the question Q1: It becomes clear that due to the place-based logic of the competition the activities that result from the implementation of S3 vary greatly across the winner regions. Technology transfer partnerships, partnerships in order to spur entrepreneurships and start-up activities, or the creation of new networking opportunities between clusters are some of the activities that frequently occurred. Intra-regional networking was spurred in the larger winner regions, including a sensitization of core–periphery relationships and associated challenges. In the winner regions with weaker institutions, various and highly idiosyncratic network activities contributed to institutional capacity building.

More interestingly, we can observe the formation of new regional partnerships as well as the deepening of regional partnerships during the length competition. Based on the empirical evidence it can be assumed that most of the partnerships that emerged during the competition are stable and that the actors will continue the collaboration. The diversity of regional actors that participate in the partnerships is rather large. Enterprises from various sectors, higher education institutes and universities, private and public R&D organizations, county administrations, economic development agencies, chambers and associations, representatives from municipalities as well as other regional and innovation intermediaries are engaged in the partnerships.

In addition to these general findings and in order to address the research question Q2 the development of the regional partnerships will be analyzed over the whole funding period. It is interesting to see the differences in the stimulation of bottom-up activities and the formation of partnerships during the length of competition. The following Figure 4.3

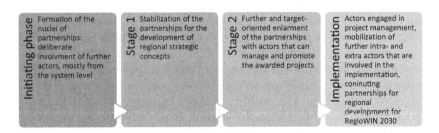

Figure 4.3 Development of regional partnerships

summarizes the key findings and provides an overview of the evolution of the intra-regional partnerships.

Triggered by the initiators, we can observe the formation of regional partnerships during the initiating phase. Most of the actors belong to the group of regional innovation intermediaries, have an official or political function in the governance system, or belong to the research system. Further actors were involved deliberately. During stage 1 those partnerships were stabilized and the regional strategy concepts were developed. An additional and very target-oriented enlargement of the partnerships occurred during the second stage. In the implementation phase, further intra- and extra-regional actors were brought into the networks for bringing the lighthouse project to life. The partnerships proofed to be stable and continue to exist. The RegioWIN network is institutionalized and ensures knowledge exchange and learning between the winner regions (cf. McCann & Ortega-Argilés, 2013).

Concerning the research question Q3, the findings from Baden-Wuerttemberg show that intra-regional disparities exist and the smart specialization approach allows sub-territories with very different characteristics to profit from the competition, however, in different ways. The policy instrument is able to support professionalization of regional innovation policy making in sparsely populated places as well as in metropolitan areas. In metropolitan areas, the competition has led to a broadening of the preexisting networks and helped the regions to gain visibility globally or to spur inner regional connectivity. In rural regions, the competition supported the formation of regional innovation networks and spurred regional intelligence concerning the innovation system and regional development potentials as well as institutional capacity building.

In order to derive policy recommendations and to address the research question Q4, it is interesting to reflect on what can be learnt from RegioWIN for future regional innovation policy making. The Baden-Wuerttemberg experience with the RegioWIN competition suggests that competitions are a successful instrument in regional innovation policy making and suited to implement S3 through EDP. A competition can be used to stimulate different activities in the territorial subregions, according to their potential. Moreover, such an instrument is suitable to activate new stakeholders and to support the formation of new and durable region partnerships, which can drive regional development. The positive response of the regional actors to the general idea of S3 and the place-based competition confirms these findings. The formation and professionalization of regional innovation partnerships through the ERDF seemed to be of pivotal importance in particular in the rural parts of Baden-Wuerttemberg. The problem of not being able to identify a certain specialization pattern (cf. Capello & Kroll, 2016) in more rural parts was overcome, by focusing on more generic aspects such as network development, institutional capacity building, or sustainability. Thus S3 can help to establish strategic development processes in sub-territories even with little strategic awareness or limited collaborative spirit. It can contribute to tailored regional development through the joint identification of different specialization domains depending on the preconditions.

Conclusion

Implications for Theory

Due to the place-based approach of the RegioWIN competition, we observe differences in the implementation practices and impacts, which can be related to the different characteristics of the places (the winner regions). The results underline the importance to take regional heterogeneity into consideration in order to support more effective policy learning (Pagliacci et al., 2020). However, it is not only important to differentiate between different types of regions but also relevant to take into account different implementation phases because the type and the number of actors change over time as Figure 3 shows. The same holds for the industrial structure and the technological specialization of the regions, which becomes more refined. To come from a static to a more dynamic perspective seems to be important in theory and practice, in particular since with the start of the new programming period 2021–2027 S3 will be assigned continuing importance.

Implications for Policy

The RegioWIN competition was constructed as a policy instrument to implement S3 in the case study region of Baden-Wuerttemberg. The aspect of self-discovery is emphasized and bottom-up approaches in regional development processes and the formation of micro-systems of innovation are spurred. Thus, the policy instrument follows in many respects the S3 concept (Foray, 2014, 2016; Hassink & Gong, 2019). The empirical evidence shows that the implementation of S3 in Baden-Wuerttemberg through the RegioWIN competition unfolds a high mobilization potential in the regional sub-territories, which were defined by the regional actors and local stakeholders, according to the requirements of a place-based approach (McCann & Ortega-Argilés, 2013).

However, the decision to organize the entrepreneurial discovery processes in form of a two-stage competition also bears drawback factors. The organizational effort seems to be quite large and the implementation takes several years. The final selection process by the ministry for the winner projects during the second stage competition is perceived as non-transparent and sometimes even as unjust and bears room for optimization. Despite the effects, S3 is not a panacea and it will be a challenge to foster the identified technological potentials with cross-sectoral impact over the next years, to maintain the high level of competitiveness, and to overcome intra-regional disparities.

Limitations

The focus of this contribution is dedicated to the investigation of the mobilizing and stimulating effects of the implementation of S3 in order to promote innovation, competitiveness, and growth in Baden-Wuerttemberg. It does so by looking at a single regional policy instrument, the RegioWIN competition in order to generate theoretical and practical insights. The contribution does not intend to analyze or measure the actual effects on regional innovation and growth or to deliver a comprehensive analysis of the regional (innovation) policy mix. Both approaches would undoubtedly be worthwhile for inquiry in other contexts.

Future Research Directions

During the research process, two new promising new research directions occurred. First, with the implementation of S3 numerous regional strategy development processes are observed in many European regions and S3 are perceived as an interesting research topic for scientist from different disciplines. However, the investigation of the development of regional innovation strategies processes from a strategic management perspective has remained underexplored in this particular research field, so far. Further interdisciplinary research in that direction could deliver interesting insights into regional managerial praxis and practices. Second, although place-based innovation policymaking has gained importance over the last decade and is now a major component in regional, national and international policy agendas there is a need for a better understanding of place in order to increase operational precision and to fully leverage the advantages of place-based policymaking. This includes the investigation of the benefits of a place-based approach to regional development by looking at its impacts on institutional capacity building, place leadership, and social capital building in different types of places. In particular, the latter deserves additional attention.

Appendix A

The structure of the interview guide (the exhaustive original interview guide was in German):

1. Basic information about the interview participants, the regional strategy of the winner region.
2. Questions about bottom-up approaches in the first stage of the competition: Generation of project ideas, the formation of regional partnership and formulation of the objectives; development of a regional strategy based on an assessment of strengths, weaknesses, opportunities, and risks, identification of future sectors and technologies based on existing potentials.
3. Questions about bottom-up approaches in the second stage of the competition: refinement of the strategy, additional involvement of regional actors, formation of bottom-up structures, organizational issues, and project management.
4. Questions about bottom-up approaches during the implementation phase: involvement of actors in the lighthouse or key projects and formation of new co-operations and sustainable bottom-up structures, generation of new ideas for further technological and sectoral development.
5. Questions on specific aspects of regional innovation and development support related to the objectives of the ERDF in Baden-Wuerttemberg.
6. Questions about future opportunities and risks in the winner region.

Acknowledgments

I would like to thank two anonymous reviewers for their comments, which have helped to make this contribution much richer. Additionally, I am very thankful to the VICTORIA | International University of Applied Sciences, for granting me a research sabbatical during the summer semester 2020, in order to work on the topic of regional innovation policymaking and its impacts. Further, I would like to say thank you to all my interviewees for sharing their valuable experiences with me.

Notes

1. Cf. https://ec.europa.eu/regional_policy/en/policy/what/glossary/c/cohesion-policy
2. https://ec.europa.eu/regional_policy/en/policy/what/glossary/c/cohesion-policy
3. Direct contacts were limited during the phase of the data collection (May/June 2020). Due to the government restrictions to prevent the further spread of the corona-virus all interviews were conducted over the phone or via video-calls. One expert provided written answers.
4. Nomenclature des unités territoriales statistiques (NUTS).
5. own calculation based on data from Eurostat for the year 2017.
6. data source: Eurostat database for "Science, technology and innovation", accessed 09.06.2020
7. data source: Eurostat database for "Science, technology and innovation", accessed 09.06.2020
8. data source: Regional Statistical Office; www.statistik-bw.de/BildungKultur/Hochschulen/HS_StudentenAkt.jsp; accessed 09.06.2020
9. data source: Eurostat database for "Science, technology and innovation", accessed 09.06.2020
10. https://ec.europa.eu/regional_policy/en/policy/what/glossary/t/thematic-objectives; accessed 20.06.2020.
11. cf. Gianelle, Guzzo, and Marinelli (2019).
12. It can be assumed from the interviews that not all of 37 officially participating NUTS3 regions from Baden-Wuerttemberg are likewise actively involved. Otherwise, there are some NUTS3 regions from neighbour states that were involved in the development of the regional strategies and project ideas (due to the existence of cross-border functional regions within Germany and its federal states) although they can't receive funding from the RegioWIN competition.
13. cf. https://efre-bw.de/foerderungsuebersicht/regiowin/; accessed 15.06.2020
14. Only one of the eleven networks was driven by a representative from a company.
15. In most of the cases the ministry followed the suggestions from the winner regions. In a few cases, however, priorities were changed. This caused irritation and in some cases even the withdrawal of the engagement by some of the actors.
16. cf. https://2021-27.efre-bw.de/netzwerktreffen-regiowin2030/; accessed 12.07.2020
17. cf. internal regulations https://2021-27.efre-bw.de/wp-content/uploads/Geschäftsordnung-RegioWIN-Netzwerk-Stand-19.11.2019.pdf; accessed 12.07.2020

References

Ares, C. (2020). EU regional development policy, from regional convergence to development through innovation. In M. González-López & B. T. Asheim (Eds.), *New horizons in regional science. Regions and innovation policies in Europe: Learning from the margins* (pp. 92–112). Cheltenham, UK: Edward Elgar.

Asheim, B. T. [Björn T.], Isaksen, A., & Trippl, M. (2019). *Regional innovation systems. Elgar advanced introductions.* Cheltenham, UK: Edward Elgar.

Audretsch, D. B., Lehmann, E. E., & Schenkenhofer, J. (2018). Internationalization strategies of hidden champions: Lessons from Germany. *Multinational Business Review*, 26(1), 2–24. https://doi.org/10.1108/MBR-01-2018-0006

Baier, E., Kroll, H., Schricke, E., & Stahlecker, T. (2012). The regional innovation system of Baden-Württemberg reconsidered: Path dependency and technological leadership. In Fraunhofer Institute for Systems and Innovation Research (Ed.), *Innovation system revisited* (pp. 171–192). Stuttgart: Fraunhofer Verlag.

Barca, F. (2009). *An Agenda for a Reformed Cohesion Policy: A place-based approach to meeting European Union challenges and expectations.* Retrieved from https://ec.europa.eu/regional_policy/archive/policy/future/pdf/report_barca_v0306.pdf

Capello, R., & Kroll, H. (2016). From theory to practice in smart specialisation strategy: Emerging limits and possible future trajectories. *European Planning Studies*, 24(8), 1393–1406.

Cooke, P. (2001). Regional innovation systems, clusters and the knowledge economy. *Industrial and Corporate Change*, 945–974.

Cooke, P., Heidenreich, M., & Braczyk, H.-J. (Eds.). (2004). *Regional innovation systems: The role for governance in a globalized world* (2nd Ed.). London and New York: Routledge.

Cooke, P., & Morgan, K. (1994). The Regional Innovation System in Baden-Württemberg. *International Journal of Technology Management*, 9(3–4), 394–429.

Crescenzi, R. [Riccardo], & Giua, M. (2016). The EU Cohesion Policy in context: Does a bottom-up approach work in all regions? *Environment and Planning a*, 48(11), 2340–2357.

Esparza Masana, R., & Fernández, T. (2019). Monitoring S3: Key dimensions and implications. *Evaluation and Program Planning*, 77, 101720. https://doi.org/10.1016/j.evalprogplan.2019.101720

European Commission. (2009). *Knowledge for growth: Prospects for science, technology and innovation.* Brussels: European Commission. Retrieved from www.kowi.de/Portaldata/2/Resources/fp/report-knowledge-for-growth.pdf

European Commission. (2010). *EUROPE 2020: A strategy for smart, sustainable and inclusive growth.* Brussels: European Commission.

Fitjar, R. D., Benneworth, P., & Asheim, B. T. (2019). Towards regional responsible research and innovation? Integrating RRI and RIS3 in European innovation policy. *Science and Public Policy*, 46(5), 772–783.

Foray, D. (2014). From smart specialisation to smart specialisation policy. *European Journal of Innovation Management*, 17(4), 492–507.

Foray, D. (2016). On the policy space of smart specialization strategies. *European Planning Studies*, 24(8), 1428–1437.

Foray, D. (2019). In response to 'Six critical questions about smart specialisation'. *European Planning Studies*, 27(10). https://doi.org/10.1080/09654313.2019.1664037

Foray, D., David, P. A., & Hall, B. (2009). Smart specialisation: The concept. In *Knowledge for growth: Prospects for science, technology and innovation* (pp. 25–30). Brussels: European Commission. Retrieved from www.kowi.de/Portaldata/2/Resources/fp/report-knowledge-for-growth.pdf

Foray, D., Morgan, K., & Radosevic, S. (2018). *The Role of Smart Specialisation in the EU Research and Innovation Policy Landscape.* Brussels: European Commission.

Gertler, M. S. (2018). Institutions, geography and economic life. In G. L. Clark, M. P. Feldman, M. S. Gertler & D. Wójcik (Eds.), *The New Oxford handbook of economic geography* (pp. 230–242). Oxford: Oxford University Press.

Gianelle, C., Guzzo, F., & Marinelli, E. (2019). *Smart specialisation evaluation: Setting the scene.* Retrieved from https://s3platform.jrc.ec.europa.eu/documents/20182/322704/Evaluation+S3+Policy+Insights/c14f64f0-1d31-4094-853b-e8c0b3c23d43

Glückler, J., Punstein, A. M., Wuttke, C., & Kirchner, P. (2019). The 'hourglass' model: An institutional morphology of rural industrialism in Baden-Württemberg. *European Planning Studies, 8*, 1–21. https://doi.org/10.1080/09654313.2019.1693981

Grillitsch, M., & Asheim, B. (2018). Place-based innovation policy for industrial diversification in regions. *European Planning Studies, 26*(8), 1638–1662. https://doi.org/10.1080/09654313.2018.1484892

Grillitsch, M., Asheim, B., & Trippl, M. (2018). Unrelated knowledge combinations: The unexplored potential for regional industrial path development. *Cambridge Journal of Regions, Economy and Society, 11*(2), 257–274. https://doi.org/10.1093/cjres/rsy012

Häberle, M. (2016). *RegioWIN—Interregional Competition as a means of successfully involving regional stakeholders in Smart Specialisation and bottom-up approach for ITI.* Retrieved from https://efre-bw.de/wp-content/uploads/2016-08-26-BW-Paper-1st-smarter-conference-RegioWIN.pdf

Hassink, R. (2020). Advancing place-based regional innovation policies. In M. González-López & B. T. Asheim (Eds.), *New horizons in regional science. Regions and innovation policies in Europe: Learning from the margins* (pp. 30–45). Cheltenham, UK: Edward Elgar.

Hassink, R., & Gong, H. (2019). Six critical questions about smart specialization. *European Planning Studies, 27*(10), 2049–2065.

Heidenreich, M., & Krauss, G. (2004). The Baden-Württemberg production and innovation regime: Past successes and new challenges. In P. Cooke, M. Heidenreich & H.-J. Braczyk (Eds.), *Regional innovation systems: The role for governance in a globalized world* (2nd ed., pp. 186–213). London and New York: Routledge.

Hollanders, H., & Es-Sadki, N. (2017). *Regional innovation scoreboard 2017.* Brussels: European Commission, Directorate-General for Internal Market, Industry, Entrepreneurship and SMEs.

Hollanders, H., Es-Sadki, N., & Merkelbach, I. (2019). *Regional Innovation Scoreboard 2019.* Luxembourg.

Kroll, H. (2015). Efforts to implement smart specialization in practice—leading unlike horses to the water. *European Planning Studies, 23*(10), 2079–2098. https://doi.org/10.1080/09654313.2014.1003036

Mayring, P. (2015). *Qualitative inhaltsanalyses: Grundlagen und techniken* (12th ed.). Weinheim and Basel: Beltz Verlag.

McCann, P., & Ortega-Argilés, R. (2013). Some practical elements associated with the design of an integrated and territorial place-based approach to EU cohesion policy. In R. Crescenzi & M. Percoco (Eds.), *Advances in spatial science. Geography, institutions and regional economic performance* (pp. 95–118). Berlin Heidelberg: Springer-Verlag.

Ministerium für Finanzen und Wirtschaft Baden-Württemberg (2013a). *Innovationsstrategie Baden-Württemberg: Dokumentation.*

Ministerium für Finanzen und Wirtschaft Baden-Württemberg (2013b). *Schritte zur Durchführung von regionalen Entwicklungsprozessen.* Stuttgart. Retrieved from https://efre-bw.de/wp-content/uploads/Brosch%C3%BCre-Schritte-zur-Regionalentwicklung.pdf

Ministerium für Ländlichen Raum und Verbraucherschutz Baden-Württemberg (2013). *Operationelles Programm des Europäischen Fonds für regionale Entwicklung (EFRE) in Baden-Württemberg 2014–2020: Innovation und Energiewende.*

Ministerium für Wirtschaft, Arbeit und Wohnungsbau Baden-Württemberg (2020). *Innovationsstrategie Baden-Württemberg (Fortschreibung 2020).* Stuttgart.

Pagliacci, F., Pavone, P., Russo, M., & Giorgi, A. (2020). Regional structural heterogeneity: evidence and policy implications for RIS3 in macro-regional strategies. *Regional Studies, 54*(6), 765–775.

Papamichail, G., Rosiello, A., & Wield, D. (2019). Capacity-building barriers to S3 implementation: An empirical framework for catch-up regions. *Innovation: The European Journal of Social Science Research, 32*(1), 66–84. https://doi.org/10.1080/13511610.2018.1537844

Patton, M. Q. (1990). *Qualitative research & evaluation methods.* Beverly Hills: SAGE.

Sánchez-Carreira, M. d. C. (2020). An overview of the European Union innovation policy from the regional perspective. In M. González-López & B. T. Asheim (Eds.), *New horizons in regional science. Regions and innovation policies in Europe: Learning from the margins* (pp. 113–138). Cheltenham, UK: Edward Elgar.

Simon, H. (2009). *Hidden Champions des 21. Jahrhunderts: Die Erfolgsstrategien unbekannter Weltmarktführer (Hidden Champions of the Twenty-First Century: The Success Strategies of Unknown World Market Leaders).* Heidelberg: Springer-Verlag.

Stahlecker, T., & Muller, E. (2008). KIBS startups in the Stuttgart region: A surprisingly below-average rate? *International Journal of Services Technology and Management, 10*(2–4), 330–334.

Strambach, S., & Klement, B. (2013). Exploring plasticity in the development path of the automotive industry. *Zeitschrift Für Wirtschaftsgeographie,* 67–82.

Teddlie, C., & Yu, F. (2007). Mixed methods sampling: A typology with examples. *Journal of Mixed Methods Research, 1*(1), 77–100. https://doi.org/10.1177/2345678906292430

Teräs, J., Dubois, A., Sörvik, J., & Pertoldi, M. (2015). *Implementing smart specialisation in sparsely populated areas* (S3 Working Papers Series No.

No. 10/2015). Sevilla. Retrieved from https://ec.europa.eu/jrc/sites/jrcsh/files/JRC98691.pdf

Valdaliso, J. M., Magro, E., Navarro, M., Aranguren, M. J., & Wilson, J. R. (2014). Path dependence in policies supporting smart specialisation: Insights from the Basque case. *European Journal of Innovation Management, 17*(4), 390–408.

Yin, R. K. (2013). *Case study research: Design and methods*. Thousand Oaks, CA: SAGE.

5 Exploring the Relationship Between Smart Specialization Strategy (S3) and Smart City (SC) Initiatives in the Context of Inland Norway

Xiang Ying Mei and Victoria Konovalenko-Slettli

Introduction

In recent years, there has been an increased focus on regional innovation and development through Smart Specialization Strategies (S3) in numerous European regions. Smart specialization is defined as "the capacity of an economic system (a region for example) to generate new specialties through the discovery of new domains of opportunity and the local concentration and agglomeration of resources and competences in these domains" (Foray, 2014, p. 1). The concept of S3 stems from this definition and relates to the actions and measures that promote these processes (González-López & Asheim, 2020). An overarching idea of S3 is that regions identify their evidence-based innovation activities and attempt to combine them in new ways to develop and provide products and services that are attractive in the global market (Asheim, 2019; Caragliu & Del Bo, 2018; Mäenpää & Teräs, 2018; Radosevic, Curaj, Gheorghiu, Andreescu, & Wade, 2017). According to the S3 logic, in order to promote innovation and growth, regions should focus on enhancing entrepreneurial search initiatives, which can lead to the variation of activities that are highly embedded within a region and connected to other regions (McCann, 2015). At the core of S3, there are the local capabilities and innovative strategies, based on local and nonlocal actors and knowledge, and participation of key stakeholders, which are combined in the bottom-up approach (González-López & Asheim, 2020).

S3 was developed as part of the European innovation strategy approach by the European Commission's Knowledge for Growth expert group, with the aim of promoting European innovation activities by focusing on regional strengths (Barca, 2009; D'Adda, Guzzini, Iacobucci, & Palloni, 2019; McCann & Ortega-Argileés, 2013). S3 is currently a major commitment behind the European Commission's cohesion policy reforms in the field of innovation, and it must be applied by European Union member countries in order to secure funding under the 2014–2020

European Union budget (Foray, 2014, 2016, 2017; Petrin & Kotnik, 2015; Sörvik, Teräs, Dubois, & Pertoldi, 2019). Several Nordic countries displayed their interests in the strategy implementation processes as many began their S3 regional innovation processes relatively early. Interestingly, although Norway is a non-EU member, existing research reveals that some regions have developed comprehensive S3 efforts. This is despite that non-EU members are not entitled to receive EU structural funds (Mäenpää & Teräs, 2018). In general, many Norwegian regions have embraced the RIS3 (Research and Innovation Strategies for Smart Specialization) policy concept in different ways, with some adopting it, some exploring it without implementation, and others choosing not to engage (Knudsen, Schulze-Krogh, & Normann, 2019). This variation is explained by regional political cultures and institutional structures where formal and informal institutions in the counties may serve both as a barrier and a facilitator for regional development (Knudsen et al., 2019).

According to Caragliu and Del Bo (2015, 2018), the concept of Smart City (SC) has emerged as a consequence of S3. The idea of SC is essentially based on the extensive use of ICTs and digital technologies to "enhance performance and well-being, reduce costs and resource consumption" (Snow, Håkonsson, & Obel, 2016, p. 92). It also implies that different actors, including citizens, industry partners, and institutions, can co-participate and co-create to enhance the effectiveness of a local economy, integration and efficiency of the urban systems, and continuous improvement of the quality of life (Caragliu & Del Bo, 2015, 2018; van Hermert, & Nijmap, 2010). An important aspect of SC is the appearance of e-governance, where the digital technological component blends with the issues of governance. A number of SC definitions are available, highlighting different aspects of this concept. For the purposes of this chapter, the following definition of SC is adopted: the SC is characterized by a status "when investments in human and social capital and traditional (transport) and modern (ICT) communication infrastructure fuel sustainable economic growth and a high quality of life, with a wise management of natural resources, through participatory governance" (Caragliu, Del Bo, & Nijkamp, 2011, p. 70).

At present, there are scant studies on this topic as scholars tend to investigate S3 and SC as unrelated concepts (Caragliu & Del Bo, 2018). However, Caragliu and Del Bo (2018, p. 130) suggest that these two approaches (policies) have certain commonalities in terms of "origins, objectives, and implications." Based on the discussion, the purpose of this chapter is to contribute to the knowledge concerning the implementation of SC approaches in Hamar Municipality in Inland County in Norway, and their overall relationship to S3. Such purpose is to be achieved by addressing two specific research questions (RQ):

> *RQ1: Why and how can the smart policies of SC and S3 be adopted in the context of Inland County and Hamar Municipality, and how are these policies related?*

RQ2: *How are the SC initiatives used as mechanisms and tools for the regional economic development and innovation, and what is their relationship to the S3 and the overall regional development?*

To answer these questions, a brief review of the literature addressing S3, SC, and the relationship between these two concepts is provided. This is followed by an explanation of the research methods. The discussion section starts by describing the adoption of S3 in the Norwegian context in general and Inland County in particular. Further, the section presents the case of SC Hamar, followed by specific examples of SC projects. The section also explains how the principle of broad citizen inclusion and participation in the city development is realized through Bylab Hamar (Citylab Hamar). Next, the section provides observations concerning collaboration on S3 between national, county, and local municipality government, and discusses how SC projects may become a trigger for the regional development. The concluding section highlights implications for theory and policy and suggests avenues for further research.

Literature Background

S3 refers to the place-based innovations that drive "positive structural changes" (Foray, 2014), which means promoting regional industrial diversification and future competitiveness, resulting in economic growth and new jobs (Asheim, 2019). The concept of diversified specialization is at the core of S3. This means that countries need to identify strategic "domains" of existing and potential competitive advantage, where they can specialize and create capabilities in a way that is different compared to other countries and regions (Asheim, 2019). S3 implies boosting the knowledge-based development potential of a region, and referring to the European Commission (2014, p. 2), S3 "supports technological as well as practice-based innovation." It is suggested that countries and regions should diversify their economies based on existing strengths and capabilities by operating in the related and unrelated sectors. S3 builds on "each region's strengths, competitive advantage, and potential for excellence" (European Commission, 2014, p. 2).

Essentially, S3 is dependent on competitiveness through innovation and the use of existing resources rather than heavy investments in infrastructure (Marques & Morgan, 2018). Moreover, different from previous emphasis and understanding of innovation, S3 embraces a much broader understanding of innovation beyond research-intensive or technology-based activities (Gianelle, Guzzo, & Mieszkowski, 2019). Nevertheless, as with any policy and development, S3 is not immune to criticism. Marques and Morgan (2018) argue that while S3 is ambitious, peripheral regions, in particular, are unable to fully capture its potential benefits, despite that those are the regions needing the most assistance. Other studies indicate that S3 is challenging to implement in practice. Thus, some regions only choose to implement the strategies partially (Gianelle et al., 2019).

In regard to SC, the understanding and practical application of the SC concept has been diverse and multifaceted. The defining features of SC refer to digital technology, human resources, and collaborative governance (Meijer & Bolívar, 2016). In the research literature, the essence of SC has been connected to the perspectives of sustainable urbanization and development, resource efficiency, technology use, and respective benefits, and so on. For example, part of the SC literature tends to focus on the betterment of the urban system through the use of ICTs. Another part of the literature advocates that it is the (smart) citizens who are the driving force of SC, rather than new technology. In this course of thinking, urban areas with high percentage of higher education institutions and adults with higher education are typical features of SC. The literature emphasizes the governance aspect of SC focuses on the interaction between various stakeholders. In this stance, developing productive interactions and networks between urban actors is central. Although human capital, new (digital) technologies, and collaborative governance are not new characteristics of innovative practices, it is their interplay and combination that distinguishes the SC concept from other innovative initiatives.

Nilssen (2019) conceptualizes SC initiatives as urban innovations highlighting four dimensions of innovations: technological, organizational, collaborative, and experimental. The technological dimension refers to the role new technology plays in the development of new products and services such as medical services in health care, new digital services for the citizens, or mobile applications for public transportation. The organizational dimension of innovation is linked to "positive changes in daily operations in the municipal body, specifically aimed at increasing efficiency, productivity, and quality" and can imply "process innovation, strategic innovation, and governance innovation" (Nilssen, 2019, p. 101). The collaborative dimension signifies the involvement and participation of multiple actors in the societal development and more open governance structures. Finally, the experimental dimension stands for citizen-centric approach and experimentation, entrepreneurial citizens, and urban labs for facilitating innovation.

Similarly, as S3 policies, SC has also had its fair share of criticism, particularly in regard to technology. Moe (2019) argues that SC policies and projects may be too reliant on technology to simplify, automatize and increase efficiency without considering other important qualities in the society as well as focusing on smart technologies without clear, measurable goals to achieve wider development. With the increase of technological development and use, another key criticism includes the surveillance and control of citizens rather than improving their life (Krivý, 2016). Other criticisms consist of outsourcing and the reliance on global external IT companies (Krivý, 2016; Moe, 2019).

As discussed in the literature, S3 and SC are often investigated as unrelated concepts. However, they share essential commonalities. First, both approaches were unleashed by the rapid development of ICTs and the acknowledgment of their positive effect on productivity growth. Second, both concepts have abandoned a merely sector-based approach to embrace a more sophisticated idea of focusing on the region-specific characteristics as the key determinants of their effectiveness. Finally, both concepts have received a significant attention in the policy debate, which leads to redefinition of their boundaries and scopes beyond the early focus on ICTs, and encompassing additional dimensions related to urban and regional development. Despite the high significance of the S3 and SC policies, the research literature has paid scant attention to the relationship between the two policy concepts and whether they yield a mutually reinforcing effect (Caragliu & Del Bo, 2015).

Furthermore, Caragliu and Del Bo (2018) argue that development in the local economy will evidently lead to broader regional development. Similarly, although SC was not addressed in particular, Bevilacqua and Pizzimenti (2016) imply that SC-related initiatives can be used as engines for S3 and broader regional development. Furthermore, Rivas (2018) provides an additional point of view by stressing that S3 can also be considered as a driver to boost the urban agenda and economic growth at the city level. Thus, besides the common grounds of the two policies, they also complement each other.

Although S3 focuses on innovation activities to increase and improve regional strengths (Barca, 2009; D'Adda et al., 2019; McCann & Ortega-Argileés, 2013), SC policies aim to enhance the effectiveness of a local economy and sustainable urban development through co-governance (Caragliu & Del Bo, 2015, 2018; van Hermert & Nijmap, 2010). Such participatory governance emphasizes on bottom-up approaches in the urban innovation process that include the involvement and collaboration of the government, citizens, businesses, and industry representatives as well as knowledge institutions and the academia (Figure 5.1). This process is also known as the quadruple-helix innovation model.

Methodological Approach

A descriptive and exploratory design using a qualitative research methodology approach was employed. Data collection methods include one focus group interview and three individual semi-structured interviews with key representatives at various governmental levels, including those who work particularly with SC projects and initiatives, representatives from Hamar Municipality (the local government), key personnel working on IT solutions, and the digitalization part of SC initiatives as well as representative from Inland County. The focus group with three informants lasted about 2 hours and the three individual interviews lasted

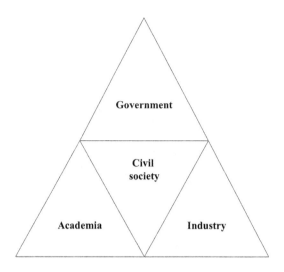

Figure 5.1 The quadruple-helix innovation model

about 1 hour. Each of them was carried out from October 2019 to January 2020. The interviews were recorded and transcribed following the GDPR policy. Analysis of the interviews, including coding and categorizing, was carried out with the help of the NVivo software. Since the interviews were carried out in Norwegian, the citations employed in the text were translated by the authors, who are both bilingual and fluent in English and Norwegian.

Nevertheless, some minor differences may still exist between the original and translated versions as languages cannot be translated word-for-word to account for linguistic and other cultural differences (Hilton & Skrutkowski, 2002). Furthermore, secondary data were obtained via available and relevant media publications, reports, websites, and social media disclosing SC and S3 well as all other regional development initiatives. In this way, a triangulation approach to data analysis contributes to the research validity (Johnson, 1997).

Result and Discussion

S3 in the Norwegian Context

In Norway, there are three levels of governance: national (state), county (regional), and municipality (local). Managing policy areas at the same time as performing functions for the community is one of the factors that challenge strategy development and strategy implementation in the public sector in general (Wilberg, 2017). As Norway is one of a few countries in Europe that is not a member of the European Union, the country is thus under no obligation to adopt S3 or even any SC strategies. Nevertheless, through the Ministry of Local Government and Modernisation, the national government endorses and encourages S3 by issuing the guide "Smart specialization as a method for regional development" aimed at various County Councils. As informed by the representative of Inland County Council, the national government through the Norwegian Research Council values projects that integrate S3 principles and issue research grants accordingly. Thus, the national government encourages regions to adopt S3 while not enforcing anything. Such encouragement may also be attributed by the fact that from 2014, all projects that were to receive funding from the European Regional Development Fund (ERDF) must have a regional development strategy based on smart specialization approved by the European Commission (Ministry of Local Government and Modernisation, 2018).

Due to these considerations, different Norwegian regions (counties) chose to adopt S3 principles to a varying degree. The official website of the Norwegian government provides some examples of such S3 adoption (see www.regjeringen.no). For instance, the most southern region of Norway Agder developed a Plan for innovation and sustainable value creation for 2015–2030, based on the Smart Specialization Analysis for Agder. This plan emphasized increased cooperation and knowledge-sharing and is complemented by 2015–2030 Strategy for research, development, and innovation and Agder's Strategy for travel and tourism industries. An in-depth study of the S3 implementation in Agder revealed that despite that the county possesses some major preconditions for realizing S3, the region displayed merely a symbolic response (Normann, Strickert, & Knudsen, 2020). This condition was explained by several reasons, including the lack of access to EU structural funding, cutbacks in national budgets causing fewer resources for R&D, and the absence of coercive or control mechanisms for S3 adoption from the national government.

Another region, Møre og Romsdal, located on the west coast of Norway, has used smart specialization in connection with their 2016–2020 Research and Innovation Strategy. Moreover, Østfold (southeast of Norway) employed smart specialization in the development of 2017–2021 Regional plan for industrial development, research, and innovation. A further example, Rogaland County, located on the southwest coast of Norway with Stavanger city in the forefront, also aims to fully adopt S3 (Rogaland County, 2019). One particular region, which has thoroughly followed the S3 principles, is Nordland County, located in Northern Norway. Nordland is an early adopter of S3. The first smart specialization analysis of the region was undertaken in 2013. A year later, Innovation Strategy for Nordland 2014–2020 was introduced. Nordland County adopted S3 "because innovation, knowledge development, markets, and research funding increasingly occur internationally, and because the society is constantly demanding specialization" (Nordland County Council, 2014, p. 7). The county focuses on three specific specialization areas consisting of fishery, manufacturing, and experience-based tourism. In cooperation with other research institutions, Nordland County carried out a smart specialization school for its employees and employees of partner organizations. One of the recent periodic reports concludes that "understanding of smart specialization is about to stick broadly in the county. At the same time, the practical implementation seems to progress slowly, which may be related to the absence of cooperation with private actors to establish the processes of entrepreneurial discoveries more systematically" (Finne, Løvland, Mariussen, Madsen, & Bjørkan, 2018, p. 3). Moreover, the same report pinpoints that "on the national level, it is important to clarify the division of tasks between the state and county levels, as well as to develop a better multilevel coordination of strategies and instruments" (Finne et al., 2018, p. 4).

Inland County

Inland County (Figure 5.2) is located in east Norway with an area of 52,072.4 km² and consisting of 34 counties and 371.385 in the population (SNL, 2020). Before the county officially became Inland County in

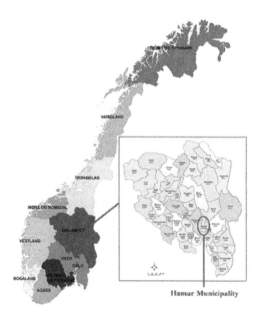

Figure 5.2 Map of Norway (without Svalbard) and Inland County
Source: Adapted from Government.no (2020) and SNL (2020).

January 2020, it consisted of Hedmark and Oppland County. Although Inland is now officially a county, it is also previously referred to as a region.

The densely populated areas are the towns and cities around lake Mjøsa, which is Norway's largest lake. Nevertheless, the county is generally characterized by low population density and the industrial activity is mainly focused on agriculture and forestry; timber-, wood- and paper industry; electricity and water supply; and health care services. According to the Regional Innovation Scoreboard 2019, Inland County performs as a "Strong—Innovator," whose innovation performance has increased by 22.1% over time (Hollanders, Es-Sadki, & Merkelbach, 2019). Furthermore, in recent years, the data on the evolution of innovation indicates that the Inland region has experienced growth in many indicators (such as trademark applications, SMEs innovating in-house, scientific co-publications, R&D expenditures in private and public sectors, product or process innovators, innovation index, etc.) (Hollanders et al., 2019).

S3 in Inland County

The role and diffusion of information regarding S3 are explained by the representative from the Inland County Council:

> It was in Bodø, in Nordland County Council. It was the first county that ran a full smart specialization strategy. And the Ministry of Local Government and Modernisation was included, and we were invited to meetings in the ministry. . . . Also, we got the impression that the actors we're related to and the Research Council, for example, is concerned with us using smart specialization. There've been many surveys, evaluations, and that kind of experience we've had with it. So, we've been informed about it, but there has never been such a formal requirement that we had to implement it. It has been strongly encouraged, at least for Hedmark (county) and probably Inland.
>
> (Representative from the Inland County Council)

Although S3 is not officially adopted by Inland County, it is revealed that the county has already adopted quite many elements of S3 and that S3 is also not regarded as something entirely "new," as the process is referred to as "emperor's new clothes" and "same content, new wrapping." This indicates that many of the S3 related processes have always existed in the regional development plan.

> Well we don't have our own smart specialization strategy in Inland. The goal, of course, is that Inland is the lighthouse but neither Hedmark nor Oppland has had it. But we've all the elements that lie in

smart specialization strategy. . . . And we see that the EU system is now concerned with adaptability and focuses on it, with that in relation to the methodology around smart specialization. We've really used it for many years. (Representative from the Inland County Council)

Sometimes it's kinda like, 'same content, new wrapping', so I think that's how you're conscious of what you're good at, what you're not good at. . . . We know the competence profile of the people in the interior part, compared to the rest of the country, we know the export share, the employment rate, we know a lot, but then there's [a thing called] smart specialization strategy, or what you call it, I don't know, but in Hedmark it was called regional development plan. And it's in many ways a smart specialization strategy. (Representative from Hamar Municipality)

Furthermore, the reason for Inland to not fully commit to S3 was further explained by the Inland County Council representative.

But I think we've had the same stability, avoiding the kind of things that many county councils might have had by running a full smart specialization strategy. It's very resource intensive if you're gonna follow the manual from A to Z. There're quite a few millions that Nordland spent on this here. But now we're in a phase where we're gonna create a regional planning strategy called the Inland Offensive, right? It should be about ready to be launched in June. And it's a bit like that, in ideal world I wished we could run smart specialization strategy for a couple of years. But it's resource consuming, and the effort doesn't exactly match what we actually have and can use, right? We have 85% of what smart specialization strategy entails, so we're there and then we cannot spend many millions to bring in the last percentages. It's not possible.

(Representative from Inland County Council)

The same informant has expressed some critiques toward the S3 regional innovation profile that maps major industry branches developed for the region:

I'll assert that we knew most part of it from before. . . . Even though I'm an old regional researcher, I've experienced it several times, and this is a bit problematic, also in regard to statistics and how we pool the industries. . . . Even though it's an international standard, it doesn't always capture everything. Also, if we look at the cultural sector, which is quite big here, at least statistically, and to some extent this is due to Norsk Tipping[1] which has a turnover of over 10 billion [NOK]. . . . But what's important is that we're off to EU, and then one will apply for projects, for example, and therefore one will consider the coverage of other strong milieus. . . . Hence, in relation to R&D, and if you look at commercialization of research projects and similar things, Hamar and Hedmark have a strong position in AR VR technology . . . Statistics that are used for different categories makes them perhaps not so interesting in relation to what we're actually engaged in.

(Representative from the Inland County Council)

In the case of Inland region, the measurement approach based on the employment rate in the sector does not seem to reflect the industries with the strongest potential for innovation. In particular, biotechnology and AR/VR technology are considered as the most rapidly developing and innovative areas in the region. Although scoring comparatively low on the number of employees, these sectors perform high on value creation, world-class academic, research community, and commercialization of research projects. Although these sectors are not mapped on the official innovation scoreboard profile, it is exactly these attributes that should be considered as priority areas according to the S3 policy.

The Case of Smart City Hamar

The municipality of Hamar is referred to both as a city and as a municipality.[2] It is considered a middle-sized municipality in Norway and the largest city and the administration center in Inland County, with a population of 31,156 citizens (Statistics Norway, 2020). Hamar City already has digital technology available to support a vast of SC efforts, including interactive maps, guides, information about the water temperature for bathing in the lake, and so on (Hamar Municipality, 2019). In SC Hamar's strategy, it was emphasized that Hamar aims to become Inland's "urban heart" through SC initiatives (Hamar Municipality, 2020). Hamar's key reason for adopting SC is explained by the representative from Hamar Municipality:

There's competition for everything. Everyone [every municipality] wants more residents, more jobs, and if you wanna get there, you've got to have as good [public] services as possible, so we've to try to make projects that make us visible, attractive.

(Representative from Hamar Municipality)

According to the municipality itself, SC projects must consist of positive climate and environmental effects, using technology in an innovative manner, and collaboration with the academic, the local industry, and public sector as well as the citizens in a quadruple-helix approach (Hamar Municipality, 2020).

> There's also a parameter in this Smart City project in Hamar that we should involve academia in the quadruple helix model. . . . There was very interesting discussion that arose regarding the establishment of a sort of cluster of actors with Hamar municipality. . . . It started as a business development case, where Hamar Municipality had some requests from some local players in biotechnology. It's a bit like relationships and that someone who knows someone and worked somewhere before. It's also very interesting that we went quite a bit to see if it's possible to establish something that's a purely professional network.
>
> (IT leader and member of the SC Hamar working group)

Although some of such processes are still in infancy, there are many ideas and activities occurring, indicating that there are strong initiators among relevant stakeholders. Furthermore, the majority of SC projects contain some elements of digitalization or digitalization is a key instrument to implement the SC projects. However, key personnel behind SC initiatives suggest that not all projects containing the element of digitalization are perceived as "SC projects." Hence, some key differences were clarified:

> We distinguish between digitalization and smart city. Digitalization is something that the municipality has, right? After all, the municipality must be concerned with its case management and stuff like that. Smart city should be something much more. It might as well be a resident building an app, right? That you take the initiative for innovation and smart things happening in Hamar. It may be internal to get better services, business can get better services, or you can get business in developing smart services. As said, it's the smart city that's for everything and everyone.
>
> (SC project manager)

As further explained by one of the key personnel working with IT and digitalization in the municipality as well as being a member of the SC Hamar working group:

> We have created a kind of smart city strategy on which we make municipal government decisions, etc. But in establishing that, it was quite difficult [to decide] what makes it a smart city project and not just a digital transformation project, or an improvement project that using digitalization. . . . I don't think it's simple, to simply define smart city [projects]. But as we've said, we've tried to concentrate

on something that has a clear impact on the citizens. It's about supporting one or more UN sustainability goals and other similar goals. (IT leader and member of the SC Hamar working group)

Hence, while it may be difficult to distinguish digitalization projects from SC projects due to the many overlaps, the main difference is that SC projects need to benefit the citizens living in the city. This concurs with the purpose of SC initiatives as the key feature of SC is to bring technology and infrastructure together to improve the quality of life of citizens (Caragliu, Del Bo, & Nijkamp, 2011). To provide an idea of the smart city projects, the sections subsequently describe three specific projects that have gained the "SC stamp."

Current Projects as Part of Hamar's SC initiative

Urban Development Through Augmented Reality (AR)

This is a research project in collaboration with the local industry, which facilitates the development of SC using AR. An app is being developed for smartphones to illustrate models of future and ongoing urban development projects, which are integrated into their real surroundings. AR and VR are areas that Hamar Municipality invests heavily in, as Hamar is already Norway's leading VR and gaming environment due to a close collaboration with the local university, Inland Norway University of Applied Sciences. The city is also the organizer of the largest gaming conference in the Nordic countries and has a biotechnology environment that generates more than 3.5 billion NOK annual revenue (Smart Cities Norway, 2016).

Smart Health

The second area of focus is smart health and primarily on welfare, where better and more effective systems for medicine management are developed. Such project is a direct response to the aging population in the Inland region. A commitment to develop welfare technology leads to various tools to assist the elderly population in terms of medicine intake and automatic dosage of medication as well as trace their movement should they have problems to locate their whereabouts. Much of welfare technology involves the use of smart sensors.

> Because we see that when we work with welfare technology, it's quite obvious that the water meter and electricity meter at the home of a service recipient in Hamar Municipality, an elderly person or whoever it may be, are actually signal senders in a welfare technological universe. We, as a municipality, may want to form the best possible

picture of what's the situation at home with Mrs. Hansen, right? She hasn't pressed any security alarm, she hasn't given any active signal about anything, but we've some sensors in her house that can say something. That is, you've such typical welfare technology sensors that say whether she's lying in bed or not, whether she fell, fall sensors, that kind of things. The fact that she has used water or not used water over a period of time is also very, very relevant information.

(IT leader and member of the SC Hamar working group)

Much of such effort is thus always dependent on collaboration with various actors and network, including HelseINN, which is a network focusing on health and working with interaction and service innovation between the public and private sectors for a smarter organization of the health and public health services in Inland (HelseINN, 2020).

Of course, in collaboration with HealthINN, which is concerned with how to use digital solutions. One must try to use the smart city concept in elderly care, right? With a refrigerator that registers if it has been opened, bed mats that register when you get up from bed at night. Yes, so we try to learn a little from them.

(Representative from Hamar Municipality)

Smart Winter Roads

The project is a collaboration between "the Mjøsa municipalities" of Gjøvik, Hamar, Lillehammer, and Ringsaker, together with suppliers, R&D partners, and others, which focuses on finding new and innovative solutions for winter operation of roads and properties. The purpose is to create better and more efficient winter operations in terms of snow removal, which are coordinated, timely, faster, and more value for money. Moreover, the project would result in fewer accidents and injuries and minimizes delays in winter traffic. Other more sustainable focus includes less pollution and greenhouse gas emissions as well as higher user satisfaction and more effective interaction between winter operators (Smarte Mjøsbyer, 2020).

The previous discussion indicates that all three projects are official SC projects, and S3 was not considered in any of the initiatives. It is evident that the development is well beyond the local and city level as the results aim to benefit the entire Inland region. This indicates that when such projects are initiated at the local level, a bottom-up approach is adopted along with collaboration between the local government, the academia (the local university), and local businesses as well as citizen and community involvement. These elements are at the heart of S3 (European Union, 2019).

Citizen Inclusion and Participation Through ByLab Hamar

Citizens' broad inclusion, involvement, and participation are some of the key elements in SC Hamar initiatives. Participation and interaction can consist of everything from information about planning processes to the fact that the residents themselves participate in and contribute to the design of the city's developmental plans (Bylab Hamar, 2019; Hamar Municipality, 2020). An arena used to initiate such a process in various developmental projects is Bylab Hamar (Citylab Hamar), which was opened in summer 2018. Bylab Hamar is a physical meeting arena with the aim to contribute to a democratic and innovative city development process. It is located in a historical building right in the heart of Hamar city. With its glass walls, the Bylab conveys physical and symbolic transparency of the municipality development projects. In addition, Bylab Hamar is utilized as a strategic tool to achieve ambitious goal of securing Hamar the position as Inland's urban heart. The site is open to the employees of the municipality, external actors, as well as the general public on a daily basis (Bylab Hamar, 2019). Although Bylab Hamar was established independently from SC, it is used as the main arena to present and communicate all relevant projects, including SC projects, making such projects visible and accessible to everyone who is interested.

> Bylab is an arena, a physical arena . . . which makes us visible in terms of presenting our plans. In order to engage the citizens and to receive the inputs. And we use this arena absolutely . . . consciously to arrange for easier communication with the citizens. To involve citizens in all our municipality development projects is required by law. Everything from the private regulations, everything we do must be available to the public. But it's very few available initiatives similar to this that are working well. You need to log in, to search on the webpage, and the municipality city hall is quite a closed arena. So here, we've established a position centrally located and with a transparent office. We're working with different types of methods to try to convey in a best possible way what we're doing. Then, we've everything from public meetings, to workshops, to the physical models, and VR models. . . . So we've a fantastic arena to show the projects, and also we're sitting and working here and making things available so that people can drop-in in the premises. In addition, we're testing different things. The idea is to test things at the early stage.
>
> (City development manager at Hamar Municipality)

It is believed that through a bottom-up approach, which focuses on interaction and citizen participation in a quadruple-helix approach, user-driven innovation will occur and benefit all parties involved. This was, however, not a common way adopted by municipalities in terms of local development.

> We've had quite a few ambitious development projects. And we've left behind decades of fairly large, heavy investments in both private and public sectors of the city. And instead of just sitting there and being passive and confined as one can quickly be. . . . [W]e've decided to take an active role in creating a vibrant city because it's not only created by us, but it's also created with the hearts of the citizens. And there're grounds that initiatives can just as easily come from the citizens and other actors. We think that's right. So we created an arena for the interaction to be made as simple as possible, by being visible and go further into the private sphere than what we normally might do . . . We've also challenged the working approaches in this area, and we need to be even more interdisciplinary. Because it's rare for us to get good projects when you just work within your own sectors, which you easy do in a municipality.
>
> (City development manager at Hamar Municipality)

By making themselves available to the broad public through the Bylab, municipality workers broke the traditional communication pattern and went out of their ways. Such change requires a shift in the mindset and organizational culture of the municipality. The Bylab became not only a physical place for municipality employees to meet citizens, business representatives, and farmers in order to inform them about the new projects, but it is also a place where the emphasis is put on participative design in problem-solving and co-creation of solutions.

> We've tested and have some examples of how this arena physically invites in a quite another way to a non-planned engagement and planned workshops that deal with broad citizens' involvement. We've used the word 'co-creation', a word, which has been used a lot in the last two years. I think it's good, because 'cooperation' is less obligatory, but co-creation' carries more obligations. This is because one is involved in new ways and makes industrial actors more responsible in a closer collaboration where we also have an active role. And when one sees that, it's easier to succeed, to get the processes started.
>
> (City development manager at Hamar Municipality) (see Figure 5.3)

Although not all city development projects are SC projects, the idea that SC projects must benefit the citizens and improve their quality of life suggests that such a bottom-up approach is well-integrated into Hamar's SC initiatives.

Figure 5.3 Example of citizen involvement and participation in Bylab Hamar

Collaboration Between National, County, and Local Municipality Government

In the early stages of data collection, it was evident that SC initiatives occurred at the municipality level, without directive or instructions from the national or county government as a true bottom-up approach.

> [F]or example, this GIS collaboration (project one) I think is more like bottom-up collaboration. There're professionals sitting in the individual municipalities, who meet at all kinds of professional forums. At the conferences and with suppliers. There're not that many suppliers in the Norwegian market. It's a bit like everyone knows everyone. So it's really collaboration that has come from below, from professionals who see it. There has been no political decision or anything from above.
>
> (IT leader and member of the SC Hamar working group)

In fact, some of the key personnel working directly with SC in Hamar were not aware of any S3 initiative at all or collaboration with other governmental levels in regional development projects.

> Very little. And I don't quite know why. I know, for example in Agder, ICT Agder, is the IT organization for these municipalities

plus the County municipality. While we aren't. . . . We've very little to do with the county government. But we've a lot to do with the county governor, specifically in relation to the support system and [grant] applications. You can apply for some funds and we cooperate with the county governor in relation to welfare technology for some national funds. But it's the national, not the county [government]. At least I haven't talked to the County Council at all.

(IT leader and member of the SC Hamar working group)

There is a clear distinction between the county government and county governor in Norway, as the county governor is not a part of the county government but rather as a representative of the national government. The county governor is thus understood as the national government's extended arm in the municipalities to ensure that municipalities carry out what the national government has decided (Lægland, 2016). Hence, as indicated by the findings, while there are no particular collaboration or SC policy guidelines from the county government, some collaboration efforts with the national government are found through the county governor in terms of funding. Moreover, despite some challenges in regard to collaboration with higher governmental levels, it was also revealed that there is a positive sharing culture among various municipalities.

So we work a lot on how to lubricate the machinery there. And try to make the municipalities appear as unity. But there's less that of the kind of collaboration and reuse of solutions in reality than I might have hoped. But it's a very big development. It's actually very positive. Very large degree of sharing culture in the municipality sector or in the public sector at all really. I've been a consultant and supplier (in the private sector) for many years myself, so I'm used to everything costing money. Time costs money not at least. Good ideas are valuable and have a price. But there's a great deal of experience and exchange between the municipalities.

(IT leader and member of the SC
Hamar working group)

It can be argued that sound collaboration between various municipalities sets the precedence for further "smart" regional development, as such bottom-up approach is of the key principles of S3. Additionally, this may lead to inter-regional collaborations, which is also an S3 effort (European Union, 2020), as municipality collaboration is not necessarily limited to one county or region.

SC as a Mechanism for Regional Development

From the previous discussion, it appears that the relationship between S3 and 3C is not obvious and this is also somewhat recognized by the Hamar Municipality:

> There's one, there's a big gap between smart specialization strategy at the regional level and Smart City strategy. . . . But it would be nice if you could connect them.
>
> (Representative from Hamar Municipality)

Bevilacqua and Pizzimenti (2016) indicate that cities can be used as an engine of S3 as the local actors at the city level are argued to be valuable sources of local development in terms of identity and innovation, which in turns leads to greater regional development and development toward S3. Although the study did not specify SC in the discussion, it is evident that SC initiatives would also lead to similar positive results toward S3. In addition, a correlation between S3 and SC would also provide positive policy outcomes and economic growth (Caragliu & Del Bo, 2018). In the case of SC Hamar, while no direct connection has been found at the political, administrative, and practical levels between S3 at the regional level and SC at the local level, SC initiatives contain many of the key elements, which are at the heart of S3 including the bottom-up approach through partnership and interactions in a quadruple-helix approach. Furthermore, many SC projects as well as the municipality's strategic plan for Hamar City to become the Inland's urban heart, indicate that SC initiatives go beyond the city itself as the entire Inland region is thought to benefit from such initiatives.

Figure 5.4 summarizes the observed practice in a theoretical model representing interconnection between S3 and SC. The model can be read

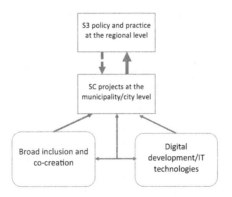

Figure 5.4 Theoretical model representing interconnection between S3 and SC

as follows: at the bottom level, broad inclusion of different actors such as citizens, business actors, academia, and so on, resulting in co-creation of solutions, and use of digital technologies, provide inputs for SC projects at the local level. The dotted arrow pointing downwards from the S3 policy and practice box suggests some conceptual elements (policies and principles) of the S3 to be adopted in SC initiatives at the city level. The thick arrow pointing upwards from the SC at the local level implies there is potential for bottom-up innovation through the spreading of smart practices initiated at the city level to the scope of the whole region.

Conclusion

This chapter has addressed two specific research questions. The RQ1 investigated why and how smart policies of SC and S3 could be adopted in the context of Inland County and Hamar Municipality, and how these policies are related.

The findings indicate that while S3 is not officially adopted by Inland County and that SC policies were initially adopted without much consideration of S3, such initiatives and projects still contain many of the key elements and principles of S3. The main reason for not adopting S3 entirely is due to resource constraint purposes. It is still too early to tell whether the chosen approach will succeed in the long run. However, very few development projects can guarantee success. Perhaps such an approach is positive for the current context as much of the knowledge of S3 can be gained and shared from other regions, while Inland County is able to pick and choose parts of S3, which the county sees fit for its circumstances.

The RQ2 posed in this chapter is how the SC initiatives were used as mechanisms and tools for regional economic development and innovation, and what was their relationship to the S3 and the overall regional development. It can be argued that many of the projects with the "SC stamps" are, in fact, focused on a much larger context, beyond the city borders. Such a bottom-up approach of focusing on the region's competitive advantages to achieve innovative regional development is at the core of S3. Although many of the development projects are not officially named and recognized as S3, cities and SC initiatives at the micro and local level with the involvement of private and public actors in a network would serve as engines to wider regional development. After all, the most important matter is that region using their specialization for development through innovation. Thus, whether such an innovative approach and practice should be officially referred to S3 may well be secondary as long as the desired outcomes are achieved.

This chapter adds to the body of knowledge about various Norwegian responses to S3 described in the recent scholarly works (Knudsen et al., 2019; Normann et al., 2020). In line with the previous research

(Knudsen et al., 2019), this study confirms that Inland County has chosen not to implement S3 fully despite the institutional capacity, many years of regional innovation experience, and relevant knowledge base. As discussed, one of the reasons is the costs associated with S3 implementation (see also Normann et al., 2020). Another reason might be the local cultural (somewhat skeptical) understanding of S3 as a new wording of a known innovation approach.

Inland County has been described as a region where administrative governance prevails and formal governance structures take a leading role in formalized partnership agreements with local business and industry (Knudsen et al., 2019). The adoption of S3 requires the principle of participatory governance and a bottom-up approach to innovation. To turn this around, a change in the local political and cultural mindset is required. The case of SC Hamar illustrates how Hamar Municipality workers are embracing new ideas of participatory governance and testing it through the Bylab Hamar initiative.

Subsequently, not only can SC projects serve as engine for regional development and innovation but also has the potential of becoming an example and inspiring source of innovative approaches, such as the shift from the customary administrative governance to a more participative form at the county level. By adopting a new understanding and practice of participatory governance at the regional level, a closer step toward implementing S3 is achieved.

Implications for Theory

This original piece of research contributes to the scant knowledge about the relationship between SC and S3 policies. In particular, it further specifies the nature of such relationship, which was firstly described by Caragliu and Bo (2018) as "positively correlated." This study does not support that SC initiatives are the results or outcomes of S3 regional innovation policy. On the contrary, it provides evidence of SC serving as an engine for regional innovation and development. An important theoretical contribution to the understanding of the relationship between S3 and SC is the upwards (bottom-up) direction of possible innovation from the local to the regional level (see Figure 5.4). In this view, SC initiatives at the urban level may feed S3 development in the region.

In relation to the adoption of S3, local cultural perception of S3 in the region may serve either as a barrier or as a promoter for S3. In addition, the type of governance and structure in the region plays a crucial role in the successful adoption of S3. A certain skepticism toward S3 combined with the administrative governance would require a change in the mindset, which may be enabled through innovative participatory governance practices of SC initiatives. In addition, the chapter contributes to a better understanding of the SC concept by distinguishing general digitalization projects from SC projects with their criteria of being beneficial for the citizens and contribution to the sustainability of solutions.

Implications for Policy

According to S3, an important stage in the policy implementation is defining sectors, which have the best potential for competitiveness and value creation. Indicators that are often used to define such sectors include export level, employment rate, and value creation. As the present study suggests, not all these indicators, or their combination may reveal the real picture of the potentially innovative sectors/industries. Thus, the sectors that are experienced as most innovative in Inland region are not listed in any regional innovation profile or scoreboard because they do not score high either on employment rate or on export. The IT sector, including AR/VR technology and data security, and the biotechnology sector are both knowledge-intensive sectors and priority areas in terms of investments and innovation in the region. The experienced high innovative performance in these sectors is a result of the efforts of several actors: individual entrepreneurs, academics, and public investments. The implication of this observation might be the choice of the particular indicators for defining potentially innovative sectors.

Although employment rate and export level might be indicators that are most useful for the manufacturing low-technology industries in the knowledge-intensive high-technology sectors, a different set of criteria such as R&D expenditure might be more appropriate in the public and other business sectors. Some other highly relevant criteria may include indicators of knowledge base in terms of codified engineering and scientific knowledge, elements of intellectual capital (human, structural, and relational capital), and indicators of the institutional framework (Smith, 2000).

As a full implementation of S3 may be challenging due to resource constraints, it may therefore be appropriate to establish mechanisms for specifying bottlenecks in the S3 process and provide incentives for the regions, which strive toward full S3 implementation. In addition, this study reveals a lack of coordinated and purposeful interaction between different government levels in the implementation of local and regional smart policies and practices. It is thus recommended to clarify the possible roles, which each government level may take on and arrange for common knowledge-sharing and communication arenas that would help to promote bottom-up innovation practices.

Limitations and Future Research Directions

The study has provided further knowledge that contributes to the understanding of the relationship between S3 and SC. Various smart initiatives at the regional and local level can assist regions to achieve innovation and development, regardless of whether S3 is formally adopted. The current study presents a "snapshot" describing the state of S3 and SC adoption in a specific region, and the nature of connection between the two. Future studies should conduct a longitudinal research to explore the progression and outcome of various SC projects and their impact on the wider region. In addition, this study has mainly presented the viewpoints of county and municipality employees and does not incorporate the viewpoints of citizens, other residents in the wider region, and industry representatives. Hence, as SC projects have the goal to benefit the citizens, the citizens' perspectives should be investigated in greater details. The entrepreneurs' perspective could shed light on the entrepreneurial discovery process and how the innovation priority areas emerge in the region. Further, it would be of interest to investigate the opinions of business partners and industrial actors concerning their experience of S3 policies and their role in promoting innovation in the private sector. Finally, since the study addresses the case of one region, it is thus suggested that future research may employ the same theoretical lenses by looking at several regions from a national or international perspective.

Notes

1. A state-owned company-monopolist offering a wide range of lottery, sports and instant games in the Norwegian market; it is administered by Norwegian Ministry of Culture. Norsk Tipping has headquarters in Hamar.
2. In the case of Hamar, the latter is referred to as both "municipality" and "city", and hence the concepts are used interchangeably. In some other cases, municipality may encompass several populated places, such as towns and villages.

References

Asheim, B. T. (2019). Smart specialisation, innovation policy and regional innovation systems: what about new path development in less innovative regions? *Innovation: The European Journal of Social Science Research, 32*(1), 8–25. https://doi.org/10.1080/13511610.2018.1491001

Barca, F. (2009). *An agenda for a reformed cohesion policy: A place-based approach to meeting European Union challenges and expectations. Independent Report, Prepared at the Request of the European Commissioner for Regional Policy*. Retrieved from http://ec.europa.eu/regional_policy/archive/policy/future/pdf/report_barca_v0306.pdf

Bevilacqua, C., & Pizzimenti, P. (2016). Living lab and cities as smart specialisation strategies engine. *Procedia—Social and Behavioral Sciences, 223*, 915–922. https://doi.org/https://doi.org/10.1016/j.sbspro.2016.05.315

Bylab Hamar. (2019). Bylab Hamar. Retrieved from www.bylabhamar.no

Caragliu, A., & Del Bo, C. (2015). Smart specialization strategies and smart cities: An evidence-based assessment of EU policies. In K. Kourtit, P. Nijkamp &

R. R. Stough (Eds.), *The rise of the city: Spatial dynamics in the urban century* (pp. 55–84). Cheltenham: Edward Elgar.

Caragliu, A., & Del Bo, C. (2018). Much ado about something? An appraisal of the relationship between smart city and smart specialisation policies. *Tijdschrift voor Economische en Sociale Geografie, 109*(1), 129–143. https://doi.org/10.1111/tesg.12272

Caragliu, A., Del Bo, C., & Nijkamp, P. (2011). Smart cities in Europe. *Journal of Urban Technology, 18*(2), 65–82. https://doi.org/10.1080/10630732.2011.601117

D'Adda, D., Guzzini, E., Iacobucci, D., & Palloni, R. (2019). Is smart specialisation strategy coherent with regional innovative capabilities? *Regional Studies, 53*(7), 1004–1016. https://doi.org/10.1080/00343404.2018.1523542

European Commision. (2014). *National/regional innovation strategies for smart specialisation (RIS3)*. Brussels: European Union.

European Union. (2019). *Smart Specialisation Platform*. Retrieved from https://s3platform.jrc.ec.europa.eu/regions

European Union. (2020). *Interregional cooperation*. Retrieved from https://s3platform.jrc.ec.europa.eu/interregional-cooperation

Finne, H., Løvland, J., Mariussen, Å., Madsen, E. L., & Bjørkan, M. (2018). *Blir Norland mer nyskapende? [Is Nordland becoming more innovative?]*. Retrieved from www.nfk.no/_f/ic206dc3b-e371-4cdc-afd8-f6e174f9e50f/blir-nordland-mer-nyskapende.pdf

Foray, D. (2014). *Smart specialisation: Opportunities and challenges for regional innovation policy*. New York: Routledge.

Foray, D. (2016). On the policy space of smart specialization strategies. *European Planning Studies, 24*(8), 1428–1437. https://doi.org/10.1080/09654313.2016.1176126

Foray, D. (2017). The economic fundamentals of smart specialization strategies. In S. Radosevic, A. Curaj, R. Gheorghiu, L. Andreescu & I. Wade (Eds.), *Advances in the theory and practice of smart specialization* (pp. 38–50). Cambridge: Academic Press.

Gianelle, C., Guzzo, F., & Mieszkowski, K. (2019). Smart Specialisation: what gets lost in translation from concept to practice? *Regional Studies*, 1–12. https://doi.org/10.1080/00343404.2019.1607970

González-López, M., & Asheim, B. T. (Eds.). (2020). *Regions and innovation policies in Europe: Learning from the margins*. Cheltenham: Edward Elgar.

Government.no. (2020). Nye Fylker [New counties]. Retrieved from www.regjeringen.no/no/tema/kommuner-og-regioner/regionreform/regionreform/nye-fylker/id2548426/

Hamar Municipality. (2019). *Temaplan 2019–2025 Kultur [Theme plan 2019–2025 culture]*. Retrieved from Hamar Municipality: www.hamar.kommune.no/getfile.php/13466157-1570523761/Bilder/Hamar/Artikkelbilder/Temaplan%202019-2025%20Kultur%20_endelig%2025.9.19.pdf

Hamar Municipality. (2020). *Hamar Kommune: Strategi Smart Hamar [Hamar Municipality: Strategy Smart Hamar]*. Retrieved from www.hamar.kommune.no/getfile.php/13496440-1590476520/Bilder/Hamar/Nyhetsbilder/Teknisk/Smart%20Hamar%20%28kortversjon%29.pdf

HelseINN. (2020). HelseINN. Retrieved from https://helseinn.net/

Hilton, A., & Skrutkowski, M. (2002). Translating instruments into other languages: Development and testing processes. *Cancer Nursing, 25*(1), 1–17.

Hollanders, H., Es-Sadki, N., & Merkelbach, I. (2019). *Regional Innovation Scoreboard 2019.* Retrieved from https://ec.europa.eu/growth/sites/growth/files/ris2019.pdf

Johnson, B. R. (1997). Examining the validity structure of qualitative research. *Education, 118*(2), 282–292.

Knudsen, J. P., Schulze-Krogh, A. C., & Normann, R. (2019). Smart Specialisation—Norwegian adoptions. *Journal of the Knowledge Economy,* 1–21. https://doi.org/ 10.1007/s13132-019-00610-7

Krivý, M. (2016). Towards a critique of cybernetic urbanism: The smart city and the society of control. *Planning Theory, 17*(1), 8–30. https://doi.org/10.1177/1473095216645631

Lægland, M. (2016). Hva er forskjellen på fylkeskommunen og Fylkesmannen? [What's the difference between county government and the county governor?]. Retrieved from www.itromso.no/nyheter/2016/08/24/Hva-er-forskjellen-p%C3%A5-fylkeskommunen-og-Fylkesmannen-13233209.ece

Mäenpää, A., & Teräs, J. (2018). In search of domains in Smart Specialisation: Case study of three Nordic regions. *European Journal of Spatial Development, 68,* 1–20.

Marques, P., & Morgan, K. (2018). The heroic assumptions of smart specialisation: A sympathetic critique of regional innovation policy. In A. Isaksen, R. Martin & M. Trippl (Eds.), *New avenues for regional innovation systems—Theoretical advances, empirical cases and policy lessons* (pp. 275–293). Cham: Springer International Publishing.

McCann, P. (2015). *The regional and urban policy of the European Union: Cohesion, results-orientation and smart specialisation.* Cheltenham: Edward Elgar.

McCann, P., & Ortega-Argileés, R. (2013). Modern regional innovation policy. *Cambridge Journal of Regions, Economy and Society, 6,* 187–216.

Meijer, A., & Bolívar, M. P. R. (2016). Governing the smart city: A review of the literature on smart urban governance. *International Review of Administrative Sciences, 82*(2), 392–408. https://doi.org/10.1177/0020852314564308

Ministry of Local Government and Modernisation. (2018). *Smart spesialisering som metode for regional næringsutvikling [Smart specialization as method for regional development].* Oslo: Ministry of Local Government and Modernisation.

Moe, T. B. (2019). Smartby Stavanger uten retning [Smart City Stavanger without direction]. Retrieved from www.aftenbladet.no/meninger/debatt/i/dO0db1/smartby-stavanger-uten-retning

Nilssen, M. (2019). To the smart city and beyond? Developing a typology of smart urban innovation. *Technological Forecasting and Social Change, 142,* 98–104. https://doi.org/10.1016/j.techfore.2018.07.060

Nordland County Council. (2014). *Et nyskapende Nordland: Innovasjonsstrategi for Nordland 2014–2020 [An Innovative Nordland: Innovationstrategies for Nordland 2014–2020]* Retrieved from www.nfk.no/_f/p34/if7a0e349-8d24-464f-8c32-3b82d1bf11f4/vedtattft15oktris.pdf

Normann, R., Strickert, S., & Knudsen, J. P. (2020). The Agder region: An innovation policy case study. In M. González-López & B. T. Asheim (Eds.), *Regions and innovation policies in Europe: Learning from the margins* (pp. 252–270). Cheltenham: Edward Elgar.

Petrin, T., & Kotnik, P. (2015). Implementing a smart specialisation strategy: An evidence-based approach. *International Review of Administrative Sciences, 83*(1), 85–105.

Radosevic, S., Curaj, A., Gheorghiu, R., Andreescu, L., & Wade, I. (2017). *Advances in the theory and practice of smart specialization.* Cambridge: Academic Press.

Rivas, M. (2018). *Smart Specialisation at City Level. URBACT- InFocus final report.* Retrieved from www.grupotaso.com/wp-content/uploads/2018/08/s3atcitylevel_taso.pdf

Rogaland County. (2019). *Smart spesialisering* [Smart specialization]. Retrieved from www.rogfk.no/vare-tjenester/planlegging/smart-spesialisering/

Smart Cities Norway. (2016). *Hamar på det digitale Norgeskartet* [Hamar on the digital Norwegian map] Retrieved from www.smartebyernorge.no/nyheter/2016/10/31/digitale-hamar

Smarte Mjøsbyer. (2020). *Smart vinterveg* [Smart winter roads]. Retrieved from www.smartemjosbyer.no/aktuelt/smart-vinterveg.1551.aspx

Smith, K. (2000). *What is the 'knowledge economy'? Knowledge intensive industries and distributed knowledge bases.* Retrieved from www.knowledge4all.com/admin/Temp/Files/95c9162b-b420-4b49-9b2b-5a7bac1c5539.pdf

SNL. (2020). *Innlandet* [the Inland]. Retrieved from https://snl.no/Innlandet

Snow, C. C., Håkonsson, D. D., & Obel, B. (2016). A smart city is a collaborative community: Lessons from smart Aarhus. *California Management Review, 59*(1), 92–108. https://doi.org/10.1177/0008125616683954

Sörvik, J., Teräs, J., Dubois, A., & Pertoldi, M. (2019). Smart Specialisation in sparsely populated areas: Challenges, opportunities and new openings. *Regional Studies, 53*(7), 1070–1080. https://doi.org/10.1080/00343404.2018.1530752

Statistics Norway. (2020). *Facts about municipality* [Kommunefakta]. Retrieved from www.ssb.no/kommunefakta/hamar

van Hermert, P., & Nijmap, P. (2010). Knowledge investments, business R&D and innovativeness of countries. A qualitative meta-analytic comparison. *Technological Forecasting and Social Change, 77*, 369–384.

Wilberg, E. (2017). *Strategi i praksis [Strategy in practice].* Bergen: Vigmostad & Bjørke AS.

6 City Smart Specializations in Tourism

The Cases of Kraków, Poland, and Košice, Slovakia

Jacek Gancarczyk, Vanda Maráková, and Ewa Wszendybył-Skulska

Introduction

This chapter assumes a bottom-up perspective in the implementation of smart specialization (SS), focusing on cities and the development of tourism as industry with high potential for branching out toward specialized (related) diversification (EOCIC, 2019; European Cluster Observatory, 2012, 2015). We also acknowledge the multi-scalar context for this industry growth in cities, presenting the relationships with the context of countries and regions, as well as related policy instruments (Bianchi & Labory, 2018). The experience in making SS real is still in its early phase, and relevant policy is predominantly designed at the level of regions and countries (Reimeris, 2016; Iacobucci & Guzzini, 2016). Correspondingly, the majority of research studies explore the processes of planning, implementation, and evaluation of smart specialization strategies (S3) from country and regional perspectives (Radosevic et al., 2017; Crescenzi et al., 2018; Cai et al., 2018; Varga, 2018; D'Adda et al., 2019).

The conceptual background of SS and policy recommendations strongly emphasize the inclusion of local communities, local governments, as well as networks and entrepreneurial discovery into territorial development processes (Foray, 2016; McCann & Ortega-Argilés, 2015; Grillitsch, 2019; Aranguren et al., 2019; Grillitsch & Asheim, 2018; Borrás & Jordana, 2016). Nevertheless, the analyses and evaluations still lack sufficient granularity in understanding the micro-foundations of the progress in smart specialization strategies (S3), particularly considering urban territorial units and individual industries (Grillitsch & Asheim, 2018; Grillitsch, 2019). By focusing on these units, it is possible to find out whether and how the bottom-up approach addresses the assumptions of SS. Additionally, an attempt can be made to consider the relevance of SS and its policy instruments for the growth of individual industries and cities, assuming their interconnections with wider industrial base and contexts of regions and countries (Barzotto et al., 2019; Crescenzi et al., 2018).

Against the previous background and research gaps, the *aim of this chapter is to present the tourism industry as an element of the city smart specialization and to evaluate the coherence of this industry development with the major assumptions of SS in two cities—Kraków, Poland, and Košice, Slovakia.* The major research method will be multiple, comparative case studies of the development of tourism and related public policies in the referred cities in the years 2014–2020, that is, the first EU programming period guided by the SS policy direction. The two case studies are relevant to investigate industrial growth and policy development because they refer to two Central European cities undergoing a transformation to the EU structures and policies and toward knowledge-intensive and service industries.

Our findings reveal the coherence with the SS assumptions of the tourism development and related policy in Kraków, while only partial reflection of SS in the case of Košice. Nevertheless, the narrow focus on the industrial policy in Kraków and underdeveloped policies for sustainable development and quality of life may impede further industry growth. The Košice city demonstrates high potential in smart specialization in tourism, based on the growth of cultural and creative business activities. This potential is underexploited due to the lack of the city government policy for tourism, unfavorable country-level conditions in the area of doing business, and inefficiency of institutional framework.

The theoretical contribution from this study includes analytical generalization about the relevance of SS as the concept for single industry growth in the local government unit. Based on the Krakow case, we reveal a positive relationship between the tourism industry compliance with SS and high performance of this industry. Moreover, our findings add to the policy practice by identifying barriers and stimulants as well as mutual lessons for tourism growth in two Central European cities facing challenges of economic transformation.

In the following sections, we present the Literature Background and a major research question, the Methodological Approach, and Results. The Discussion and Conclusion include the analytical generalization from the findings as well as contributions to theory and practice.

Literature Background

Smart specialization (SS) comprises both the concept of development at different levels of territorial units and the concept of public intervention implemented through smart specialization strategies (S3) (Foray, 2014, 2017; Rodrik, 2014; McCann & Ortega-Argilés, 2015). As a concept of a country, region, or city development, SS emphasizes sustainable growth based on shaping the industrial profile toward *specialized (related) diversification* (Foray et al., 2012, p. 17, 2019, 2020). The idea of SS rests upon two rationales. One rationale is to avoid rigid and excessive specialization of a region or a city (thus the promotion of related diversification). The other rationale is to channel the development pathway toward some prospective activities (specialization), which demonstrate adjacency (industrial relatedness). This approach brings the advantage of the focus and necessary selectivity in public spending, as well as synergies and added value from sharing the resources, such as knowledge, including technology, qualified human resources, brands, and markets. Entrepreneurial discovery leading to innovations is emphasized as mechanism of implementing the SS concept (Foray, 2014; Stam, 2015; Grillitsch, 2019). Entrepreneurial processes in a particular territorial unit should combine exploitation of extant resources and capabilities, that is, activities with significant knowledge and input to regional economies, with exploration of new areas, that is, launching areas of activity (Gancarczyk, Najda-Janoszka, & Gancarczyk, 2020; Gancarczyk & Ujwary-Gil, 2020; Grillitsch & Asheim, 2018; Foray, 2014; McCann & Ortega-Argilés, 2015; Grillitsch, 2019).

As a concept of public intervention, SS departs from a purely top-down approach in the implementation and encourages the bottom-up approach of an organization, network, and smaller territorial units in a multi-scalar context (Morgan & Marques, 2019; Foray, 2016; McCann & Ortega-Argilés, 2015). This suggests the design and implementation of 3S at the level of cities as well, acknowledging their relationships with a wider economic context of a region, country, and the EU (Barzotto et al., 2019).

In the case of low-technology and mature industries, such as tourism, the innovative absorption of high-technologies, for example, ICT, is particularly important (D'Adda et al., 2019; Iacobucci & Guzzini, 2016; Barzotto et al., 2019). The potential of tourism to absorb new technologies leads to innovations—both in the area of efficiency gains from the extant tourism products and services (exploitation) and in the area of new tourism products and services (exploration). At the same time, tourism belongs to the group of industries that demonstrate a high potential for relatedness and synergies with many other areas of activity (Foray, 2014; Lin & Wang, 2020). The referred adjacent areas might include leisure and culture industries, creative industries, as well as social and religious institutions and events that attract people's mobility (Bianchi & Labory, 2018). These relationships benefit tourism and adjacent activities, thus generating synergies. Moreover, they stimulate product and service innovations and, ultimately, branching out and related diversification to new tourism segments, such as cultural tourism and religious tourism (EOCIC, 2019). These characteristics make tourism a high potential industry in implementing smart specialization at the level of cities, with direct input to local and regional development (European Cluster Observatory, 2012, 2015).

Consequently, the tourism industry is often an element of city development strategies and city smart specializations (Chen et al., 2019). The specificity of urban destinations points to the value of leisure offerings (culture heritage and events, entertainment, theme parks, and other adjacent leisure activities), professional and social events (conferences, congresses), as well as some unique elements of city natural environment (yellow zones, nature parks) (OECD, 2018). Leisure activities are then a natural target to seek industrial relatedness and synergies for tourism development within the framework of 3S (EOCIC, 2019).

Based on the previous considerations, this research addresses the research gaps in the area of implementation of SS at the level of cities and industries in the multi-scalar context. Therefore, we formulate the major research question (RQ) as follows:

RQ: Do the tourism industry development and related public policies in the studied cities implement the concept of smart specialization?

Methodological Approach

Our major research question is comprehensive in nature and requires disentangling into a plethora of variables. Similar to the evaluations of the SS design and implementation, it needs to tackle a number of qualitative and quantitative dimensions, as well as contexts of particular territories—cities, but also their parent regions and countries, as well as the EU framework. Such characteristics of research objects justify the adoption of the case study method that is adequate for complex phenomena, in which the context matters as one of explanatory dimensions (Yin, 2018; Eisenhardt & Graebner, 2007). We will undertake comparative investigation of two cities, Kraków in Poland and Košice in Slovakia. In doing so, we seek conclusions regarding common and differing pathways toward smart specializations (Marschan-Piekkari & Welch, 2011). Particularly, we focus on the evaluation of their level of advancement toward SS, as well as mutual lessons regarding good practice and barriers in this process (Crescenzi et al., 2018).

The choice of the city cases was purposeful and based on similarities to clearly identify commonalities and idiosyncrasies in development paths (Yin, 2018). The cities demonstrate similarities in relation to their geopolitical locations, industrial profiles, and roles in their source regions and countries. Košice and Kraków are cities in Central European countries experiencing similar history of socialist and centralized government policy, and later transforming to democratic society and market economy. Moreover, they jointly accessed the EU in 2004, participating in the European industrial and innovation policies, including SS policies. Although Košice and Kraków differ in size, they have similar structural characteristics and profile as important cultural and tourism centers, as well as concentrations of creative and leisure industries. Additionally, both cities have been transforming from heavy industries, such as steelworks, toward knowledge-intensive and creative services that can develop synergies with tourism industry.

Our research procedure involves: (1) the evaluation of tourism industry development and related policy according to the criteria of SS, over 2014–2020 in each city; (2) the comparative analysis of two cities regarding their consistency with the SS concept; (3) drawing conclusions as to stimulants and barriers in the SS implementation, as well as mutual lessons for both cities.

On the basis of the conceptual background of SS, we disentangle the major research question into the following evaluation criteria:

- developing synergies—an evaluation of whether tourism in the researched cities established links with and benefits from synergies with other adjacent industries;
- combining exploitation and exploration activities to accomplish specialized diversification—an evaluation whether in the referred cities; (1) tourism industry exploited the extant products and services through growth and increased their efficiency through innovations (e.g., with the use of ICT); (2) tourism industry developed new products and services based on advanced technologies and on branching out toward other related industries;
- enhancing competences and growth of incumbent enterprises and entrepreneurial activity (launching new tourism firms)—an evaluation of dynamics of extant and start-up tourism enterprises in the studied cities;
- organizing bottom-up agency—an evaluation whether local institutions and bottom-up initiatives (business and local development associations and agencies, chambers of commerce and industry, stakeholder lobbying, etc.) support tourism development according to SS directions;
- targeting policy measures—an evaluation of whether policy instruments are well adjusted to develop tourism according to SS in both cities.

In order to perform the analysis according to the indicated criteria, we used secondary data sources and the method of desk research (Wadham & Warren, 2014; Wright et al., 2018). These sources included:

- policy documents, such as development and innovation strategies of the cities, regions, and countries in connection with the EU policy statements;
- evaluations of policy programs targeting the development of Kraków and Košice;
- public statistics regarding tourism and related industries, as well as their innovative performance;

- documents and webpages of industrial associations and institutions promoting the development of tourism in both cities;
- research publications related to the development of cities and industries under study.

We used selective coding and structuring of the previously mentioned data, following the template of the evaluation criteria stated previously. The coding of data was selective in focusing on the phenomena and relationships derived from the theory (Wadham & Warren 2014; Wright et al. 2018). Three researchers cross-reviewed the coded information, discussed, and resolved ambiguities. Finally, the comparative analysis was subsumed with conclusions.

Results

Case Study Kraków

The Tourism Industry in Poland

Poland is recognized as a leader in the Central European region when it comes to the number of foreign visitors. The number of foreigners coming to Poland in 2018 was 19.6 million. It increased by 3.6 million in comparison with 2014. However, the dynamics of the tourism share in the country's GDP demonstrated only small increases in 2014–2019. In 2019, this share was 4.7%, and compared to 2014, it increased by 0.5 percentage point (WTTC, 2020).

In 2018, tourism enterprises in Poland accounted for approx. 6% of enterprises in the nonfinancial business economy (Table 6.1).

Table 6.1 Key economic indicators for the tourism industry in Poland in 2018

	Number of enterprises	Number of persons employed	Turnover (in million EUR)	Value-added at factor cost (in million EUR)
Total nonfinancial business economy	1,960,361	9,822,046	1,124,830	247,281
Tourism industry (total)	116,707	338,304	19,309	5,471.7
Tourism industry (total) in total nonfinancial business economy (%)	5.95	3.4	1.72	2.2

Source: Based on Eurostat (2020).

The population of 116,707 tourism enterprises employed 338,304 persons in 2018. Enterprises in industries with tourism-related activities accounted for 3.4% of employment in the nonfinancial business economy. The tourism industry share in total turnover and value added at factor cost was relatively lower, accounting for 1.72% of the turnover and 2.2% of the value added of the nonfinancial business economy (Eurostat, 2020). Poland is ranked 42nd in the Tourist Attractiveness and Competitiveness Index. The key factors determining the value of Polish tourism include hygienic conditions and healthcare, cultural heritage resources, and international openness (Calderwood & Soshkin, 2019). The potential of Kraków, which is by far the most popular tourist destination in Poland, has a significant impact on the value of the previously mentioned economic indicators. This is largely due to one of the country's largest tourist attractions, the number and variety of cultural events, and a well-developed accommodation base.

The Tourism Industry and Its Synergies in Kraków

Kraków is one of the most important European metropolises. The city is located in the southern part of the country in the Małopolska region, which in 2019 had 3.36 million inhabitants, with a significant concentration in Kraków (23.2% of the inhabitants of the region live in the city of Kraków) (KCGO, 2020). Kraków is the metropolitan center of the region and the second largest city in Poland according to gross domestic product (GDP). In 2017, the city GDP amounted to 66,487 million PLN, which accounted for more than 40% of Małopolska's GDP. The average level of GDP per 1 inhabitant of Kraków amounted to 86,715 PLN and was more than 83% higher than the regional average and by more than 67% higher than the national average (Statistics Poland, Local Data Bank, 2020). The unemployment rate in Kraków alone (2%) is significantly lower than the rates in Małopolska (4.15%) and at the same time also lower than in Poland (5.2%) (KCGO, 2020).

Kraków is also a city characterized by international openness, manifested in the number of organized events, cultural, sports, and business events of international importance. Kraków's openness to the world is also evidenced by its position as the leading business services center in Europe (ABSL, 2018). In the years 2014–2019, the number of business process offshoring, shared services centers, IT, and R&D centers increased from 85 to 234. There are about 78,000 people working in the service centers in Kraków, which translates into 23% of the city's share in the employment structure of the industry in the country (ABSL, 2020).

Krakow hosts more than 146,00 business companies and about 5,000 companies with foreign capital that have invested more than 4.6 billion PLN (KCGO, 2016a). The city is the location of international banks, associations that support business activities, and chambers of commerce. Its position is confirmed by high creditworthiness ratings and international rankings. In 2017, it was ranked second in Europe and eighth in the world in the Tholons Services Globalization City Index (KCGO, 2020).

In recent years, the fastest growing industries in Kraków have been IT, business services, as well as creative and cultural activities. These industries have been included in the set of the Małopolska smart specializations (Gancarczyk et al., 2020). Kraków is one of the oldest cities in Poland, where tradition is intertwined with modernity. The historical heritage of Kraków consists of around 6,000 monuments dated from all ages. About 2.5 million works of art collected in Kraków's museums, churches, and archives, accounting for 25% of Poland's museum resources. In addition, the historic center of Kraków is on the World List of Cultural and Natural Heritage (KCGO, 2017). Kraków position as an important European tourist and cultural center is evidenced by the dynamics of tourist traffic and development of accommodation facilities (Table 6.2).

Table 6.2 Capacity and performance of accommodation facilities in the city of Kraków

Year	Accommodation facilities	Beds in total	Visitors	Overnight stays of visitors
2019	264	30,969	2,727,247	6,082,877
2018	258	31,022	2,513,799	5,579,275
2017	254	27,863	2,389,414	5,270,648
2016	248	27,243	2,277,582	4,999,278
2015	231	24,037	2,122,091	4,573,896
2014	224	23,734	1,996,404	4,247,477

Source: Based on Statistics Poland, Local Data Bank (2020).

The continuous increase in tourist traffic in the city translates into the city's GDP. However, at the same time, it also meets physical congestion and social problems. The phenomenon of over-tourism (excessive number of tourists in the city) is becoming more and more noticeable. On average, there are 146 tourists per 100 inhabitants in the city per year (Orłowski et al., 2019). The constantly rising prices of services, flats, rents, and excessive noise cause dissatisfaction of the inhabitants in historical districts, and even some reluctance toward visitors. The result is a gradual depopulation of the city's central districts (KCGO, 2016d). The underdeveloped and dysfunctional transportation system hardly meets the challenges of congestion. The city authorities, noticing this problem, are trying to take measures to reduce these dysfunctions.

Specialized Diversification in Kraków

The Kraków tourism industry has been exploiting its potential through growth and ICT-based innovations. Newly built or modernized tourist facilities in Kraków (including hotels, museums, conference centers, and fair centers) are equipped with intelligent management systems. These solutions are also provided by Kraków ICT companies, including the vibrant community of start-ups. Thanks to these innovations, Kraków tourism entities can develop and modernize their offer, as well as increase the efficiency of processes (Gancarczyk et al., 2020).

The examples include Comarch S.A. offering the "Pilgrim" application for participants of the World Youth Day in Kraków. The company HG Intelligence S.A. developed a mobile application that facilitates planning a visit to the MOCAK Jewish Museum and serves as a guide to the exhibition. Amistad Sp. z o. o. created a dedicated application for the Kraków Airport. It also operates the website www.Kraków.travel, the city information system "Treespot Kraków," and a multimedia guide to the Sacrum Profanum Festival. Ailleron SA has launched modern specialized iLumio and Ligahotel systems for hotel services used not only in Kraków but also around the world. The company Startup Base Lab has developed modern solutions facilitating the management of the customer base and sales. This start-up subsidiary of the Dutch company made a significant contribution to the modernization of the tourist offer in Kraków. It developed an original website that offers up to 25% discount on competitors' prices (including Booking.com and Expedia) for hotel reservations, without charging a commission from hoteliers. The solution of the start-up has already been used by 155,000 hotel facilities around the world, including 123 hotels located in Kraków. Bidroom.com was announced as the most innovative tourism start-up in the world during the World Tourism Forum in Lucerne in 2017 (Bidroom, 2020). These examples not only refer to the development of extant tourism businesses by increasing their efficiency and market reach but they also reflect explorative branching out in the city—from tourism to new segments of the ICT sector that are specialized in the solutions for the tourism industry.

Therefore, not only is tourism in Kraków developing in terms of quantity but also in terms of quality ensured by innovative solutions. The development of innovation on the Kraków tourism market seems to be a natural phenomenon, given that the city is the center of research and development activities in the region (Statistics Poland, Local Data Bank, 2020). The latest progress in the Małopolska R&D expenditure by business sector, non-R&D innovation expenditures, and design applications have been accomplished due to the business and R&D activity concentrated in the region's capital (MRGO, 2012).

Another explorative pathway can be observed in tourism branching out to new, adjacent market segments. We observe the synergy with adjacent industries operating on the Kraków market, based on new tourism products diversifying to such industrial segments as cognitive tourism, cultural, business, medical, sports, religious, and culinary tourism. For years, the main purpose of tourists has been to visit places that are elements of heritage, such as the institutions of culture, old architecture, and monuments.

However, along with the increased number of foreign direct investments in business services, business tourism has also developed (KCGO, 2014, 2016f). The city has invested in the development of modern and innovative infrastructure. Therefore, there is a visible link between tourism and the developing sector of service centers. The tourist sector of Kraków was also able to see the potential of the city as a scientific and medical center that does not only attract business but also tourists with a large number of clinics at the European level. In recent years, linking the medical sector with tourism has allowed for the development of a new innovative tourist product of the city, that is, medical tourism (KCGO, 2020).

The Dynamics of Enterprise Growth and New Ventures in the Kraków Tourism

The share of tourism in Kraków's GDP (taking the indirect and induced effects into account) is more than 8%. The share of the tourism economy in terms of employment in relation to employment in the entire economy of Kraków is more than 10% (Seweryn et al., 2017). The number of tourist enterprises in the city is systematically growing. Between 2014 and 2019, their number increased by 16%, with the dynamics showing a constant upward trend until 2017. Then, it slightly weakened in 2018 (from 3.2% in 2017 to 2.7% in 2018) to increase again in 2019 (Statistics Poland, Local Data Bank, 2020).

Every year, more than 1,200 new tourism enterprises are created in Kraków. Until 2018, their dynamics showed an upward trend, at a level that was higher than ever recorded in the modern history of the city (Figure 6.1) (Statistics Poland, Local Data Bank, 2020).

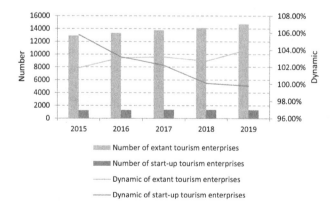

Figure 6.1 Number and dynamics of extant and start-up tourism enterprises in Kraków 2015–2019

*Organized Agency and Partnerships for Tourism Development
in Kraków; Targeting Policy Measures*

The development of entrepreneurship and innovation in the tourism sector in Kraków is supported by the city and regional ecosystems that provide access to qualified human resources, financing, business services, and networks among entrepreneurs. There are 23 universities and 37 research institutes, and research and development (R&D) centers in Kraków (KCGO, 2020). Technology transfer centers, technology incubators, clusters, such as the Life Science Cluster Kraków, the Kraków Gastronomic Cluster, the Culture and Free Time Industries Cluster, the European Game Center Cluster, and regional development agencies offer various forms of support for business, including tourism. Entrepreneurs benefit from training, workshops, networking meetings, and hackathons organized by both public agencies and private investors. These business-oriented organizations and activities are often launched by tourism business associations and chambers of commerce, notably Krakow Chamber of Tourism and Krakow Chamber of Commerce and Industry (KCGO, 2016c).

The referred bottom-up agency of public and private organizations and activities has been complemented, and also to some extent coordinated, by the city government. The latter policy acts as a hub for organized efforts of individuals, enterprises, and business support organizations. The city government bridges academic and business communities and adds own efforts, as exemplified by the Kraków Science–Business–Residents–Local Government Forum that reflects the triple helix idea. The aim of this initiative is to stimulate dialogue and initiate cooperation among science, business, residents, and local government (KCGO, 2016c).

The city treats tourism as one of the most important areas of its development, supporting tourism entrepreneurship with grants and subsidies. The priority activities include creating competitive tourism products and building a network of tourism partnerships with other industries (KCGO, 2016a). One of the planned activities in this regard was to involve the city in the implementation of events of international, scientific, cultural, and sports importance, as well as the development of congress, business, and religious tourism. In the years 2016–2018, the city government organized international events, such as the International Medical Tourism Congress (three editions), Historical Cities as part of the project "Historical Cities 3.0," and the International Congress of Religious and Pilgrimage Tourism.

None of the city's programmatic documents directly declares the implementation of SS. However, the development of leisure sectors, including tourism, is indicated as the strength of the city, contributing to the region's smart specialization (KCGO, 2016a). The city government development strategy declares the implementation of ICT in business and financial services, as well as leisure and creative industries that are natural inspiration for tourism movement (KCGO, 2016a, p. 75). Moreover, the tourism development policy is supported by evaluation and research reports, publicly available online. These reports confirm the upward trend in implementing policies and measures between 2016 and 2019 (KCGO, 2020).

Several programmatic documents have been developed that address the development of the city (KCGO, 2016a, 2016b), its promotion (KCGO, 2016f), as well as particular areas of its functioning, including tourism (KCGO, 2014), culture (KCGO, 2017), safety (KCGO, 2016e), transport (KCGO, 2016d), and entrepreneurship (KCGO, 2016c). The city development strategy seeks to accomplish sustainability and reduce the dysfunctions that lower the quality of life, that is, over-tourism and air pollution.

Overall, we acknowledge effective and SS-driven policy of the city government, coordinating and supporting the efforts of the bottom-up agency in the area of entrepreneurship and innovation development in tourism. This policy is also strongly targeted at attracting external foreign direct investors, city visitors, and potential residents. The quality of life policy has been strongly emphasized in the latest policy declarations (KCGO, 2020). However, it was largely neglected during the earlier periods of business-oriented growth. The city suffers from such disadvantages as inefficient communication system, air pollution, and congestion that threaten further industrial development and city reputation, particularly in the area of tourism. The claims of over-tourism lowering the quality of residents' lives are rather outcomes than causes of problems.

Case Study Košice

Tourism Industry in Slovakia

Slovakia has a great potential for tourism development because a number of attractions are concentrated in a relatively small country area. Moreover, each region offers a unique experience. Hence diversity and variety of destinations form the country's competitive advantage. The major objective of *New Strategy of Tourism Development in the Slovak Republic until 2020* (MTCRD, 2020) is "to increase competitiveness of tourism by better exploitation of its potential with intent to balance regional disparities and create new jobs." In the *Travel and Tourism Competitiveness Report* (WEF, 2019), Slovakia was placed as the 60th among 140 monitored countries, with an evaluation score of 4.0. Compared to the last rated period, there was a slight increase in total score

(59th position in 2017 with a score of 3.9, and 61st position in 2015 with a score of 3.8).

Despite the earlier mentioned potential, the competitiveness of Slovakia's tourism is largely undermined by considerable drawbacks. The major disadvantages include the lack of government support for tourism and unfavorable legal conditions of doing business. Slovakia is also lagging behind in transport availability, particularly air transport infrastructure, macro-marketing capabilities, trustworthy police services, qualified human resources, and high-capacity sports stadiums (WEF, 2019). On the other hand, the strength of the country is the ability to minimize terrorist threats and other external shocks through efficient signaling by mobile operators. Furthermore, the country is rich in natural and cultural heritage, highly concentrated in East Slovakia, with a central city of Košice.

In 2018, 24,414 tourism enterprises with the employment of 74,469 (4.5% share on employment in nonfinancial business economy) operated in Slovakia (Table 6.3). The tourism industry shares in total turnover and value added at factor cost were relatively low, with the figures of 1.6% and 2.1%, accordingly. This modest performance is largely due to the predominance of micro, small, and medium-sized enterprises, as well as considerable part-time employment in many tourism segments (Eurostat, 2020).

Tourism has the potential to play a significant role in the economic aspirations of many EU regions and can be of particular importance in peripheral regions. This is also true in the case of Košice Region located

Table 6.3 Key economic indicators for the tourism industry in Slovakia in 2018

	Number of enterprises	*Number of persons employed*	*Turnover (in million EUR)*	*Value-added at factor cost (in million EUR)*
Total nonfinancial business economy	493,636	1,652,546	212,337	40,141
Tourism industry (total)	24,414	74,469	3,386	844
Tourism industry (total) in total nonfinancial business economy (%)	4.95	4.5	1.6	2.1

Source: Based on Eurostat (2020).

in Eastern Slovakia. Transport infrastructure and facilities created for tourism contribute to local and regional development. The jobs generated in that industry largely help counteract industrial decline and rural decline.

The Tourism Industry and Its Synergies in Košice

The Košice Region, with an area of 6,754 km² occupies 13.8% of Slovak territory. The number of inhabitants in the region is the second largest in Slovakia, and the area is the fourth largest among eight Slovak regions. Košice is the region's capital and the second biggest city of Slovakia, situated only 20 km from Hungary, 80 km from Ukraine, and 90 km from the Polish border. The city covers an area of 243.7 km², with 239,141 inhabitants (Košice CGO, 2019). It is well equipped with the infrastructure to provide a wide spectrum of public services and commercial activities. Košice is the location of public country-level and regional administration offices and international consulates. A network of banking and financial institutions, universities, research and development institutes, administrative and cultural facilities, hospitals, and a wide range of services distinguish Košice from other Slovak urban agglomerations. Moreover, more than 600 companies with foreign ownership are active in the region (Košice CGO, 2019).

Regarding basic macroeconomic indicators, regional GDP is lower, while the unemployment rate is higher than the Slovak national average (Eurostat, Regional Statistics, 2020). The main industries driving the development of the region are downstream chemical products, forestry, leather, and related products, metal mining, automotive, metal manufacturing, electric goods, and textile manufacturing. Košice is an industrial city with a strong tradition in steel production, currently represented by the company US Steel Košice. This enterprise is the largest employer in Eastern Slovakia with more than 12,000 jobs, and the largest steel producer in Central Europe. Besides this mature industry, the IT sector is growing, as evidenced by the IT Valley cluster. The number of this cluster occupations has accomplished more than 10,000 in the year 2018 (Košice CGO, 2019).

Unemployment rate of around 5% is lower than the regional and national average (Statistical Office of Slovak Republic, 2020a). The transport infrastructure, including road, rail, and an international airport, is well developed, and Košice acts as the most important transport hub in the eastern part of the country. Located at the intersection of two main crossings of transnational roads, Košice represents an important European transportation node. The primary west–east direction extends from the Czech Republic and Austria to and in the eastward direction to Ukraine, and further to other states of the former Soviet Union.

Table 6.4 Capacity and performance of accommodation facilities in the city of Košice in 2014–2019

Year	Accommodation facilities	Beds in total	Visitors	Overnight stays of visitors
2019	117	6,987	240,345	560,580
2018	84	5,817	200,277	417,209
2017	67	5,054	195,890	367,725
2016	67	5,648	184,467	350,145
2015	71	5,065	154,012	305,620
2014	67	5,011	140,011	262,112

Source: Based on Statistical Office of Slovak Republic: Data cube statistics (2020b).

The second important direction runs to the north–south, from Poland to Hungary.

Table 6.4 presents the key economic indicators regarding the tourism industry in Košice in 2014–2019.

In 2014–2019, there has been an increase in the offer (number of accommodation facilities, number of beds) as well as in the demand (the number of visitors and overnight stays). These figures need to be placed within the context of the country specificity. Like Austria, Croatia, and Greece, Slovakia belongs to the narrow group of destinations, where overnight stays are not concentrated in cities but in rural areas, towns, and suburbs (WTTC, 2020).

It is worth to mention that the city was awarded several statues of "European." In 2013, Košice was the European Capital of Culture. Since 2017, Košice has been a member of the UNESCO Creative Cities Network in the field of media art. Moreover, it was announced as a UNESCO Creative City of Media Arts in 2018. In 2016, Košice became the European City of Sport (KCGO, 2020).

Besides housing and construction, cultural and creative industries are another booming sector in Košice. In 2017, Košice was included in the Creative Cities Monitor (EU Science Hub, 2017), based on favorable evaluation of governance quality, potential road accessibility, graduates in ICT, integration of foreigners, and theater arts. These advantages were summed up as highly enabling environment, cultural vibrancy, and strong cultural economy that potentially can contribute to tourism growth (EU Science Hub, 2017).

The dynamics of tourism and related services has been evidenced in Table 6.5.

The data reveal more than doubled the number of employees in professional, scientific, and technical activities, both in the region and in the

Table 6.5 The average number of registered employees in tourism and tourism-related services in the Košice region and the Košice city 204–2014–2019

		Average registered number of employees								
		2010	2011	2012	2013	2014	2015	2016	2017	2018	2019
Košice region	Professional, scientific, and technical activities	2,023	3,383	3,899	3,248	3,535	4,099	4,423	5,013	6,518	5,499
	Arts, entertainment, and recreation	2,310	2,803	2,219	2,020	1,715	2,046	1,805	1,935	2,480	3,024
	Accommodation and catering services	3,318	3,158	2,507	1,812	1,831	2,017	1,533	2,349	2,480	4,829
Košice City	Professional, scientific, and technical activities	1,682	2,909	3,120	2,474	2,884	3,319	3,359	3,842	4,995	4,445
	Arts, entertainment, and recreation	1,184	1,437	1,169	1,372	1,176	1,343	1,267	1,398	1,813	1,841
	Accommodation and catering services	1,839	2,039	1,368	717	1,466	971	1,019	1,834	1,815	2,755

Source: Based on Statistical Office of Slovak Republic, Data cube statistics (2020b).

Košice city. Nevertheless, arts, entertainment, and recreation, as well as accommodation and catering, report considerable decrease in the region. Still, moderately positive dynamics was recorded for these activities in the city in 2014 (SOSR, Data cube statistics, 2020).

The Košice city created a hub for supporting creative and cultural potential development, Creative Industry Košice, responsible for the local creative and cultural development. The hub conducts projects with broad public participation, in particular with tourism organizations, international partner cities, Ministry of Culture SR, Technical University in Košice, US Steel Košice, as well as local clusters, such as BITERAP, Klaster AT+R (the IT innovation in the automation and robotics), and Košice IT Valley (KCGO, 2020).

Specialized Diversification in Košice

There are examples of interconnections between the ICT sector and tourism services in the city. The most promising are the digital environment (PC games and software) and advertising industry, which are largely dedicated to tourism organizations in public and private sectors (Košice CGO, 2019). Orientation on smart solutions is the most visible in the segment of hotels and spatial mobility. Ecohotel Dalia in Košice not only is the best practice in sustainable solutions, unique holder of the European award "Green label," but also has pioneered automation processes and robots in hotel services. The ICT-enhanced family-owned wineries in Tokaj regions represent another innovative approach that contributes to the Košice region appealing brand (KCGO, 2020). Unfortunately, these positive examples of ICT–tourism interconnections do not outweigh limited innovativeness of the population of tourism SMEs. The causes of this shortcoming include underdeveloped infrastructure, as well as lack of a regional innovation ecosystem and efficient management of regional innovation policy (KRGO, 2016; Košice CGO, 2019).

Strong links can also be observed between culture and tourism supported by ICT and multimedia technologies. The status of Košice as a European Cultural Capital has stimulated the development of new and modernization of existing infrastructure that is also available for the visitors of the city. A notable project in this area was the renovation of an old army barracks into a cultural center, Kultur Park, to establish an arena for presentation and support of art and other creative industries. The Steel Park, a science part being a part of the cultural center, is dedicated to the interactive exhibition of steel production. The development of cultural and creative industries stimulated a cyclical event, "White night," regularly organized from 2010. It is a unique cultural project combining light shows, sculptures, animations, architectures, and performances. The event originally started in Paris in 2002. Košice was the only city in Slovakia and neighboring V4 countries that acquired the license from

Paris to organize this prestigious international arts project. Currently, it is the biggest and the most-visited festival of modern art in the Slovak Republic. Another unique event is a festival USE THE C!TY. It involves the residents, artists, visitors to the interactive architectural interventions into public spaces (Košice CGO, 2019).

Overall, we observe a promising background for synergies between tourism and related industries that might benefit further synergetic growth of all these activities. There are prospective undertakings that prove viability of tourism innovation to upgrade the effectiveness of extant industries (exploitation) and to create new tourism segments oriented on adjacent activities (exploration). Nevertheless, these initiatives are at the nascent stage, and both innovative performance and the dynamics of new tourism projects were only marginal in the period under study (SOSR, Financial database, 2020).

The Dynamics of Enterprise Growth and New Ventures in Košice

There are limited statistics on new tourism firms in Košice city. The general data are provided by the national financial, statistical portal Finstat for the region and industry (SOSR, Financial database, 2020). The available data are monitoring the Košice region, and in the tourism industry data, the segment of gastronomy is also included. By analyzing the data, we can confirm that the majority of incumbent enterprises were firms in gastronomy rather than in the tourism industry in the last years. Indirectly, we can infer tourism enterprise dynamics from the employment dynamics in this industry (Table 6.5), which was moderately positive in 2014–2017. This matched with considerable increases in the number of visitors and facilities in 2014–2019 (Table 6.4) provides for positive performance of incumbent businesses that increase their capacity with moderate employment growth. Still, the growth of new tourism ventures remained modest in the studied period.

Both macro-environmental conditions (unfavorable conditions of doing business and contract legal enforcements) and lack of local and regional institutions for entrepreneurship support, explain underperformance of the tourism enterprise. Slovak Business Agency created such an institutional network at the national level, but its units are absent in the Košice city. On the other hand, there are some positive examples of green and smart start-ups. Cleantech Slovakia (Cleantech Slovakia, 2020) is one of new ventures whose main objective is the transformation toward zero-carbon economy in the field of tourism, transportation, and technology. So far, the ecology-oriented start-ups have implemented 37 innovative solutions in the three industries in focus (Cleantech Slovakia, 2020).

*Organized Agency and Partnerships for Tourism Development
in Košice; Targeting Policy Measures*

Košice represents a vibrant city, where development has been strongly supported by local residents and bottom-up initiatives. The leader and coordinator of these initiatives are the Regional Tourism Organization— Košice Tourism Region, operating as a public–private partnership. It is one of seven regional tourism organizations (RTOs) established at the national level and entitled to receive subsidies from public funds (Tourism Support Act Law, 2010). The membership of regional government each RTO is obligatory. The main role of the RTO Košice Tourism Region comprises coordination of the development, marketing, and distribution of tourism products in cooperation with local tourism organizations to accomplish regional identity and destination branding. Other responsibilities comprise financial support for ecotourism and communication with relevant partners in tourism development, such as Slovak railways, Slovak tourist club, and Slovak forest governance. Moreover, the RTO creates a mutual system of reservations and integrated communication of ecotourism products.

The RTO gathers local tourism entities, such as Visit Košice representing Košice area and surrounding. Visit Košice acts as a local tourism organization (LTO), associating private businesses and municipalities, including the region' capital. It is one of 34 LTOs operating in the country and financially supported by member fees and state subsidies (Tourism Support Act, 2010). LTO Visit Košice seeks to develop local tourism products and invest in related infrastructure in cooperation with its members, that is, local residents, businesses, local development organizations, and municipalities. It also distributes and markets ecotourism products, represents the interests of its members in the regional organization, and offers financial support for ecotourism development. The members of the local organization not only participate in the major initiatives but also offer their opinions and recommendations regarding further development of the city, as well as initiate project proposals for external funding.

The tourism governance in the region and city is a top-down, centrally coordinated system rather than a bottom-up agency that originates from local-level initiatives of a variety of actors. Although the system seems clearly organized in terms of competencies and functions, it is determined by the hierarchical structure of decision-making and financing that predominantly comes from top tiers and state budget. These characteristics may support the coherence of multiscalar strategies and measures. However, its downside risks are overlong decision processes and policy measures that do not fully target local specific needs. Less popular is the approach represented by the Košice IT Valley, a city-level clustering initiative that promotes the development of entertainment industries through IT solutions and thus benefits tourism as well.

Košice city has not developed any strategy for tourism development. Nevertheless, the strategy *The city of culture and sport* (Košice CGO, 2019) promotes the areas relevant for tourism development, such as innovation, creative economy, logistics center for agro-accommodations, and labor market in the ICT sector. The funds targeted at these areas almost doubled in 2019 from around 5 million euros in 2014 (Košice CGO, 2019). Within the city strategy in culture and sport, there are some indirect measures that might be relevant for tourism development in Košice. However, there are no measures directly targeted at this industry. Moreover, these documents do not refer to smart specialization as a local development concept nor they declare any contribution to the regional SS policy.

The urban tourism can also benefit from the Košice region development strategy that emphasizes ecotourism 2020–2024 and cross-industrial cooperation to launch new tourism products (KRGO, 2013, 2016). Other significant objectives include transport and ICT infrastructure development in rural areas, municipalities, and tourism resorts (KRGO, 2014, 2016). These documents are consistent with the country's strategies (Slovak Government, 2014, 2020). Although the regional measures may support urban tourism as well, they cannot be deemed targeted at the Košice place-based needs.

Discussion

Following the aim of this chapter, we have conceptually presented the tourism industry as element of the city smart specialization, and evaluated the coherence of this industry development and related policy with the major assumptions of SS in two Central European cities of Kraków and Košice. Our case study investigations responded to the evaluation criteria driven by the SS concept.

Regarding the Krakow case in the referred period 2014–2020, the findings reveal positive evaluations of the tourism industry development. This development is an effect of synergy with other industries in the city's economy (Aranguren et al., 2019). Thanks to this synergy, there has been a gradual diversification of Krakow's tourist product and development of its innovativeness (Foray, 2014; 2020). The city has accomplished specialized diversification both through exploitation of extant industrial base that effectively innovates with the use of ICT solutions and through exploration of new tourism products launching new industrial segments (Foray, 2019; 2020). We also find other industries, such as ICT, using the opportunities to branch out toward tourism-related segments (MCann & Ortega-Argilés, 2015; Grillitsch & Asheim, 2018). In the period under study, Krakow recorded high dynamics of the growth of incumbent tourism enterprises (about 14%), and the entrepreneurial activity in tourism (more than 6%), featured by the number of innovative start-ups.

These processes are the results of a well-developed network of organizations and policies supporting the development of tourism at the local and regional levels (Asheim, 2019). The city government assumes the role of the strategic planner and a hub, coordinating the efforts of varied and dense networks of public and private institutions that are involved in the development of local entrepreneurship.

Therefore, addressing the main research question, we can confirm that the development of tourism in Kraków and related public policies followed the principles of smart specialization industrial policy in the studied period. Nevertheless, focusing on economic growth of the city over the referred and earlier periods of transformation and EU accession, the local government largely neglected other important policy areas. In particular, this refers to the transportation infrastructure, air pollution, and space planning that would acknowledge both future economic growth and increasing demand for quality of life from inhabitants and business community. Although the latest development strategy recognizes these needs, it is still delayed and challenged by the claims of congestion and "over-tourism" that threaten future development of this industry. Still, the claimed "over-tourism" can be treated as an outcome rather than a cause of current problems.

In the case of Košice, tourism development and related public policies follow the principles of SS only marginally. Tourism is not a driving force for the Košice socioeconomic development, but it rather benefits from synergies with and advancements in other industries. These industries are both related to tourism, such as culture and creative industries, including the ICT, and unrelated, such as steel industry (D'Adda et al., 2019). Specialized diversification is a potential development trajectory, but not a real case by now. There are prospects for both exploitation in terms of extant enterprise growth, and exploration, that is, launching new tourism products and segments based on adjacent industries (Iacobucci & Guzzini, 2016). Nevertheless, the available data reveal low dynamics of entrepreneurial activity, that is, launching new tourism firms in the city, as well as modest dynamics of extant tourism enterprises. More significant dynamics of growth have been prevented by unfavorable conditions of business environment, especially in the area of new job creation. These conditions are one of the causes of differences in the overall tourism industry dynamics between Slovakia and Poland.

There is a valuable bottom-up network of local tourism organizations coordinated by the regional and country public–private partnerships (Estensoro & Larrea, 2016). Still, these efforts require more targeted and place-based support measures to ensure the dynamics of exploitation and exploration of the city tourism entrepreneurship (Grillitsch & Asheim, 2018). In this vein, financial resources allocated to ecotourism as well as culture and sport should be regarded as positive but insufficient.

The positive aspects of the regional strategic planning are the acknowledgment of ecological aspects. Moreover, public–private partnerships in tourism organizations might serve as efficient mechanisms for tourism development in the future (Estensoro & Larrea, 2016). To sum up, we find the development of Košice tourism industry and related policies as only marginally consistent with the assumptions of SS. The major barriers and drawbacks in this regard are unfavorable country-level conditions for doing business and legal enforcement, lack of tourism-targeted strategy and measures at the city level, and underdeveloped business support institutions.

Conclusion

Implications for Theory

This study contributes to the micro-level and bottom-up perspectives on the implementation of the SS concept, which represents a research gap in the current literature in regional development (Aranguren et al., 2019; Grillitsch & Asheim, 2018; Grillitsch, 2019). Particularly, we provide a comparative perspective of a local government unit and one industry. The policy lessons highlighted in the next section can be treated as a natural generalization about specific industrial development of peripheral and transforming territorial units (Yin, 2018; Crescenzi et al., 2018). Moreover, by proposing the adoption of the SS concept to other units than regions and countries, we broaden its applicability and validity as a theoretical construct and policy direction (Foray, 2019, 2020). The case of Krakow tourism development, as a success story and a benchmark of tourism development, is consistent with the assumptions of SS, despite the fact that 3S is not recalled in the policy programmatic documents. This case serves as a confirmatory test for the SS approach based on pattern-matching between the real-life processes and the concept of smart specialization (Yin, 2018; Eisenhardt & Graebner, 2007). The Košice case additionally supports this confirmatory test. It reveals less developed and less dynamic industry, with the characteristics, supporting agency and policies that are only marginally consistent with the SS concept.

Implications for Policy

The cases also offer practical lessons for the development of tourism and related policy in the studied cities. Contrary to Košice, Kraków noticed the need for sustainable development matched with industrial development overly late. Košice has started this development pathway in the beginning of its planning, emphasizing ecotourism, which may further alleviate dysfunctions, such as congestion and over-tourism. Still, the lack of policy measures targeted at innovation and enterprise development, as well as limited bottom-up activities in designing innovation-oriented growth of tourism represent important impediments to the smart development of Košice tourism.

Kraków can be perceived as a best practice example of tourism industry being a part of the city smart specialization, supported with targeted policy measures. The city is not only cultural center and one of the most visited metropoles in Europe but also a unique example of creating a vibrant business environment gathering enterprises, foreign investors, researchers, scientists, academic community, and students. Based on the Kraków case, other cities striving to support tourism development in the vein of SS strategy might consider such key success factors like international openness of the city, a variety and density of cultural, sport and business events, modern infrastructure for science and R&D development, diversified portfolio of tourism products, a number of business support institutions and policy measures relevant for tourism and its promotion at an international scale.

Besides regional and city-level strategies and policies, we also need to acknowledge wider, country-level institutional contexts for the smart tourism development in both cities. The legal enforcement for credible commitments and laws directly regulating business activities represent a critical framework that may either enable or prevent local-level and bottom-up initiatives for sustainable growth.

Limitations and Future Research

The major limitation of this research stems from the secondary and selective nature of data. We used only secondary data sources, while the primary data, based on interviews or survey among key stakeholder groups, such as entrepreneurs, tourists, city residents, and policy makers might have deepened our evaluations and conclusions (Grillitsch & Asheim, 2018; Grillitsch, 2019). Another drawback is selective data use. Nevertheless, the selectivity was enforced by the comprehensive and complex nature of the SS concept and evaluation criteria. Acknowledging both limitations, we ensured the comparability of data and information for both cities, and the objectivity of processing and synthesizing them. Three researchers coded and structured the data, discussed results and resolved inconsistencies to avoid biases. Nevertheless, based on these limitations, we recommend that future research performs primary investigations and data sources to verify the current findings.

Another drawback is the threat of post hoc reasoning and binding results to theory when the case study uses deductive pattern-matching (Yin, 2018). We addressed this limitation by performing multiple, comparative case study instead of a single case. Two different development pathways in different settings allowed for a nuanced approach and being sensitive to alternative evaluations and conclusions (Yin, 2018;

Wadham & Warren, 2014; Wright et al., 2018). Moreover, the work of the research team instead of a single investigator enabled the conclusions based on reconciling different views and interpretations. Still, the potential biases in the results might be addressed by future research using a larger sample of case studies and quantitative methods to test the adherence of real-life processes to the SS policy principles.

References

ABSL. (2018). *The sector of modern business services in Poland*. Warsaw: ABSL

ABSL. (2020). *Business services sector in Poland 2020*. Retrieved from https://investinpomerania.pl/wp-content/uploads/2020/06/ABSL-Report-2020.pdf

Aranguren, M. J., Magro, E., Navarro, M., & Wilson, J. R. (2019). Governance of the territorial entrepreneurial discovery process: Looking under the bonnet of RIS3. *Regional Studies*, *53*(4), 451–461.

Asheim, B. T. (2019). Smart specialisation, innovation policy and regional innovation systems: What about new path development in less innovative regions?. *Innovation: The European Journal of Social Science Research*, *32*(1), 8–25.

Barzotto, M., Corradini, C., Fai, F. M., Labory, S., & Tomlinson, P. R. (2019). Enhancing innovative capabilities in lagging regions: An extra-regional collaborative approach to RIS3. *Cambridge Journal of Regions, Economy and Society*, *12*(2), 213–232.

Bianchi, P., & Labory, S. (2018). *Industrial policy for the manufacturing revolution: Perspectives on digital globalization*. London: Edward Elgar Publishing.

Bidroom. (2020). Retrieved from https://bidroom.com/pl

Borrás, S., & Jordana, J. (2016). When regional innovation policies meet policy rationales and evidence: A plea for policy analysis. *European Planning Studies*, *24*(12), 2133–2153.

Cai, Y., Normann, R., Pinheiro, R., & Sotarauta, M. (2018). Economic specialization and diversification at the country and regional level: Introducing a conceptual framework to study innovation policy logics. *European Planning Studies*, *26*(12), 2407–2426.

Calderwood, L. U., & Soshkin M. (2019). *The travel & tourism competitiveness report 2019*. Retrieved from http://www3.weforum.org/docs/WEF_TTCR_2019.pdf

Chen, M., Sui, Y., Liu, W., Liu, H., & Huang, Y. (2019). Urbanization patterns and poverty reduction: A new perspective to explore the countries along the Belt and Road. *Habitat International*, *84*, 1–14.

Cleantech Slovakia. (2020). Retrieved from www.cleantech.sk/en/

Crescenzi, R., de Blasio, G., & Giua, M. (2018). Cohesion Policy incentives for collaborative industrial research: Evaluation of a Smart Specialisation forerunner programme. *Regional Studies*, 1–13. https://doi.org/10.1080/00343404.2018.1502422

D'Adda, D., Guzzini, E., Iacobucci, D., & Palloni, R. (2019). Is Smart Specialisation Strategy coherent with regional innovative capabilities?. *Regional Studies*, *53*(7), 1004–1016.

Eisenhardt, K. M., & Graebner, M. E. (2007). Theory building from cases: Opportunities and challenges. *Academy of Management Journal*, *50*(1), 25–32.

EOCIC (European Observatory for Clusters and Industrial Change). (2019). *European cluster and industrial transformation trends report.* Luxemburg: Publications Office of the European Commission.

Estensoro, M., & Larrea, M. (2016). Overcoming policy making problems in smart specialization strategies: Engaging subregional governments. *European Planning Studies, 24*(7), 1319–1335.

European Cluster Observatory. (2012). *Emerging industries. Report on the methodology for their classification and on the most active, significant and relevant new emerging industrial sectors.* Luxemburg: Publications Office of the European Commission.

European Cluster Observatory. (2015). *Report. European cluster trends.* Luxemburg: Publications Office of the European Commission.

Eurostat. (2020). *Regional Statistics.* Retrieved from https://ec.europa.eu/eurostat/statistics-explained/index.php/Tourism_industries_-_economic_analysis

EU Science Hub. (2017). *Cultural and creative cities monitor,* 2017 edition. Retrieved from https://ec.europa.eu/jrc/en/publication/eur-scientific-and-technical-research-reports/cultural-and-creative-cities-monitor-2017-edition

Foray, D. (2014). *Smart specialisation: Opportunities and challenges for regional innovation policy.* New York: Routledge.

Foray, D. (2016). On the policy space of smart specialization strategies. *European Planning Studies, 24*(8), 1428–1437.

Foray, D. (2017). The economic fundamentals of smart specialization strategies. In S. Radosevic, A. Curaj, R. Gheorghiu, L. Andreescu & I. Wade (Eds.), *Advances in the theory and practice of smart specialization* (pp. 37–50). Cambridge, MA: Academic Press.

Foray, D. (2019). In response to 'Six critical questions about smart specialisation'. *European Planning Studies, 27*(10), 2066–2078.

Foray, D. (2020). Six additional replies—one more chorus of the S3 ballad. *European Planning Studies, 28*(8), 1685–1690.

Foray, D., Goddard, J., Beldarrain, X. G., Landabaso, M., McCann, P., Morgan, K., & Mulatero, F. (2012). *Guide to research and innovation strategies for smart specialisations* (RIS 3). Brussels: European Commission.

Gancarczyk, M., & Ujwary-Gil, A. (2020). Revitalizing industrial policy through smart, micro-level and bottom-up approaches. In A. Ujwary-Gil & M. Gancarczyk (Eds.), *New challenges in economic policy, business, and management* (pp. 11–29). Warsaw: Institute of Economics, Polish Academy of Sciences.

Gancarczyk, M., Najda-Janoszka, M., & Gancarczyk, J. (2020). Regional innovation system and policy in Malopolska, Poland: An institutionalised learning. In M. González-López & B. T. Asheim (Eds.). *Regions and innovation policies in Europe* (pp. 225–251). Cheltenham, U.K.: Edward Elgar Publishing.

Grillitsch, M. (2019). Following or breaking regional development paths: On the role and capability of the innovative entrepreneur. *Regional Studies, 53*(5), 681–691.

Grillitsch, M., & Asheim, B. (2018). Place-based innovation policy for industrial diversification in regions. *European Planning Studies, 26*(8), 1638–1662.

Iacobucci, D., & Guzzini, E. (2016). Relatedness and connectivity in technological domains: Missing links in S3 design and implementation. *European Planning Studies, 24*(8), 1511–1526.

KCGO. (2016a). *Krakow's development strategy "Here I want to live. Krakow 2030" (Krakow development strategy. "This is where I want to live. Krakow 2030").* Krakow: Krakow City Government Office. Retrieved from www.bip. krakow.pl/plik.php?zid=212318&wer=0&new=t&mode=shw

KCGO. (2016b). *Krakowski program wspierania przedsiębiorczości i rozwoju gospodarczego miasta 2016–2020 (The Krakow programme for supporting entrepreneurship and economic development of the city 2016–2020).* Krakow: Krakow City Government Office. Retrieved from www.bip.krakow.pl/plik.php ?zid=176469&wer=0&new=t&mode=shw

KCGO. (2014). *Tourism development strategy in Krakow for 2014–2020.* Krakow: Krakow City Government Office.

KCGO. (2016c). *Krakowski program wspierania przedsiębiorczości i rozwoju gospodarczego miasta 2016–2020 (The Krakow program for the support of entrepreneurship and economic development 2016–2020).* Retrieved from www.bip.Kraków.pl/?sub_dok_id=22598

KCGO. (2016d). *Transport policy for the city of Krakow for 2016–2025 (Polityka transportowa dla miasta Krakowa na lata 2016–2025).* Krakow: Krakow City Government Office.

KCGO. (2016e). *The safety improvement programme for the city of Kraków for 2018–2020 "Safe Kraków".* Krakow: Krakow City Government Office.

KCGO. (2016f). *Strategic programme for the promotion of the city of Kraków for 2016–2022.* Krakow: Krakow City Government Office.

KCGO. (2017). *The culture development program in Kraków until 2030 (Program rozwoju kultury w Krakowie do roku 2030).* Krakow: Krakow City Government Office.

KCGO. (2020). *City state report 2019.* Krakow: Krakow City Government Office.

Košice CGO (Košice City Government Office). (2019). *Expenses for the program—The city of culture and sport 2014–2021.* Budget of Košice City.

KRGO (Košice Regional Government Office). (2016). *Program of economic and social development of košice region for the period of 2016–2022.* Retrieved from https://web.vucke.sk/sk/uradna-tabula/rozvoj-regionu/program-hosp-socialneho-rozvoja/phsr_2016-2022.html

KRGO. (2013). *Regional innovation strategy of Košice region 2013–2020.* Retrieved from https://web.vucke.sk/sk/uradna-tabula/rozvoj-regionu/program-hosp-socialneho-rozvoja/dokumenty-publikacie/

KRGO. (2014). *Regional integrated territorial strategy 2014–2020.* Retrieved from https://web.vucke.sk/sk/uradna-tabula/rozvoj-regionu/program-hosp-socialneho-rozvoja/dokumenty-publikacie/

Lin, J. Y., & Wang, Y. (2020). Structural Change, Industrial Upgrading, and Middle-Income Trap. *Journal of Industry, Competition and Trade, 20*(2), 359–394.

Marschan-Piekkari, R., & Welch, C. (Eds.). (2011). *Rethinking the case study in international business and management research.* Cheltenham, U.K.: Edward Elgar Publishing.

McCann, P., & Ortega-Argilés, R. (2015). Smart specialization, regional growth and applications to European Union cohesion policy. *Regional Studies, 49*(8), 1291–1302.

Morgan, K., & Marques, P. (2019). The Public Animateur: Mission-led innovation and the "smart state" in Europe. *Cambridge Journal of Regions, Economy and Society*, 12(2), 179–193.

MRGO (Malopolska Regional Government Office). (2012). *Program strategiczny "Regionalna Strategia Innowacji Wojewodztwa Malopolskiego 2013–2020" (Strategic programme, "Regional Innovation Strategy of the Malopolska Region 2013–2020"); updates approved by the Management Board of the Malopolska region in 2012, 2013, 2014, 2015, 2016.* Krakow: MRGO.

MTCRD (Ministry of Transport, Construction, and Regional Development, Slovak Republic). (2020). Bratislava: Construction and Regional Development of the Slovak Republic.

OECD. (2018). *Rethinking urban sprawl: Moving towards sustainable cities.* Retrieved from https://read.oecd.org/10.1787/9789264189881-en?format=pdf

Orłowski, W., Gajewska, A., Smolensk, D., & Bartczak, Z. (2019). *Report on the state of Polish metropolises: Kraków.* PwC. Retrieved from www.pwc.pl/pl/publikacje/2019/raport-o-polskich-metropoliach-2019.html

Radosevic, S., Curaj, A., Gheorghiu, R., Andreescu, L., & Wade I., (Eds.). (2017). *Advances in the theory and practice of smart specialization.* Cambridge, MA: Academic Press.

Reimeris, R. (2016). New rules, same game: The case of Lithuanian Smart specialization. *European Planning Studies*, 24(8), 1561–1583.

Rodrik, D. (2014). Green industrial policy. *Oxford Review of Economic Policy*, 30(3), 469–491.

Seweryn, R., Berbeka, J., Niemczyk, A., & Borodako, K. (2017). *Economic impact of tourism on the economy of Krakow.* Cracow: Małopolska Tourist Organization.

Slovak Government. (2014). *National strategy of regional development in Slovak Republic.* Retrieved from www.vlada.gov.sk//data/files/6951_narodna_strategia_.pdf

Slovak Government. (2020). *Strategy of Tourism development in Slovak Republic for 2020.* Bratislava.

Stam, E. (2015). Entrepreneurial ecosystems and regional policy: A sympathetic critique. *European Planning Studies*, 23(9), 1759–1769.

Statistical Office of Slovak Republic. Financial database Finstat. (2020a). Retrieved from https://finstat.sk/analyzy/statistika-poctu-vzniknutych-a-zaniknutych-firiem#kosicky-kraj

Statistical Office of Slovak Republic. Data cube statistics. (2020b). Retrieved from https://finstat.sk/analyzy/statistika-poctu-vzniknutych-a-zaniknutych-firiem#kosicky-kraj

Statistics Poland. (2020). *Local data bank.* Retrieved (10 September 2020) from https://bdl.stat.gov.pl/BDL/start.

Tourism Support Act no. 91/2010 Col. Retrieved from www.zakonypreludi.sk/zz/2010-91

Varga, A., Sebestyén, T., Szabó, N., & Szerb, L. (2018). Estimating the economic impacts of knowledge network and entrepreneurship development in smart specialization policy. *Regional Studies*, 1–12. https://doi.org/10.1080/00343404.2018.1527026

Wadham, H., & Warren, R. C. (2014). Telling organizational tales: The extended case method in practice. *Organizational Research Methods* 17(1), 5–22.

WEF (World Economic Forum). (2019). *Travel and tourism competitiveness report*. Retrieved from http://www3.weforum.org/docs/WEF_TTCR_2019.pdf

Wright, A. L., Middleton, S., Hibbert, P., & Brazil, V. (2018). Getting on with field research using participant deconstruction. *Organizational Research Methods*, 1–21. https://doi.org/10.1177/1094428118782589

WTTC (World Travel & Tourism Council). (2020). Global Economic Impact & Trends 2020. Retrieved from https://wttc.org/Research/Economic-Impact

Yin, R. K. (2018). *Case study research and applications. Design and methods.* Los Angeles: Sage.

Part 3

Smart Growth of Enterprises, Clusters, and Networks

7 The Quadruple Helix Partnerships for Enterprise Eco-Innovation in Italian Macro-Regions Under the Lens of Smart Specialization Strategy

Ivano Dileo and Marco Pini

Introduction

Since its origin, the Europe 2020 Strategy indicated the strong link between growth and sustainable investments as key for implementing the smart specialization strategy (European Commission, 2017). In order to respond to the global socioeconomic challenges and facilitate a more efficient and greener economic ecosystem for citizens, the EU has promoted innovation models through the improvement of synergies between the private and the public sectors (European Commission, 2019). The green transition has proven to be crucial across all industrial sectors through the concept of eco-innovation by renewing many forms of products and technologies, also involving behaviors and cultural approaches. Over the years, eco-innovation has become increasingly connected to green growth under the lens of global climate change.

However, shifting growth trajectories from innovation-standard models to eco-innovation approaches is not easy. This is because the new technological paradigm and innovation-driven green strategies depend on complex issues, including the collaboration and relationships between actors and stakeholders at various levels (Fabrizi, Guarini, & Meliciani, 2018).

Enhancing cooperation through the perspective of the Quadruple Helix (QH) (Carayannis & Campbell, 2009; Leydesdorff, 2012) may be a consistent long-term strategy for achieving sustainable growth and increasing knowledge flows among partners via a mutual exchange of practices (Gouvea, Kassicieh, & Montoya, 2013). Unlike Triple Helix collaborations, which focus on the relationships between three components—industry, institutions, and firms, a QH collaboration has a fourth component: civil society. The inclusion of civil society in the collaboration process could enable knowledge to be shared more quickly and provide more responsible approaches to help firms to support internal innovation and also create greater social benefits.

From the smart specialization strategy (S3) point of view, the QH could strongly contribute to the development of regions (Kolehmainen et al., 2016; Lindberg, Danilda, & Torstensson, 2012). S3 models are based on innovation approaches in which, besides companies, research and innovation stakeholders, and public institutions, citizens should also be present as the main recipients and users of innovations. In this vein, implementing Smart Specialization strategies requires a quadruple-helix model in which an innovation includes users of products and services, placing them at the center in each step of the innovation process. This latter is increasingly important as new responses to the major environmental challenges necessarily require changes in cultural patterns and behaviors both at an individual and societal scale.

However, how well the QH model works may depend on the context and the innovation stages of a geographical region. In fact, the exploitation of collaborative networks relies on economic geography (Backman & Lööf, 2015; Ascani, Balland, & Morrison, 2020). In this regard, eco-innovation process, like other forms of innovation, is related to the regional context (Doloreux & Parto, 2005).

In Italy, regional innovation patterns depend not only on the technological performances of firms but also on the type of interactions between the actors in that region (Evangelista, Iammarino, Mastrostefano, & Silvani, 2002). Traditionally, the best-performing knowledge and institutional systems in Italy are located in the north (Camagni & Capello, 2017; Evangelista et al., 2002), where forms of proximity (geographical, technological, and cognitive) are more structured and lead to more established relationships among stakeholders.

This chapter explores whether and to what extent the QH model works differently and supports firms to achieve sustainable growth, which is one of the main targets of the S3. We examine the influence of the institutional support provided by public institutions (government and agencies), universities, and civil society on Italian SMEs in achieving eco-innovation. To the best of our knowledge, currently, there is no systematic empirical research focused on the relationship between eco-innovation and the QH model in the framework of the S3.

Our results highlight the differences between the more developed center–north and the less developed south. They indicate that the collaboration between firms and public institutions is crucial for investing in eco-innovation for firms located in southern Italy, and the collaboration with universities and civil society is more effective in the north. These results provide insights into decision-making for the implementation of the S3 (Grillitsch & Asheim, 2018; Ujwary-Gil, 2019). This is because the new environmental paradigm cannot ignore the importance of simultaneous forms of collaboration and geographical factors in the achievement of both sustainability and innovation in the new economic era, also when faced with complex and unexpected exogenous shocks.

The chapter is organized as follows. Literature background discusses the links between S3, eco-innovation, QH, and sets out our research questions. The methodological approach describes the data set and variables used in our analysis and the method. Finally, the results and discussion present the summary statistics, estimation results, and discussion. The chapter ends with the conclusion.

Literature Background

The Italian Context of the S3

Smart specialization strategy (S3) is an innovative model that is helping various parts of Europe to achieve long-term sustainable growth aimed at increasing firms' competitive advantages (European Commission, 2010). The concept of S3 was launched to contribute to smart growth for Europe 2020. Italy, like other EU countries, started to adopt the model in order to better qualify and benefit from structural funds. Italy is currently facing significant challenges from economic, social, and environmental points of view. However, according to the EU Innovation Union Scoreboard (European Commission, 2020), Italy is still considered as a Moderate Innovator due to a performance that is below the European average.

The contribution of the Italian S3 is thus to promote innovation and help to convert the results of R&I activities through the concentration of interventions and measures. The strategy relies on a multilevel and multistakeholder approach, with a focus also on the collaboration between private and public sectors aimed at exploiting the potential of firms and the knowledge assets of the regions. Crescenzi, de Blasio, and Giua (2020) focused on the importance of S3 for increasing the collaborative dimension of innovation policies. They also highlighted that these collaborations should take into consideration the differences in the needs of local innovation actors.

The analysis of Smart Specialization Strategies at the regional level has also identified the most significant areas and development trajectories for implementation plans. The National Strategy thus identifies five thematic areas (smart and sustainable industry, energy and environment; health, nutrition, quality of life; digital agenda, smart communities, intelligent mobility systems; tourism, cultural heritage and the creative industry; aerospace and defense) which lead in technological innovation of the regions, and represented by 12 areas of regional specialization (aerospace; agrifood; blue growth; green chemistry; design, creativity and made in Italy; energy; smart industry; sustainable mobility; health; smart, secure and inclusive communities; technologies for life environments; technologies for cultural heritage) (Ministry of Economic Development & Ministry of Education, University and Research, 2016).

One of the pioneering studies detecting the main priority areas of the S3 in Italy (Iacobucci, 2014) highlighted the need for better identification of the S3 theoretical framework and the related practical implementation. Another study (Iacobucci & Guzzini, 2016) showed that the priorities of the S3 proposed by the regions in Italy refer to broad domains and that regions have not yet established a joint classification method. Gianelle, Guzzo, and Mieszkowski (2020) underlined that a large number of priorities might hinder selective actions in some regions in Italy.

An empirical study by MET (2019) showed that of the 12 areas of Smart Specialization, those concerning design, creativity, and made in Italy comprise the highest share of businesses, which are mostly in the northwest. Conversely, southern regions seem to show similar strategies with a prevalence related to agri-food, energy (environment), life sciences, and sustainable mobility (Pellegrini & Di Stefano, 2017). Recently, the Italian Territorial Cohesion Agency, in collaboration with the Italian Union of Chambers of Commerce (Unioncamere), analyzed the strengths and weaknesses of the Italian regions under the lens of the S3. The main goal was to provide detailed and updated information on S3 for policy makers (Territorial Cohesion Agency & Unioncamere, 2020).

As indicated previously, most studies on the Italian S3 have concentrated on the coherence between technological domains and priorities between the regions. Currently, we are not aware of any study that has investigated the connection between eco-innovation and the QH in terms of the S3. This chapter is a first attempt to highlight the importance of firms' external support for innovation in increasing their propensity toward green investments from the perspective of long-term sustainable growth.

Smart Specialization Strategy and Eco-Innovation

Since 2012 the S3 has focused on tackling the structural weaknesses and potential of three priority areas: smart growth (based on knowledge and innovation); sustainable growth (for a greener and competitive economy); and inclusive growth (European Commission, 2017). Of these three priorities, eco-innovation is one of the most promising. In fact, the European Commission (2009) states that the socioecological transition is one of the greatest challenges for current and future societies, also recently emphasized with the European Green Deal (European Commission, 2019). According to the Eco-Innovation Action Plan (European Commission, 2011, p. 2), eco-innovation leads to more sustainable development, thanks to the more responsible use of natural resources.

Innovation is crucial for smart and green sustainable growth (Carayannis, Barth, & Campbell, 2012), as the green transition requires technological changes that foster productivity (Cassetta & Pini, 2017), disrupt conventional practices (Cassetta, Monarca, Dileo, Di Berardino, & Pini, 2020), and also involves institutional changes (Gouvea et al., 2013). Consequently, local and regional governmental authorities need to understand the advantages of emerging sectors because sustainable development should be addressed in the context of the gloCal knowledge economy and society (Carayannis & Campbell 2011, p. 329; Carayannis & von Zedtwitz 2005; Carayannis & Alexander 2006). Among scholars, Ghisetti and Montresor (2019) highlight the strict relationship between eco-innovation and investments in design.

As part of their innovation strategies for smart specialization, public authorities at regional and local levels need to design interventions that help to overcome specific market failures in this area, as well as improve the supply of green innovation, technologies, and solutions. This strategy thus represents an attempt to reorganize policy in order to combine new processes of entrepreneurial discovery and diversification across sectors (Foray et al., 2012; McCann & Ortega-Argilés, 2013). The latter can be developed through "a partnership-based policy process of discovery and learning on the part of both policy makers and entrepreneurs" (McCann & Ortega-Argilés, 2013, p. 10). Collaborative leadership favors a flexible decision-making process where actors play a key role according to their specific characteristics, background, and capacities (Foray et al., 2012). Innovation development for sustainable and green growth requires new coordination, alliances, and external links for firms as well as cross-cutting models.

Quadruple Helix and S3

The S3 developed in the post-linear era relies on a new knowledge and innovation base characterized by the transition toward the QH model. According to Carayannis and Rakhmatullin (2014), the Quadruple Helix Innovation System could lay the foundation for implementing Smart Specialization Strategies and strengthen the user-centric approach through multilevel collaborations and cooperation. The European Commission has encouraged the adoption of the QH approach for the second round of RIS3 (Research and Innovation Strategies for Smart Specialization) assessments (Foray et al., 2012), whose importance has also been highlighted by several scholars (Carayannis & Grigoroudis, 2016; Carayannis & Rakhmatullin, 2014; Cavallini, Soldi, Friedl, & Volpe, 2016).

The QH model (Carayannis & Campbell, 2009; Leydesdorff, 2012) was launched in an attempt to extend previous interaction models for innovation that involved industry, academia, and government (Triple Helix) (Etzkowitz, 2003). Basically, the S3 adopts the Mode 3 knowledge production system, enhancing bottom-up civil society initiatives to generate more effective and efficient cooperation (Carayannis & Campbell,

2012). Specifically, the QH model highlights the role of universities as they provide new knowledge and expertise across the community at different levels, thus generating competitive advantages (D'Este, Mahdi, Neely, & Rentocchini, 2012; Wang & Lu, 2007). The relationship with universities also helps firms to access basic and advanced information on green issues. This, in turn, helps to expand long-term research activities, thus obtaining proprietary technology through licensing, agreements, leverage funding through matching grant projects, and collaborating with research labs, which are the source of new recruits.

Furthermore, the QH model also highlights the role of government in terms of its ability to generate a more favorable local environment for innovation (Mars & Rios-Aguilar, 2010), by establishing the right conditions for businesses, research centers, and universities, as well as establishing how to best address public funds for research and development. Government (including also public agencies) plays a critical role by favoring the development of new green technologies through regulations (e.g., green standards) and incentives, as well as changes in consumer preferences and behavior via carbon pricing and taxation (Lash & Wellington, 2007). There are many ways by which government can encourage firms toward eco-innovation by strengthening cooperation even further (e.g., Boardman, 2009), thus promoting knowledge exchange between different sectors and actors (e.g., Archer & Cameron, 2009); helping to increase awareness about the advantages of the green economy; reducing uncertainty and, at the same time, increasing trust (Molina-Morales, Martínez-Fernández, & Torlò, 2011; Lundvall, 1992).

Finally, the QH model states that the interaction between industry, institutions, and academia, requires a fourth component, that is, civil society (Carayannis & Campbell, 2011). The QH model emphasizes the involvement of civil society as it is considered capable of strengthening the interaction among actors on the basis of cross-functional cooperation among diverse fields, bridging technological gaps in the codesign of research and innovation strategies (Deakin, Mora, & Reid, 2017). Civil society includes citizens, NGOs, labor unions that are more growth-oriented as consumers, and includes individuals characterized by interests such as environmental and social ones, rather than economic interests (Hock Heng, Mohd Othman, Md Rasli & Jawad Iqbald, 2012).

Overall, civil society represents the foundation on which innovations are developed by the interplay between academia, industry, and government (Leydesdorff & Etzkowitz, 2003; Leydesdorff, 2005; Lindberg, Danilda, & Torstensson, 2012). It is worth to mention that civil society encourages the eco-innovation of firms (Yang & Holgaard, 2012): indirectly, by raising community's awareness about environmental problems (Betsill & Corell, 2001) in relation to lifestyles and consumption habits and favoring green technologies with cultural settings (Yang & Holgaard, 2012); and directly, by impacting firm's innovation strategies through the influence of particular stakeholders (Luxmore & Hull, 2011). Due to its less formalized character, civil society may be more capable of giving voice to marginalized entrepreneurs and firms in nontraditional industries. This may depend on the institutionalized character of the region as well as the specific development stage (Dileo & García Pereiro, 2019).

The interplay among all actors has long been underestimated or ignored in innovation processes (Ivanova, 2014). In line with the QH model, innovation evolves according to an inclusive and pluralistic process involving all the stakeholders as active players in experimenting with new ways of production, products, and services in a global context (Gancarczyk, & Gancarczyk, 2018), which is strongly characterized by sustainability (Chaaben & Mansouri, 2017; Yang & Holgaard, 2012). In this regard, the green quadruple helix (Gouvea et al., 2013) indicates the involvement of industry, government, university, and civil society along the entire green economy value chain, which boosts the global green economy and green firms' competitiveness (Gouvea et al., 2013; Nidumolu, Prahalad, & Rangaswami, 2009; Porter & Reinhardt, 2007). Nevertheless, many regions may be insufficiently developed in terms of innovation due to having a relatively weaker university system in terms of fostering knowledge exchange and transfer process.

The impact of the QH may depend on the geographical location of firms, which in turn may influence the entrepreneurial potential, development, and levels of wealth of the region. Also, the need for firms to improve their competitiveness depends on the characteristic of regions where they operate, which in turn influences the efficient functioning of the QH (Nordberg, 2015; Höglund & Linton, 2018).

Therefore, innovation policy in the EU needs to consider the specific resources, governance, and institutional capacity of each region (Rodrigues & Teles, 2017) and boost the collaborative networking that is at the basis of any smart specialization (Gertler, 2003; Morgan, 2016). This is why collaborations between industry and public institutions (government and agencies) work in some regions, and in others, the interplay with universities and civil society may be more important. In such regions, social and community groups often play a dominant role. The impact of civil society on sustainable growth is likely to take place in more developed regions where the basic elements of the QH model are present and the involvement of civil society in consultation and decision-making processes is more evolved. In less developed regions, where firms are less equipped, public institutions may be critical in helping them to engage in competitiveness issues (Kolehmainen et al., 2016).

Based on all these considerations, we formulated our research questions (RQ):

RQ1: Does the collaboration with public institutions impact differently on the probability of SMEs engaging in eco-innovation practices when they are located in less developed regions compared to more developed regions?

RQ2: Does the collaboration with universities impact differently on the probability of SMEs engaging in eco-innovation practices when they are located in less developed regions compared to more developed regions?

RQ3: Does the collaboration with civil society impact differently on the probability of SMEs engaging in eco-innovation practices when they are located in less developed regions compared to more developed regions?

Methodological Approach

Data and Variables

The data were drawn from two surveys carried out by Unioncamere (Italian Union of Chambers of Commerce) in 2018 and 2019. Each survey is based on a representative sample of 3,000 Italian manufacturing firms with at least five employees (Unioncamere, 2018; 2019).

We merged the two data sets and obtained almost 6,000 firms, corresponding to 4.7% of the whole Italian population in terms of firms and 6.5% in terms of employees. The survey was conducted by CATI (Computer-Assisted Telephone Interviewing) with the aim of gathering both qualitative and quantitative information on the firm, including the structural characteristics. The maximum sampling error is small (e = 1.8%; α = 0.95%).

The stratification has taken into account three dimensions of the firm: (i) industry (24 divisions of the section C—manufacturing sector—of the Nace Rev.2 classification); (ii) size class in terms of employees (5–9, 10–19, 20–49, 50+); (iii) geographical location (northwest, northeast, center, south). Data set also includes information on product and process innovation and digitalization, green innovation, R&D, and external cooperation. We focused on SMEs as they form the backbone of the European economy, make diverse contributions to economic and social well-being and provide around 50% of the value added by manufacturing (OECD, 2019; Matt & Rauch, 2020).

We divided the whole sample on the basis of the geographical location of firms. Specifically, we investigated the impact of the QH on firms located in the less developed south and on those firms located in the more developed center–north. Our dependent variable is *Eco-innovation*, which captures one of the main targets of the S3 related to sustainable growth (European Commission, 2017). One of the most common interpretation of eco-innovation refers to process and product green innovation:

"develop new ideas, behavior, products, and processes, apply or introduce them and which contribute to a reduction of environmental burdens or to ecologically specified sustainability targets" (Rennings, 2000, p. 322; for a review, see Horbach, 2008). Accordingly, *Eco-innovation* takes value 1 whether a firm invested in green technologies involving sustainable products and/or processes (energy efficiency; emissions, raw materials, and waste reduction; recycling).

To measure the role of the QH (Carayannis & Campbell, 2009; Leydesdorff, 2012), we included three variables: (i) *Public institutions*, coded 1 whether the firm has strong relationships with public institutions (Chambers of Commerce, local public authorities, government, public agencies, etc.), (ii) *University*, coded 1 whether the firm has a strong relationship with universities, for example, for research projects, cooperation agreements, and technological transfer; (iii) *Civil society*, coded 1 whether the firm has a strong relationship with civil society such as social groups, NGOs, community-based organizations, voluntary organizations and cultural organizations (Yang & Holgaard, 2012). Finally, we included one more variable (Quadruple Helix) approximating for the simultaneous effect of each helix; it takes value 1 whether the firm has strong relationships with public institutions, universities, civil society.

We control for the investments in R&D through a dummy variable (*R&D*) taking value 1 whether the firm invested in R&D (Cuerva, Triguero-Cano, & Córcoles, 2014): this variable is mostly used as a proxy of technological push factor (e.g., Sáez-Martínez, Díaz-García, & Gonzalez-Moreno, 2016). Then, we distinguished the firms according to Pavitt sectoral taxonomy by using the two-digit activities Nace rev.2 Classification (Bogliacino & Pianta, 2016): *Suppliers dominated, Scale intensive, Specialized suppliers, Science based*.

We also control for firm's age. Thus, we included a continuous variable (*Age*) accounting for the years since its establishment (e.g., Del Río, Romero-Jordán, & Peñasco, 2017). This variable is a proxy that captures the impact of firms' knowledge and experience that are meaningful for the choice to invest in eco-innovation (Rave, Goetzke, & Larch, 2011).

Finally, we control for firm's size. We included a continuous variable (*Size*) that accounts for the number of employees (e.g., Del Río et al., 2017). Firm's size has been found to be positively related with eco-innovation, as in larger firms factors such as the presence of higher skilled human capital and more financial resources (Kammerer 2009; Rave et al. 2011), economies of scale (Mazzanti & Zoboli, 2009), and lower constraints, are likely to be associated with the decision to invest in green technologies (De Marchi, 2012). A description of the variables is included in Table 7.1.

Table 7.1 Variables description

Dependent variable	
Eco-innovation	Dummy variable: 1 whether the firm invested in green technologies involving sustainable products and/ or processes (energy efficiency; emissions, raw materials, and waste reduction; recycling)
Independent variables	
Public Institutions	Dummy variable: 1 whether the firm has strong relationships with public institutions (e.g., Chambers of Commerce, local public authorities, government, and agencies)
University	Dummy variable: 1 whether the firm has a strong relationship with universities
Civil society	Dummy variable: 1 whether the firm has a strong relationship with civil society such as social groups, NGOs, community-based organizations, voluntary organizations, and cultural organizations
Quadruple Helix	Dummy variable: 1 if the firm has a strong relationship with public institutions, universities, civil society
Control variables	
R&D	Dummy variable: 1 whether the firm invested in R&D
Suppliers dominated	Dummy variable: 1 whether the firm belongs to Suppliers dominated sector (Pavitt Taxonomy)
Scale intensive	Dummy variable: 1 whether the firm belongs to Scale intensive sector (Pavitt Taxonomy)
Specialized suppliers	Dummy variable: 1 whether the firm belongs to the Specialized suppliers sector (Pavitt Taxonomy)
Science based	Dummy variable: 1 whether the firm belongs to Science-based sector (Pavitt Taxonomy)
Age	Continuous variable: Number of years since the establishment
Size	Continuous variable: Number of employees

Methods

For modeling such a binary dependent variable, a suitable econometric model is a probit model (Wooldridge, 2010, pp. 453–459). Although the standard linear regression is a model where the conditional mean of the outcome is the linear combination of the predictors, the probit model is a nonlinear model that modeling the conditional probability of a successful outcome. In this chapter, probit models were specified for modeling the conditional probability that a sample of Italian manufacturing SMEs has invested in eco-innovation through the support of the QH. In particular, we used the following probit specification:

$$P\left(EI_i = 1 \mid PI_i, UN_i, CS_i, S_i,\right) = P\left(\beta_0 + \beta_1 PI_i + \beta_2 UN_i + \beta_3 CS_i + \beta_4 S_i + \varepsilon_i > 0\right)$$
$$= \Phi\left(\beta_0 + \beta_1 PI_i + \beta_2 UN_i + + \beta_3 CS_i + \beta_4 S_i\right)$$

where *EI* represents the probability that the firm *i* invested in eco-innovation. The main independent variables are *PI*, *UN*, and *CS* indicating if the firm has a strong relationship with Public institutions, University, and Civil Society, respectively. *S* is a vector including the control variables (for more details, see Table 7.1). Φ is a standard normal cumulative distribution function and ε is the normally distributed random error that captures any other unknown factors.

However, to get more accurate and precise analyses, in our model, the predictors are measuring for how much the mean of the outcome variable change when that predictor is varying while holding all the other predictors constant at some values. This is what we call the *marginal effect* of the specific predictor. The most common marginal effects reported are those where all the other predictors are set to their mean values, that is, the so-called marginal effects at the means (MEMs). Specifically, for binary independent variables, marginal effects show how $P(Y = 1)$ changes as the independent variable changes from 0 to 1, after controlling for the other variables in the model. For categorical variables with more than two possible values, marginal effects show how $P(Y = 1)$ changes for cases in one category relative to the reference category. For continuous independent variables, marginal effects show how $P(Y = 1)$ changes as the independent variable changes by a one unit (Cameron & Trivedi, 2010; Williams, 2012). Stata version 15 was used for all the estimates.

Results and Discussion

Table 7.2 displays summary statistics. More than 30% of firms surveyed invested in eco-innovation, both in south (35.3%) and in central–north (38.0%). About 14% has strong relationships with public institutions both in the south and central–north (13.1% and 13.9%, respectively); 10–12% has strong collaborations with university whereas 7–8% has strong relationships with civil society.

Table 7.2 Summary statistics

	South (Obs. 886)				Center–North (Obs. 4,824)			
	Mean	Std. Dev	Min	Max	Mean	Std. Dev	Min	Max
Dependent variable								
Eco-innovation	0.353	0.478	0	1	0.380	0.485	0	1
Independent variables								
Public institutions	0.131	0.338	0	1	0.139	0.346	0	1
University	0.102	0.302	0	1	0.122	0.327	0	1
Civil society	0.072	0.259	0	1	0.079	0.270	0	1
Quadruple helix	0.021	0.145	0	1	0.027	0.161	0	1
Control variables								
R&D	0.326	0.469	0	1	0.371	0.483	0	1
Suppliers dominated	0.583	0.493	0	1	0.571	0.495	0	1
Scale intensive	0.273	0.446	0	1	0.208	0.406	0	1
Specialized suppliers	0.114	0.318	0	1	0.174	0.379	0	1
Science based	0.029	0.169	0	1	0.046	0.210	0	1
Age	32.919	11.221	5	110	36.377	12.465	3	118
Size	22.216	33.007	5	245	30.278	42.223	5	249

The percentage of firms invested in R&D is slightly higher in the center–north (37.1%) than in the south (32.6%). Firms located in center–north are relatively older if compared to those located in the south (average age: 36 years old versus 33 years old), larger (average size in terms of employees: 30 versus 22); more concentrated in specialized suppliers (17.4% versus 11.4%) and science-based (4.6% versus 2.9%) sectors; however, the suppliers dominated category involves almost 60% of the firms in both regions.

Tables 7.3 and 7.4 report the correlation matrices. Collinearity problem does not emerge because correlation coefficients are all below the critical value of 0.7 (Tabachnick & Fidell, 1996) and variance inflation factor (VIF) is below the critical value of 10 (Yoo et al., 2014).

Table 7.5 shows the estimates of our binary probit regression. Columns 1 and 3 report the results for firms located in southern Italy, whereas columns 2 and 4 present the results related to firms located in central–north. We also report the Wald chi-square. The Wald chi-square test statistic for the intercepts is significant in both models and associated with a p value <.0001. The probability of Wald chi-square suggests that there is a significant effect of the predictors, that is, at least one of the regression

Table 7.3 Correlation matrix: South (Obs. 886)

	1	2	3	4	5	6	7	8	9	10	11
1. Public institutions	1.000										
2. University	0.224	1.000									
3. Civil society	0.448	0.325	1.000								
4. Quadruple helix	0.381	0.440	0.530	1.000							
5. R&D	0.108	0.236	0.169	0.163	1.000						
6. Suppliers dominated	0.070	0.064	0.041	0.094	-0.115	1.000					
7. Scale intensive	-0.050	-0.055	-0.005	-0.056	0.076	-0.726	1.000				
8. Specialized suppliers	-0.045	-0.015	-0.059	-0.053	0.008	-0.425	-0.220	1.000			
9. Science based	0.012	-0.014	0.003	-0.026	0.122	-0.206	-0.107	-0.062	1.000		
10. Age	0.033	-0.043	-0.011	-0.002	-0.053	0.003	0.019	-0.018	-0.027	1.000	
11. Size	0.146	0.238	0.149	0.127	0.181	-0.039	0.018	-0.009	0.082	-0.006	1.000
VIF	1.28	1.22	1.35		1.12		1.09	1.07	1.05	1.01	1.10

Table 7.4 Correlation matrix: Center–North (Obs. 4824)

	1	2	3	4	5	6	7	8	9	10	11
1. Public institutions	1.000										
2. University	0.277	1.000									
3. Civil society	0.399	0.294	1.000								
4. Quadruple helix	0.411	0.443	0.563	1,000							
5. R&D	0.186	0.173	0.142	0.119	1.000						
6. Suppliers dominated	-0.009	-0.068	0.003	-0.013	-0.111	1.000					
7. Scale intensive	-0.020	-0.002	-0.039	-0.021	0.044	-0.592	1.000				
8. Specialized suppliers	-0.005	0.054	0.007	0.016	0.049	-0.530	-0.236	1.000			
9. Science based	0.068	0.066	0.056	0.044	0.089	-0.254	-0.113	-0.101	1.000		
10. Age	0.015	-0.003	0.010	-0.031	0.019	-0.010	0.018	-0.012	0.010	1.000	
11. Size	0.257	0.234	0.184	0.183	0.278	-0.150	0.046	0.100	0.083	0.070	1.000
VIF	1.28	1.17	1.25		1.12		1.10	1.10	1.05	1.01	1.19

Table 7.5 Marginal effects at the means for eco-innovation

	South	Center–North	South	Center–North
	dy/dx (1)	dy/dx (2)	dy/dx (3)	dy/dx (4)
Independent variables				
Public institutions	0.193***	0.009		
	(0.054)	(0.024)		
University	0.002	0.055**		
	(0.062)	(0.023)		
Civil society	0.033	0.128***		
	(0.074)	(0.030)		
Quadruple helix			0.042	0.132***
			(0.107)	(0.047)
Control variables				
R&D	0.248***	0.215***	0.259***	0.223***
	(0.036)	(0.015)	(0.036)	(0.015)
Scale intensive	−0.008	0.078***	−0.020	0.074***
	(0.039)	(0.019)	(0.038)	(0.019)
Specialized suppliers	0.066	−0.027	0.051	−0.028
	(0.054)	(0.019)	(0.053)	(0.019)
Science based	−0.149*	0.101***	−0.155**	0.108***
	(0.080)	(0.036)	(0.079)	(0.036)
Age	0.001	0.000	0.001	0.000
	(0.002)	(0.001)	(0.001)	(0.001)
Size	0.002***	0.001***	0.002***	0.001***
	(0.001)	(0.000)	(0.001)	(0.000)
Obs.	886	4,824	886	4,824
Wald chi-square	95.85***	438.6***	78.37***	415.34***
Pseudo R^2	0.0879	0.0755	0.0724	0.0710

Note: (a) Dependent variable: eco-innovation = 1 if the firm invest invested in green technologies. (b) The table displays marginal effects at the means (MEMs). (c) Robust standard errors in parentheses. (d) Wald test for all the explanatory variables is reported. (e) Reference Pavitt category: Suppliers dominated. *** $p < 0.01$, ** $p < 0.05$, * $p < 0.1$.

coefficients in the model is different from zero. McFadden's pseudo R^2 statistic is very small (0.088 in south and 0.075 in center–north, respectively). However, interpretation of this statistic should be made with great caution because it simply measures the level of improvement over the intercept model offered by the full model.

A positive/negative coefficient means that an increase/decrease in predictor will result in an increase/decrease in the predicted probability. For measuring the effects of predictors on the dependent variable, one of the marginal effects methods should be used. Marginal effects in Table 7.5 are calculated using the predictors' mean values.

We found that having strong relationships with public institutions positively affects the likelihood for firms of investing in eco-innovation in Southern Italy. The marginal effects of public institutions are positive and significant at 1% ($p < 0.01$; Model 1). This finding is in line with Zhang, Wang, Zhao, and Zhang (2017), who found a positive effect of the institutional support for product and process innovation. Our results may be explained by the fact that in less developed regions, due to their structural constraints (credit access, risk aversion, low internationalization), the relationship with public institutions may be more determinant and the support more effective. SMEs' investments to develop a new technology or new technology practices can be hindered by project scale and cost, low expertise, and technical and business risk. Thus, in less developed regions, public institutions can contribute to the development of the overall industrial process that, otherwise, might not emerge spontaneously.

Concerning the relationships with universities, we found that firms having a strong relationship with universities are more likely to make investments in eco-innovation when located in northern regions ($p < 0.01$). This finding is in line with Bellucci and Pennacchio (2016), who highlighted the importance of universities as a source of knowledge for firm's innovation activities.

Lagging behind the average wealth levels, in less developed regions, it is more likely that the collaboration with public institutions represents the efficacy solution to firms' structural burdens; conversely, in northern regions, the collaboration between university and industry may be the efficient solution for bypassing their innovation frontiers and undertake new technological trajectories, involving firms that are less constrained by structural burdens. About the relationships with civil society, this helix seems to work only in the case of firms located in northern regions. In fact, marginal effects are positive (M.E. = 0.128; Model 2) and statistically significant at 1%. This probably happens more in the north, where the inclusion of civil society in the decision-making mechanism is around more time, and the knowledge system is stronger. In this environment, the relationships between firm and civil society are more pervasive and the awareness of sustainability issues also increases.

Overall, these results show that the QH exerts its power differently depending on the geographic location of firms and the actors involved in the collaboration. In fact, by analyzing the overall effect of the QH, we show that the quadruple helix variable is statistically significant only in the center–north ($p < 0.01$; Model 4). This result corroborates the fact that in the center–north, the joint effect of the four helices positively influences eco-innovations than in the south, where it is more likely that a lack of coordination mechanisms among actors seems to be emerged more heavily.

Concerning control variables, marginal effects of R&D proved to be crucial in influencing the probability of investing in eco-innovation both for firms located in south and those located in center–north (M.E. = 0.248

and = 0.215, respectively; Models 1 and 2). Their marginal effects are both statistically significant at 1%. Our findings corroborate the results found in previous research (e.g., Horbach, Rammer, & Rennings, 2012; Muscio, Nardone, & Stasi, 2017).

Furthermore, Italian firms belonging to scale-intensive and science-based industrial sectors are more likely to be associated with the likelihood for firms of investing in eco-innovation only in northern regions (M.E. = 0.078 and = 0.101, respectively; Model 2). Marginal effects are positive and statistically significant at 1%. Only for firms located in southern Italy, the marginal effects for specialized suppliers are negatively related to eco-innovation at 10% (M.E. = –0.149; Model 1).

Finally, size seems to be a good predictor for all the firms surveyed. Despite its low marginal effects, size is positive and statistically significant at 1%. These results are in line with Horbach et al. (2012) and Cuerva et al. (2014).

Conclusion

Implications for Theory

In this chapter, we examined how the QH works differently and supports firms located in less (southern) and more developed (central–northern) macro-regions in their quest for sustainable growth, which is one of the main targets of the smart specialization strategy (Carayannis & Grigoroudis, 2016; Carayannis & Rakhmatullin, 2014). Our results indicate that in the more developed macro-region (center–north), the direct effects of single helices and the overall impact of QH seem to be emerging. In particular, the relationships with university and civil society exert a higher significant effect than in the south. It is more likely that the context characterized by higher quality and effectiveness of universities, the relatively more advanced technological regime as well as the stronger knowledge production system have over the years favored the consolidation of a networking system. Conversely, in the less developed macro-region (South), only the basic supportive functions of industry–government collaboration seem to be implemented. Thus, the efficacy of the collaboration proves to be place-based according to the characteristics of the region (Höglund & Linton, 2018; Nordberg, 2015; Doloreux & Parto, 2005; Evangelista et al., 2002).

Phenomena such as corruption but also uncertainty regarding the importance of the interrelations among various actors may, directly and indirectly, influence the social role of the QH. These factors weaken the active participation of the community in the interaction with other helices. In fact, user-oriented innovations may be more effective if the national response to social challenges includes structural, cultural, and behavioral changes in civil society (Yang & Holgaard, 2012). Another important factor that differentiates the impact of the QH is the composition of the participant group. Certain groups and sectors might require some competences, more tailored approaches.

Our chapter contributes to filling the gap in the literature by empirically exploring the different QH support on the adoption of environmental practices by firms (Gouvea et al., 2013) in more and less developed macro-regions, thus supporting policy makers in the attempt to better implement the S3 (Grillitsch & Asheim, 2018; Ujwary-Gil, 2019).

Implications for Policy

The policy measures aimed at reinforcing the relationships between actors should take into account the features and the level of effectiveness of the actors (Foray et al., 2012; European Commission, 2019). This means that before fostering relationships, the strength of that particular actor needs to be understood. The involvement of civil society in the collaboration road to an eco-innovation revolution is of great importance (Yang & Holgaard, 2012) as it provides direct support in the implementation of government policies, helps the dissemination of information, and increases the eco-awareness that is crucial for spreading the importance of the green transition. Eco-innovation implies not only effective use of new technologies but also an increase in quality and efficiency with regard to the mitigation of environmental impacts. The latter requires the support of diverse stakeholders, including communities that need to increase their awareness regarding the importance of their involvement in the process of creation of (eco) innovation. Eco-innovation is transversal and can be introduced across economic sectors and with great potential in fostering strategic and cross-collaboration. Regions should consider both requests from the demand and supply sides when planning for eco-innovation.

Limitations and Future Research

Our approach presents some limitations. First, the cross-sectional nature of the analysis impedes the cause–effect mechanism from being investigated in depth. Second, we focused only on manufacturing. Third, we did not consider firm's characteristics related to governance. Finally, we did not investigate the potential presence of nonlinear effects. Future research should investigate what type of expertise may be more suitable in multi-stakeholder collaboration. Scholars could also further investigate these relationships through panel model analyses, also including agricultural and services. Cross-country analyses that take into account, for instance, family governance could also be conducted.

Acknowledgments

We wish to thank Alessandro Rinaldi, who provided us the possibility to realize this chapter. The views expressed in the chapter are those of the authors and not of the institution they are affiliated with.

References

Archer, D., & Cameron, A. (2009). *Collaborative leadership—How to succeed in an interconnected world*. Oxford: Butterworth- Heinemann.
Ascani, A., Balland, P. A., & Morrison, A. (2019). Heterogeneous foreign direct investment and local innovation in Italian provinces. *Structural Change and Economic Dynamics, 53*(2020), 388–401. https://doi.org/10.1016/j.strueco.2019.06.004
Backman, M., & Lööf, H. (2015). The geography of innovation and entrepreneurship. *The Annals of Regional Science, 55*(1), 1–6. https://doi.org/10.1007/s00168-015-0713-x
Bellucci, A., & Pennacchio, L. (2016). University knowledge and firm innovation: Evidence from European countries. *The Journal of Technology Transfer, 41*(4), 730–752. https://doi.org/10.1007/s10961-015-9408-9
Betsill, M. M., & Corell, E. (2001). NGO influence in international environmental negotiations: A framework for analysis. *Global Environmental Politics, 1*(4), 65–85. https://doi.org/10.1162/152638001317146372
Boardman, P. C. (2009). Government centrality to university—industry interactions: University research centers and the industry involvement of academic researchers. *Research Policy, 38*(10), 1505–1516. https://doi.org/10.1016/j.respol.2009.09.008
Bogliacino, F., & Pianta, M. (2016). The Pavitt Taxonomy, revisited: Patterns of innovation in manufacturing and services. *Economia Politica, 33*(2), 153–180. https://doi.org/10.1007/s40888-016-0035-1
Camagni, R., & Capello, R. (2017). Regional innovation patterns and the EU regional policy reform: Towards smart innovation policies. In *Seminal studies in regional and urban economics* (pp. 313–343). Cham: Springer.
Cameron, A. C., & Trivedi, P. K. (2010). *Microeconometrics using stata*. College Station, TX: Stata Press.
Carayannis, E., & Alexander, J. (2006). *Global and local knowledge: Glocal transatlantic public-private partnerships for research and technological development*. London: Palgrave Macmillan.
Carayannis, E. G., Barth, T. D., & Campbell, D. F. (2012). The Quintuple Helix innovation model: Global warming as a challenge and driver for innovation. *Journal of Innovation and Entrepreneurship, 1*(1), 1–12. https://doi.org/10.1186/2192-5372-1-2
Carayannis, E. G., & Campbell, D. F. (2009). 'Mode 3' and 'Quadruple Helix': Toward a 21st century fractal innovation ecosystem. *International Journal of Technology Management, 46*(3–4), 201–234.
Carayannis, E. G., & Campbell, D. F. (2011). Open innovation diplomacy and a 21st century fractal research, education and innovation (FREIE) ecosystem: Building on the quadruple and quintuple helix innovation concepts and the

"mode 3" knowledge production system. *Journal of the Knowledge Economy*, 2(3), 327–372. https://doi.org/10.1007/s13132-011-0058-3

Carayannis, E. G., & Campbell, D. (2012). *Mode 3 knowledge production in quadruple helix innovation systems: 21st-Century democracy, innovation, and entrepreneurship for development*. New York: Springer.

Carayannis, E. G., & Grigoroudis, E. (2016). Quadruple innovation helix and smart specialization: knowledge production and national competitiveness. *Foresight and STI Governance*, 10(1), 31–42. http://dx.doi.org/10.17323/1995-459X.2016.1.31.42

Carayannis, E. G., & Rakhmatullin, R. (2014). The quadruple/quintuple innovation helixes and smart specialisation strategies for sustainable and inclusive growth in Europe and beyond. *Journal of the Knowledge Economy*, 5(2), 212–239. https://doi.org/10.1007/s13132-014-0185-8

Carayannis, E. G., & Von Zedtwitz, M. (2005). Architecting gloCal (global—local), real-virtual incubator networks (G-RVINs) as catalysts and accelerators of entrepreneurship in transitioning and developing economies: lessons learned and best practices from current development and business incubation practices. *Technovation*, 25(2), 95–110. https://doi.org/10.1016/S0166-4972(03)00072-5

Cassetta, E., Monarca, U., Dileo, I., Di Berardino, C., & Pini, M. (2020). The relationship between digital technologies and internationalisation. Evidence from Italian SMEs. *Industry and Innovation*, 27(4), 311–339. https://doi.org/10.1080/13662716.2019.1696182

Cassetta, E., & Pini, M. (2017). The green investments and competitiveness of the Italian manufacturing system. *Sinergie Italian Journal of Management*, 35(Jan-Apr), 141–163. https://doi.org/10.7433/s102.2017.11

Cavallini, S., Soldi, R., Friedl, J., & Volpe, M. (2016). *Using the quadruple helix approach to accelerate the transfer of research and innovation results to regional growth*. European Union Committee of the Regions. Retrieved from http://cor.europa.eu

Chaaben, N., & Mansouri, F. (2017). Quadruple innovation helix model: An engine for a smart growth. In *Challenges of Europe: International Conference Proceedings* (pp. 175–191). Split, Croatia: University of Split.

Crescenzi, R., de Blasio, G., & Giua, M. (2020). Cohesion policy incentives for collaborative industrial research: Evaluation of a smart specialisation forerunner programme. *Regional Studies*, 54(10), 1341–1353. https://doi.org/10.1080/00343404.2018.1502422

Cuerva, M. C., Triguero-Cano, Á., & Córcoles, D. (2014). Drivers of green and non-green innovation: Empirical evidence in Low-Tech SMEs. *Journal of Cleaner Production*, 68(1), 104–113. https://doi.org/10.1016/j.jclepro.2013.10.049

D'Este, P., Mahdi, S., Neely, A., & Rentocchini, F. (2012). Inventors and entrepreneurs in academia: What types of skills and experience matter? *Technovation*, 32(5), 293–303. https://doi.org/10.1016/j.technovation.2011.12.005

De Marchi, V. (2012). Environmental innovation and R&D cooperation: Empirical evidence from Spanish manufacturing firms. *Research Policy*, 41(3), 614–623. https://doi.org/10.1016/j.respol.2011.10.002

Del Río, P., Romero-Jordán, D., & Peñasco, C. (2017). Analysing firm-specific and type-specific determinants of eco-innovation. *Technological and Economic*

Development of Economy, 23(2), 270–295. https://doi.org/10.3846/2029491
3.2015.1072749

Deakin, M., Mora, L., & Reid, A. (2017, August). Smart specialisation strategies in the post-linear era on research and innovation. In *10th International
Conference for Entrepreneurship, Innovation, and Regional Development
(ICEIRD 2017): University-Industry Links: Coproducing Knowledge, Innovation and Growth. Conference Proceedings, Thessaloniki* (pp. 529–540).
Retrieved from www.napier.ac.uk/~/media/worktribe/output-998412/smart-
specialisation-strategies-in-the-post-linear-era-of-research-and-innovation.
pdf

Dileo, I., & García Pereiro, T. (2019). Assessing the impact of individual and
context factors on the entrepreneurial process. A cross-country multilevel
approach. *International Entrepreneurship and Management Journal, 15*,
1393–1441. https://doi.org/10.1007/s11365-018-0528-1

Doloreux, D., & Parto, S. (2005). Regional innovation systems: Current discourse and unresolved issues. *Technology in Society, 27*(2), 133–153. https://
doi.org/10.1016/j.techsoc.2005.01.002

Etzkowitz, H. (2003). Innovation in innovation: The triple helix of university-
industry-government relations. *Social Science Information, 42*(3), 293–337.
https://doi.org/10.1177/05390184030423002

European Commission. (2009). *The World in 2025. Rising Asia and socioecological transition*. Brussels: European Commission. Retrieved from http://
ec.europa.eu/research/social-sciences/pdf/the-world-in-2025-report_en.pdf

European Commission. (2010). *Regional policy contributing to smart growth
in Europe 2020*. Retrieved from https://ec.europa.eu/regional_policy/sources/
docoffic/official/communic/smart_growth/comm2010_553_en.pdf

European Commission. (2011). *Communication from the Commission to
the European Parliament, the Council, the European Economic and Social
Committee and the Committee of the regions*. Innovation for a sustainable
Future—The Eco-innovation Action Plan (Eco-AP), Retrieved from https://eur-
lex.europa.eu/legal content/EN/TXT/PDF/?uri=CELEX:52011DC0899&from
=EN

European Commission. (2017). *Strengthening innovation in Europe's regions:
Strategies for resilient, inclusive and sustainable growth*. Retrieved from https://
ec.europa.eu/regional_policy/sources/docoffic/2014/com_2017_376_2_en.pdf

European Commission. (2019). *The European Green Deal*. Retrieved from
https://eur-lex.europa.eu/resource.html?uri=cellar:b828d165-1c22-11ea-
8c1f-01aa75ed71a1.0002.02/DOC_1&format=PDF

European Commission. (2020). *European Innovation Scoreboard 2020*.
Retrieved from https://ec.europa.eu/docsroom/documents/42981

Evangelista, R., Iammarino, S., Mastrostefano, V., & Silvani, A. (2002). Looking for regional systems of innovation: Evidence from the Italian innovation
survey. *Regional Studies, 36*(2), 173–186. https://doi.org/10.1080/003434002
20121963

Fabrizi, A., Guarini, G., & Meliciani, V. (2018). Green patents, regulatory policies and research network policies. *Research Policy, 47*(6), 1018–1031. https://
doi.org/10.1016/j.respol.2018.03.005

Foray, D., Goddard, J., Goenaga Beldarrain, X., Landabaso, M., McCann, P.,
Morgan, K., Nauwelaers, C., & Ortega-Argilés, R. (2012). *Guide to research*

and innovation strategies for smart specialisations (RIS3). Luxembourg: Publications Office of the European Union.

Gancarczyk, M., & Gancarczyk, J. (2018). Proactive international strategies of cluster SMEs. *European Management Journal*, 36(1), 59–70. https://doi.org/10.1016/j.emj.2017.03.002

Gertler, M. S. (2003). Tacit knowledge and the economic geography of context, or the undefinable tacitness of being (there). *Journal of Economic Geography*, 3(1), 75–99. https://doi.org/10.1093/jeg/3.1.75

Ghisetti, C., & Montresor, S. (2019) Design and eco-innovation: Micro-evidence from the Eurobarometer survey. *Industry and Innovation*, 26(10), 1208–1241. https://doi.org/10.1080/13662716.2018.1549475

Gianelle, C., Guzzo, F., & Mieszkowski, K. (2020). Smart Specialisation: What gets lost in translation from concept to practice? *Regional Studies*, 54(10), 1377–1388 https://doi.org/10.1080/00343404.2019.1607970

Gouvea, R., Kassicieh, S., & Montoya, M. J. (2013). Using the quadruple helix to design strategies for the green economy. *Technological Forecasting and Social Change*, 80(2), 221–230. https://doi.org/10.1016/j.techfore.2012.05.003

Grillitsch, M., & Asheim, B. (2018). Place-based innovation policy for industrial diversification in regions. *European Planning Studies*, 26(8), 1638–1662. https://doi.org/10.1080/09654313.2018.1484892

Hock Heng, L., Mohd Othman, N. F., Md Rasli, A., & Jawad Iqbald, M. (2012). Fourth pillar in the transformation of production economy to knowledge economy. *Procedia—Social and Behavioral Sciences*, 40, 530–536.

Höglund, L., & Linton, G. (2018). Smart specialization in regional innovation systems: A quadruple helix perspective. *R&D Management*, 48(1), 60–72. https://doi.org/10.1111/radm.12306

Horbach, J. (2008). Determinants of environmental innovation—New evidence from German panel data sources. *Research Policy*, 37(1), 163–173. https://doi.org/10.1016/j.respol.2007.08.006

Horbach, J., Rammer, C., & Rennings, K. (2012). Determinants of eco-innovations by type of environmental impact—The role of regulatory push/pull, technology push and market pull. *Ecological Economics*, 78, 112–122. https://doi.org/10.1016/j.ecolecon.2012.04.005

Iacobucci, D. (2014). Designing and implementing a smart specialisation strategy at regional level: Some open questions. *Scienze Regionali*, 13(1), 107–126.

Iacobucci, D., & Guzzini, E. (2016). Relatedness and connectivity in technological domains: Missing links in S3 design and implementation. *European Planning Studies*, 24(8), 1511–1526. https://doi.org/10.1080/09654313.2016.1170108

Ivanova, I. (2014). Quadruple helix systems and symmetry: A step towards helix innovation system classification. *Journal of the Knowledge Economy*, 5(2), 357–369. https://doi.org/10.1007/s13132-014-0201-z

Kammerer, D. (2009). The effects of customer benefit and regulation on environmental product innovation: Empirical evidence from appliance manufacturers in Germany. *Ecological Economics*, 68(8–9), 2285–2295. http://dx.doi.org/10.1016/j.ecolecon.2009.02.016

Kolehmainen, J., Irvine, J., Stewart, L., Karacsonyi, Z., Szabó, T., Alarinta, J., & Norberg, A. (2016). Quadruple helix, innovation and the knowledge-based development: Lessons from remote, rural and less-favoured regions.

Journal of the Knowledge Economy, 7(1), 23–42. https://doi.org/10.1007/s13132-015-0289-9

Lash, J., & Wellington, F. (2007). Competitive advantage on a warming planet. *Harvard Business Review, 85*(3), 94–102.

Leydesdorff, L. (2005). The triple helix model and the study of knowledge-based innovation systems. *International Journal of Contemporary Sociology, 42*(1), 12–27. http://hdl.handle.net/10150/106148

Leydesdorff, L. (2012). The triple helix, quadruple helix,. . ., and an N-tuple of helices: Explanatory models for analyzing the knowledge-based economy? *Journal of the Knowledge Economy, 3*(1), 25–35. https://doi.org/10.1007/s13132-011-0049-4

Leydesdorff, L., & Etzkowitz, H. (2003). Can 'the public' be considered as a fourth helix in university-industry-government relations? Report on the Fourth Triple Helix Conference, 2002. *Science and Public Policy, 30*(1), 55–61. https://doi.org/10.3152/147154303781780678

Lindberg, M., Danilda, I., & Torstensson, B. M. (2012). Women Resource Centres—a creative knowledge environment of quadruple helix. *Journal of the Knowledge Economy, 3*(1), 36–52. https://doi.org/10.1007/s13132-011-0053-8

Lundvall, B. A. (1992). *National innovation system: Towards a theory of innovation and interactive learning.* London, England: Pinter Publishers.

Luxmore, S. R., & Hull, C. E. (2011). Innovation and NGOs: A framework of interaction. *The International Journal of Entrepreneurship and Innovation, 12*(1), 17–27. https://doi.org/10.5367/ijei.2011.0017

Mars, M. M., & Rios-Aguilar, C. (2010). Academic entrepreneurship (re) defined: Significance and implications for the scholarship of higher education. *Higher Education, 59*(4), 441–460. https://doi.org/10.1007/s10734-009-9258-1

Matt, D. T., & Rauch, E. (2020). SME 4.0: The role of small- and medium-sized enterprises in the digital transformation. In D. Matt, V. Modrák & H. Zsifkovits (Eds.), *Industry 4.0 for SMEs.* Cham: Palgrave Macmillan. https://doi.org/10.1007/978-3-030-25425-4_1

Mazzanti, M., & Zoboli, R. (2009). Embedding environmental innovation in local production systems: SME strategies, networking and industrial relations: Evidence on innovation drivers in industrial districts. *International Review of Applied Economics, 23*(2), 169–195. https://doi.org/10.1080/02692170802700500

McCann, P., & Ortega-Argilés, R. (2013). Smart specialization, regional growth and applications to European Union Cohesion policy. *Regional Studies, 49*(8), 1291–1302. doi.org/10.1080/00343404.2013.799769

MET. (2019). *Ambiti tecnologici della Smart Soecialisation Strategy nell'industria italiana* [Technological areas of the Smart Specialisation Strategy in the Italian Industry]. Report realized for the Territorial Cohesion Agency. Retrieved from www.agenziacoesione.gov.it/wp-content/uploads/2019/11/Report_MET_ambiti-tecnologici.pdf

Ministry of Economic Development & Ministry of Education, University and Research. (2016). *Strategia nazionale di specializzazione intelligente* [National Strategy of Smart Specialization]. Retrieved from https://s3platform.jrc.ec.europa.eu/documents/20182/223684/IT_RIS3_201604_Final.pdf/085a6bc5-3d13-4bda-8c53-a0beae3da59a

Molina-Morales, F. X., Martínez-Fernández, M. T., & Torló, V. J. (2011). The dark side of trust: The benefits, costs and optimal levels of trust for innovation performance. *Long Range Planning, 44*(2), 118–133. https://doi.org/10.1016/j. lrp.2011.01.001

Morgan, K. (2016). Nurturing novelty: Regional innovation policy in the age of smart specialisation. *Environment and Planning C: Government and Policy, 35*(4), 569–583. https://doi.org/10.1177/0263774X16645106

Muscio, A., Nardone, G., & Stasi, A. (2017). How does the search for knowledge drive firms' eco-innovation? Evidence from the wine industry. *Industry and Innovation, 24*(3), 298–320. https://doi.org/10.1080/13662716.2016.12 24707

Nidumolu, R., Prahalad, C. K., & Rangaswami, M. R. (2009). Why sustainability is now the key driver of innovation. *Harvard Business Review, 87*(9), 56–64.

Nordberg, K. (2015). Enabling regional growth in peripheral non-university regions—The impact of a quadruple helix intermediate organisation. *Journal of the Knowledge Economy, 6*(2), 334–356. https://doi.org/10.1007/s13132-015-0241-z

OECD. (2019). *Strengthening SMEs and Entrepreneurship for Productivity and Inclusive Growth: OECD 2018 Ministerial Conference on SMEs, OECD Studies on SMEs and Entrepreneurship.* Paris: OECD Publishing. https://doi.org/10.1787/c19b6f97-en

Pellegrini, G., & Di Stefano, R. (2017). La Strategia di Specializzazione Intelligente Nazionale e Regionale in Italia: Analisi di coerenza. *Rivista Economica del Mezzogiorno, 31*(4), 959–980. https://doi.org/10.1432/90203

Porter, M. E., & Reinhardt, F. L. (2007). Grist: A strategic approach to climate. *Harvard Business Review, 85*(10), 22–26. Retrieved from www.hbs.edu/faculty/Pages/item.aspx?num=31309

Rave, T., Goetzke, F., & Larch, M. (2011). *The determinants of environmental innovations and patenting: Germany reconsidered* (Ifo Working Paper No. 97). Retrieved from www.econstor.eu/bitstream/10419/73719/1/IfoWorking-Paper-97.pdf

Rennings, K. (2000). Redefining innovation—eco-innovation research and the contribution from ecological economics. *Ecological Economics, 32*(2), 319–332. https://doi.org/10.1016/S0921-8009(99)00112-3

Rodrigues, C., & Teles, F. (2017). The fourth helix in smart specialization strategies: The gap between discourse and practice. In S. P. De Oliveira Monteiro & E. G. Carayannis (Eds.), *The quadruple innovation helix nexus: A smart growth model, quantitative, empirical validation and operationalization for OECD countries* (pp. 111–136). New York: Palgrave Macmillan.

Sáez-Martínez, F. J., Díaz-García, C., & Gonzalez-Moreno, A. (2016). Firm technological trajectory as a driver of eco-innovation in young small and medium-sized enterprises. *Journal of Cleaner Production, 138*, 28–37. https://doi.org/10.1016/j.jclepro.2016.04.108

Tabachnick, B. G., & Fidell, L. S. (1996). *Using multivariate statistics* (3rd ed.). New York, NY: Harper Collins.

Territorial Cohesion Agency & Unioncamere. (2020). *Data and information on the socio-economic situation and trend: Regional reports.* Retrieved from www.agenziacoesione.gov.it and www.unioncamere.gov.it

Ujwary-Gil, A. (2019). Organizational network analysis: A study of a university library from a network efficiency perspective. *Library & Information Science Research*, *41*(1), 48–57. https://doi.org/10.1016/j.lisr.2019.02.007

Unioncamere. (2018). *First survey on Italian manufacturing firms*. Retrieved from www.unioncamere.gov.it/

Unioncamere. (2019). *Second survey on Italian manufacturing firms*. Retrieved from www.unioncamere.gov.it/

Wang, Y., & Lu, L. (2007). Knowledge transfer through effective university-industry interactions. *Journal of Technology Management in China*, *2*(2), 119–133. https://doi.org/10.1108/17468770710756068

Williams, R. (2012). Using the margins command to estimate and interpret adjusted predictions and marginal effects. *Stata Journal*, *12*(2), 308–331. https://doi.org/10.1177/1536867X1201200209

Wooldridge, J. M. (2010). *Econometric analysis of cross section and panel data* (2nd ed.). Cambridge, MA: London, England: MIT Press.

Yang, Y., & Holgaard, J. E. (2012). The important role of civil society groups in eco-innovation: A triple helix perspective. *Journal of Knowledge-based Innovation in China*, *4*(2), 132–148. https://doi.org/10.1108/17561411211235730

Yoo, W., Mayberry, R., Bae, S., Singh, K., He, Q. P., & Lillard Jr, J. W. (2014). A study of effects of multicollinearity in the multivariable analysis. *International Journal of Applied Science and Technology*, *4*(5), 9–19.

Zhang, S., Wang, Z., Zhao, X., & Zhang, M. (2017). Effects of institutional support on innovation and performance: Roles of dysfunctional competition. *Industrial Management & Data Systems*, *117*(1), 50–67. https://doi.org/10.1108/IMDS-10-2015-0408

8 Smart Specialization through Cluster Policy

Evidence from Poland and Germany

Anna Maria Lis, Arkadiusz Michał Kowalski, and Marta Mackiewicz

Introduction

Smart specialization, which centers on the definition and promotion of regional specialization, is closely related to the concept of clusters. Hence, in S3 strategies elaborated by European regions, cluster promotion plays a central role (Benner, 2017b). The identification of smart specializations is one of the objectives of the document "Europe 2020: A strategy for smart, sustainable and inclusive growth." As recommended by the European Commission, each region should have a strategy for the development of smart specialization in order to enable the implementation of the Europe 2020 assumptions at the regional level. Each smart specialization strategy needs actors that participate in the entrepreneurial discovery process and form an adequate innovation ecosystem. Hence, the S3 implementation depends on the ability to find such actors and bring them together. This is where S3 is linked to clusters, as they group key players (local business, scientific, and political institutions), stimulating cooperation, and leading to synergy effects. Therefore, clusters may be treated as a prerequisite of S3, and especially as instruments for the conception and implementation of regional innovation strategies. As clusters represent sectoral concentrations in the regional economy, they can be used to identify the industrial strengths and assets in a region. Hence, in the S3 formulation phase, cluster mapping and benchmarking may constitute useful tools that can be applied to identify regional specialization patterns and compare position of the region in different sectors in relation to other regions. Furthermore, in the S3 implementation phase, the existing clusters may be used to foster cooperation and mobilize collective actions between local actors. If there are no clusters in the identified areas of smart regional specialization, establishing new cluster initiatives may be considered, together with appropriate budgetary provisions (Anastasopoulos, 2017).

The chapter aims at investigating the interlinks and commonalities between clusters and regional smart specialization strategies, both from the theoretical point of view and through the prism of practical experiences of Poland and Germany. The rationale for this research comes from the observation that clusters themselves are the building blocks of regional economies, representing the areas of specializations rooted in a region's knowledge base. Despite the fact that clusters and smart specialization are strongly related to the territorial context and they aim at exploiting the advantages of proximity to stimulate innovation and competitiveness, the question arises "whether and how cluster policies can be exploited to support implementation of smart specialization strategies."

Poland and Germany have been selected for comparison due to several reasons. These two neighboring countries have become increasingly close partners in recent years, with a lot of cultural similarities. For recent years, Germany has been Poland's biggest trade partner, whereas Poland has been Germany's biggest trade partner in Central and Eastern Europe. They are comparable countries in terms of size, as both represent the most populous countries in their regions: Germany in Western Europe, whereas Poland in Central and Eastern Europe. Moreover, these countries share some similarities, including geographical location and the number of regions, a policy focused on clusters that perform well and are selected in a competitive procedure (National Key Clusters in Poland and Leading-Edge Clusters in Germany). The number of such clusters is 15 in both countries. On the other hand, there are significant differences in the cluster policy. Germany is an example of successful implementation of cluster policy at the regional level, while in Poland, it is at a much lower level of development. Therefore, the comparison between these countries has not only a cognitive but also educational value.

The chapter consists of several related parts. The first part presents the literature background of both cluster and smart specialization strategy; the second one describes the methodological approach, the third one presents the main findings of the comparative case studies conducted in selected regions of Poland and Germany and discussion, and the last part—main conclusion, including implications for theory and policy, limitations and directions for future research.

Literature Background

Introduction Into Theoretical Background of Clusters and Cluster Policy

The classical definition states that clusters are "geographic concentrations of interconnected companies, suppliers, service providers, firms in related industries, and associated institutions (e.g., universities, standards agencies, and trade associations), in particular fields that compete but also cooperate" (Porter, 1998, p. 197). The previously mentioned definition indicates two important characteristics of clusters (Kowalski, 2016):

- geographical concentration of specific sectors, connected with the phenomenon of the regional specialization;
- coopetition (simultaneous cooperation and competition) between cluster actors.

Clusters have become a very important research area, with cluster structures being seen as a key factor influencing entrepreneurship (Pascal, 2005), innovativeness, and regional development (Porter, 1998; 2000). The popularity of the concept of clusters is linked to the observation of geographical concentration of economic activity, especially in high-tech industries, around metropolitan areas, and in specialized regional clusters (Sölvell, 2008; Glaeser et al., 2010; Gallego & Maroto, 2013; Delgado et al., 2014; Qi, 2019; Delgado, 2020). Economic successes of many regions, which have developed prosperous clusters, are an incentive for regional and national governments to prepare strategies and implement programs that support clustering processes. Development with the use of clusters as a policy tool is reflected in the cluster-based economic development policy concept, formulated in the OECD documents (Roelandt & den Hertog, 1999). It is understood as a set of activities and instruments used by the authorities at various levels to improve the competitiveness of the economy by stimulating the development of the existing cluster systems or creating new systems, primarily at the regional level.

It is important to distinguish between clusters and cluster initiatives, the latter being "organized efforts to enhance competitiveness of clusters within a region, involving cluster firms, government and/or the research community" (Sölvell et al., 2003, p. 9). In practice, there are different practices and models of public intervention adopted by governments, with two dominant cluster policy models: bottom-up model with clusters driven mostly by market forces, where the key role is played by enterprises, and top-down model, where clusters are emerging and developing mostly as a result of government actions, or a mixed model (Sölvell et al., 2003; Fromhold-Eisebith & Eisebith, 2005; Iritié, 2018; Kiese, 2019). The classic approach to clusters is generally in line with the first, bottom-up approach. Porter (2007) points out that in cluster theory, all clusters are perceived as good, so cluster-based policies, unlike sectoral or industrial policies, should be neutral in relation to industry or type of economic activity. However, there is a growing gap in analytical rigor between cluster theory focusing mostly on bottom-up clusters and cluster policy run by practitioners, who often adopt the top-down approach (Lehmann & Benner, 2015).

One of the challenges in research on clusters is the ambiguity of the cluster concept itself. According to some representatives of economic geography (Martin & Sunley, 2003), "Porter's cluster metaphor is highly generic in character, being sufficiently indeterminate to admit a very wide spectrum of industrial groupings and specialization." They put forward the following questions, to which the cluster theory does not give a precise answer: At what level of industrial aggregation should a cluster be defined, and what range of related or associated industries and activities should be included? How strong linkages between firms are required? What level of economic specialization must be achieved by a local concentration of firms so that they could constitute a cluster? The difficulties in precisely addressing these challenges are reflected in Porter's (1998, p. 204) recognition that "cluster boundaries rarely conform to standard industrial classification systems, which fail to capture many important actors in competition as well as linkages across industries."

Whereas traditionally the concept of clustering served to explain business success of industrial regions, recent research on cluster theory has shifted toward innovation-related effects of clustering (Tallman, Jenkins, Henry, & Pinch, 2004; Casanueva et al., 2013; Kowalski, 2013; Anokhin et al., 2019; Ferras-Hernandez & Nylund, 2019; Belso-Martínez et al., 2020). The importance of clusters for innovation is connected with the contemporary innovation economics paradigm; new products are mainly the result of cooperation and interactions between the three types of actors forming triple helix model of innovation, as described by Etzkowitz and Leydesdorff (1995), namely industry, university, and government. Turkina, Oreshkin, and Kali (2019) find that an important driver for innovation is connectedness to highly performing firms. An important ingredient behind the success of industrial clusters is also informal knowledge networks (Balland et al., 2016).

The impact of clusters on the innovativeness of the economy is related to the fact that new technologies in specific industrial branches are created in units located in close proximity to each other. Geographical proximity of enterprises and other units helps to build interactions and links between partners, creating significant added value and leading to different effects of synergy. Cooperation among different cluster actors encourages the flow of knowledge, technology transfer, constant learning as well as generation and absorption of innovations. The effectiveness of the innovation processes in the regional economy is determined by its innovation abilities, with especially important role in clustering played by soft factors, such as high quality of human and social capital, including relational capital and trust, technological advancement of scientific and research units, entrepreneurship-friendly environment, support from local government and appropriate innovative milieu. All these elements cannot be analyzed separately, but they must constitute one whole system, which is often ensured by developing cluster structure (Kowalski, 2010).

Concept of Smart Specialization Strategy

Smart specialization is a policy concept elaborated in 2008, which aims to address the relations between R&D and innovation ability on the one hand and the sectoral structure of the economy on the other hand. It recognizes the importance of focusing on identified regional strengths in order to realize the potential for scale, scope, and spillovers in knowledge production and utilization, and consequently increase the productivity of innovation-related activities (Foray et al., 2009). Smart specialization strategy should be perceived as a regional initiative useful in the exploration and discovery of technological and market opportunities leading to a sustainable competitive advantage, upon which related policy actions will be conceptually based and implemented (Foray & Goenaga, 2013).

S3 represents a relatively new strategic orientation of regional innovation policy, reflecting a shift from a "redistributive" toward a "developmental" logic of regional policy, which aims to promote innovation-based endogenous development (Capello & Kroll, 2016). The rationale to introduce S3 approach is to avoid critical failures of policy developments in the past, like "one-size-fits-all" approach (Tödtling & Trippl, 2005) and ignoring the problems of path dependency and lock-in in the analysis of regional innovation systems (Morgan, 2013; 2016). In addition to the category of path extension reflecting the continuation of an existing trajectory, Belussi and Trippl (2018) identified the following patterns of change:

- new path creation, which is about the emergence of new specializations or sectors deriving from breakthrough innovations;
- new path entry of established industries, which is about setting up of an established industry that is new for the region, often based on the inflow of foreign direct investment (FDI);
- path ramification, which is about "speciation" of knowledge by existing industries into new but related industries;
- path upgrading and renewal, which is about a major change of an industrial path into a new direction based on innovation.

According to the study conducted by Belussi and Trippl (2018), advanced regions gain the most benefits from S3, owing to technological variety of companies, the capacity to prioritize a set of clusters and sectors, organizational thickness, high quality of government, institutional diversity, and well-developed culture of cooperation and stakeholder involvement in policymaking. Intermediate regions are also in good position to benefit from S3, which advances regional practices, facilitating the inclusion of SMEs. On the contrary, smart specialization processes tend to be undermined in less-developed regions due to weak innovation systems and inadequate experience with regionalized innovation policies. According to the study of Papamichail et al. (2019), the barriers to implement S3 in catchup regions are the shortcomings in the absorptive capacity of companies that are incapable of exploiting scientific knowledge, critical to meet the objectives of S3. In practice, this is translated into limitations in gathering a sufficient number of science–business propositions that could be implemented in the S3 framework. Another problem is presented by the inefficiencies in building institutional networking and interorganizational connectivity, as catchup regions experience lack of cooperative culture at an institutional level and weak linkages among companies, scientific units, and regional authorities. Also, Hassink and Gong (2019) are skeptical about the abilities of weak regions to benefit from S3, as there are insufficient existing structures on which the smart specialization can build. In addition, there may be poor institutional capabilities when it comes to the selection of the right entrepreneurial discovery process (EDP), understood as a systematic effort of public–private dialogue that draws on quantitative and qualitative evidence, focuses on prioritization and action planning, and enables codifying of an emerging regional consensus on cross-sectoral economic development in smart specialization strategies (Benner, 2019). In general, Hassink and Gong (2019) argue that the rent-seeking behavior of interest groups and strong dependence on the existing economic structures make the EDP a rather illusory hope. Additionally, Balland et al. (2019) point out that the operationalization of S3 has been limited because a coherent set of analytical tools to guide the policy directives remains elusive.

Complementarities and Differences between Cluster Policy and S3 Approaches

The concepts of cluster policy and S3 are not exactly the same. There are significant differences between them. However, it possible to recognize similarities and synergies between the two policy constructs. Both of them are policy approaches exemplifying place-based policy, aimed at exploiting the advantages of proximity to promote economic growth and efficiency. They focus on productivity and innovation as the key drivers of economic growth and emphasize the need to utilize regional embeddedness in exploitation of the advantages of proximity (European Commission, 2013). Saha et al. (2018) claim that both S3 and cluster policy approaches are seen as a source of continued innovation-driven territorial growth that leads to sustainable regional value creation, which not only increases regional competitiveness but also makes it possible to identify the best method of exploiting local resources. Hassink and Gong (2019) even state that S3 is a continuation of cluster policies, rather than a brand-new policy instrument, as both of them encourage concentration, which enables to achieve critical mass, agglomeration economies, and knowledge spillovers.

However, there are still some important conceptual differentiations between cluster policy and S3 approaches. The most notable are different objectives, as S3 aims at structural transformation of regional economies around new knowledge-based activity domains, whereas the explicit goal of cluster actions is to create competitive advantages of groups of companies and enhance the performance of local businesses. Another difference between cluster policy and S3 is about how they strive to achieve an economic upgrade, either for regions or for groups of clustered companies. S3 emphasizes the exploration of emerging, often hidden economic opportunities, which are identified through an EDP. Contrarily, cluster actions are not intended to disclose new economic domains, but they primarily build on a critical mass of geographically concentrated economic activities. S3 and cluster policy also place different emphasis on economic diversification, while both recognizing it as an important process in increasing regional competitiveness. In the case of clusters, economic diversification is meant to be a variety within a limited number of economic and institutional actors, so it is supposed to support solely cluster insiders. S3 perspective on diversification is about ensuring the stability of regional economies in the event of unexpected shocks in individual sectors so that they take place between related sectors and so that regional economies can benefit from more diverse, positive externalities (Pronestì, 2019). Hence, S3 refers to the process of regional, rather than sectoral specialization, and it aims at leading regions toward a pattern of specialized (Santoalha, 2016), or smart diversification, where regions identify areas or domains of existing or potential competitive advantage and differentiate themselves from others (Hassink & Gong, 2019). Regions may achieve diversification by specializing in a limited number of prioritized economic activities to take advantage of knowledge spillovers and economies of scale and scope. This means that territories should take advantage of transformation opportunities in order to meet structural challenges by combining their existing capacities into unique innovative activities expressed in smart specialization (Keller et al., 2019). According to the research of Balland et al. (2019), diversification into complex technologies may be difficult for regions, although this process is easier when such technologies are more closely related to the existing knowledge core of the region.

Taking into account synergies and differentiations between S3 and cluster policies, Caloffi and Mariani (2018) claim that both approaches are useful in the policy mixes understood as a combination of policy objectives and instruments. They note that clusters, along with S3, can generate the necessary social, cultural, and institutional conditions with different specializations in the process of development and application of new technologies, especially key enabling technologies. Benner (2017a) argues that both cluster policy and smart specialization can be of considerable value for territorial institution-sensitive sectoral development that provides a set of instruments for establishing public–private dialogue platforms and prevents a dangerous lock-in situation. However, the study of Rocha et al. (2019) reveals that clusters with positive economic performance do not necessarily lead to regional social cohesion as in some cases they fail to integrate different groups, such as migrant or local workers, and embed new and large firms within the region.

Cluster support is a part of the concept of smart specialization by regions, which is an important element of the Europe 2020 strategy, under which member states are expected "to reform national (and regional) R&D and innovation systems to foster excellence and smart specialization, reinforce cooperation between universities, research, and business, implement joint programming and enhance cross-border cooperation in areas with EU value added and adjust national funding procedures accordingly, to ensure the diffusion of technology across the EU territory" (European Commission, 2010). The use of clusters to carry out the smart specialization strategy is expected to enable:

- concentration of resources in several priority sectors of key importance to the regional economy where regions enjoy a competitive advantage;
- increase of synergies between policies implemented at the EU level and in individual member states and regions;
- more effective use of public funds by achieving the necessary critical mass of investment instead of scattering funds around many different areas;
- strengthening regional innovation systems, R&D efficiency, and knowledge flows.

According to European Commission (2013), cluster policies can provide a basic set of tools to engage and develop economic sectors in which the region enjoys comparative advantages. Moreover, they have the ability to manage concentration and integration of economic policies around specific economic areas. It was highlighted that cluster policies may constitute the key building blocks in developing and implementing S3, especially if:

- S3 integrates cluster policies into a broader transformation agenda for the entire regional economy;
- S3 complements cluster policies with other cross-cutting and technology/knowledge-domain-specific activities;
- S3 cluster measures move beyond the current cluster policy practice and they address emerging new domains cutting across sectors.

The reasons for selecting regions in Germany and Poland for a comparative case study in the empirical analysis are presented in Introduction;

however, it is also worth to mention that such selection adds to the body of knowledge in the field of S3 and clusters. According to the bibliometric research, Scopus database includes only five publications linking the following terms in the title, abstract, or keywords: smart specialization, clusters, Germany and Poland, none of which focusing on two regions discussed in detail in this chapter: Pomeranian Voivodeship and Saxony. Similarly, in the Web of Science, there are only two publications, including (in all fields) all the terms specified previously, without any literature with reference to these regions.

Methodological Approach

We report the outcomes of our study aimed at finding the answer to the following research question: "if and how cluster policies can be exploited to support implementation of smart specialization strategies." We strive to answer this question based on the study in two countries of the European Union: Poland and Germany. The selection of the countries was dictated by different conditions with regard to the development of both cluster policy and S3 implementation. A comparison of both countries has a great cognitive value.

On the one hand, there are some similarities between Poland and Germany. Their cluster policies have common roots—it is largely a consequence of their membership in the European Union. In addition, the administrative division of Poland and Germany is quite similar: 16 regions (voivodeships in Poland, federal states in Germany) in which cluster policy is implemented. In both regions, there are leading clusters, classified among the most mature cluster structures on a national scale. On the other hand, there are also visible differences in the level of cluster policy development between the analyzed countries, which may be interesting in the context of achieving the research aim. This applies especially to the cluster policy implemented at the regional level, which in Germany is at a much higher level of development than in Poland. Further, some more in-depth analyses (case studies) have been carried out in regions of a similar size (both in terms of area and population): in the Pomeranian Voivodeship and the Federal State of Saxony.

The main research strategy was international comparative analysis of areas of cluster activity and smart specialization, and the basic technique for the collection of data was an analysis of documents, including web resources, research reports, reports published by public authorities, and cluster documents. The four-level procedure of selecting documents for desk research consisted of (1) identification of specific information about the cluster policy in Poland and Germany; (2) gathering the content of Regional Smart Specializations in all the 16 regions in Poland and 16 lands in Germany; (3) finding details on the functioning of all the leading clusters that were selected in the competitive procedure in both countries, and (4) finally, identification of specific information about two regions selected for in-depth research in the form of a case study (Pomerania and Saxony).

The research procedure consisted of three stages. In the first stage, the development of cluster policy in Poland and Germany was analyzed. In the second stage, a comparative case study was carried out. This method involved the analysis and synthesis of the similarities, differences, and patterns across two countries with respect to their cluster policies. Such an approach enabled the compilation of the data and translated it to the mapping tool. The objective of mapping clusters and smart specializations in Poland and Germany was to select regions for case studies. The analysis focused on national clusters, an important element of a regional innovation ecosystem, which can undertake activities to foster the development of regions. In the case of Poland, those included National Key Clusters (NKCs), in the case of Germany—Leading-Edge Clusters (LEC). The list of clusters is presented by the Ministry of Economic Development (in Poland) and by the Ministry of Education and Research (in Germany). The information about the main areas of cluster activity was collected by means of Web scraping (30 websites of 15 NKCs and 15 of LECs). In order to link clusters to smart specialization, an overview of S3 in all the regions (16 in Poland and 16 in Germany) was prepared. The objective was not to benchmark the countries and their strategic approaches but rather to classify and systematize the identified thematic priorities and fields of action. In view of the more detailed subcategories, clear coding is often not possible. According to Sörvik and Kleibrink (2015), this can be attributed to most broad designs and descriptions of the specialization fields in the strategy documents, which often cannot be reduced to one category. This also means that the encodings usually cover only a subarea of the specialization fields. The data were analyzed and adjusted, considering the limitations described. Subsequently, the main areas of cluster activity were assigned to the domains of smart specializations. The matrix created in the mapping process shows whether clusters contributed to defining smart specializations. In the third stage, an analysis of two selected regions was carried out: Pomerania and Saxony.

Results and Discussion

Development of Cluster Policy in Poland and Germany

Cluster policy in the EU has been developing since the beginning of the 21st century, which was influenced by various strategic programs launched at the EU level and then transferred to the level of individual countries and regions. Germany belongs to the group of European countries with strong cluster policy (similarly to Austria, Norway, Denmark, Sweden, France, and Spain). Germany is also a precursor of cluster policy in the EU—experience related to clusters was accumulated at the level of federal states as early as in the 1980s, and organized system support for clusters in Germany was launched in the mid-1990s as part of an innovation policy. In turn, Poland, like other countries of Central and Eastern Europe (such as the Czech Republic, Hungary, and Bulgaria) has a less developed cluster-based policy. Nevertheless, a similar evolution of cluster policy is observed in both Germany and Poland, and the distinguished phases of its development coincide to a large extent with the adopted programming periods at the EU level. One can clearly see a gradual transition from launching cluster initiatives, which was associated with their initial identification and mapping (until 2007), through supporting the established cluster organizations (2007–2013), to strengthening the selected, most developed cluster organizations, especially in the area of innovation and internationalization (2014–2020). In Germany, as well as in other countries with a strong cluster policy, there is also an increasing emphasis on the development of intersectoral cooperation, intensification of cooperation between clusters and the promotion of world-class clusters which have the potential to become internationally visible growth centers, regardless of technological field. Both in Poland and Germany, the cluster support system is based on national and regional programs. However, there are clear differences between the two countries in this respect. While in Poland, cluster support programs are prepared and implemented mainly at the central level, in the case of Germany, cluster policy is implemented mainly in the federal states, which employ their own programs focused on cluster development.

At present, however, cluster policy is stagnating in both analyzed countries (as well as in the entire EU). Within the cluster-based economic development policy, there is a shift away from financing the clusters in favor of implementing regional innovation and development policies. In both analyzed countries, a system of categorization of cluster organizations was created, which enabled distinguishing the most mature organizations with documented experience (NKCs and LECs).

In Poland, the assumption of the cluster assessment process and granting of the status of a National Key Cluster (NKC) is to select clusters that have significant potential for the development of the Polish economy and are competitive in international terms. The NKC selection system is the result of several years of work and is based on a document "Directions and assumptions of cluster policy in Poland until 2020" (Dzierżanowski, 2012) developed by the working group on Cluster Policy, operating in 2010–2012 under the leadership of the Ministry of Economic Development. The NKC status is granted through a competition procedure. The evaluation criteria relate to the cluster's potential, quality of operations, and development prospects. The NKC status makes the clusters eligible for public support under the Smart Growth Operational Programme 2014–2020, which is aimed at strengthening the international expansion of NKCs. Obtaining NKC status is a quality mark, which increases the cluster's recognition on the domestic and international market and raises the prestige of the entities operating in it. As a result, NKCs become important partners in the dialogue between the sphere of enterprises, scientific institutions, and administration.

In Germany, the Leading-Edge Cluster program started in 2007. The basis for choosing the Leading-Edge Clusters was the stage of an implementation of the joint strategic goals and the definition of future development projects in a specific technological area. An important condition was the involvement of key actors in the field of innovation. The competition was open to all technological and industrial sectors. It was required for the cluster to meet a number of criteria, for example, high technological advancement, the minimum number of cluster members, a strong position on international markets, and a cluster strategy. In the LEC program, it was possible to obtain financing mainly for joint R&D projects (implemented jointly by the companies) in order to initiate research and development cooperation among cluster participants. LEC could also receive funding under the "Internationalization of top clusters, future projects, and comparable networks" program.

In the context of a further focus on S3, the need for more efficient use of available public funds requires stronger concentration of public intervention on specific fields and specializations and coordination between different areas of public policy. It enables the support of enterprises that are most beneficial for the economy. For this reason, Poland and Germany, like some other EU countries, have decided to use leading clusters as one of the public support flow channels for S3.

Matching Leading Clusters and RSS in Poland

In Poland, the process of emergence of smart specializations was based on the assessment of endogenous resources of voivodeships, carried out on the basis of foresight research, industry analyses, and technology mapping. Public consultations were also held in the regions in the form of expert panels as well as meetings and workshops. The experience gained in the regions in the field of cluster policy has also proved valuable. The process of identification of the priority areas was based on knowledge on significant industry clusters and maturity of launched cluster organizations, the previous achievements of these organizations in the area of institutional relationships development, and participation of cluster representatives who were invited to participate in expert panels. In order to investigate the linkages between the existence of clusters and RSS, the voivodeships in which NKCs operate were distinguished. The selection of regions for case studies was based on identification of those voivodeships in which the matching between NCS's activity and RSS fields was noted (Table 8.1).

Table 8.1 Regional Smart Specializations matching National Key Clusters' specializations in Polish voivodeships

No.	Voivodeship	Regional Smart Specializations (SS)	Clusters matching the SS of the region	Main areas of cluster activity
1.	Kuyavian-Pomeranian	Tools, injection molding, products from plastics	Bydgoszcz Industrial Cluster	Injection molding and other tools for processing polymer materials Production of plastic products for many sectors of the economy Recycling polymer materials
2.	Lublin	Information science and automation	Eastern ICT Cluster	ICT
3.	Lesser Poland	Life sciences	Life Science Kraków Cluster	Technologies for health and quality of life
		Sustainable energy	Sustainable Infrastructure Cluster	Intelligent energy-saving and passive construction Low-energy buildings Energy efficiency in construction
4.	Subcarpathian	Aviation and space technology	Aviation Valley Cluster	Production, maintenance, repair, and overhaul of aircraft Propulsion and components
5.	Podlaskie	Metal and machine industry, boat-building, and sectors combined with a value chain	Metal Processing Cluster	Production of machines, devices, tools for industry Specialized services related to metalworking Cooperative services based on processes related to automation and robotization

(Continued)

No.	Voivodeship	Regional Smart Specializations (SS)	Clusters matching the SS of the region	Main areas of cluster activity
6.	Pomeranian	Offshore and port logistic technologies	North–South Logistics and Transport Cluster	Design and construction of hybrid—electric vessels
		Interactive technologies in information-saturated environment	Interizon— Pomeranian ICT Cluster	Telecommunications systems electronics production Software development Industry 4.0; Internet of Things, Artificial Intelligence Augmented Reality Space and satellite technologies
7.	West Pomeranian	Environmentally friendly packaging	West Pomeranian Chemical Cluster	Chemical and biotechnology industries
		Chemical and material engineering products		Packaging Energy and Materials Recovery Healthy Food
		Modern agri-food processing		

Sources: Dolina Lotnicza, n.d.; Klaster Obróbki Metali, n.d.; Mazowiecki Klaster ICT, n.d.; Polski Klaster Budowlany, n.d.; Bydgoski Klaster Przemysłowy, n.d.; Polska Grupa Motoryzacyjna, n.d.; Klaster Gospodarki Odpadowej i Recyklingu, n.d.; Klaster LifeScience Kraków, n.d.; Klaster Logistyczno Transportowy Północ-Południe, n.d.; Interizon—Pomorski Klaster ICT, n.d.; Silesia Automotive & Advanced Manufacturing, n.d.; Śląski Klaster Lotniczy, n.d.; Wschodni Klaster ICT, n.d.; Zielona Chemia, n.d.; Klaster Zrównoważona Infrastruktura, n.d.; Związek Pracodawców Klastry Polskie.

As the research results show, currently, there are 15 National Key Clusters in Poland located in 10 regions (out of 16). In some voivodeships, there are even three NKCs (Lesser Poland) or two NKCs (Podlaskie, Silesian, Pomeranian). NKSc represents various industries—most of them operate in the ICT, aviation, and automotive industry. The number of RSSs identified in Polish voivodeships is also very diverse (it ranges from 3 for Subcarpathian to 8 for Kuyavian-Pomeranian and West Pomeranian voivodship), just like is their thematic scope. The ICT industry is the most common one (present in almost all voivodships). Other most popular fields include energy, agri-food/safe food, metal industry, logistics, as well as broadly understood quality of life, including life science, medicine, and health. The findings indicate that clusters were not the basis for the emergence of smart specializations in all analyzed regions. In the regions where NKC is located, in most cases, at least one smart specialization is related to the area of activity (main specialization) of the cluster. However, this does not apply to three voivodeships: Masovian, Silesian, and Holy Cross. Moreover, out of 15 NKCs, 6 are still not related to smart regional specialization. In turn, in one voivodeship—Pomerania—clusters' specialization areas were the basis for the emergence of two smart regional specializations.

Pomerania belongs to one of the best-developed voivodeships of Poland, with a large share of the SME sector in the structure of the economy. The main industries in Pomerania include wood–paper, petrochemical, electrotechnical, and construction industries. High-tech industries, including ICT and biotechnology, are also being developed in the region. In the Pomeranian Voivodeship, there are strong academic centers, business environment institutions, including business incubators, science, and technology parks, centers of technology transfer, and cluster organizations.

Pomerania is an example of a region in which a bottom-up and partner RSS selection process was adopted (e.g., Agencja Rozwoju Pomorza S. A., n.d.; Departament Rozwoju Gospodarczego, n.d.; Interizon, n.d.; Pomorskie w Unii Europejskiej 2020; Serwis Regionalnego Programu województwa Pomorskiego, n.d.). It was based on an internal debate between the representatives of various sectors, including business and science, organized in Partnerships for Pomeranian Smart Specializations. The role of the Partnerships was to define the most promising directions for the development of innovative products and services which, with the participation and investment of public funds, could become internationally competitive. This type of partnership-based approach should be considered as an innovative way of participation and making decisions regarding the allocation of funds for research and development. A key element of this approach was the competition for the best concepts of cooperation in thematic areas relevant to the regional economy, with the potential to create high added value in the future, as announced in 2014. The competitive mode of selecting Pomeranian Smart Specializations has launched an active process of entrepreneurial discovery, involving various partners from the region, including enterprises, R&D institutes, and universities, nongovernmental organizations, business environment institutions, as well as cluster organizations. The culmination of the smart specialization identification process was the signing in 2016 of four Agreements for the Smart Specialization of Pomerania. In order to organize a permanent dialogue within smart specializations, the Pomeranian Smart Specialization Councils (one for each of the specializations) were created, which in cooperation with the regional government determine the directions of development of the specialization. They comprise the representatives of different sectors, including cluster organizations.

The large involvement of clusters in the RSS selection process is the result of previous experience of cooperation between administration and business, among other things, in the field of animating the development of clusters in Pomerania. As a result of activities carried out under "the Regional Program for Support of Clusters in the Pomeranian Province for the Period 2009–2015," several cluster initiatives were launched. Inventory of clusters in Poland (Buczyńska et al., 2016) showed that there are five clusters operating in Pomerania, formed in the period 2007–2015.

Cluster organizations operating in Pomerania have actively joined the process of establishing Partnerships for RSS—North–South Logistics and Transport Cluster operates under "Offshore and port logistic technologies" (PSS1), while Interizon-Pomeranian ICT Cluster coordinates the Pomeranian Smart Specialization called "Interactive technologies in an information-saturated environment" (PSS2). The Interizon Foundation, the coordinator of the cluster, is the leader of the PSS2. The goal of this specialization is to build and strengthen international competitiveness and accelerate the growth rate of enterprises in the ICT sector in the Pomeranian Voivodeship. This is carried out through the implementation of R&D results and building intellectual potential for creating innovative products and services in the area of interactive technologies in an information-saturated environment. As part of this specialization, horizontal projects are planned, related to the development of models for the functioning of Smart City solutions, the creation of the Pomeranian Laboratory of Crisis Management at Gdańsk University of Technology, and the creation of the Smart City Living Lab. As a coordinator, the Interizon Foundation launches activities (e.g., information meetings, workshops, networking meetings) addressed to the Cluster members. Because the strategy and action plan of PSS2 and the Interizon Cluster are correlated, their activity enables building numerous synergies and gradual activation of new entities present in the ICT industry in Pomerania. A visible advantage resulting from S3 in Pomerania and the large involvement of clusters, both in the process of selection and coordination of RSS, is the further development of cooperation among key regional entities.

Matching Leading Clusters and RSS in Germany

In Germany, conditions for the implementation of S3 were very favorable, especially at the regional level. Before assumptions regarding S3 were developed at the European level, federal states already had many years of experience in the scope of regional innovation strategies and implementation of cluster policy, which may form the basis for S3. In addition, the general approach of federal states to development strategies focuses on consensus, assuming the integration of various stakeholder groups. In the German federal system, stakeholder consultation processes and decentralized strategic governance are common practice, which had a positive impact on the SS selection process. In Germany, there are big differences between the regions, resulting from the size, history, decentralized education, and research system, which are visible both in smart specializations and in the main areas of leading-edge clusters activity. The results of matching of SS and areas of activity of leading clusters at the state level are presented (Table 8.2).

In Germany, as in Poland, there is an uneven deployment of Leading-Edge Clusters—there are 15 LECs, located in 8 (out of 16) federal states. This means that half of the states do not have a single leading cluster. The industry range of LECs is very wide and includes, among other things, ICT, biotechnology and medicine, energetics, aviation and automotive industry, printing technologies, and logistic. The number of RSS identified in the eight federal states analyzed are very diverse, with most (10) RSS found in Saxony-Anhalt, and least (4) in Baden-Württemberg. The scope of RSS is very broad; however, ICT, life sciences, and energy are the most frequently recurring areas. With regard to the degree of convergence of specialization and leading clusters areas, the situation is somewhat different in the German federal states as compared to Polish voivodships. All federal states in which leading-edge clusters are located have at least one smart specialization that corresponds to the cluster's specialization. Only one cluster is not associated with smart regional specialization.

Saxony—selected for further analysis—is one of the most innovative regions of Eastern Germany. Saxony is a technological and industrial center, with several regional universities and public research institutes being among the nation's leaders. Saxony's regional economy, characterized by an above-average SME participation, demonstrates relevant technological and economic potential to develop priority areas on which S3 could focus. Significant industrial clusters can be observed, in particular, in the automotive, microelectronics, and machine-building industries.

The smart specialization approach has not introduced a new way of thinking about Saxony's innovation policy (e.g., Baier et al., 2013; Fraunhofer ISI, n.d.; Kroll et al., 2016; Saxony.de, n.d.; Vlčková et al., 2018). Moreover, in contrast to other federal states, Saxony had no formal innovation strategy defining priority areas throughout the 1990s and 2000s. Nevertheless, the aspects considered to be one of the most important in S3, namely strong priority on innovation and focus on investments, were already visible in Saxony in the early nineties. The set of key Saxony technology fields was laid down in the 1992 "Guidelines for Technology Policy." This document identified nine technology fields that are worth further support because of their potential to establish a leading position in Germany. Thus, the aforementioned document formulated the key assumptions of the smart specialization strategy much earlier than they

Table 8.2 Regional Smart Specializations matching leading-edge clusters' specializations in the German states

No.	State	Regional Smart Specializations (SS)	Clusters matching the SS of the region	Main areas of cluster activity
1.	Baden-Württemberg	Sustainable mobility concepts ICT, green IT, and intelligent products Health	Elektromobilität Süd-West microTEC Südwest	Automotive industry Microsystems technology Industry 4.0
2.	Bavaria	Life sciences	BioRN Münchner Biotech Cluster Medical Valley EMN	Biotechnology Biotechnology Pharmaceutical industry Healthcare
		New materials, nano, and micro technology ICT	M A I Carbon Medical Valley EMN	Carbon fiber reinforced plastics fiber-reinforced composites Medicine Digital Health
3.	Hamburg	Aviation	Hamburg Aviation	Aviation industry Aircraft production
4.	Hessen	ICT Life sciences and bioeconomy and health economics	Software Cluster Cluster für Individualisierte ImmunIntervention	Software development Medicine
5.	North Rhine-Westphalia	ICT	it's OWL—Intelligente Technische Systeme OstWestfalenLippe EffizienzCluster LogistikRuhr	artificial intelligence digital platforms digital twins and Industry 4.0 Logistic
6.	Saxony	Mobility and logistics Nanotechnology Microelectronics, including organic and polymer electronics	Cool Silicon	Micro- and nanoelectronic energy-efficient solutions in the areas of computing, mobile communication, and sensor technology ICT
7.	Saxony-Anhalt	Chemistry and bioeconomy	BioEconomy Cluster	Biotechnology
8.	Thüringen	Sustainable energy and resource use	Solarvalley Mitteldeutschland	Renewable energies Solar energy

Sources Die Spitzencluster—BMBF Spitzencluster, n.d.; BioRN Network e.V., n.d.; BioEconomy Cluster eV, n.d.; Cluster for Individualized Immune Intervention (Ci3) e.V., n.d.; Cool Silicon e. V., n.d.; Digital Hub Logistics, n.d.; Cluster Elektromobilität Süd-West, n.d.; InnovationLab, n.d.; Hamburg Aviation, n.d.; it's OWL, n.d.; Medical Valley EMN e.V., n.d.; MicroTEC Südwest, n.d.; BioM Biotech Cluster Development GmbH—BioM, n.d.; Software-Cluster, n.d.; So ar Valley, n.d.; Smart Specialisation Platform—Europa EU.

were formally introduced. As a result of adapting to S3 conditions, seven key enabling technologies of the state related to its industrial orientation were defined. The government of Saxony has taken actions to promote selected fields of technology as part of the adopted political concept, which resulted in launching some important initiatives, including the association "Silicon Saxony e.V.," "Biotechnology-offensive Saxony" as well as the innovation cluster "Nano for Production."

In Saxony, S3 was implemented as part of interministerial consultations and it was disseminated to external stakeholders. To enable a coordinated policy design within S3 framework conditions, cooperation between ministries (based on working groups) was implemented, involving representatives of the science and business sector, as well as the federal government and the European Commission. Saxony has extensive experience in designing, implementing, and adapting instruments in consultation with regional stakeholders. Already in 2010, the Saxon government had started to establish a continuous and structured dialogue based on "innovation fora" to analyze the needs and requirements of regional stakeholders. The objective was to identify major problems and develop the necessary support instruments, as well as to ensure the stakeholders' participation in the strategy development process. Business networks (referred to as "Saxon Cluster Initiatives") also took part in this dialogue.

From the outset of regional technology and innovation policy in the 1990s, Saxony has focused on key structural challenges related to supporting research and development projects in SMEs, connecting SMEs with R&D institutions, and promoting joint projects of public research and private enterprise. Great emphasis was also placed on the development of business environment infrastructure by creating science and technology parks, incubators, technology transfer centers, as well as various types of consultancy facilities. And although the previous challenges and actions are combined with the cluster concept, there is no organized regional cluster policy in Saxony. Regional network policy in the context of cluster policy is considered obsolete. However, Saxony actively participates in national cluster initiatives such as leading-edge cluster initiative. Saxony is also involved in the promotion of selected cluster initiatives, an example of which is Silicon Saxony e. V. (with 350 members)—the largest high-tech network in Saxony, also considered to be one of the largest microelectronics and IT clusters in Germany and Europe. The cluster has an international reputation in its sector, and the extensive public support for cluster was anchored at the highest political level (both at federal and European levels). In 2009, as part of Silicon Saxony, the national leading-edge cluster Cool Silicon e. V. was launched, associating 60 companies and research institutes from the leading microelectronics Silicon Saxony region. Its main goal is to increase energy efficiency within the field of information and communications technology.

Discussion

The findings show that the cluster policy, although established at the EU level, has been implemented and developed in individual countries in various ways and with diverse effects—this can be seen in the example of Poland and Germany. The matrix mapping of the areas of cluster activity and smart specializations demonstrates that both in Poland and Germany S3 priority domains are broader than leading clusters. It is understandable as S3 is more oriented toward structural change and the cluster's business growth. Research results also confirm that in both studied countries, clusters are important as the building blocks of smart specialization strategies. However, the ways and extent to which clusters are involved in the development and implementation of S3 vary among the regions and reveal opportunities for cluster initiatives in the process that were not fully utilized.

It is difficult to state unequivocally which of the analyzed countries is using cluster policies to a greater extent in order to implement smart specialization strategies at the regional level. Considering the differences in the development of cluster policy in the analyzed countries, it can be argued that a better organized cluster system in Germany creates more favorable conditions for the implementation of S3. However, the research showed that it depends on the approach taken by a concrete region. German regions have implemented S3 in a non-standardized way, which is associated with the heterogeneity of the framework conditions of economic policies. The analyzed case of Saxony shows that the S3 implementation can rely on the previous experience related to innovation rather than to cluster policy. In turn, the example of Pomeranian Voivodship and Interizon-Pomeranian ICT Cluster shows that clusters can serve as means for the implementation of S3. First of all, clusters embrace all relevant actors of the innovation process and provide important information about the needs and ongoing transformations. Furthermore, clusters usually have a triple helix platform configuration and for this reason, they are the right body to coordinate and facilitate working groups on specific S3 priority domains. The research results confirm the findings of Mikhaylov (2020) that clusters are complex cross-sectoral structures stretching beyond the statistical industrial classifications, which brings up new challenges for S3. As such, clustering approach provides a rationale to build a place-based smart specialization policy (Thissen et al. 2013), which goes beyond a concept of a place-based development as explained, for example, by McCann and Ortega-Argilés (2011), who emphasize the complexity of regional systems and economic networks. Moreover, comparative case study conducted in this chapter confirms the arguments of Kroll (2019) that "place-based economic transformation agendas," promoted by the smart specialization, provide a new framework to assess strategic regional innovation policy, which faces a number of regionally specific obstacles that need to be overcome. Integrating clusters into S3 constitutes a leading concept, which acts as a vital stimulant for the individual and group competency development in order to accomplish sustainable entrepreneurial and regional economic growth (Saha & Saha 2017).

Conclusion

Implications for Theory

The study broadens the knowledge of clusters and cluster policies, and their role in smart specialization strategies based on a relatively new and complex academic framework. In this respect, an attempt is made to translate it into policy practice. The originality of the study comes from the comparative analyses of Polish and German experiences, which provide real-life evidence on how clusters correlate and contribute to the implementation of smart specialization strategies in the regional context. This adds to previous studies, for example, D'Adda, Guzzini, Iacobucci, and Palloni (2019), which provide an empirical assessment of the coherence between the specialization domains chosen by Italian regions and those in which they show actual innovative capabilities.

The study provides better recognition of the approach applied by the analyzed countries while developing smart specializations. It also finds the answer to the question of whether smart specialization strategies are developed with the focus on clusters with the purpose of pursuing the innovation potential and developing a region's knowledge base. On this basis, it is also possible to assess the degree of consistency among the main areas of cluster activity and domains of smart specializations. This enables public authorities to identify and develop those sectors of economy in which the region has a significant position. These are primarily sectors at the intersection of clusters and smart specializations. Finally, it confirms that while specialization is a broader notion than clustering, clusters can still be major pillars of S3, as postulated by, for example, Rehfeld (2013) and Benner (2017a, 2017b).

As the research indicates, both in Poland and in Germany, there is an uneven deployment of leading clusters, and their scope is much narrower compared to RSS. The research also showed that in both analyzed countries, clusters are used to implement S3 with the participation of various stakeholder groups, although it is more visible in the example of German regions, where the degree of coherence between leading clusters and RSS seems to be higher than in Polish voivodships. Furthermore, the example of German regions proves that not only cluster policy can be the basis for implementation of S3 but also innovation policy. The findings from our study are also consistent with Barca, McCann, and Rodríguez-Pose (2012), according to which regions are expected to identify their strengths in terms of research and innovation, which provide opportunities for the development of new products and services. Innovation policy, just as cluster policy, can be used to identify fields of smart specialization while preventing too strong specialization, which may involve the use of a cluster approach. Both innovation and cluster policies can ensure consistency in action through integration with preexisting strategies and policies.

Implications for Policy

The empirical findings can also provide some practical implications, especially for policy makers responsible for implementing S3. Cluster policies may be used as tangible inputs into the development of the smart specialization strategy. Close alignment with regional smart specializations allows for more integrated use of European Structural and Investment Funds to increase the impact of cluster's activities, as postulated by Benner (2014). The case of Pomerania and Saxony shows that it is valuable for the development of regional economies as clusters can connect the different actors and measures and build bridges and synergies. However, the smart specialization policy recommendations should vary in different regions, taking into account their specificity and trajectories. This complements the proposition of Capello and Kroll (2016), who postulate that a one-size-fits-all policy needs to be overcome. Moreover, the S3 approach should promote specialization and facilitate diversification into new sectors, which can be achieved in domains closely related to the existing knowledge base (D'Adda et al., 2019). As proved by the experiences of regions analyzed in this chapter, regardless of the use of the cluster approach, the successful implementation of smart specializations requires commitment from all relevant stakeholders in the process of their selection and further coordination. This should become a partnership-based policy process of discovery and learning that involves both policy makers and entrepreneurs.

Limitations and Future Research Directions

The research conducted has some limitations, resulting primarily from the research method applied which is based only on the analysis of secondary data. In our study, we did not apply methods triangulation, which would ensure a higher quality of research and significantly enrich the obtained research material. The second limitation results from the fact that only two European countries were included in the study, which narrows the field of analysis, despite the differences in the level of development of the cluster policy in these countries. The third limitation is associated with the fact that smart specialization is a fairly new policy concept. However, at the current stage of implementing S3, it is possible to analyze the process of choosing smart specializations in selected EU countries and regions.

In some preliminary work, our study can contribute to understanding how cluster policies can be used to support the implementation of smart specialization strategies at regional level. For a better understanding of this issue, it is necessary to carry out both quantitative and qualitative research on a larger, more representative sample, taking into account additional European countries. It would be worthwhile to establish how earlier clustering experiences affect the effectiveness of S3 implementation by comparing RSS that is based on leading clusters and those that have emerged independently of the clusters. Furthermore, in future research, the possibility and legitimacy of using cluster initiatives as a driving force for regional innovation strategies should be given even more consideration.

References

Agencja Rozwoju Pomorza S. A. (n.d.). *Inteligentne Specjalizacje Pomorza.* Retrieved from www.arp.gda.pl/1189,inteligentne-specjalizacje

Anastasopoulos, D., Brochler, R., & Kalentzis, A. L. (2017). Smart specialisation strategy and the role of strong clusters: As a development leverage in Asia. *World Technopolis Review, 6*(2), 102–112. https://doi.org/10.7165/WTR17A1217.17

Anokhin, S., Wincent, J., Parida, V., Chistyakova, N., & Oghazi, P. (2019). Industrial clusters, flagship enterprises and regional innovation. *Entrepreneurship & Regional Development, 31*(1–2), 104–118. https://doi.org/10.1080/08985626.2018.1537150

Baier, E., Kroll, H., & Zenker, A. (2013). *Templates of smart specialisation: Experiences of place-based regional development strategies in Germany and Austria.* Arbeitspapiere Unternehmen und Region (No. R5/2013). Karlsruhe: Fraunhofer ISI.

Balland, P. A., Belso-Martínez, J. A., & Morrison, A. (2016). The dynamics of technical and business knowledge networks in industrial clusters: Embeddedness, status, or proximity?. *Economic Geography, 92*(1), 35–60. https://doi.org/10.1080/00130095.2015.1094370

Balland, P. A., Boschma, R., Crespo, J., & Rigby, D. L. (2019). Smart specialization policy in the European Union: Relatedness, knowledge complexity and regional diversification. *Regional Studies, 53*(9), 1252–1268. https://doi.org/10.1080/00343404.2018.1437900

Barca, F., McCann, P., & Rodríguez-Pose, A. (2012). The case for regional development intervention: Place-based versus place-neutral approaches. *Journal of Regional Science, 52*(1), 134–152. https://doi.org/10.1111/j.1467-9787.2011.00756.x

Belso-Martínez, J. A., Mas-Verdu, F., & Chinchilla-Mira, L. (2020). How do interorganizational networks and firm group structures matter for innovation in clusters: Different networks, different results. *Journal of Small Business Management, 58*(1), 73–105. https://doi.org/10.1080/00472778.2019.1659673

Belussi, F., & Trippl, M. (2018). Industrial districts/clusters and smart specialisation policies. In *Agglomeration and firm performance* (pp. 283–308). Cham: Springer.

Benner, M. (2014). From smart specialisation to smart experimentation: Building a new theoretical framework for regional policy of the European Union. *Zeitschrift für Wirtschaftsgeographie*, 58(1), 33–49.

Benner, M. (2017a). From clusters to smart specialization: Tourism in institution-sensitive regional development policies. *Economies*, 5(3), 26. https://doi.org/10.3390/economies5030026

Benner, M. (2017b). Smart specialization and cluster emergence: Elements of evolutionary regional policies. In D. Fornahl & R. Hassink (Eds.), *The life cycle of clusters* (pp. 151–172). Cheltenham, UK: Edward Elgar Publishing.

Benner, M. (2019). Smart specialization and institutional context: The role of institutional discovery, change and leapfrogging. *European Planning Studies*, 27(9), 1791–1810, https://doi.org/10.1080/09654313.2019.1643826

Buczyńska, G., Frączek, D., & Kryjom, P. (2016). *Raport z inwentaryzacji klastrów w Polsce 2015*. Warszawa: PARP.

Caloffi, A., & Mariani, M. (2018). Regional policy mixes for enterprise and innovation: A fuzzy-set clustering approach. *Environment and Planning C: Politics and Space*, 36, 28–46. https://doi.org/10.1080/08985626.2018.1537149

Capello, R., & Kroll, H. (2016). From theory to practice in smart specialisation strategy: Emerging limits and possible future trajectories. *European Planning Studies*, 24, 1393–1406. https://doi.org/10.1080/09654313.2016.1156058

Casanueva, C., Castro, I., & Galán, J. L. (2013). Informational networks and innovation in mature industrial clusters. *Journal of Business Research*, 66(5), 603–613. https://doi.org/10.1016/j.jbusres.2012.02.043

D'Adda, D., Guzzini, E., Iacobucci, D., & Palloni, R. (2019). Is Smart Specialisation Strategy coherent with regional innovative capabilities?. *Regional Studies*, 53(7), 1004–1016. https://doi.org/10.1080/00343404.2018.1523542

Delgado, M. (2020). The co-location of innovation and production in clusters. *Industry and Innovation*, 1–29, https://doi.org/10.1080/13662716.2019.1709419

Delgado, M., Porter, M. E., & Stern, S. (2014). Clusters, convergence, and economic performance. *Research Policy*, 43(10), 1785–1799. https://doi.org/10.1016/j.respol.2014.05.007

Departament Rozwoju Gospodarczego. (n.d.). *Inteligentne Specjalizacje*. Retrieved from https://drg.pomorskie.eu/inteligentne-specjalizacje

Dzierżanowski, M. (Ed.). (2012). *Kierunki i założenia polityki klastrowej w Polsce do 2020 roku. Rekomendacje Grupy roboczej ds. polityki klastrowej*. Warszawa: PARP.

Etzkowitz, H., & Leydesdorff, L. (1995). The Triple Helix: university—industry—government relations. A laboratory for knowledge-based economic development. *EASST Review*, 14, 14–19. https://doi.org/10.1007/s13132-019-00595-3

European Commission. (2010). *EUROPE 2020 – A strategy for smart, sustainable and inclusive growth*. Retrieved from http://europa.eu/press_room/pdf/complet_en_barroso___007_-_europe_2020_-en_version.pdf

European Commission. (2013). *The role of clusters in smart specialisation strategies*. Luxembourg: Publications Office of the European Union.

Ferras-Hernandez, X., & Nylund, P. A. (2019). Clusters as innovation engines: The accelerating strengths of proximity. *European Management Review*, 16(1), 37–53. https://doi.org/10.1111/emre.12330

Foray, D., & Goenaga, X. (2013). *The goals of smart specialization*. European Commission: JRC Scientific and Policy Report, S3 Policy Brief Series

No. 01/2013. Retrieved from https://s3platform.jrc.ec.europa.eu/documents/20182/115084/JRC82213_The_Goals_of_Smart_Specialisation.pdf/f5908687-6a34-42d7-bfd1-735e882e3681

Foray, D., David, P., & Hall, B. H. (2009). *Smart specialization—The concept.* Knowledge Economists Policy Brief, Number 9, June. European Commission: DG Research, Brussels. Retrieved from http://ec.europa.eu/invest-in-research/pdf/download_en/kfg_policy_brief_no9.pdf?11111

Fraunhofer ISI. (n.d.). *Cluster policy adjustment in the context of smart specialization? First impressions from Germany.* Retrieved from www.isi.fraunhofer.de/content/dam/isi/dokumente/ccp/vortragsfolien/regionale-innovationssysteme/Presentation_Koschatzky_Cluster_policy_adjustments.pdf

Fromhold-Eisebith, M., & Eisebith, G. (2005). How to institutionalize innovative clusters? Comparing explicit top-down and implicit bottom-up approaches. *Research Policy, 34*(8), 1250–1268. https://doi.org/10.1016/j.respol.2005.02.008

Gallego, J., & Maroto, A. (2013). The Specialization in Knowledge-Intensive Business Services (KIBS) across Europe: Permanent co-localization to debate. *Regional Studies, 49*, 644–664. https://doi.org/10.1080/00343404.2013.799762

Glaeser, E. L., Kerr, W. R., & Ponzetto, G. A. (2010). Clusters of entrepreneurship. *Journal of Urban Economics, 67*(1), 150–168. https://doi.org/10.1016/j.jue.2009.09.008

Hassink, R., & Gong, H. (2019). Six critical questions about smart specialization. *European Planning Studies, 27*(10), 2049–2065. https://doi.org/10.1080/09654313.2019.1650898

Interizon. (n.d.). *Inteligentne specjalizacje.* Retrieved from https://interizon.pl/pl/o-nas/inteligentne-specjalizacje

Iritié, B. J. J. (2018). Economic issues of innovation clusters-based industrial policy: A critical overview. *Global Business and Economics Review, 20*(3), 286–307. https://doi.org/10.1504/GBER.2018.10010995

Keller, M., Reinbruber, I., Dermastia, M., Bersier, J., & Meier zu Köcker, G. (2019). Implementing S3 with clusters—an innovation model for transformative activities. *Journal for Research and Technology Policy Evaluation, 47*, 23–34. https://doi.org/10.22163/fteval.2019.325

Kiese, M. (2019). Regional cluster policies in Germany: Challenges, impacts and evaluation practices. *The Journal of Technology Transfer, 44*(6), 1698–1719. https://doi.org/10.1007/s10961-017-9589-5

Kowalski, A. M. (2010), The role of clusters in enhancing ties between science and business, In M. A. Weresa (Ed.), *Poland: Competitiveness Report 2010. Focus on Clusters* (pp. 305–316). Warsaw: Warsaw School of Economics—Publishing.

Kowalski, A. M. (2013). The impact of industrial clusters on the innovativeness of business firms in Poland. *World Journal of Social Sciences, 3*(1), 73–84. http://dx.doi.org/10.2139/ssrn.2129190

Kowalski, A. M. (2016). Territorial location of ICT cluster initiatives and ICT-related sectors in Poland. In H. Drewello, M. Bouzar & M. Helfer (Eds.), *Clusters as a driving power of the European economy* (pp. 49–66). Baden-Baden: Nomos.

Kroll, H. (2019). Eye to eye with the innovation paradox: Why smart specialization is no simple solution to policy design, *European Planning Studies, 27*(5), 932–951, http://dx.doi.org/10.1080/09654313.2019.1577363

Kroll, H., Böke, I., Schiller, D., & Stahlecker, T. (2016). Bringing owls to Athens? The transformative potential of RIS3 for innovation policy in Germany's Federal States. *European Planning Studies*, 24(8), 1459–1477.

Lehmann, T., & Benner, M. (2015). Cluster policy in the light of institutional context—a comparative study of transition countries. *Administrative Sciences*, 5(4), 188–212. http://dx.doi.org/10.3390/admsci5040188

Martin, R., & Sunley P. (2003). Deconstructing clusters: Chaotic concept or policy panacea? *Journal of Economic Geography*, 3(1), 5–35.

McCann, P., & Ortega-Argilés, R. (2011). *Smart specialization, regional growth and applications to EU cohesion policy*. Economic Geographic Working Paper: Faculty of Spatial Sciences, University of Groningen.

Mikhaylov, A. S. (2020). Cross-border clustering across the Baltic region: Relating smart specialization and cluster categories. In *Baltic region—The region of cooperation* (pp. 99–108). Cham: Springer.

Morgan, K. (2013). Path dependence and the state. In P. Cooke (Ed.), *Re-framing regional development* (pp. 318–340). London: Routledge.

Morgan, K. (2016). Nurturing novelty: Regional innovation policy in the age of smart specialisation. *Environment and Planning C: Government and Policy*, 35, 569–583. https://doi.org/10.1177/0263774X16645106

Papamichail, G., Rosiello, A., & Wield, D. (2019). Capacity-building barriers to S3 implementation: An empirical framework for catch-up regions. *Innovation: The European Journal of Social Science Research*, 32(1), 66–84. https://doi.org/10.1080/13511610.2018.1537844

Pascal, V. (2005). Clusters and entrepreneurial intnesity: The influence of economic clusters on entrepreneurial activity. *Journal of Research in Marketing and Entrepreneurship*, 7, 5–27. https://doi.org/27. 10.1108/1471520058000 1348

Pomorskie w Unii Europejskiej. (2020). *Inteligentne Specjalizacje Pomorza*. Retrieved from https://pomorskieregion.eu/inteligentne-specjalizacje-pomorza-p230

Pronestì, G. (2019). *Life cycle of clusters in designing smart specialization policies*. Berlin: Springer International Publishing.

Porter, M. E. (1998). Clusters and the new economics of competition. *Harvard Business Review*, 76(6), 77–90.

Porter, M. E. (2000). Location, competition, and economic development: Local clusters in a global economy. *Economic Development Quarterly*, 14(1), 4–6.

Porter, M. E. (2007). *Clusters and Economic Policy: Aligning Public Policy with the New Economics of Competition*. White Paper, Institute for Strategy and Competitiveness, Harvard Business School, Harvard.

Qi, H., Liu, S., Qi, W., & Liu, Z. (2019). Geographical concentration of knowledge-and technology-intensive industries and city innovation in China. *Sustainability*, 11(18), 4840. https://doi.org/10.3390/su11184840

Rehfeld, D. (2013). *Clusterpolitik, intelligente Spezialisierung, soziale Innovationen—neue Impulse in der Innovationspolitik*. Forschung Aktuell 04/2013, Institut Arbeit und Technik (IAT), Gelsenkirchen. Retrieved from http://nbn-resolving.de/urn:nbn:de:0176-201304012

Rocha, H., Kunc, M., & Audretsch, D. B. (2019). Clusters, economic performance, and social cohesion: A system dynamics approach. *Regional Studies*, 1–14. https://doi.org/10.1080/00343404.2019.1668550

Roelandt, T. J. A., & den Hertog, P. (1999). Cluster analysis and cluster-based policy making: The state of the art. In Idem (Ed.), *Cluster analysis and cluster-based policy: New perspectives and rationale in innovation policy*. Paris: Organisation for Economic Cooperation and Development.

Saha, N., & Saha, P. (2017). The synergies influence of clustering and smart specialization strategy: Do they really stimulate entrepreneurship and regional development?, *Global Journal of Business, Economics and Management: Current Issues, 7*(1), 159–168. https://doi.org/10.18844/gjbem.v7i1.1365

Saha, N., Sáha, T., & Sáha, P. (2018). Cluster strategies and smart specialisation strategy: Do they really leverage on knowledge and innovation-driven territorial growth?. *Technology Analysis & Strategic Management, 30*(11), 1256–1268. https://doi.org/10.1080/09537325.2018.1444747

Santoalha, A. (2016). *New indicators of smart specialization: a related diversification approach applied to European regions* (TIK Working Papers on Innovation Studies No. 20161220). Centre for Technology, Innovation and Culture, University of Oslo.

Saxony.de. (n.d.). *Smart Specialisation*. Retrieved from www.innovationsstrategie. sachsen.de/en/smart-specialisation.html#:~:text=Smart%20Specialisation%20 made%20in%20Saxony&text=The%20smart%20specialisation%20of%20 the,intensive%20participation%20of%20numerous%20stakeholders

Serwis Regionalnego Programu województwa Pomorskiego. (n.d.). *Inteligentne specjalizacje*. Retrieved from www.rpo.pomorskie.eu/inteligentne-specjalizacje

Sölvell, Ö., Lindqvist, G., & Ketels, Ch. (2003) *The cluster initiative greenbook*. Stockholm: Ivory Tower AB.

Sölvell, O. (2008). *Clusters balancing evolutionary and constructive forces*. Stockholm: Ivory Tower Publishing.

Sörvik, J., & Kleibrink, A. (2015). *Mapping innovation priorities and specialisation patterns in Europe*. Brussels, Belgium: European Commission.

Tallman, S., Jenkins, M., Henry, N., & Pinch, S. (2004). Knowledge clusters, and competitive advantage. *The Academy of Management Review, 29*, 258–271. https://doi.org/10.5465/AMR.2004.12736089

Thissen, M., Van Oort, F., Diodato, D., & Ruijs, A. (2013). *regional competitiveness and smart specialization in Europe: Place-based development in international economic networks*. Cheltenham, UK: Edward Elgar Publishing.

Tödtling, F., & Trippl, M. (2005). One size fits all? Towards a differentiated regional innovation policy approach. *Research Policy, 34*(8), 1203–1219. https://doi.org/10.1016/j.respol.2005.01.018

Turkina, E., Oreshkin, B., & Kali, R. (2019). Regional innovation clusters and firm innovation performance: An interactionist approach. *Regional Studies, 53*(8), 1193–1206.

Vlčková, J., Kaspříková, N., & Vlčková, M. (2018). Technological relatedness, knowledge space and smart specialisation: The case of Germany. *Moravian Geographical Reports, 26*(2), 95–108.

Internet sources

(n.d.). https://ci-3.de/

BioEconomy Cluster eV. (n.d.). www.bioeconomy.de/

BioM Biotech Cluster Development GmbH—BioM. (n.d.). www.bio-m.org/

BioRN Network e.V. (n.d.). www.biorn.org/
Bydgoski Klaster Przemysłowy. (n.d.). www.klaster.bydgoszcz.pl
Cluster Elektromobilität Süd-West. (n.d.). www.emobil-sw.de/
Cluster for Individualized Immune Intervention (Ci3) e.V.
Cool Silicon e. V. (n.d.). www.cool-silicon.de/start/
Die Spitzencluster—BMBF Spitzencluster. (n.d.). www.spitzencluster.de/
Digital Hub Logistics. (n.d.). https://digitalhublogistics.de/effizienzcluster/
Dolina Lotnicza. (n.d.). www.dolinalotnicza.pl
Hamburg Aviation. (n.d.). www.hamburg-aviation.de/
InnovationLab. (n.d.). www.innovationlab.de/gedruckte-elektronik-flexible-drucksensoren/
Interizon—Pomorski Klaster ICT. (n.d.) www.interizon.pl
it's OWL. (n.d.). www.its-owl.de/home/
M.A.I. Carbon. (n.d.). www.mai-carbon.de/
Klaster Gospodarki Odpadowej i Recyklingu. (n.d.). www.klasterodpadowy.com
Klaster LifeScience Kraków. (n.d.). www.lifescience.pl
Klaster Logistyczno Transportowy Północ-Południe. (n.d.). www.klasterlogtrans.pl
Klaster Obróbki Metali. (n.d.). www.metalklaster.pl
Klaster Zrównoważona Infrastruktura. (n.d.). www.klasterzi.pl
Mazowiecki Klaster ICT. (n.d.). www.klasterict.pl
Medical Valley EMN e.V. (n.d.). www.medical-valley-emn.de/
microTEC Südwest. (n.d.). www.microtec-suedwest.de/
Polska Grupa Motoryzacyjna. (n.d.). www.pgm.org.pl
Polski Klaster Budowlany. (n.d.). www.budowlanyklaster.pl
Silesia Automotive & Advanced Manufacturing. (n.d.). www.silesia-automotive.pl
Śląski Klaster Lotniczy. (n.d.) www.aerosilesia.eu
Smart Specialisation Platform—Europa EU. (n.d.). https://s3platform.jrc.ec.europa.eu/
Software-Cluster. (n.d.). http://software-cluster.org/
Solar Valley. (n.d.). www.solarvalley.org/
Wschodni Klaster ICT. (n.d.). www.ecict.eu
Zielona Chemia. (n.d.). www.zielonachemia.eu
Związek Pracodawców Klastry Polskie. (n.d.). www.klastrypolskie.pl

9 Municipality Digital Platforms and Local Development in the Warmia and Mazury Region

Implications for Smart Specialization

Aleksander Jakimowicz and Daniel Rzeczkowski

Introduction

Strong regions are the foundation of any national economy. The emergent result of all forces operating at the local level is revealed at the macroeconomic level. Smart specialization strategy (S3) seeks to ensure a competitive advantage for a region or country by developing and combining its strengths in the form of research and innovation (Foray, 2015; 2016). The expected benefit is a coherent local development under conditions of rational human and material resources management. Rather than on individual industries, smart specialization strategy focuses on technological fields with particular emphasis on digital technology (Foray, 2017; McCann & Ortega-Argilés, 2015). It can be argued that the importance of ICT entails the necessity to introduce the fundamental principles of wikinomics to the implementation of S3. Wikinomics is an emergent field of research that emphasizes the economic and social impact of digital technologies (Tapscott & Williams, 2006; 2012). Considering a premature experience in the implementation of the smart specialization concept, the insights from wikinomics can contribute to the understanding of the role of ICT in the adoption of smart specialization (SS).

This research focuses on studying the importance of information and communication technologies on the advancement of local governments. In particular, its aim is to identify the relationship between the development of municipality digital platforms and the development of their respective territories in the Warmia and Mazury region, Poland, and to derive implications for the implementation of smart specialization strategies at the local level. The considerations presented here are carried out within the framework of the smart specialization strategy, enhanced by the principles of wikinomics. The object of the research is the Warmia and Mazury region in northeastern Poland. This region is characterized by a low level of entrepreneurship, which requires establishing a collaborative public–private partnership to stimulate economic and social cohesion (Tapscott & Williams, 2006; 2012). From the perspective of wikinomics, the websites of municipal public administration offices may serve as germs of participative platforms that would initiate a public–private collaboration to enhance entrepreneurial discovery processes.

To explore the link between the quality of local digital platforms and local development, this study has identified spatial growth poles and development axes in Warmia and Mazury, based on an original research methodology comprising dual graphs. The findings reveal that the most developed municipality digital platforms overlap with infrastructural growth poles and development axes in the studied region. Moreover, the comparison of the information contained in the empirical dual graphs with the information base of the dual graph corresponding to the four-color theorem was used to develop a completely new measure of regional economic development (Jakimowicz & Rzeczkowski, 2021). Our research proposes the conceptual advancement and practical recommendations as to the implementation of S3 at the local level. The conceptual contribution consists of integrating the assumptions of wikinomics, combined with the theories of growth poles and development axes, to the guidelines of adopting SS at the local level. The referred concepts are proposed as useful in explaining the role of the ICT infrastructures and competences in the establishment of public–private partnership networks for entrepreneurial discovery processes. Second, we identify the current and potential impacts of ICT instruments in the local government context, and we formulate recommendations regarding their use in mobilizing local capabilities toward S3.

The chapter structure is as follows. The literature background section discusses the concepts of wikinomics, growth poles, and development axes as ideas that may enhance the understanding of how to implement S3. Moreover, it identifies the related research gaps. The following sections present research methods and results. The discussion and conclusions highlight the implications for theory and practice, limitations, and future research directions.

Literature Background

The concept of smart specialization defines the capacity of the economic system, such as a region, to initiate specialties and development directions through creative, previously unknown combinations of resources and competences (Foray, 2015). Smart specialization strategy is also an economic development policy based on targeting and supporting research and innovation in such a way as to encourage regions to discover new economic niches or specializations (Foray, 2016; 2017). The purpose of this policy approach is to introduce into the system structural changes, such as diversification, transition, modernization, which would contribute to the improvement of existing or the creation of new branches of production or service sectors. A smart specialization process is based on local capabilities and production structures, but their improvement may also require new resources, technologies, and competences from within or outside the region (Carayannis & Grigoroudis, 2016). Smart specialization complements existing productive assets with new, innovative solutions (Foray, 2015).

According to the smart specialization concept, the entrepreneurial discovery process is of great importance, as it reveals the potential of a given country or region in R&D and innovation (Foray, 2017; Carayannis & Grigoroudis, 2016). During the process, companies, technologies, or areas that should be supported are identified. For this purpose, a bottom-up policy based on entrepreneurial trial and error is used (McCann & Ortega-Argilés, 2015). Entrepreneurs are relevant partners to designate new fields or areas in which the region has the best chance of success, as they have the appropriate understanding of current market trends and knowledge of existing capabilities and productive assets. The innovation policy is built on this basis, considering not only the strengths and potential of each region but also a sufficiently large group of economic entities and their knowledge of local markets. There is no central planning in this process, priorities are set by the market sector, the government assesses the development potential and supports those who can make the best use of it (Foray, 2017).

Smart specialization strategy should be understood as the process of developing new specializations on the basis of existing production structures, which is the result of targeted governmental intervention (Foray, 2015). It is about supporting the most promising solutions through experimentation, learning from mistakes, expected spillovers, and structural changes. This concept should not be equated with smart specialization, which can sometimes appear spontaneously due to the independent activity of economic entities and coordination capacities of the market sector. In other words, processes of smart specialization can occur without any government policy. The essence of smart specialization strategy is the focus on two issues: capacity building in selected strategic areas and driving structural change (Foray, 2015, 2017).

Until recently, entrepreneurial discovery processes emphasized techno-economic potentials, but it soon emerged that the institutional context was equally important. The implementation of smart specialization in individual regions should be associated with the identification and elimination of certain institutional barriers that could inhibit economic development. Benner (2019) understands the institutional context as a set of existing institutions in the form of stable patterns of social practice, their interaction with prescriptive rules and organizations, as well as institutional change caused by mutual interactions between the private sector and the public sector. It can be noticed that economic performance depends largely on the type of feedbacks that occur in public–private networks. Kuznetsov and Sabel (2017) create a new framework for discussing the efficiency of smart specialization, emphasizing the aspect of gradual changes in the private and public sectors. Heterogeneity of institutions is recommended, which consists of improving inefficient institutions by efficient institutions and diagnostic monitoring. Another proposal in this respect is the strengthening of cooperation between regional and subregional governments in order to create new sources of knowledge in a given territory (Estensoro & Larrea, 2016). Thus, there is a rapprochement between smart specialization policy and prosumption, which is one of the basic wikinomics business patterns.

Wikinomics is a relatively young but dynamically developing field of economic research, which looks into the influence of digital computing technologies on the growth of economies and societies (Tapscott & Williams, 2006, 2012). Digital technology has brought about a significant change in the conditions for running a business, which has been reflected in the emergence of completely new business rules and business models. The mass and spontaneous cooperation of people, facilitated by modern information technologies, has fundamentally changed the course of modern economic processes. The basic principles of wikinomics include openness, peering, sharing, and acting globally. The concept of competitiveness based on companies' refusal to share some of their resources is becoming obsolete, as this prevents them from benefiting from external sources of human innovation and ingenuity. Partial openness is nowadays a factor increasing the competitiveness of companies. A new form of economic organization, with a horizontal structure, in which a partnership is born and gradually blurs the boundaries between employers and employees, is becoming increasingly popular. In line with the new intellectual property economy, the supply of resources by knowledge producers upgrades their potential to create value. Modern ICT technologies make companies operate more frequently in global markets. A new way in which enterprises operate, resulting from the spread of information technologies and computer networks, inevitably changes traditional business strategies. Wikinomics models of global cooperation include (Tapscott & Williams, 2006; 2012):

- peer pioneers—people who spontaneously create new products and services, often better and more sophisticated than their market counterparts;
- ideagoras—new markets for ideas, innovations, and people with unique skills that are developing on the Internet beyond the boundaries of traditional businesses. They enable enterprises to benefit from the potential of the global scientific community without having to hire new staff;

- prosumers—a new category of economic operators combining consumer and producer functions. They actively participate in designing, creating, and manufacturing a new product through their innovation and creativity (Toffler, 1980; Toffler & Toffler, 2007);
- new Alexandrians—people actively participating in multiplying, collecting, systematizing, and instantly sharing human knowledge;
- platforms for participation—advanced websites with product information and relevant technological infrastructure, which are made available to the large communities of partners in order to develop new values and launch innovative projects;
- global plant floor—systems for designing and producing goods or services resulting from global cooperation;
- wiki workplace—a new organizational culture of the enterprise breaking with hierarchy and linking internal enterprise teams with external social networks; it includes new technologies in the workplace to enhance people's creativity and social connectivity and to promote friendly relationships within and outside the company.

It should also be noted that wikinomics inspired Degerstedt (2015) to develop the notion of social competitive intelligence, which is used by the networking organization to gather, analyze, and transform information into actionable intelligence.

The literature indicates that entrepreneurial discovery process must consider geographic conditions, such as the characteristics of a given region, interregional links, local entrepreneurial cultures, governance structures, and institutional forms. It is emphasized that the level of entrepreneurship is higher in regions with higher population density, less specialized, less dominated by a small number of large firms, with more multinational companies actively participating in foreign trade, and in regions with large market potential. Furthermore, it is noted that the ICT implementation has deepened development disparities between core and noncore regions, rather than reducing them (McCann & Ortega-Argilés, 2015). As the simulations show, regional conditions determine the effectiveness of smart specialization policy (Varga, Sebestyén, Szabó, & Szerb, 2020). It is very important to attentively observe the relation between economic geography and smart specialization; however, it may still be not enough to obtain an accurate perspective. A more complete use of the geographic potential by the smart specialization policy may occur when the local growth poles and development axes are considered.

The theory of growth poles was developed by a French economist, François Perroux (1964), who formulated it in the 1950s. Regional growth poles are considered to be driving forces, such as fast-growing companies or industrial sectors that support economic activity in their environment and contribute to the better economic performance of other companies and industries. From the point of view of wikinomics, it may be argued that a growth pole is created where economic activity is supported by advanced digital technology. Such a pole in the examined region may be the website of a municipality public administration office, which integrates and strengthens the economic forces operating in the given municipality. The higher the quality of the municipal website is, the greater the chance that it will act as a regional growth pole.

The theory of growth poles is supplemented by the concept of development axes, proposed by Pottier (1963). The idea of the axis indicates that economic development is transferred through trade routes and transport networks connecting the major industrial centers. Regions between the growth poles receive additional growth drivers in the form of increased flows of goods and services, the spread of innovation, or the development of transport infrastructure. Therefore, they turn into development axes or corridors, forming an integral whole with poles of growth and define the spatial framework for the economic growth of entire regions or countries. In the digital economy, information routes are at least as important as traditional trade routes. The spatial distribution of high or very high-quality municipality websites might be considered as representing wikinomics growth poles in the region, makes it possible to learn the ways in which economic growth is spread in the examined region and to identify the places where barriers to this growth emerge. When compared to the established growth poles and development axis in the region. Consequently, the identification and explanation of the links between the distribution of advanced municipality platforms and the distribution of growth poles and development axes in the region enable the implications for future development directions and drivers of S3 implementation.

Therefore, we formulate the following research questions:

RQ1: *What is the relationship between the distribution of high-quality municipality platforms and the distribution of local growth poles and development axes?*

RQ2: *What implications for future development directions and conditions of S3 implementation at the local level can be derived from the referred relationship?*

These research questions and study design address the following research gaps. First, smart specialization strategy requires a specification at the local level since the extant research predominantly focuses at the level of regions and countries. In particular, the experience as to technology-enhanced public–private partnerships for entrepreneurial discovery processes is under-researched. Second, S3 assumes integration and recombination of extant development concepts to enhance its implementation (Foray, 2016). However, the principles and models of wikinomics have not been recognized in the set of relevant concepts to date, while they are relevant to understand the role of ICT in entrepreneurial discovery processes. Third, there is a shortage of effective methods to monitor S3, especially regarding the role of digital technology. Fellnhofer (2017) reviewed 131 scientific articles devoted to the topic and found that 84 publications use qualitative methods, 26 articles focus on quantitative approaches, and only 21 use both methodologies. The reports classified to the qualitative stream usually contain research on smart specialization from a policy perspective. Manuscripts using the quantitative approach mainly explain regional diversification processes and statistics and define smart specialization policy on their basis. The conclusions of the review of the scientific literature are that researchers are advised to use mixed methods, using a combination of qualitative and quantitative approaches because the results obtained in such a way are considered as more rigorous. Therefore, addressing the aforementioned research gaps requires an interdisciplinary research approach and application of an integrated set of qualitative, as well as economic, mathematical, and econophysics methods. These will be discussed in detail in the next section.

Methodological Approach

Both qualitative and quantitative methods have been applied in this research. The qualitative method refers to the evaluation of advancement of municipality electronic platforms as digital growth poles and germs for public–private partnership in their respective territories. To identify the local growth poles and development axes, the quantitative approach was designed, including the methods of the k-means algorithm, the four-color theorem, and the reduction of the dual empirical graphs.

In a nutshell, the research design was as follows. The first step was to apply the binary method to assess municipal websites based on 16 quality criteria. Next, using the k-means algorithm, four quality classes of these websites were determined. Each quality class was assigned a color, which was used to mark individual municipalities on the provincial map. The four-color theorem and the resulting dual graph performed the role of the absolute reference system in the conducted studies. The next step was to draw up maps of the region for 2009, 2012, and 2015 and to determine empirical dual graphs for these maps. They were found to be reduced in comparison to the graph corresponding to a map meeting the conditions of the four-color theorem. The reduction of the dual empirical graphs made it possible to construct the complementary graphs, which, in turn, made it possible to determine the growth poles and development axes. The following paragraphs explain the details of the aforementioned methodological design.

In the first step, this study has applied the binary method to assess municipal websites based on 16 quality criteria. In our previous studies, we have identified 16 criteria in line with the principles of wikinomics (Table 9.1). The acquisition of information about the quality of websites

Table 9.1 Criteria for the functionality of the municipal websites in 2009, 2012, and 2015

Number	Website functionality criteria
1	Website is updated on a regular basis
2	The postal address of the office is included, directions are provided
3	The office publishes chat lines and/or discussion lists for the citizens
4	The structure of the office has been posted
5	Current information is published on a regular basis
6	There is a possibility to search for necessary information
7	A calendar of posts is published
8	The user can fill and send a form online
9	Other than Polish language versions are available
10	Website provides icons that help the user to use the website
11	The website address of the office is intuitive
12	Archive exists
13	A map of the municipality is published
14	Tourist attractions are indicated
15	Link to "digital office" provided
16	Link to ePUAP (Electronic Platform of Public Administration Services) provided

Source: Based on Jakimowicz and Rzeczkowski (2016).

was possible with the use of the binary method, which consisted in assigning a value of 1 when a criterion was met or 0 if the criterion was not satisfied. Thus, the abundance indicator of the website was expressed as a number from the closed interval between 0 and 16 (Jakimowicz & Rzeczkowski, 2016). In this way, all 116 municipalities in the Warmia and Mazury Region were assessed, and the study was carried out three times. The data concern 2009, 2012, and 2015. Next, based on the k-means algorithm, four quality classes of these websites were determined.

In order to divide websites into homogeneous subsets representing their quality classes, the k-means algorithm was used. The task consisted of dividing the data set $X = (x_1, x_2, \cdots, x_n)$ into a predetermined number of k clusters with the greatest possible distinction (Everitt, Landau, Leese, & Stahl, 2011). The calculation should lead to such a set of k cluster centroids that each point of the X set should be assigned to one cluster. At the same time, the distances of all points belonging to a cluster from its centroid must be smaller than the distances of these points from all other centroids. The corresponding mathematical formula takes the following form:

$$\arg \min \sum_{i=1}^{k} \sum_{x_n \in C_k} \| x_n - \mu_k \|^2,$$

where C_k and μ_k stand for clusters and centroids, respectively. The division of the set of observations into $k \leq n$ clusters is obtained by minimizing the within-cluster sum of squares, that is, variance. This method, despite its apparent simplicity, belongs to NP-hard problems (Aloise, Deshpande, Hansen, & Popat, 2009; Mahajan, Nimbhorkar, & Varadarajan, 2009). The term is used to describe the complexity class containing the set of decision problems that can be solved by a nondeterministic Turing machine in polynomial time (Zhao, Pan, Thomas, Jekjantuk, & Ren, 2013, p. 56).

In practice, difficulties associated with k-means clustering can be overcome using an iterative method called Lloyd's algorithm. It consists of repeating two mathematical operations (Lloyd, 1982):

1. After the establishment of a set of centroids μ_k, the C_k clusters are updated by reducing—inside each cluster—the distance of points from the centroid;
2. Once the clusters have been established, the centroids, which are the means of all points belonging to the respective clusters, are recalculated.

The calculations included in the algorithm are as follows:

$$C_k = \left\{ x_n : \left\| x_n - \mu_k \right\| \leq \text{all} \left\| x_n - \mu_l \right\| \right\},$$

$$\mu_k = \frac{1}{C_k} \sum_{x_n \in C_k} x_n.$$

The calculations are continued until the results stop changing. The convergence usually occurs after a few steps, but a certain limitation of this method should be kept in mind. It consists of the fact that the solution may contain a local minimum.

After determining four quality classes of websites, each class was assigned a color. These colors were used to mark individual municipalities on the provincial map and to derive a four-color theorem. The next step was to draw up maps of the region for 2009, 2012, and 2015, and to determine empirical dual graphs for these maps. They were found to be reduced in comparison to the dual graph corresponding to a map meeting the conditions of the four-color theorem (Jakimowicz & Rzeczkowski, 2018, 2021). The reduction of the dual empirical graphs made it possible to construct the complementary graphs, which, in turn, enabled the identification of the growth poles and development axes. The four-color theorem and the corresponding dual graph performed the role of the absolute reference system in the conducted studies.

To identify regional growth poles and development axes, the four-color theorem and the dual graph reduction method were used. According to the four-color theorem, the regions on each planar map can be colored with only four colors so that every two adjacent areas have different colors (Wilson, 2014). The importance of this theorem in research lies in the fact that it acts as an absolute reference system. Determination of such a reference system requires coloring the map of the Warmia and Mazury region with the municipalities identified in a manner consistent with the conditions of the four-color theorem. In this way, all adjacent municipalities are colored with different colors. The resulting map is a kind of planar graph, in which the faces are municipalities, the edges form inter-municipal boundaries and the vertices are delimited by the boundary points of contact.

Next, on the basis of such a map, a dual graph is drawn, referred to as the reference graph. To this end, the main towns of all municipalities are marked on the map of the region, and the main towns of adjacent municipalities are then connected by roads crossing their common borders. These roads are sections of straight lines and form the edges of a dual graph. They divide the plane into triangles (called faces) of the dual graph. The main towns of municipalities, on the other hand, are the vertices of the dual graph and correspond to the municipalities marked on the original map. Replacing a map colored according to the conditions of the four-color theorem with a dual graph allows solving a very important problem of identifying inter-municipal cooperation. This cooperation is based on the websites of municipal public administration offices, which should increasingly provide platforms for participation. With their assistance, the municipalities, as the basic units of local government, can not only support entrepreneurship but also enhance entrepreneurial discovery processes through creativity and innovation of the inhabitants as prosumers. Hence, the quality of these websites is one of key factors in regional economic growth.

Empirical maps were created in such a way that individual municipalities were marked with colors corresponding to the quality classes of their websites. The method used to construct dual graphs corresponding to empirical maps is identical to that of dual graphs determined based on a map satisfying the conditions of the four-color theorem. On empirical maps, it often happens that adjacent municipalities have the same color, which means that their websites belong to the same quality class. In this case, their main towns are not connected by the edges of a dual graph. If bordering municipalities have websites belonging to the same quality class, they are treated as one region. Before drawing the empirical dual graph, the conventional main towns of all such regions are then designated. The main towns of adjacent municipalities or regions are then connected by sections of straight lines passing through the common borders of these areas. The resulting object is referred to as an empirical dual graph. Three such graphs were drawn up in the course of the research, corresponding to 2009, 2012, and 2015.

The reference dual graph corresponds to a theoretical case with no inter-municipal cooperation. On the other hand, empirical dual graphs contain information about such cooperation. If neighboring municipalities have websites belonging to the same quality class, which is shown by the same color of these municipalities on the map, it is assumed that these municipalities cooperate with each other. This fact is indicated by the absence of edges on the dual graph connecting the main towns of these municipalities. In other words, the existence of edges connecting the main towns of adjacent municipalities proves the lack of cooperation between them, while the absence of edges indicates cooperation. Thus, a reference dual graph, which has the maximum number of edges, means that there is no inter-municipal cooperation.

This does not happen in the case of empirical maps and corresponding dual graphs. The reduction of empirical dual graphs compared to the reference dual graph permits identifying regional growth poles and development axes. If adjoining municipalities have the same colors and these colors stand for a high or very high-quality class of their websites, the municipalities concerned form spatial growth poles or, in the case of a longer chain of such municipalities, growth and development axes. In order to determine them, complementary graphs were used in relation to the empirical dual graphs for 2009, 2012, and 2015, which were created by supplementing reduced edges. Strictly speaking, graph H is called the complement of graph G if both graphs H and G contain the same vertices, and an edge exists between the vertices of graph H if, and only if, there is no edge between the same vertices in graph G (Diestel, 2000, p. 4). The next step was to draw up maps of the region for 2009, 2012, and 2015 and to determine empirical dual graphs for these maps.

Results

The Characteristics of the Warmia and Mazury Region

The Warmia and Mazury region is one of the least economically developed administrative units in Poland (Czyżewska-Misztal & Golejewska, 2016). Industries of key importance for the region include the wood and furniture sectors, food processing, and tourism. Local entrepreneurship is very underdeveloped. In 2010–2015, the level of information infrastructure in this region was very low, although changes in the synthetic ICT index between 2010 and 2015 in comparison to the average value for Poland indicate the occurrence of convergence (the catching-up effect) (Wierzbicka, 2018). In 2015, a large investment was completed in this region, consisting of constructing a fiber-optic backbone distribution network to provide broadband Internet access to subscribers. However, the absence of last-mile networks might be responsible for the low level of IT infrastructure indicated in the aforementioned studies. This investment, which is a driving force for the socioeconomic development of the region, was carried out as part of a public–private partnership based on the design, build, operate, transfer (DBOT) model (Sieć Szerokopasmowa Polski Wschodniej, 2018; Krzyżanowski, 2015). Ultimately, the network should cover more than 90% of the population of the region after the inclusion of telecommunications operators already operating in the project.

The project was implemented as a public–private partnership based on the DBOT (design, build, operate, transfer) model. Under this model, the Warmia and Mazury region is the owner of the created infrastructure, while the duties of the private partner include implementation of the project against remuneration and incurring a part of the related expenses. In particular, this involves designing and building the infrastructure, followed by performing management and operation functions, and thus providing services with its use. The private partner is also obliged to carry out training in Internet use for the inhabitants of the region at risk of digital exclusion. In addition, the private partner will pay the lease rent for the use of the network until the end of 2025 and then return all of the assets produced to the public partner. The agreement also provides for a detailed division of investment risk between the public and private partners. As studies show, the success of public–private partnerships depends to a large extent on the experience of the public entity in this field (Węgrzyn, 2018). In this case, it proved sufficient as the investment was successfully completed.

More than 20 towns in the region belong to the Polish National Cittàslow Network, which promotes such values as improving the quality of life of the inhabitants, protecting the natural environment, spreading the culture of hospitality, promoting local products, local crafts, and cuisine, as well as improving the work of local administration and adjusting the operation of institutions to the needs of the inhabitants (Wierzbicka, 2020). Such initiatives are certainly part of the smart specialization strategy and demonstrate the need to take into account the wikinomics models in city economics. However, alarming changes are taking place in the municipalities of the Warmia and Mazury region, consisting of their shrinking due to adverse demographic changes. This is reflected in lower budgetary revenues. In 2012–2017, the population was reduced in 95 out of 116 municipalities in the region (Wichowska, 2019).

In 2013, as part of the nationwide project of defining smart specializations using a foresight methodology, eight areas were designated for the Warmia and Mazury region: water economy, high-quality food (agricultural and food sector), wood and furniture industry, ICT, fairs and promotion, safety, logistics, and finance sector (Miller, Mroczkowski, &

Healy, 2014; Wyrwa, 2014). However, the latest research proves that there has been no significant progress in these areas, and some studies even indicate that there was a regress in innovation in these fields. In the studied region, a steady decrease in the value of the synthetic measure of regional innovation development has been observed since 2009. This index in 2009 was 0.27, in 2014 it dropped to 0.24, and in 2019 it was only 0.22. This means that throughout this period there was a high risk of supporting solutions that could ultimately occur to be ineffective. A partial explanation of these issues may be the fact that some of the mentioned smart specializations are based on innovations that use the natural environment, often also on eco-innovations, which may result in a long-term lack of profitability of such investments (Kogut-Jaworska & Ociepa-Kicińska, 2020).

Tourism in the Warmia and Mazury region, despite the existence of many lakes, rivers, forests, nature monuments, and recreation centers, is not smart specialization, although from an economic point of view, it is an important sector for the region. However, smart specialization may emerge in this sector when new applications of information and communications technology (ICT) contribute to the improvement of services and enrichment of the tourist offer. A prerequisite for achieving this goal is the commitment of enough efforts and resources to create new competitive advantages by properly linking the tourism sector with ICT.

The literature review shows that not much research has been carried out so far in the Warmia and Mazury region. In particular, lacking is a comprehensive approach that would comprise a set of such methods to investigate the grounding for S3 at the local level. Based on this review, we can expect historically and politically conditioned local growth poles and development axes. These poles and axes are closely linked to the transport network: road, rail, and inland waterway. Considering the previous characteristics of the region, public–private partnership networks at the municipality level, construction of a fiber-optic backbone distribution network, the 2025 Digital Plan for Warmia and Mazury, and the government's investment in infrastructure might be considered useful ways to achieve sustainable economic growth.

The Identification of the Quality of Municipality Participative Platforms in Warmia and Mazury

As a result of applying Lloyd's algorithm, four clusters representing the following quality classes of websites of municipal public administration offices were distinguished: low-quality, average quality, high quality, and very high quality (Table 9.2). The number four is not a random number here. This division is natural in the topological sense that can be justified on the basis of catastrophe theory, which is a kind of method allowing for the classification of stable forms (Jakimowicz, 2010; Jakimowicz &

Table 9.2 Four clusters representing the wikinomics categories of quality of the websites of the municipal administrative authorities in 2009, 2012, and 2015

Characteristics	Low quality	Average quality	High quality	Very high quality
Year	**2009**			
Points (min–max)	0–4	5–9	10–11	12–16
Centroid	0	7.72	10.45	13.35
Number of municipalities	17	22	37	40
Year	**2012**			
Points (min—max)	0–6	7–10	11–13	14–16
Centroid	0	9	11.75	14.45
Number of municipalities	6	11	49	50
Year	**2015**			
Points (min–max)	0–6	7–11	12–13	14–16
Centroid	0.47	8.69	11.75	14.65
Number of municipalities	10	32	35	39

Source: Based on Jakimowicz and Rzeczkowski (2018).

Kulesza, 2018; Thom, 1975; Trotman & Zeeman, 1976). As it will be demonstrated subsequently, the regional economic growth research uses maps of Warmia and Mazury, where individual municipalities are marked with colors representing quality classes of their websites. In addition, dual graphs are prepared for these maps. Based on the dual graphs, the complementary graphs are drawn, which, in turn, are used for the identification of growth poles and development axes. Furthermore, the study is not only static but also dynamic because it covers three points in time, that is, the years of 2009, 2012, 2015.

Determining Growth Poles and Development Axes by Dual Graph Reduction

Figure 9.1 presents a map of Warmia and Mazury with a division into municipalities, which shows growth poles, development axes, and transport networks. As it can be observed, the development axes, which have been marked out with straight lines, based on the high and very high quality of the municipalities' websites, almost exactly coincide with the transport infrastructure. Seven main development axes have been identified in this region, numbered from 1 to 7. The growth poles are mostly located at the intersections of the development axis and include the major towns of the region, such as Elbląg, Iława, Ostróda, Olsztyn, Orzysz, and Ełk. It is also evident that the local growth poles are linked to four road

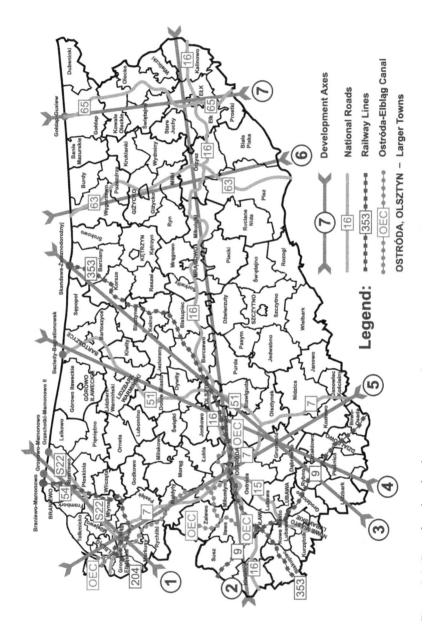

Figure 9.1 Growth poles, development axes, and communication routes in the Warmia and Mazury Region

and two rail border crossing points facilitating passenger and freight traffic between Poland and Russia.

The first development axis is located on the southwest–northeast line and crosses the towns of Elbląg and Braniewo. It includes two roads, national road No. 54 and express road No. S22, as well as railroad No. 204, which leads from Malbork through Elblag to the railway border crossing Braniewo-Mamonowo. Two towns, Elbląg and Frombork, feature seaports and sea border crossing points. Both ports are located on the Vistula Lagoon, from where the Baltic Sea can only be reached through the Strait of Baltiysk, located in the Kaliningrad Oblast belonging to Russia. This represents a serious restriction on passenger and freight traffic from both ports. For the northwestern part of the region, this is an important barrier to growth and economic development, hence the idea of a government investment called "Construction of a waterway connecting the Vistula Lagoon with the Gulf of Gdańsk," which is related to the crosscut of the Vistula Spit. The investment is already underway and is intended to provide Poland with free access from the Vistula Lagoon to the Baltic Sea, excluding the Strait of Baltiysk.

The second development axis is located on the west–east line and is related to national road No. 16, which runs through the entire Warmia and Mazury Region, and then continues through the Podlaskie Region, up to the border with Lithuania in Ogrodniki. This road is the main communication route of the region and connects its major cities, such as Iława, Ostróda, Olsztyn, Orzysz, and Ełk, which all are growth poles.

The third development axis runs southwest–northeast and is related to railway line No. 353, which connects the Poznań East junction station with the railway border crossing Skandawa-Żeleznodorożnyj. It runs through such towns as Iława, Ostróda, Olsztyn, and Korsze.

The fourth development axis has a similar geographical location as the third axis and is linked to national road No. 51. This road is one of the most important communication routes in the region. It starts in Olsztynek, where it connects with national road No. 7, then runs through the towns of Olsztyn, Dobre Miasto, Lidzbark Warmiński, Bartoszyce and ends with the road border crossing Bezledy-Bagrationowsk. A part of national road No. 15 is parallel to the fourth axis, so it can be treated as part of this axis. This road connects Nowe Miasto Lubawskie, Lubawa, and Ostróda.

The fifth development axis runs from the southeast to the northwest and is related to the national road No. 7 and the Ostróda-Elbląg Canal. It is worth mentioning that the Ostróda-Elbląg Canal was built in the 19th century, and since then, it has been considered a pearl of world hydraulic engineering (Rewitalizacja Kanału Elbląskiego, 2015). The fifth axis is parallel to railway line No. 9, which connects Warszawa Wschodnia with Gdańsk Główny, so it can be included in its structure according to the same principle as before.

The sixth development axis runs from south to north and is related to national road No. 63. It runs through the towns of Pisz, Orzysz, Giżycko, and Węgorzewo, and then ends at the Polish–Russian border. The road border crossing Perły-Kryłowo has been planned there for a long time now, which is particularly important for the residents of the surrounding towns located on both sides of the border, in view of the expected economic revival of border municipalities.

The seventh development axis runs parallel to the sixth axis, so it is also situated on the south–north line. It is related to national road No. 65 and runs through the towns of Ełk, Olecko, Gołdap, and then ends with the road border crossing Gołdap-Gusiew.

Discussion

Wikinomics Assumptions Complementing the Smart Specialization Strategy at the Local Level

The basic principle of smart specialization strategy is coherent development of markets while avoiding duplication and fragmentation of efforts. At present, digital technology functions as a top technique in Hicks's terms (1965, p. 221). Therefore, it not only provides the highest rate of return but also makes it possible to put the regional economy on a balanced growth path with the maximum rate of growth. It is the basis for the operation of the digital economy both at local and global level. One of the most important business strategies of wikinomics is the creation and improvement of participation platforms, as this enables the practical implementation of other models. As previously mentioned, all the activities undertaken in the framework of wikinomics are global in nature and enable the development of those industries that can be controlled by software. Therefore, investing in digital technology is currently the best way to avoid duplication and fragmentation of efforts. We do not have to duplicate operations by initiating the development of different branches of industry separately and focusing too much on their specificity because we can control them all by means of rules and models applied in wikinomics. The principles and models of wikinomics are not limited to the private sector, but can also improve the functioning of the public sector and cooperation between the two sectors. In this paper, we focused on the municipal websites of public administration offices in the Warmia and Mazury region, which should initiate and strengthen local entrepreneurial discovery processes.

Many issues connected with the entrepreneurial discovery process are related to the necessity to acquire new knowledge about the potential of a given country or region in the field of R&D and innovation, in order to be able to correctly designate enterprises, technologies, or areas that should be supported. Undoubtedly, entrepreneurs have an

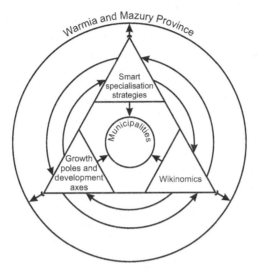

Figure 9.2 The policy space of smart specialization strategies supplemented with wikinomics, growth poles, and development axes

important role to play here; nevertheless, wikinomics indicates other, until recently unknown, ways to improve this process. The most important of these methods is prosumption, which represents the involvement of consumers in the design and production of new products or services. From the smart specialization point of view, prosumers are an important source of economic information, as they combine the functions of a producer and a consumer. It is well known that the ideas and concepts obtained from them are very original and innovative. The problem, however, is that knowledge from prosumption is dispersed, so it is necessary to find methods to collect and process it. The websites of municipal governments are best suited for this purpose, as one of their most important tasks is to organize the economic life in municipalities. When transformed into wikinomics platforms for participation, these websites will focus and strengthen the economic forces operating in the area. In such a case, standard prosumption becomes digital, which signifies that the information obtained can be easily processed. Knowledge acquired in this way by local governments complements the entrepreneurial discovery process because it stems not only from entrepreneurs but also from the entire society. Thus, expanded knowledge with the sources both in the market sector and the nonmarket sector is obtained.

Figure 9.2 explains our proposed conceptual framework of smart specialization strategies supplemented with wikinomics, growth poles, and development axes. The three basic elements of the study are marked with small equilateral triangles, which are located at the vertices of another, larger equilateral triangle. The large triangle indicates that all three concepts form an integrated and functional whole. There are interactions between the small triangles, symbolized by the semicircular arrows. All three concepts combined determine what happens in the municipalities represented by the small circle, and the productive sum of all the economic forces operating in the municipalities determines the development of the whole region represented by the large circle.

Growth Poles and Development Axes in the Warmia and Mazury Region

The research on the quality classes of websites of municipal public administration offices has led to the identification of growth poles and development axes in Warmia and Mazury. Based on empirical maps for the years of 2009, 2012, and 2015 a specific feature of this region was established, consisting of historically and politically conditioned infrastructural growth poles and development axes. The driving forces of regional growth and development are directly linked to the road, rail, and inland waterway infrastructure in the area (Jakimowicz & Rzeczkowski, 2018, 2021). The foundations of the current transport infrastructure were created in previous centuries, while the source of political conditions is the complex history of statehood in this area. For this reason, the region under examination is an excellent confirmation of the theory of the growth poles by François Perroux (1964) and the development axes of Pierre Pottier (1963).

Technologically advanced municipal digital platforms overlap with physical growth poles and development axes. The findings show that computer networks and communication paths are mirror images of each other and there are feedbacks between them in the studied region. The earlier mentioned creation of the fiber-optic backbone distribution network based on the public–private partnership is a necessary condition, yet not sufficient for the development of the information society in the Warmia and Mazury region. It is still necessary to build the last-mile networks, that is, the access networks that will connect end users to the main network (O rozwoju sieci "Ostatniej mili" na Warmii i Mazurach, 2017). The solution to this problem is to be provided by the Digital Plan 2025 for Warmia and Mazury, whose aim is to eliminate or reduce economic barriers hindering the construction of the last mile network (Plan Cyfrowy 2025 dla Warmii i Mazur. . ., 2017). In Poland, this is a unique agreement between the regional government and the authorities of districts and municipalities from the entire region. It will unify and reduce charges for locating telecommunications infrastructure along public roads and exempt it from property tax. According to the intentions of the provincial authorities, the Digital Plan is to provide a driving force for the social and economic development of the region and ensure the development of a low-carbon economy and entrepreneurship oriented toward a digital economy.

From the point of view of entrepreneurial discovery process, the creation of public–private networks is a basic condition for the success of smart specialization strategies (Estensoro & Larrea, 2016). The fiber-optic backbone distribution network and the related Digital Plan 2025 for Warmia and Mazury, which aims to build the last mile networks are a useful example of this. All local governments and telecommunications operators are involved in creating this computer network. The principles and business models of wikinomics were also applied. Prosumers were involved in the development and implementation of this huge investment, which was reflected in allowing all inhabitants of the region to report their needs for access to broadband Internet. This led to the development of a map of access networks covering over 5000 households. The knowledge obtained in this process is valuable not only for local governments but also for telecommunications operators. This is a good example of support given to one of the smart specializations in the form of ICT development, which was established for the region already in 2013.

Conclusion

Implications for Theory

The conceptual contribution of this research comprises the integration of wikinomics assumptions, combined with the theories of growth poles and development axes, to the guidelines of adopting SS at the local level. In particular, these concepts are proposed as useful in explaining the role of digital technologies in the establishment of public–private partnership networks for entrepreneurial discovery processes (Foray, 2015; McCann & Ortega-Argilés, 2015; Carayannis, & Grigoroudis, 2016). The extension of the policy space of smart specialization strategies to the principles and models of wikinomics and to the growth poles and development axes gives new guidelines for the construction of the quadruple helix model, which explains the processes of knowledge creation and innovation development in the contemporary European economy. It consists of four interrelated elements: education subsystem, economic subsystem, political subsystem, and civil society (Carayannis & Grigoroudis, 2016). During the mutual interactions between these social subsystems, knowledge is produced, which increases the level of innovation and know-how in the economy. The quadruple helix model already contains the foundations of what we now call prosumption, however, incorporating the principles and business patterns of wikinomics into this model enables the codification of knowledge from various sources and facilitates its use (Tapscott & Williams, 2006, 2012). In addition, participation platforms make the gathered knowledge more accessible to all interested stakeholders. As shown in this chapter, this approach can also include the growth poles and development axes that will interact with other subsystems, leading to a sextuple helix (six-helix model). Such a model provides an appropriate basis for the development of smart specialization strategies, therefore, it deserves to be implemented despite increased efforts related to it (Carayannis, Barth, & Campbell, 2012).

Implications for Policy

This study also provides a contribution to practice. Namely, it has identified the current and potential impacts of ICT instruments in the local government context, and it formulates recommendations regarding their use in mobilizing local capabilities toward S3. According to wikinomics, high and very high-quality websites can be considered as the germs of participation platforms (Tapscott & Williams, 2006, 2012). Ultimately, these sites should act as platforms for grassroots action and include platforms for public disclosure and platforms for neighborhood knowledge. An example of this is the Górowo Iławeckie Town Hall, which receives submissions from the LocalSpot application, designed to enable the contact of residents with public administration offices of towns and municipalities. It is a type of digital prosumption, allowing residents to notify local authorities of problems in the public space. One of the best directions for the development of municipal websites is to transform them into web services mashups. This is the name given to websites that use various ready-made services or applications made available by other websites to create a brand new service of much higher quality, with additional functionalities. We are dealing here with an innovative activity consisting of remixing data and software into recombinant creations. At present, the websites of municipal public administration offices are much less developed as compared to platforms for commerce. This is one of the reasons why extensive sources of public information that could contribute to the development of entirely new public services are not exploited. It is almost certain that such services would become significant additional factors of regional economic growth.

Moreover, some possible threats for the sustainable and coherent development can be identified regarding the identified relationships between municipality platforms as growth poles and the established development axes. Namely, the current distribution of the quality platforms might be considered as petrifying the earlier established historically and politically development axes, and thus strengthen the regional polarization and uneven development at the local level (McCann & Ortega-Argilés, 2015; Varga et al. 2020). Another threat might be the persistence of the current structures and lack of spillover effects from the growth poles and development axes. The technological investment requires additional efforts at the level of economic and social structures to ignite other joint initiatives of public–private actors that would make use of the current infrastructures. Therefore, the referred digital infrastructures should be treated as important resource that needs to be integrated into components and relationships in the quadruple helix model of innovation to fully exploit potential for spillovers (McCann & Ortega-Argilés, 2015; Varga et al. 2020).

Limitations

The method of diagnosing inter-municipal cooperation based on dual graph reduction may have some limitations. They consist of identifying potential opportunities for municipalities to carry out joint ventures, which do not actually have to be undertaken in all cases. Nevertheless, if neighboring municipalities have websites that are of high or very high quality, the likelihood of cooperation is high. Moreover, the existence of discrepancies in quality classes of the adjacent municipalities does not exclude their cooperation in the implementation of economic projects, which is best illustrated by the example of the Digital Plan 2025 for Warmia and Mazury. The growth poles and development axes were, in fact, identified from the complementary graphs in relation to the three empirical dual graphs plotted for 2009, 2012, and 2015. Complementary graphs were present wherever there was a reduction in the dual graphs. In spite of this, the method presented here proved to be effective, and its best test was to identify the existing historically and politically conditioned infrastructural growth poles and development axes.

Future Research Directions

An interesting direction for future research would be to explore the policy space of smart specialization strategies by building multi-helical models. One example is the quintuple helix innovation model, which introduces an additional element into the quadruple helix model in the form of natural environments of society (Carayannis et al., 2012). By adding the rules and patterns of wikinomics as well as the growth poles and development axes to this model we obtain feedbacks occurring between the seven subsystems. The Septuple Helix (seven-helix model) is certainly much more complex than the previous ones, but nevertheless closer to reality. Wikinomics provides the potential to collect, process, and share knowledge with interested stakeholders, while the growth poles and development axes introduce appropriate spatial and regional context. However, as it appears, the more nuanced and comprehensive approach to the implementation of S3 comes at the cost of increasing the complexity of the underlying models.

References

Aloise, D., Deshpande, A., Hansen, P., & Popat, P. (2009). NP-hardness of Euclidean sum-of-squares clustering. *Machine Learning*, 75, 245–248. https://doi.org/10.1007/s10994-009-5103-0

Benner, M. (2019). Smart specialization and institutional context: The role of institutional discovery, change and leapfrogging. *European Planning Studies*, 27(9), 1791–1810. https://doi.org/10.1080/09654313.2019.1643826

Carayannis, E. G., Barth, T. D., & Campbell, D. F. J. (2012). The Quintuple Helix innovation model: Global warming as a challenge and driver for innovation. *Journal of Innovation and Entrepreneurship*, 1(2). https://doi.org/10.1186/2192-5372-1-2

Carayannis, E. G., & Grigoroudis, E. (2016). Quadruple Innovation Helix and smart specialization: Knowledge production and national competitiveness. *Foresight and STI Governance*, 10(1), 31–42. https://doi.org/10.17323/1995-459x.2016.1.31.42

Czyżewska-Misztal, D., & Golejewska, A. (2016). The least innovative regions in Poland in the process of smart specialization. *Optimum. Studia Ekonomiczne*, 5(83), 123–137. https://doi.org/10.15290/ose.2016.05.83.08

Degerstedt, L. (2015). Social competitive intelligence: Sociotechnical themes and values for the networking organization. *Journal of Intelligence Studies in Business*, 5(3), 5–34. Retrieved from https://ojs.hh.se/index.php/JISIB/article/view/135

Diestel, R. (2000). *Graph theory*. New York: Springer-Verlag.

Estensoro, M., & Larrea, M. (2016). Overcoming policy making problems in smart specialization strategies: Engaging subregional governments. *European Planning Studies*, 24(7), 1319–1335. https://doi.org/10.1080/09654313.2016.1174670

Everitt, B. S., Landau, S., Leese, M., & Stahl, D. (2011). *Cluster analysis* (5th ed.). Chichester, United Kingdom: John Wiley and Sons.

Fellnhofer, K. (2017). Evidence revisited: Literature on smart specialisation calls for more mixed research designs. *International Journal of Knowledge-Based Development*, 8(3), 229–248. https://doi.org/10.1504/IJKBD.2017.086407

Foray, D. (2015). *Smart specialisation: Opportunities and challenges for regional innovation policy*. New York, NY: Routledge—Taylor & Francis Group.

Foray, D. (2016). On the policy space of smart specialization strategies. *European Planning Studies*, 24(8), 1428–1437. https://doi.org/10.1080/09654313.2016.1176126

Foray, D. (2017). The economic fundamentals of smart specialization strategies. In S. Radosevic, A. Curaj, R. Gheorghiu, L. Andreescu & I. Wade (Eds.), *Advances in the theory and practice of smart specialization* (pp. 37–50). London, UK: Academic Press. https://doi.org/10.1016/B978-0-12-804137-6.00002-4

Hicks, J. R. (1965). *Capital and growth*. New York: Oxford University Press.

Jakimowicz, A. (2010). Catastrophes and chaos in business cycle theory. *Acta Physica Polonica A*, 117(4), 640–646. https://doi.org/10.12693/APhysPolA.117.640

Jakimowicz, A., & Kulesza, S. (2018). The mechanism of transformation of global business cycles into dynamics of regional real estate markets. *Acta*

Physica Polonica A, 133(6), 1351–1361. https://doi.org/10.12693/APhysPolA. 133.1351

Jakimowicz, A., & Rzeczkowski, D. (2016). Prosumption in the public administration sector. *Acta Physica Polonica A, 129*(5), 1011–1017. https://doi. org/10.12693/APhysPolA.129.1011

Jakimowicz, A., & Rzeczkowski, D. (2018). Application of the four colour theorem to identify spatial regional poles and turnpikes of economic growth. *Acta Physica Polonica A, 133*(6), 1362–1370. https://doi.org/10.12693/ APhysPolA.133.1362

Jakimowicz, A., & Rzeczkowski, D. (2021). New measure of economic development based on the four-colour theorem. *Entropy, 23*(1), 61. https://doi. org/10.3390/e23010061

Kogut-Jaworska, M., & Ociepa-Kicińska, E. (2020). Smart specialisation as a strategy for implementing the regional innovation development policy—Poland case study. *Sustainability, 12*(19), 7986. https://doi.org/10.3390/su12197986

Krzyżanowski, P. (2015, September 20). Koniec budowy sieci szerokopasmowej na Warmii i Mazurach. *Komputer Świat.* Retrieved from www. komputerswiat.pl/artykuly/redakcyjne/koniec-budowy-sieci-szerokopasmowej-na-warmii-i-mazurach/6pxxn4m

Kuznetsov, Y., & Sabel, C. (2017). Managing self-discovery: Diagnostic monitoring of a portfolio of projects and programs. In S. Radosevic, A. Curaj, R. Gheorghiu, L. Andreescu & I. Wade (Eds.), *Advances in the theory and practice of smart specialization* (pp. 51–72). London, UK: Academic Press. https:// doi.org/10.1016/B978-0-12-804137-6.00003-6

Lloyd, S. P. (1982). Least squares quantization in PCM. *IEEE Transactions on Information Theory, 28*(2), 129–137. https://doi.org/10.1109/ TIT.1982.1056489

Mahajan, M., Nimbhorkar, P., & Varadarajan, K. (2009). The planar *k*-means problem is NP-hard. In S. Das & R. Uehara (Eds.), *WALCOM: Algorithms and Computation. Third International Workshop, WALCOM 2009, Kolkata, India, February 18–20, 2009. Proceedings* (pp. 274–285). Berlin: Springer-Verlag. https://doi.org/10.1007/978-3-642-00202-1_24

McCann, P., & Ortega-Argilés, R. (2015). Smart specialization, regional growth and applications to European Union cohesion policy. *Regional Studies, 49*(8), 1291–1302. https://doi.org/10.1080/00343404.2013.799769

Miller, M., Mroczkowski, T., & Healy, A. (2014). Poland's innovation strategy: How smart is 'smart specialisation'? *International Journal of Transitions and Innovation Systems, 3*(3), 225–248. https://doi.org/10.1504/ IJTIS.2014.065697

O rozwoju sieci "Ostatniej mili" na Warmii i Mazurach. (2017, May 22). *Regionalny Portal Informacyjny Wrota Warmii i Mazur.* Retrieved from https:// warmia.mazury.pl/rozwoj-regionu/informatyzacja/162-o-rozwoju-sieci-ostatniej-mili-na-warmii-i-mazurach

Perroux, F. (1964). *L'Économie du XXe Siècle.* Paris, France: Presses Universitaires de France.

Plan Cyfrowy 2025 dla Warmii i Mazur—stan na 6 marca 2017. (2017, May 22). *Regionalny Portal Informacyjny Wrota Warmii i Mazur.* Retrieved from https://warmia.mazury.pl/rozwoj-regionu/informatyzacja/165-plan-cyfrowy-2025-dla-warmii-i-mazur-stan-na-6-marca-2018

Pottier, P. (1963). Axes de communication et développement économique. *Revue Économique, 14*(1), 58–132. https://doi.org/10.3406/reco.1963.407543

Rewitalizacja Kanału Elbląskiego. (2015). Gdańsk, Poland: Regionalny Zarząd Gospodarki Wodnej w Gdańsku.

Sieć Szerokopasmowa Polski Wschodniej. (2018, April 6). *Regionalny Portal Informacyjny Wrota Warmii i Mazur.* Retrieved from www.warmia.mazury.pl/rozwoj-regionu/informatyzacja/158-siec-szerokopasmowa-polski-wschodniej

Tapscott, D., & Williams, A. D. (2006). *Wikinomics: How mass collaboration changes everything.* New York: Portfolio.

Tapscott, D., & Williams, A. D. (2012). *Macrowikinomics: Rebooting business and the world.* New York: Portfolio/Penguin.

Thom, R. (1975). *Structural stability and morphogenesis. An outline of a general theory of models.* Reading, MA: W.A. Benjamin.

Toffler, A. (1980). *The third wave.* New York: William Morrow and Company.

Toffler, A., & Toffler, H. (2007). *Revolutionary wealth: How it will be created and how it will change our lives.* New York: Doubleday.

Trotman, D. J. A., & Zeeman, E. C. (1976). The classification of elementary catastrophes of codimension $\leq$ 5. In P. Hilton (Ed.), *Structural Stability, the Theory of Catastrophes, and Applications in the Sciences. Proceedings of the Conference Held at Battelle Seattle Research Center 1975* (pp. 263–327). Berlin: Springer-Verlag.

Varga, A., Sebestyén, T., Szabó, N., & Szerb, L. (2020). Estimating the economic impacts of knowledge network and entrepreneurship development in smart specialization policy. *Regional Studies, 54*(1), 48–59. https://doi.org/10.1080/00343404.2018.1527026

Węgrzyn, J. (2018). Does experience exert impact on a public-private partnership performance? The case of Poland. *Equilibrium. Quarterly Journal of Economics and Economic Policy, 13*(3), 509–522. https://doi.org/10.24136/eq.2018.025

Wichowska, A. (2019). Shrinking municipalities and their budgetary revenues on the example of the Warmian-Masurian Voivodeship in Poland. *Oeconomia Copernicana, 10*(3), 419–432. https://doi.org/10.24136/oc.2019.020

Wierzbicka, W. (2018). Information infrastructure as a pillar of the knowledge-based economy—an analysis of regional differentiation in Poland. *Equilibrium. Quarterly Journal of Economics and Economic Policy, 13*(1), 123–139. https://doi.org/10.24136/eq.2018.007

Wierzbicka, W. (2020). Socio-economic potential of cities belonging to the Polish National Cittaslow Network. *Oeconomia Copernicana, 11*(1), 203–224. https://doi.org/10.24136/oc.2020.009

Wilson, R. J. (2014). *Four colors suffice: How the map problem was solved. Revised color edition.* Princeton, NJ: Princeton University Press.

Wyrwa, J. (2014). Smart specialisation—a novel approach towards region development in Poland. *Acta Scientiarum Polonorum. Oeconomia, 13*(3), 143–154.

Zhao, Y., Pan, J. Z., Thomas, E., Jekjantuk, N., & Ren, Y. (2013). Ontology languages and description logics. In J. Z. Pan, S. Staab, U. Aßmann, J. Ebert & Y. Zhao (Eds.), *Ontology-driven software development* (pp. 51–68). Berlin: Springer-Verlag. https://doi.org/10.1007/978-3-642-31226-7_3

Index

Note: Page numbers in *italics* indicate figures and page numbers in **bold** indicate tables on the corresponding page.

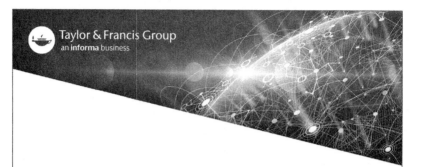

Printed in the United States
by Baker & Taylor Publisher Services